D0445256

Molto Agitato

Also by

JOHANNA FIEDLER

Arthur Fiedler: Papa, the Pops, and Me

The
Mayhem

Behind the Music

at the *Metropolitan Opera*

NAN A. TALESE
Doubleday
NEW YORK   LONDON   TORONTO   SYDNEY   AUCKLAND

Molto Agitato

JOHANNA FIEDLER

Published by Nan A. Talese

an imprint of Doubleday

a division of Random House, Inc., 1540 Broadway, New York, New York 10036

DOUBLEDAY is a trademark of Doubleday, a division of Random House, Inc.

Book design by Terry Karydes

Library of Congress Cataloging-in-Publication Data

Fiedler, Johanna.

    Molto agitato : the mayhem behind the music at the Metropolitan Opera / Johanna Fiedler.

    p.   cm.

    1. Metropolitan Opera (New York, N.Y.) 2. Opera—New York (State)—

New York—

History and criticism. I. Title.

    ML1711.8.N3 M427 2001

782.1'09747'1—dc21   2001027158

ISBN 0-385-48187-X

Copyright © 2001 by Johanna Fiedler

All Rights Reserved

Printed in the United States of America

November 2001

First Edition

10 9 8 7 6 5 4 3 2 1

In memory of my father,

who loved music, books, and dogs

CONTENTS

Contents

CHRONOLOGY

1854   The Academy of Music opens.

1883   The Metropolitan Opera opens with a performance of *Faust* in the new opera house at Broadway and Thirty-ninth Street.

1903   Enrico Caruso makes his debut in *Rigoletto*. Otto Kahn joins Met board; he will become its most influential member for the next quarter-century.

1908   Opening of the twenty-fifth anniversary season and debut of new general manager Giulio Gatti-Casazza and conductor Arturo Toscanini.

1931   First Met radio broadcast; *Hänsel und Gretel* is broadcast nationwide.

1935   Mrs. August Belmont, the first woman named to the Metropolitan board, founds the Metropolitan Opera Guild.

1941   After the bombing of Pearl Harbor, the United States enters World War II; *Madama Butterfly* is banned for the duration of the war.

1949   Rudolf Bing named as general manager, remaining in the position for the next twenty-three years.

1955   Marian Anderson makes her Metropolitan Opera debut in *Un Ballo in Maschera*, becoming the first African-American principal artist in the Met's history.

1961   Bitter labor dispute develops between Met board, administration, and orchestra; strike averted by the last-minute intervention of secretary of labor Arthur Goldberg.

1966   New Opera House opens at Lincoln Center with world premiere of Samuel Barber's *Antony and Cleopatra*; only just before the performance, the Met reaches a settlement with its recalcitrant musicians.

1968   Plácido Domingo makes his Met debut as a last-minute substitute for Franco Corelli in *Adriana Lecouvreur*. Luciano Pavarotti makes his debut in *La Bohème*.

1969   Labor impasse with Met Orchestra forces latest opening night in the company's history.

1970   Goeran Gentele named to succeed Bing. He chooses Rafael Kubelik as his music director.

1971   James Levine makes his Met debut conducting *Tosca* at the June Festival. Shortly afterward, he is named principal conductor, to assist Kubelik.

1972   Gentele is killed in an automobile accident: his assistant, Schuyler Chapin, is named acting general manager.

1975   Board dismisses Chapin, leaving Anthony Bliss in charge. James Levine is named music director, part of a triumvirate including Bliss and John Dexter (director of production).

1977   First *Live from the Met* telecast of *La Bohème*, with Renata Scotto and Luciano Pavarotti.

1980   Violinist Helen Hagnes murdered backstage; Craig Crimmins, a stagehand, is eventually arrested and convicted of the crime. Labor dispute with the orchestra shuts down the first three months of the 1980–81 season. Joseph Volpe emerges from the shambles of the management's negotiations to become a major player.

1981   Zeffirelli's new *La Bohème* ushers in new Met aesthetic of flamboyant, conservative productions, many underwritten by Mrs. Donald D. Harrington.

1983   James Levine named artistic director at start of the Centennial season.

1983   The Met celebrates its one hundredth anniversary with a two-part marathon concert televised live nationally and internationally.

1984   Bruce Crawford named new general manager, replacing Anthony Bliss. Mrs. Gilbert W. Humphrey replaces him as board president, becoming the first woman to hold that position.

1988   Crawford unexpectedly resigns as general manager.

1990   Joseph Volpe is named general director, a substitute title for general manager.

1991   James Levine conducts John Corigliano's *The Ghosts of Versailles*, the Met's first world premiere in a quarter-century. This began an era of new experimentation in repertory and production style.

1992–93 Joseph Volpe finally is given the title of general manager, a vote of confidence from the formerly dubious board.

1994   Volpe fires Kathleen Battle, one of Levine's favorite singers, producing speculation that he has won the supposed power struggle between himself and Levine.

1997   The Met announces the appointment of Valery Gergiev to the newly created
         position of principal guest conductor.

1998   Alberto Vilar makes a gift of $25 million to launch the Met's new $300 million
         endowment campaign. It is the first well-publicized gift that Vilar has made; in
         the next three years, he will become a famous arts philanthropist.

Preface

The fifteen years I spent at the Metropolitan Opera were among the most interesting of my life. From the first day I walked in the stage door, I felt at home in the opera house. Life there was lived on a lavish scale; it was a world populated by larger-than-life characters who behaved as though they lived in an opera. Tempers raged, love affairs flourished, rivalries thrived, all at top volume. There was cruelty but there was also kindness, greed but also generosity, ambition but also self-sacrifice. The one thing there never was was silence.

This is not a book about opera; it is a study of the politics of an institution. I have made an attempt to open up the Metropolitan's world and study the three main forces that propel it: the artistic, the financial, and the social. The singers who have been included are a rather arbitrary list; several of my own favorites have been left out. But the singers who are in the book are all people who have influenced what has happened at the Met, usually because of their power to fill the theater.

The Metropolitan Opera has been described often as a closed world, as impervious to outsiders as the Kremlin or the Vatican. As the company's general press representative, I saw all aspects of the company from the stage crew to the orchestra to the board of directors. Behind the gold curtain is a world that is very human, although human on a grand scale. It was a privilege to be part of that world for the time I was at the Met.

Molto Agitato

*P*rologue

THE LONGEST CONCERT

So many singers were at the Met on the evening of April 27, 1996, when James Levine stepped into the orchestra pit, that the audience openly speculated what other opera houses could possibly be doing the same evening. The occasion was the celebration of Levine's twenty-fifth anniversary at the Metropolitan Opera. Twenty-five years earlier, when he was twenty-eight, he had made his first appearance, leading Puccini's *Tosca*. During the intervening years, Levine had presided over fifteen hundred performances of sixty-eight operas, a record unlikely to be surpassed.

Everyone in the opera house had wondered which work he would choose to celebrate his silver anniversary—his repertory at the Met had covered almost every style and school. But Levine savors excess in all parts of his musical life; any man capable of conducting a matinee of Verdi's five-hour *Don Carlo* and an evening performance of Wagner's six-hour *Götterdämmerung*, and afterward pronouncing himself invigorated, would have trouble selecting a single opera to celebrate such an important anniversary. Levine decided that he didn't want to do what he has done more than any other man in the history of the Metropolitan Opera. He didn't want to conduct an opera; instead, he conducted a concert.

But what an operatic concert it was in repertory, length, scope, and ambition: the evening began at 6:00 P.M. with Wagner's Overture to *Rienzi* and ended eight hours later with the finale from the same composer's *Die*

Meistersinger von Nürnberg. In the hours between, sixty of the world's best-known opera singers, accompanied by the Met Orchestra and Chorus, sang forty-three selections that spanned most of the operatic repertory. All of the artists had come to New York to pay tribute to one conductor: James Levine, artistic director of the Metropolitan Opera.

Everyone knew the whereabouts of the few singers not at the Met: Luciano Pavarotti was in bed with the flu; Ben Heppner was fulfilling a longtime engagement with the Seattle Opera; Cecilia Bartoli had succumbed to her famous fear of flying.

Confronted with the elite of opera, few listening, either in the Opera House or watching the live telecast broadcast internationally, worried about who was not there. Instead, they wallowed in an operatic orgy that included Wotan's Farewell from *Die Walküre,* Isolde's Narrative and Curse from *Tristan und Isolde,* the septet from *Les Contes d'Hoffmann,* the final scene of *Eugene Onegin,* the final trio from *Der Rosenkavalier,* the sextet from *Don Giovanni,* the Watch Duet from *Die Fledermaus,* the Cherry Duet from *L'Amico Fritz,* and the Immolation Scene from *Götterdämmerung*—as well as arias from operas by Verdi, Puccini, Johann Strauss II, George Gershwin, Gounod, Donizetti, Charpentier, Rossini, Bizet, and Saint-Saëns.

The singers who swept on to the stage either alone or in collegial ensembles included Renée Fleming, Gabriela Benackova, Dawn Upshaw, Nicolai Ghiaurov, Thomas Hampson, Angela Gheorghiu and Roberto Alagna, James Morris, Deborah Voigt, Plácido Domingo, Mirella Freni, Bryn Terfel, Frederica von Stade, Alfredo Kraus, Jessye Norman, Catherine Malfitano, Sherrill Milnes, Waltraud Meier, Carlo Bergonzi, Gwyneth Jones, Samuel Ramey, Carol Vaness, Jane Eaglen, Hakan Hagegard, Karita Mattila, and Kiri Te Kanawa.

There were many, many others, but the musical affection for Levine truly crystallized when Birgit Nilsson, the legendary Wagnerian soprano, came onstage just before the end of the evening. Wearing spike heels and a tight evening dress in celebration of her almost seventy years, Nilsson gave a touching tribute to Levine, who had brought her back to the Met fifteen years earlier after a long absence. Then, for probably the last time in her career, and hitting every note, she sang Brünnhilde's famous battle cry

"Ho yo to ho!," landing the high note at the end as cleanly as she ever had over her forty-year career. She received the loudest ovation of the evening; even the final scene of *Meistersinger,* which ended the concert, was anticlimactic.

Before the concert, the Met's artistic administration took a hard look at the staggering length and scope (and expense) of this concert and gently suggested to Levine—to Jimmy, as he is known by everyone, from superstars to stagehands—that he might want to start with a shorter, snappier overture than the lengthy *Rienzi.* Levine, beaming as always, shook his head. He wanted to do *Rienzi.*

Just as he wanted, *Rienzi* opened the program. It was his night. For twenty-five years, twenty-one as either music director or artistic director, he was the man who had shaped the Met's artistic profile and he wanted his concert to reflect every facet of that quarter-century. "Leave them wanting more" was an epigram Levine never understood. For years, he had conducted nearly two-thirds of each Met season, and even when he cut back to about half, he was in the opera house almost every day. This was the achievement he wanted to celebrate, and celebrate he did, in his favorite way. This man, who lives to conduct, led the entire eight hours.

Levine is called "His Smilingness" by the Met Orchestra because of his enthusiasm, but his serene appearance masks an ardent determination and steely will that have served him advantageously over a life in the treacherous trenches of the opera world. The evening of his twenty-fifth anniversary was a striking symbol of his domination of the world's largest and busiest opera house. On the evening of April 27, 1996, Levine was the primary figure at the Met. But in the flux of life in the theater, there are other major forces at work, aside from the artistic. At any given moment, one or another may be in the ascendant.

As Levine conducted that night, his sturdy figure silhouetted against the light from the stage, a man watched from the darkness of the auditorium. Seated in the Diamond Horseshoe, the ancestral domain of New York society, was Joseph Volpe, the company's general manager, the first man in the Met's history who had risen from the ranks to the top position. He watched from his own box on the parterre level, where for over one hundred years, in the old Met at Broadway and Thirty-ninth Street and the new Met at Lincoln Center, the wealthy and prominent had come to see the opera and to be seen themselves. The rich and powerful, who represented and embodied the Met's financial strength and social influence, were also in the darkened boxes, but this was not their night. Tonight belonged to Levine and to the music.

Volpe did not wear his power as graciously as Levine. He was tall and solidly built, and his shoulders seemed to push against the confines of his well-cut tuxedo; his eyes under their dark brows were, as always, working, watching, and evaluating. Perhaps he was thinking of tomorrow, which could well belong to him.

These were the normal posts of the two men at performances: Levine on the podium, Volpe watching from the general manager's box. But away from the auditorium, in the backstage maze of hallways, offices, rehearsal studios, workshops, and dressing rooms, their roles were less clearly defined. The history of the balance of power at this opera house stretches back to the company's very beginning in 1883. There has always been a struggle for power between the Met's primary elements—artistic, social, and financial. Through world wars, economic depressions, and bountiful times, the conflicts backstage at the Met have taken place, the present ones often eerily mirroring those of the past.

Levine, like many powerful men, has enemies, and some viewed the gala as an eight-hour celebration of himself, wearing out his orchestra and most of the world's great opera singers in the process. But a high school friend who had watched him for forty years saw the evening differently. "All I could think of was that the whole evening was so typical of Jimmy, celebrating his anniversary by working his heart out."

Afterward, Volpe was host of a party for the whole company—about a thousand singers, orchestral players, choristers, dancers, stagehands. Levine, still filled with energy, bounded into the party and stayed until the very end, while everyone around him was drooping with exhaustion. Volpe gave a lengthy speech at some point about the wonders of the company he headed, but the image that remained for everyone there was of Levine smiling, hugging, and kissing. And then, when the time came, he vanished, as is his custom, to celebrate at home on his own.

Chapter One

THE BOXHOLDERS

Mrs. William K. Vanderbilt was furious, and that was how the Metropolitan Opera began. In the late 1870s, she had applied for a box at the Academy of Music, then New York's premier opera presenter and social venue, and she had been turned down by the directors of the Academy. Mrs. Vanderbilt, whose fortune was estimated at $200 million, regarded this decision as completely unacceptable.

To have a box at the Academy—and there were only eighteen—was to attain the highest rung on the city's social ladder. As Edith Wharton wrote, "The world of fashion was still content to reassemble every winter in the shabby red and gold boxes of the sociable old Academy. Conservatives cherished it for being small and inconvenient, and thus keeping out 'the new people.' "

But society in New York was, as it always is, in transition. The city's wealth and power had increased vastly in the second half of the nineteenth century, and this had catapulted families such as the Vanderbilts, Astors, Morgans, Roosevelts, Goelets, Iselins, and Goulds to vast fortunes. The men who amassed these fortunes acquired an equally vast desire for social standing. Certainly, with only eighteen boxes at the Academy, this ultimate symbol of social triumph was tantalizingly out of reach. There was no room—or no box—for the newly wealthy.

The new elite believed that there was no obstacle that could not be surmounted by money. If the directors of the Academy refused them entry, they would solve that problem by building their own opera house. This new house would be designed with a virgin set of boxes, available to those who had been snubbed by the Academy of Music. In 1880, $600,000 was raised from a group of subscribers, each of whom would own their own box, and a site was purchased at Thirty-ninth Street and Broadway. And so the Metropolitan Opera was founded—essentially tiers of boxes with an opera house built to surround them.

On October 22, 1883, the new theater was inaugurated with Gounod's *Faust*. The basic administrative organization of the new opera house was simple, and lasted for a quarter-century. The boxholders, who became known in 1893 as the Metropolitan Opera Real Estate Company, were co-operative owners of the opera house. They hired an impresario to produce what went onstage. This division between the Real Estate Company and the actual opera presenters would create serious problems in the future, but for the first few years, progress was smooth.

Henry E. Abbey, the first impresario, received his instructions from the boxholder-stockholders. He was bidden "to provide first-class opera," or at least opera that was so defined by the boxholders. Abbey put together a fourteen-week season of nineteen operas, all in Italian. When, at the end of the first season, he had lost $300,000, he was dismissed. The boxholders were not interested in losing money.

The boxholders next turned to Leopold Damrosch, conductor of the New York Symphony Orchestra, and a close friend of Wagner and Liszt, and engaged him as both impresario and music director. Damrosch brought in an experienced company of singers from Central Europe to produce German opera. The directors were impressed by the small budget he presented—German singers were considerably less expensive than Italians. So for the second Metropolitan Opera season, all operas were sung in German, including works from the Italian and French repertories. This new programming brought in a new audience of German opera lovers to the Metropolitan; many of these were members of New York's large immigrant population who thronged to the less-expensive seats. They went to the Met because they loved the music. The boxholders, in marked contrast, went to be seen by the other boxholders.

The first German season was a success, but it took a grievous toll on Leopold Damrosch—he conducted every performance from opening night until he collapsed from overwork in February 1885, caught pneumonia, and swiftly died. He was immediately replaced by his son, Walter, and the season ended with only a small deficit. Despite the death of their music director, the boxholders were content.

For the next seven seasons, the Metropolitan was primarily a German house. By 1890, all ten widely performed Wagner works, from *Rienzi* to *Götterdämmerung,* had been presented, including the first performance in the United States of the *Ring* cycle, which took place during the 1898–99 season. Meanwhile, to the great satisfaction of the boxholders, the Academy of Music, which had continued with the Italian repertory, went bankrupt.

But, aside from the satisfaction of revenge, the boxholders found new reasons to be unhappy. The German-only policy and lengthy Wagner operas bored the wealthy patrons and left them no opportunity to converse between arias, as they enjoyed doing. So the company announced a switch to the Italian and French repertories. At this point, a rift that had been developing deepened between the wealthy boxholders and the music lovers who sat in regular seats. These ticket buyers were outraged over the change in policy, and they signed petitions and crowded into the remaining Wagner performances before the new policy went into effect. The boxholders were unmoved. They wanted to go in a new direction and they regarded themselves as the owners of the Metropolitan Opera.

They brought back Henry E. Abbey, the first general manager, whom they had dismissed after the first season. In partnership with one of his theatrical collaborators, Abbey decided on a season based on opera's brightest stars singing a primarily Italian repertory. In an about-face, the German operas were now presented in Italian translations, although some French works were done in the original language. Sometimes the confusion led to performances of Meyerbeer's operas in which the soloists sang in French while the chorus stuck to Italian. But despite the mélange of languages, the Metropolitan did begin to embody a more international tone.

The New York newspapers delighted their readers with stories about the opera-going robber barons who had built the house and dictated its artistic policy. In Europe, the social hierarchy had been set for centuries; in the United States, this hierarchy was still fluid, and opulence became the defining standard of what came to be known as the Gilded Age. Journalists pounded on the excesses of this recently arrived upper class. Mrs. Vanderbilt's gowns and Mrs. Astor's guest lists, which were often adorned with titled Europeans, received frequent mention. The glaze of glamour around the Metropolitan and glitter of the wealthy boxholders made it easy to forget that the majority of the seats were filled with people who came to the opera because they loved music.

In 1892–93, the Metropolitan closed for an entire season after a fire that gutted the auditorium. When the house reopened with a gala performance in November 1893, the auditorium had been redecorated with cream-colored walls and newly installed electric lights. There was also a new sense of artistic vigor. For the next fifteen years, the Metropolitan was visited by all the famous singers, including Lillian Nordica, Jean and Edouard de Reszke, Emma Calvé, Francesco Tamagno, Nellie Melba, Milka Ternina, Ernestine Schumann-Heink, Enrico Caruso, Antonio Scotti, and Pol Plançon. The season ran until April, when the boxholders left the hot city for the country. The cosmopolitan company now performed almost the entire standard repertory in the original languages, as was the custom in most major international theaters.

Competing for attention with the singers were the boxholders who had now incorporated the Metropolitan Opera Real Estate Company with the Metropolitan Opera Company. The thirty-five boxes in the rebuilt house, the Diamond Horseshoe, were for the most part owned by the Vanderbilt and Morgan dynasties and the old guard Knickerbocker families. When the directors met, they did so at the home of J. P. Morgan.

These families were not socially liberal. Catholics, Jews, and foreigners (unless titled, of course) were prevented from owning boxes in the Diamond Horseshoe. The opera house was actually repainted in 1903 because the cream walls were deemed unflattering to the elaborate jewelry worn by the Diamond Horseshoe women in their evening dresses. The new color scheme, gold and maroon, was probably not by coincidence the Astor colors.

Caroline Astor, née Schermerhorn, born into one of New York's

Knickerbocker families who were descended from the original Dutch settlers, was the acknowledged doyenne of Metropolitan society. Draped in diamonds that reportedly had been owned by Marie Antoinette, she arrived in Box 7 promptly at nine, regardless of the time the opera began. Her husband, William Astor, rarely joined her; he spent most of his time on his yacht. Her jewels were so blazing that she was compared to an ambulatory chandelier. Her custom was to receive guests during intermissions, so she stayed for one or two before departing with her usual sangfroid. No other boxholder dared leave before Mrs. Astor.

Mrs. Astor returned to her mansion at the corner of Fifth Avenue and Thirty-fourth Street, where she entertained every Monday night after the opera. These were not light after-performance suppers: the average meal consisted of ten courses served on gold plates with gold flatware, the centerpieces of orchids so elaborate that the tables had to be reinforced. After dinner, Mrs. Astor showered her guests with extravagant party favors. One night, the guests were presented with a pile of sand on the dining room table, and given silver trowels for digging. Buried in the sand was expensive jewelry, set with diamonds, sapphires, and rubies.

If Mrs. Astor had a rival, it was Mrs. Cornelius Vanderbilt, who held court in Box 4. She was a more serious opera aficionado, and stayed until the evening's finale was at least started; then she, too, left. As Edith Wharton's novels confirm, going to the opera was a way for well-bred young men and women to meet. Unaccompanied gentlemen were not neglected and there was a section of the opera house reserved for "Male penguins only," as well as clubrooms. On special occasions, women were allowed to enter the clubrooms, but they were well hidden behind a large corner screen.

The boxholders each paid an annual assessment of $1,200 (which rose to $4,500 in the 1930s) and had their names engraved in brass plaques on the doors to their boxes; other people were allowed to enter only on invitation. Since it was considered ill form to leave a box empty, and since the boxholders certainly didn't want to attend every performance, some of them rented out their boxes on a nightly basis. They determined who was eligible to rent the boxes and fixed the rental price, much in the manner of present-day cooperative apartment house boards.

Refreshments were delivered from a restaurant on Sixth Avenue, and the boxholders enjoyed having both the house lights turned up all evening and the intermissions lengthier to provide time for their socializing. They ignored the rest of the audience, not caring that the evenings were now interminable and exhausting for those who had to go to work the next morning.

The boxholders also never let their general manager forget that the opera house was run at their sufferance. Many were successful businessmen who understood that the other seats in the theater had to be filled in order to balance the books. The number of "stars" was stipulated by contract, as was the amount of Wagner. The general managers quickly learned as long as the deficits were small and the number of star singers large, their positions were secure.

Disaster struck on several fronts in 1906 and 1907. From the very first season, touring had been an important part of the Met season, and the company was on tour in San Francisco in the spring of 1906 at the time of the great earthquake. Although no one was seriously injured, all the sets, costumes, and musical instruments were destroyed. But even before that, an internal dispute threatened the delicate balance between the financial goals of the Real Estate Company and the emphasis on artistic aspirations by the Opera Company. The boxholders split into factions, one concentrating on artistic aspects, the other on financial viability. The Opera Company, more interested in music than finance, referred to the Real Estate Company boxholders with their fiscal priorities as the "fogies." "The performances are better and better, and yet the [Real Estate] boxholders are kicking like mules," wrote Opera Company board member Eliot Gregory to Henry Hyde, another board member.

The conflict crystallized over the American premiere of Richard Strauss's *Salome*. The Real Estate board was initially reluctant to schedule the opera at all because of its salacious subject matter, for despite their ostentation, many still harbored a strong strain of puritanism. A rising young board member named Otto Kahn, who had allied himself with the Opera Company faction, went to the Real Estate board to plead the case for *Salome*. He pointed out that it had been performed all over Europe and should ideally be judged as a musical work rather than a theatrical spectacle. The board eventually acquiesced, but the premiere was nonetheless a scandal, with many people walking out and the reviews condemning "the moral stench with which *Salome* fills the nostrils of mankind." The reaction of J. P. Morgan's daughter was paramount. She was so upset that she complained to her father, who responded by making sure the remaining performances were canceled. The enraged Opera Company directors saw this as an abuse of the boxholders' power, even though Morgan offered to underwrite the losses. The Opera board, under Kahn's guidance, refused to accept the money as a matter of principle.

All these elements—the *Salome* debacle, the disastrous losses in San Francisco, and the opening of a rival opera house run by Oscar Hammerstein—led Heinrich Conried, the general manager, to search for a major conductor to take over the musical aspects of the company, someone who could compete with Cleofonte Campanini, Hammerstein's popular music director. The search was not easy. Artur Nikisch, the charismatic German who directed the Berlin Philharmonic was not interested, and neither was La Scala's music director, Arturo Toscanini. Conried wrote to Hyde, "Toscanini . . . replied that no financial consideration would persuade him to accept an engagement in America."

Like Damrosch, Conried suffered exhaustion and ill health caused by the anxieties of his position. But, finally, from his sickbed, he was able to send a triumphant cable to the board: "I am happy to announce the engagement of the very best of all musical directors Gustav Mahler for three months each season at very favorable terms."

Conried had approached Mahler about coming to the Met just when the conductor and composer was desperate to get away from Europe and the painful memories of his beloved four-year-old daughter, who had recently died of diphtheria. Although he himself suffered from a serious heart condition, he found the situation at the Met restorative. "The orchestra, the singing, the house itself," his wife, Alma, wrote, "all was wonderful . . . Mahler swam in bliss."

In the fall of 1907, Conried began his fifth season as general manager, but he received little gratitude for his coup in engaging Mahler, and became, instead, a pawn in the battle between the Opera board and the Real Estate Company. When Otto Kahn and the Opera board became more and more critical of Conried's leadership, the Real Estate Company, which had formerly criticized Conried ceaselessly, switched its support to the impresario. As the struggle intensified, the ambitious Kahn, who was not eligible to own a box because of his Jewish background, built a power base that would change the face of the Metropolitan.

*W*ith the early-twentieth-century boxholders being resolutely anti-Semitic, it is ironic that when Mahler arrived, two of the company's most influential positions were held by Jews. Although Gustav Mahler had converted to Catholicism to counteract the anti-Semitism he encountered while running the Vienna Opera, he had been born a Jew. The Jewish and foreign-born Otto Kahn, who was to guide the company's destiny for over a quarter-century, could not even rent a box. Yet Mahler's European background enhanced his desirability as a Met conductor.

Mahler made his debut at the Met on January 1, 1908, with a triumphant performance of Wagner's *Tristan und Isolde.* The music critics raved about Mahler's sensitivity toward his singers and the balance he achieved with the large Wagner orchestra.

Mahler also conducted performances of *Don Giovanni, Die Walküre, Siegfried,* and *Fidelio,* and critics credited him with visionary interpretations. He made clear that he expected the leading singers to rehearse as thoroughly as the lowliest chorister. Despite this, he was revered, especially by members of the orchestra. After a five-and-a-half-hour rehearsal for *Don Giovanni,* the fifteenth for that one production, a musician said, "Tired? Yes! But I feel that at least I am a musician once more."

Otto Kahn was so excited by Mahler's success that he seriously considered the conductor as a replacement for Conried. Disillusioned with Conried's ineptness, Kahn, by the beginning of the 1907–8 season, was planning to get rid of him. J. P. Morgan, however, disliked Kahn because of his Jewish ancestry and opposed his idea. So did many of the other directors. "This we all sat on," Eliot Gregory wrote, "as we were anxious to work away from the german [sic] atmosphere and the Jew (Mahler is a J.)." Kahn, an investment banker who was a managing partner of Kuhn, Loeb & Company, already knew about discrimination. The other directors even sneered at his wife, Adeline Wolff, a cousin of James Loeb: "Socially, the Kahns 'went backwards' last year," Eliot Gregory reported to Henry Hyde. "She is impossible for any social purpose having that worst of all defects, *débineuse* [an almost untranslatable French expression describing a person who delights in malicious gossip]." The Met board members sprinkled their correspondence with as many French phrases as possible.

The Opera Company rejected the idea of Mahler leading the company. Instead, they decided to invite both Giulio Gatti-Casazza, the intendant, or general manager, of La Scala, and Arturo Toscanini, the music director, to fill the same roles at the Met. Despite Toscanini's previous reluctance to come to New York, his trust in Gatti-Casazza as an administrator led him to reconsider when he heard that Gatti was interested in the Met. The board sent one of its members to La Scala with contracts for Gatti and Toscanini and, to placate Kahn, vowed to retain Mahler for the performances of German opera. The board was jubilant: if this plan worked, the Metropolitan would have two of the world's greatest conductors under contract.

The Opera Company board had to deal with the Real Estate Company's rage at not having been consulted in these plans. Initially, the situation seemed hopeless: the Opera board representative was in Milan with the Gatti and Toscanini contracts, and both men were ready to sign. In New York, however, Conried refused to resign.

In the end, Otto Kahn negotiated a settlement that completely reorganized the Metropolitan. The board of the Opera Company took out a lease on the theater and assumed the responsibility of hiring professionals to run the company, and Kahn agreed to the Real Estate Company's employing Andreas Dippel, a former singer, as "administrative manager," promising J. P. Morgan that he would keep an eye on Gatti. Kahn made sure that Dippel never became a nuisance to the new intendant, although the situation was annoying. "Kahn really has done excellent work," one board member wrote. "I doubt if anyone else could have pulled us out of the mess we were in. But!!! There is always a but, alas! It will end in his becoming the president of the new co. . . . It will make trouble I feel almost sure."

Conried returned to Austria. Already ill, he was now also broken in spirit. In 1909, at the end of Toscanini and Gatti's first Met season, he died. Kahn and the board had kept in effect a life insurance policy on him and, after a payment to his widow, there still remained $150,000 to help pay off some of the accumulated losses.

Kahn now underwrote the debts that the reorganized Metropolitan Opera Company had incurred over the preceding four years, a total of $450,000. In this way, he achieved total control of the Opera Company, although the building itself remained the property of the Real Estate board. With Gatti, whom Kahn greatly respected, running the theater, the company began twenty-five years of relative stability, at least for the board and management. Stability in the artistic arena was harder to achieve.

Chapter Two

MAHLER AND TOSCANINI

Gustav Mahler's name was mentioned only in passing during the dispute between the Opera Company and the Real Estate Company, but, in fact, both factions wanted to ensure that Mahler would stay on after Toscanini arrived. Any awareness of Mahler's and Toscanini's temperaments, however, would have seen the futility of this hope.

Kahn was sophisticated enough to ask Toscanini, even before he was engaged, whether Mahler's presence would be a problem. Toscanini answered promptly, "But of course, I will have no difficulty at all. There is room at the Metropolitan for several conductors and I am very happy to find myself with an artist of Mahler's worth . . . and would infinitely prefer such a colleague to any mediocrity." Mahler expressed similar sentiments.

In the fall of 1908, however, Mahler returned to New York and realized that the situation was no longer ideal for him. "Gatti-Casazza was now director . . . and he had brought Toscanini over with him. The glorious days of German supremacy were over," Alma Mahler reported.

The inevitable clash between the two conductors came quickly, and it was over *Tristan und Isolde.* As part of his contract, Toscanini had insisted that he be given a new production of *Tristan;* Andreas Dippel was given the job of breaking the news to Mahler. As could have been expected, Mahler was furious and refused to agree. He considered *Tristan,* which had been his debut at the Met, to be his territory, and he threatened to resign.

For the 1908–9 season, Mahler prevailed, but in 1909, Toscanini conducted _Tristan_. Suffering renewed symptoms of his heart problem, Mahler did not have the strength to fight another battle. Later, he accepted an invitation to become music director of the newly formed Philharmonic Society of New York, while Toscanini settled in at the Met.

Mahler's relationship with the Philharmonic deteriorated quickly because of the radical programs he wanted to present that were disliked by both the press and the wealthy patrons. In addition, he became seriously ill in the late winter of 1911. He began to miss concerts, and even his adversaries expressed concern. But it was too late. In the spring, Mahler returned to Vienna, where he died on May 18, 1911; he was only fifty years old.

In 1908, when the new regime took over at the Metropolitan, all three principals were young men: Otto Kahn and Toscanini were each forty-one, and Gatti-Casazza was thirty-eight. The combination was magical. Gatti and Toscanini had worked closely at La Scala and Kahn respected their experience and authority.

Toscanini's career was helped by his appearance; he looked like everyone's image of a conductor. His profile was aristocratic, his skin translucent, and his eyes dark and dreamy. His expression alternated between intensity and spirituality, although many attributed the special quality of his gaze to his extreme near-sightedness. His myopia forced him to memorize anything he conducted and earned him the reputation for a phenomenal memory; the truth was that he could not see the music in front of him.

For his first orchestra rehearsal at the Met, Toscanini chose to work on Wagner's _Götterdämmerung_. Although he rarely suffered from insecurity, he was nervous before meeting his new orchestra. At the time, rehearsals at the Met were held in German or English. Most of the musicians were European, as was the case in most American orchestras since there was no tradition of musical education in the United States. Toscanini was not comfortable in either German or English, but he stunned the orchestra, who had heard about his legendary memory, when he rehearsed the gigantic _Götterdämmerung_ without a score. Not only did he know every note of the opera and every word of the text, he was able to correct mistakes in the printed parts that no other conductors, even the Germans, had ever noticed. At the end of the rehearsal, the musicians applauded.

His temper was also legendary; he screamed at the players and bellowed offensive names at anyone who made a mistake. When he said, "The orchestra play like pig!" the orchestra, unused to his cavalier treatment, demanded an apology. Toscanini explained that he couldn't apologize because the orchestra indeed played "like pig," although he did offer to open each rehearsal by saying "Good morning." Not reassured by this concession, the orchestra sent a delegation to Gatti to report some of Toscanini's most egregious insults. "You think that's bad," Gatti said to the musicians. "You should hear what he calls me."

Toscanini had a clear vision of the general manager's role: it was to enable Toscanini to achieve artistic excellence. He wanted Gatti to build financial security, handle all logistics, and keep the company as happy as any opera company could be. He, Toscanini, would make all artistic decisions and, although he probably never articulated this, would personify all artistic temperament. Fortunately, Gatti had an amenable nature, which was the only way he could have coexisted as he did with Toscanini for their seven years at La Scala and seven years at the Met. However, their personal relationship remained formal and they never became friends.

Toscanini's fits of temper extended as well to some of the leading singers, whom he offended by his insistence on their attendance at all rehearsals and by his zealousness in correcting them. The American soprano Geraldine Farrar was one of the Met's reigning divas at the time Toscanini arrived, and, with Caruso, one of the first classical musicians to achieve superstar status. Toscanini was not the least impressed by her fame and a clash was inevitable since Farrar was not short of temperament herself.

The two rehearsed together for the first time when Toscanini prepared a revival of *Madama Butterfly* in which Farrar sang the title role. She had performed the company premiere of the work and felt she owned the role, at least in New York. So she was astonished when Toscanini made clear that he expected her to follow him instead of the other way round. "But I am the star," she protested.

"Madame," Toscanini replied, "the only stars are in the heavens."

Eventually, Toscanini came to admire Farrar's Butterfly so much that he requested her in the role when another singer canceled in the middle of the 1908–9 season. By the end of the tour, which came late in the season, Toscanini was coming onstage to take curtain calls with Farrar, and one night in Chicago, she noted some "very unexpected and friendly overtures." Soon an affair developed and became an open secret.

Music was Toscanini's religion and it came before anything else in his life. He worked hard, drank little, and ate sparingly, yet he could not control his appetite for women. Although he had many relationships outside his marriage, besides the one with Farrar, he had also been brought up as an Italian Catholic and divorce to him was unthinkable.

Gatti was also enmeshed in a complicated romance. He had become entranced with Frances Alda, a beautiful red-haired soprano from New Zealand who made her Met debut in 1908 as Gilda in *Rigoletto*. She had already sung for Gatti and Toscanini at La Scala but had not made much of an impression; Toscanini had asked in what language she thought she was singing. Her Met debut was not particularly well received, but Gatti was smitten. Alda and Gatti married in 1910, and she left the Met to sing at the Boston Opera.

In 1911, Toscanini wanted Alda to sing Desdemona in *Otello*. Paul D. Cravath, Otto Kahn's lawyer and a member of the board, was horrified at the idea of the general manager's wife appearing on the stage. He offered a motion to the board refusing Alda permission to appear, but Kahn supported Toscanini and Gatti, and Cravath was defeated. Alda returned to the Met and continued to sing there until 1929, the year she divorced Gatti.

By the end of Toscanini's first season in New York, the press proclaimed him a genius. Gatti was turning out to be a model intendant, Otto Kahn had insured the company's financial health despite recent losses, and Toscanini had reinstated high musical standards. Tranquillity and stability seemed just over the horizon.

But tranquillity and stability were rare in any opera house that was home to Arturo Toscanini. Toscanini conducted the world premiere of Puccini's newest opera, *La Fanciulla del West*, to great acclaim, as well as the Met premiere of Gluck's _Armide_ and the American premiere of _Boris Godunov_. The orchestra and chorus were considered among the best in the world, as was the roster of international singers. Toscanini was well paid and also had the freedom to conduct anywhere else in the world.

As Toscanini was proving himself, Gatti was doing the same. His ten years at La Scala had trained him in everything from the small detail to the broad view; he was the best general manager the company had had. He was able to cut down on costs and at the same time improve production. He brought European designers and artisans, strengthened the ballet, which boasted Anna Pavlova as prima ballerina from 1910 to 1912, and engaged Michel Fokine for a new staging of _Le Coq d'Or_. Gatti's interest in the ballet was heightened when Rosina Galli became prima ballerina. The high-spirited dancer was first his mistress and then his second wife, setting a trend followed by several Met general managers.

The Met had never presented a world premiere or performed a work by an American composer. Gatti gave American and New York premieres in seasons that ran up to twenty-four weeks and often included fifty operas. To him, an opera house was not to be a museum for music of the past or of Europe.

Gatti was a colorful presence, an Italian male who never quite adjusted to the United States. He did not learn English, which often served as an excuse when he was faced with confrontations. He was liable to turn up anywhere in the opera house at any moment, and he listened closely to rehearsals over a speaker that was installed in his office.

Gatti attended nearly every performance, sitting in the general manager's box, as did Otto Kahn, content in his orchestra seat. Kahn had gained almost complete financial control of the company—he had earned stock for making up the Met's deficit from 1908 to 1910—but he did not attempt to dictate artistic policy, although occasionally he recommended a talented conductor or young singer. One of the few times he exercised authority was in helping Frances Alda during her separation from Gatti. After she told her husband that she wanted a divorce because of his affair with Galli, she heard rumors that she was not to sing again at the Met. She turned to Kahn and was soon offered a one-year renewal of her contract.

Kahn's diplomacy in artistic matters, however, did not extend to questions of finance. Kahn had made it clear that deficits such as those incurred during the first two Gatti-Toscanini seasons would never again be tolerated. His edict resulted in the erosion of Gatti's good relationship with Toscanini.

Toscanini was notoriously unsympathetic to Gatti's attempts at saving money. A major explosion occurred in 1913 over a new production of Verdi's *Un Ballo in Maschera,* part of the Met's salute to the composer's centenary. Toscanini wanted a stage band for the ball scene in the final act, but Gatti told him to use musicians playing from the pit, saving the cost of extra players. Knowing how much the principal artists, including himself, were paid, Toscanini sneered at this penny-pinching. Rumors began circulating that Toscanini had threatened to resign.

Toscanini may have been frustrated by the petty financial limitations, but he was also exhausted by the relentless pace of Met seasons. In addition, his affair with Geraldine Farrar had progressed far beyond its light-hearted beginnings. Farrar was a prima donna, but she was an American prima donna. His previous mistresses had been Italians, who had understood Toscanini's lifelong commitment to his wife and family, but Farrar did not. She always expected to have what she wanted. When she had made her Met debut in 1906 as Juliette, her European stardom was such that she could demand not to be upstaged by a tenor. Thus, the first night of the 1906–7 season was the only opening night during his tenure that Caruso did not sing. She was the only Met singer to have her own dressing room and, when she traveled with the company, her own railroad car.

Six years into her affair with Toscanini, Farrar said that unless he left his wife, their relationship would be over. Toscanini, who by religion and by heritage abhorred divorce, was so in love with Farrar that he could not conceive of having to see her at the Met after their affair ended. Toscanini began to consider leaving New York.

At a matinee performance of *Carmen* in March 1915, the tenor Giovanni Martinelli was called on to replace Caruso, who had suddenly fallen ill. Even though Toscanini had given Martinelli as hard a time as he did everyone—once telling him he "sang like a police dog"—the tenor admired him. But that afternoon he was singing Don José for the first time in French instead of Italian, and because of nervousness, he had a memory lapse. Toscanini and the orchestra managed to keep the performance going, but afterward the maestro blamed Gatti for not allowing sufficient rehearsal time.

A few days later, after another poorly sung matinee of *Carmen*, Toscanini stormed backstage and announced to Gatti that he was canceling his last six performances of the season and would return early to Italy. His misery over his affair with Farrar made his artistic frustrations seem insurmountable. This decision turned out to be great good luck. The change put him and his family aboard a ship other than the one he was originally scheduled to sail on, the *Lusitania*, which was sunk by a German submarine on that same voyage.

Gatti went to see Toscanini in Italy during the summer of 1915 and wrote to Kahn that chances for the conductor's return did not seem promising. He implored Kahn to intercede, even suggesting that allowing Toscanini one of his tantrums might clear the air.

Kahn attempted to negotiate with Toscanini, assuring him of the admiration not only of the board but also of the entire city of New York. In the end, Toscanini stayed in Italy and soon went back to La Scala. He returned to live in the United States only when the Fascist threat of World War II made music-making in Italy impossible for him. But he never again conducted an opera performance at the Metropolitan.

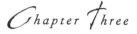

Chapter Three

Toscanini used the onset of World War I as an excuse not to come back to New York. Real consequences of the war in Europe, however, soon were felt in New York. As it became clear that the United States would be drawn into the conflict, a fierce anti-German sentiment swept through the country.

Before the United States entry into the war in 1917, Gatti had been able to resist the pressure to cancel German opera and dismiss German artists. But after war was declared on Good Friday, when the Met was halfway through a performance of *Parsifal,* he had to defer to his board. By the beginning of the 1917–18 season, the directors could no longer ignore the public's xenophobia. The board made it clear to Gatti that he would rid the Met of Teutonic influence or lose his job, even though the press deplored the directors' stand and took Gatti's side: "Bach, Beethoven, Wagner and Brahms," read an editorial in the *Sun,* "belong to the world as do Shakespeare and Dante."

Nevertheless, one week before the 1917–18 season opened, Gatti replaced forty-five German operas, nearly one out of every three performances. The company issued a statement explaining that these works had been canceled "lest Germany should make capital of their continued appearance to convince the German people that this nation was not heart and soul in the war."

Johanna Gadski, a German soprano married to a captain in the German army, had been taken off the roster at the end of the previous season, and now Gatti also fired Melanie Kurt, Margaret Ober, Johannes Sembach, Carl Braun, and Otto Goritz. To fill the gaps in the repertory, he hired the French conductor Pierre Monteux and Roberto Moranzoni, an Italian conductor.

At the same time, there was a brief flurry over an order by the federal fuel administrator that theaters should be dark one night a week. The Met was ordered to close on Mondays, which horrified the boxholders, since Monday had always been the most social night at the opera. Finally, it was decreed that the Met could save as much fuel by a dark Tuesday as a dark Monday, and, with great relief, the boxholders returned to their original schedule. They may have been patriotic, even xenophobic, but they would not countenance a disruption of their social lives.

Another consequence of the war was the difficulty of recruiting chorus and orchestra members from Europe. For the first time, American musicians began to dominate both groups, and the atmosphere in the company began to change. The Europeans were more accustomed to the traditional hierarchy of an opera house, and as the chorus, orchestra, and stage crew became Americanized, they organized into unions, and the precarious history of Met labor relations began. On a more positive side, as Americans became increasingly entrenched in the performing arts professions, an American tradition of playing and teaching started, both vocally and instrumentally.

World War I officially ended on November 11, 1918, which happened to be the opening night of the Met's 1918–19 season. Purely by chance, Gatti had planned to open with Saint-Saëns's *Samson et Dalila,* with Monteux conducting and Caruso and Louise Homer singing. This was hailed as a brilliantly prescient salute to victorious France. Gatti, who like all intendants was blamed constantly for circumstances beyond his control, must have enjoyed the undeserved acclaim for this fluke of fate. He was, however, much prouder of reintroducing the German repertory with a performance of Wagner's *Parsifal* in February 1920, although he bowed again to public opinion, which was still vociferously anti-German, by presenting the opera in English.

Opening night of the 1919–20 season was the first one during Prohibition, but the audience was more directly affected by a rise in ticket prices. This increase was part of Gatti's ongoing efforts to keep the company in the good fiscal shape demanded by Otto Kahn. The Gatti-Kahn initiative was certainly successful in financial terms, and the company's net profit increased yearly in spite of the fact that the season expanded, as did the number of operas produced. But in artistic terms, the results were less felicitous. Rehearsal time suffered as more and more operas were thrust onstage; conductors stopped even trying to get major singers to rehearse. At Lauritz Melchior's first Met appearance, he did not have any rehearsal and did not even meet the conductor. The company had signed a union contract with its musicians in 1919 that stated the players, in return for an increase in salary, could be asked to perform eight times a week. And they were asked to do just that, with the result being an exhausted and demoralized orchestra.

Sapping the Met's sense of ensemble was a policy, instituted by Gatti in 1922, of engaging singers for only half a season. The idea was to provide variety and flexibility in casting, but its effect was disastrous on the company's cohesiveness and discipline. This was also the beginning of the singers' awareness that they could mold the Met to their own schedules. As this sense developed over the years, it would give the artists a new appreciation of their own power in negotiating with the management.

Gatti and Kahn were in total agreement about the inadequacy of the Metropolitan Opera House itself. When Gatti first had arrived and expressed horror at the building's shortcomings, Kahn had promised that a new house would be built immediately. World War I made this impossible, but the prosperous 1920s that followed seemed to Kahn an ideal time to raise funds.

Kahn wanted to change more than the four walls of the house. His time as board president had been scarred by his sense that the other directors never considered him socially acceptable. Even the external perception of his power at the Met did not alter this, nor did his joining the congregation at St. Thomas, an Episcopal church on Fifth Avenue at Fifty-third Street. Kahn wanted to revise the Met's system that gave power to the private shareholders, and he did not want to build a new opera house until this evolution was guaranteed. For two decades, from 1908 until the onset of the Depression, Kahn used all his diplomatic skills to build a coalition of like-minded directors who would have the backbone to stand up to the omnipresent "old fogies" who cherished social position above artistic values.

After World War I, Kahn realized that a substantial group of well-educated music lovers who cared nothing about social standing now came to the Met and he considered their tastes and interests just as valuable as those of the boxholders. Kahn was determined that their voices be heard. To him, it was quintessentially American and democratic that a semipublic institution like the Met represent the concerns of all opera lovers, wealthy or not.

The boxholders were horrified, and some referred to Kahn as a socialist. They turned down his suggestions in the early 1920s that a new house be built, but Kahn was not dissuaded. In 1925, with his own money he bought land for the new opera house, a large plot on Ninth Avenue between West Fifty-sixth and Fifty-seventh Streets (where the Parc Vendôme apartment complex now stands). His fellow board members refused to be steamrollered despite the fact that the public and the press took Kahn's side.

There were various attempts at a compromise—Kahn would sell the land to the shareholders, who could then sell the old site at a healthy profit; the boxholders would still constitute an ownership group, but others would be allowed in the boxes on certain nights; those who didn't want the opera house would be bought out. But a determined group of boxholders, including the powerful Goelet and Vanderbilt families, refused to concede. Eventually, in 1928, Kahn gave up and put his Ninth Avenue property up for sale, and any discussion of a new theater was at an end.

Gatti and Kahn also were determined to infuse some fresh air into the company; they scheduled four contemporary operas during the 1928–29 season. One, Ernst Krenek's jazz opera, _Jonny Spielt Auf,_ had been a sensation in Europe the previous year, and in January 1929, the Metropolitan gave the American premiere. The production, underwritten by Kahn and his supporters, told the story of an African-American entertainer, although to minimize racial sensitivity, Jonny in New York was portrayed as a white entertainer in blackface. Still, this was too much for Kahn's many enemies. At the premiere, several of the anti-Semitic directors, even those who had known Kahn for twenty years, attacked him verbally, saying that this time he had gone too far. The more conservative element among the boxholders vowed to tighten their control on the company's artistic policies.

Kahn did not vent his bitterness until after his resignation from the board two years later. In an interview with Olin Downes of the *New York Times,* he excoriated the other board members for accepting the money and business expertise he poured into the Met while never letting him forget he was an outsider.

Despite Kahn's battles, Gatti concentrated on sustaining the company's artistic stature. Although daily standards and discipline were deteriorating, he still managed to produce a parade of the world's greatest singers across the Met stage: Titta Ruffo, Elisabeth Rethberg, Giacomo Lauri-Volpi, Lawrence Tibbett, Melchior, Rosa Ponselle, Ezio Pinza, Grace Moore, Gladys Swarthout, Lily Pons, Claudia Muzio, Lotte Lehmann, and Kirsten Flagstad.

After Caruso's death in 1921, Beniamino Gigli became the leading tenor, and two popular and glamorous sopranos, Amelita Galli-Curci and Maria Jeritza, made their debuts. At Jeritza's first performance as Tosca in December 1921, she created the tradition of singing "Vissi d'arte" while lying prone on the stage (she had slipped) and incited an ovation that Gatti would later call the loudest he ever heard in a theater. Puccini had rushed backstage afterward, delighted. "It was from God!" he told Jeritza. "Always do it that way!" Subsequently, Geraldine Farrar made the decision to retire from the Met at forty. She was still so popular that after her last performance, her distraught fans dragged her limousine by hand down Broadway.

The 1929–30 season, which opened on the day of the stock market crash, grossed the most money ever—$3,411,000—and the number of performances declined only slightly. Otto Kahn congratulated Gatti on this achievement, but surely both men knew this could not go on. The Metropolitan, as always, was firmly anchored in the world offstage, and that world was falling apart.

Chapter Four

THE GREAT DEPRESSION

The Metropolitan Opera proceeded into the Depression years with arrogant complacency. For almost a quarter-century, through a world war and a period of enormous social change, the capable management of Gatti-Casazza and Otto Kahn had kept the company stable. In 1930, the United States economy may have been in dire condition, but the Metropolitan had $1 million in its reserve fund.

The 1929–30 season opened with a new top ticket price of $8.25, up from $7 ten years previously. Subscription statistics remained healthy, despite the stock market crash on opening night, since those tickets had been bought long before October 29, and by the end of the season, single ticket receipts were still so good that Kahn and the board extended Gatti's contract for two years, raising his salary to $67,000. But there were signs of trouble ahead; despite the season's record profits, expenses had risen, and the Met recorded its first loss in twenty years.

At first, Gatti and Kahn did not take the deficit seriously, considering the history of fiscal well-being. But by the beginning of the 1930–31 season, the number of subscribers fell, and two of the tour sponsors dropped out. The season was cut by two weeks, but the losses mounted so fast that this money-saving maneuver was not sufficient. By the end of the season, the company had lost almost $325,000, about a third of its reserve fund.

The 1931–32 season opened with subscriptions down; many of the subscriptions that had been taken had not been paid for. Kahn's plans for a new opera house were in shambles, and so was the existing building. One reason the company had been able to build up a large reserve fund was that it had made no repairs or improvements in years; the scenery was shabby, the electrical system so old that it was dangerous, and no air-conditioning had been installed. Kahn, with his years of experience in the financial world, knew that the Depression was not a short-term economic downturn that the Met could survive by drawing on its reserves.

Kahn resigned in 1931, tired of his struggles with the other directors and embarrassed by a breach-of-contract suit brought by a young singer with whom he had been having an affair. He was replaced by Paul D. Cravath, the attorney who was Kahn's personal lawyer and who represented Bethlehem Steel, Westinghouse, and RCA. Kahn may have had difficulties with his fellow directors, but the public perceived him as a strong asset to the Met. His resignation fueled apprehension about the company's future, and subscriptions continued to drop.

Kahn's resignation had one fortunate consequence. Paul Cravath's new role spurred RCA's and Westinghouse's interest in the Metropolitan, and within a few weeks of his appointment, RCA-NBC signed the company to a contract for twenty-four national radio broadcasts. The board had long been interested in the possibility of profits from the media. Twenty years before the weekly broadcasts began in 1931, the company had experimented with broadcasting a performance. A Yale University physicist, who piqued Gatti's imagination about transmissions from the Met stage, had installed two microphones on the stage, a ship's transmitter in the opera house attic, and, as an antenna, attached two fishing rods to the flagpole on the roof. The only problem with this bold experiment was that almost no one had a radio, so almost no one heard the broadcast. But by 1931, almost everyone had a radio. The first Met national broadcast, _Hänsel und Gretel,_ took place on Christmas Day, 1931, only months before Franklin D. Roosevelt assumed office.

Still, the company's situation was desperate. Articles began to appear entitled "Is This the Twilight of Opera?" The deficit for 1931–32 reached almost $500,000; the reserve fund had vanished in just two seasons. Cravath insisted that stringent economizing be initiated, so Gatti proposed a "voluntary" pay cut of 10 percent for all salaried employees, including principal artists. This had become a standard request all over the country as the Depression deepened. Almost all the artists agreed, except for Gigli, the company's leading tenor. Gatti himself volunteered to serve without a salary (his wife, the dancer Rosina Galli, had earned over $200,000 from the Met from 1921 to 1930), but the truth was that he took only a token deduction. The 10 percent pay cut allowed the Met to start over in negotiating artists' contracts. A top fee of $1,000 was established.

Cravath knew he had to act on a higher level as well. A board member since 1910, he had never been a boxholder and had little allegiance to that sacred body. There was no question in his mind that the financial crisis must take precedence over any social tradition, so he reincorporated the Metropolitan Opera Company as the Metropolitan Opera Association. Now the institution had an "educational" and thus nonprofit status, saving entertainment taxes. Ticket prices could be reduced to 1920 levels and, as a result, single-ticket sales rose. The season was shortened from twenty-four to sixteen weeks, creating the shortest since 1903. However, the deficit was stubborn; the 1932–33 season lost $339,901.

Real power had passed to the Metropolitan Opera Association, but because the Metropolitan Opera Real Estate Company, the descendants of the original boxholders, still owned the opera house itself, the public's perception persisted that the wealthy still had control.

The conductor Artur Bodanzky summed up the situation when he implored, "There must be a plan to take opera out of the hands of the 'wealthy few' and put it in the hands of the 'appreciative public.' " The actuality was that those wealthy few had been affected by the Depression like most of the rest of the country; they could no longer even offer token support to keep the opera house open.

In 1933, the Met's fiftieth anniversary season, the directors, for the first time, made a serious plea for public funds. The situation was so bad that opening night was postponed until December 26 so as not to compete with Christmas shopping. At fourteen weeks, 1933–34 was the shortest season in forty years.

The directors realized that with the new radio series, they had access to a national audience, and they began to make appeals during the weekly broadcasts. Money, often in tiny contributions of a dollar or two, began to flow in. Eventually, these offerings from the general public who loved the Met and its music reached $100,000. This response actually inspired the directors themselves to pledge $150,000 in addition to their boxholders' fees—the first time they had shown any personal sense for the company that had served their social needs for so long.

Gatti-Casazza announced his retirement as of the 1934–35 season. He had known he would have to leave since 1930, when he had horrified the directors by marrying Rosina Galli; they had informed him at the time that he could serve out the rest of his contract but that it would not be renewed. He also had trouble making the transition from working with Kahn, a decisive and generous man, to dealing with Cravath, who had a lawyer's bent for management detail yet volunteered very little of his copious fortune to help the struggling institution he oversaw.

Even during this dreary period, the old Met glamour still surfaced from time to time. The French soprano Lily Pons, who had made her debut in 1930–31 and had become a big box office attraction, dressed so elegantly that, even in the depths of the Depression, she inspired the other singers to spruce themselves up. Kirsten Flagstad made her debut in 1934–35, and overnight became the Met's top box office attraction, despite her shy temperament and her hatred of the operatic social scene. She joined a force of eminent Wagnerians then singing with the company, among them Lotte Lehmann, Lauritz Melchior, and Friedrich Schorr. Many had come to the Met from the Chicago Opera, which had gone bankrupt in 1932 and closed.

An extraordinary woman emerged from this chaotic time. Eleanor Robson Belmont was a prominent actress who had left the stage in 1910 when she married the financier August Belmont, son of a boxholder at the Academy of Music. A woman of great energy and independence, she had channeled her vigor into raising money for the Red Cross during World War I. Once having learned the techniques of fund-raising, she saw no reason not to apply them to an artistic institution. The result was the Committee for Saving the Metropolitan Opera, formed outwardly to celebrate the company's fiftieth anniversary but in reality to keep the curtain from coming down permanently. Mrs. Belmont enlisted Lucrezia Bori,

Lawrence Tibbett, and Edward Johnson from the artists' roster to galvanize public support. Johnson announced the fund drive during a radio broadcast in 1933, and, two weeks later, NBC made an unprecedented move by giving the Met a half hour of air time in which to raise funds.

Mrs. Belmont also inaugurated a series of benefit performances, parties, and balls, an effort that has continued ever since. Although she had married a member of one of the city's most prominent families, Mrs. Belmont believed that the people of New York had the right to look at the Met as their own and as an essential component of life in the city. She actually referred to her mission as "the democratization of opera." A relative of one of those exclusionary boxholders at the Academy of Music who had inspired the creation of the Metropolitan in the first place thus became an important force in expanding the company's accessibility.

Mrs. Belmont launched a women's club for the Metropolitan. In 1935 she transformed this club into the Metropolitan Opera Guild. Its emphasis firmly on cultural support rather than social status, the Guild became the democratic fund-raising arm of the company. She named herself chairman. In 1933, in recognition of her work on behalf of the company, she was elected the first woman member of the Metropolitan Opera board.

Joining Mrs. Belmont in her efforts was Cornelius N. Bliss, a boxholder, philanthropist, and a treasurer of the Republican National Committee. Mrs. Belmont would later credit Bliss as the one man above all others who had helped the Met survive, and, with her support, he became president of the board. Bliss's father, also named Cornelius, had been a former partner of J. P. Morgan, and had made a fortune in textiles. He had also been chairman of the Republican Party and William McKinley had invited him to be his vice president, an offer Bliss turned down because his wife refused to move to Washington. Instead, he had become secretary of the interior in McKinley's administration. The elder Cornelius Bliss had come to the Metropolitan in the 1890s as the owner of Box 8, and he had passed his proprietary interest on to his son.

Cornelius N. Bliss had sold the family business at enormous profit just before the Depression, and turned to philanthropy. His sister, Lillie P. Bliss, was also a patron of the arts: she was one of the three founders of the Museum of Modern Art. When Bliss became board president in 1938, having evaluated the company over his six years on the board, he was ready to move to reduce the power of the boxholders. Bliss had one enormous advantage in dealing with these cantankerous men: he was a boxholder by inheritance. The battle to wrest power from the boxholders was now undertaken by one of their own.

Even in boxholder circles, the Depression had taken a toll. More than half the boxes were now owned by the heirs or estates of the original owners, some of whom were unwilling and probably unable to pay their assessed fees. But their stubborn pride cost them nothing; although the boxholders realized they would eventually have to sell the opera house because they could no longer afford its upkeep, they were determined to make the process as difficult and expensive as possible.

Under Bliss's guidance, the Metropolitan Opera Association offered the boxholders almost $2 million for the building, the cost of the original construction. The boxholders reluctantly agreed, so the last remaining problem for the Metropolitan Opera directors was how to pay for this purchase.

Again, they took a populist route and named Mayor Fiorello H. La Guardia as chairman of a public campaign. Money began to come in: from radio listeners, from foundations, from subscribers, from the directors themselves, and, amazingly, even some from boxholders who donated the sale price of their holdings. On May 31, 1940, the title to the opera house finally passed from the hands of the original boxholders. While no one could have mistaken the Metropolitan Opera Association as a congregation of the common man, for the first time the company was no longer, at least officially, the playing field for a small group of wealthy men.

EDWARD JOHNSON, WORLD WAR II, AND THE AMERICAN OPERA SINGER; RUDOLF BING ARRIVES

Edward Johnson had been a tenor with the Metropolitan for fifteen years when he became involved in Mrs. Belmont's campaign to save the company. Born in Canada, he had begun his career in Italy as Edoardo di Giovanni—many American singers used European forms of their names in the hope of gaining status. When Johnson came to the Met, in 1922, he switched back to his real name. While involved with the fund-raising effort, Johnson had become interested in opera administration; he so impressed Gatti-Casazza with his ability that Gatti suggested Johnson succeed him as general manager.

But, over the years, the Juilliard Music Foundation had become a major backer of the Met, and, as usual, the giving of money provided influence in return. In 1935, Juilliard gave the company a desperately needed $250,000, tied to certain conditions: the foundation had to be represented on the board; there were to be no budget deficits; subscription sales must increase; and opportunities must be provided for American artists. In order to ensure that these conditions be met, Juilliard pressured the board to name as general manager Herbert Witherspoon, the former artistic director of the defunct Chicago Opera who had been associated for years with the Juilliard Foundation. The board acquiesced; Johnson was named as Witherspoon's assistant. Johnson swallowed his pride and accepted.

In May 1935, only a few weeks after becoming general manager,

Witherspoon collapsed and died of a heart attack in his office. Suddenly, Edward Johnson had the job he had really wanted. He proved an excellent choice for the time. An elegant, charming man who inspired great loyalty in his staff, he had a healthy respect for the history and traditions of the company. The wealthy board members were comfortable with a man who seemed much like one of their own.

When World War II broke out, most European singers could not get to New York, so Johnson turned by necessity into a tireless promoter of American artists. In addition, the budgetary restrictions made homegrown singers appealing, since their fees tended to be lower than those of their European colleagues.

Johnson also proved inventive in sparking the public's interest in the Met. He launched the Metropolitan Auditions of the Air, a popular vocal competition whose winners included Leonard Warren, Eleanor Steber, Robert Merrill, Patrice Munsel, and Regina Resnik, who went on to become Met favorites. Johnson also presented the debuts of Helen Traubel, Risë Stevens, Jan Peerce, Blanche Thebom, Astrid Varnay, Dorothy Kirsten, and Richard Tucker. He gradually lengthened the season to its former span.

Johnson had fewer difficulties during World War II than Gatti had in World War I. This time, there was little pressure to censor the German repertory, although *Madama Butterfly* was not performed after Japan attacked the United States in 1941. But the sets and costumes, already in terrible shape after the financial crisis, continued to deteriorate because needed materials were unobtainable during the war. To make up for the poor visual aspects, Johnson reduced ticket prices, and the company played to mostly full houses during the war. Members of the armed forces were given free tickets when seats were available, and uniforms became more common than tuxedos.

The war brought to the company numbers of experienced European conductors and musicians: Erich Leinsdorf, George Szell, Bruno Walter, Max Rudolf, Sir Thomas Beecham, and others became Met regulars, raising the musical standards. Also, the company remained relatively intact during the war years and developed a sense of ensemble that had been missing during the seasons when European singers came for only part of the year.

The directors, like most people in the country, were distracted by the war efforts, and, once he proved trustworthy as a fiscal strategist, they left the urbane Johnson alone to run the company. There was some criticism that he overused certain American singers, putting them in roles for which their voices were not suited in order to fill gaps in casting and thus shortening their careers. Although he had been a singer himself, he frequently placed singers in roles that were too heavy or demanding. Many of the Americans, relatively inexperienced, did not protest when they were badly cast or thrust into roles for which they were unprepared.

But by promoting and incorporating, if occasionally overusing, important Americans, Johnson managed to maintain unity through a troubled period. It was an era in which the social and political change brought about by the Depression and a world war could have set off a downward spiral for the Met. Although quality did slip, Johnson kept the company enthusiastic, the finances intact, and the curtain up.

By the end of the war, the Metropolitan was in relatively sound financial condition; Johnson balanced its budget between 1944 and 1947. But now his weaknesses as general manager were becoming apparent. One reason that Johnson had rapport with the directors was that he was an easygoing man who avoided confrontations with either his board members or artists. He enjoyed his prestigious position and his reputation for making the Met an American theater. But running an opera house takes an unwavering administrative purpose and an iron hand; Johnson had neither.

And Johnson was perhaps too easily swayed by public opinion. After World War II ended, the question arose of Kirsten Flagstad's return to the Met. In 1941, the great Wagnerian soprano had left the company and returned to Norway to be with her husband, who would later be imprisoned for having collaborated with the Nazis. Flagstad herself had spent the war years almost entirely in Norway; aside from an occasional performance, her main role was that of docile wife. But her name had been tainted, and when the Met considered inviting her back, the public was outraged. Even the influence of Mrs. Belmont, who gave a courageous speech to the Women's National Republican Club praising Flagstad, could not change the misperception of Flagstad's political leanings. Eventually, the U.S.

government issued Flagstad a visa, and she began making concert tours in the United States, but Johnson still would not invite her back to the Met.

Mrs. Belmont, who never lacked the courage of her convictions, gave a dinner party in 1949 and invited both Flagstad and Johnson. Johnson gave a gracious toast to the soprano but said nothing about a possible return to the Met. Even when the board's executive committee cleared the way for Flagstad, Johnson did nothing. Aware that his popularity stemmed in part from his avoidance of controversy, he did not want to take on the press and public on behalf of an artist of Flagstad's stature.

Other company problems grew worse: the decrepit theater, the shabby sets and costumes, the overtaxed singers, and the demanding labor unions, with whom Johnson was clumsy. Like all his predecessors, Johnson became weary. He accepted an extension of his contract to 1950 so he could retire with a service of a full fifteen years, and the directors began to look for a successor.

It was Edward Johnson who found Rudolf Bing. Bing came to New York in the late 1940s to study the possibilities of a tour by a company that performed at the Glyndebourne Festival in England, and Johnson, on meeting him, immediately saw his talents. The board had begun a desultory search for a new intendant, but had made little progress. Johnson suggested Bing.

Slender and elegant, clad in suits tailored in London and married to a Russian ballerina, Rudolf Bing considered himself the complete European. Born in Vienna, the son of a Jewish-Austrian industrialist, he had become fascinated by music and had chosen opera administration as his career, to the horror of his financier father. His first post was at the opera house in Darmstadt, one of the many provincial companies in Germany. It was in these small houses that ambitious young singers, conductors, and administrators served their apprenticeships before going on to the more prestigious posts. Even in Darmstadt, Bing knew why he was drawn to a life in the theater. An opera company, he wrote, was a "microcosmos," a little world unto itself. He enjoyed the power of controlling this tiny world, "without the evil that [real] political power so often entails."

After a few seasons in Darmstadt, Bing moved to Berlin's Municipal Opera. But by 1934, he had become concerned about the Nazis' growing power and he eagerly accepted an offer from England to help establish the Glyndebourne Festival.

Glyndebourne quickly became a success, but the festival was forced to suspend operations for most of World War II, and Bing, impoverished, was reduced to working in a London department store. This interlude, humiliating for a proud man, ended in 1945, and Bing went on to found and run the Edinburgh Festival, the job he held when he first met Edward Johnson.

Many of the board members, who had close ties to England, quickly learned of Bing's excellent reputation as an administrator. He was forty-eight years old in 1949, ambitious and eager to come to New York. Johnson introduced Bing to several of the directors, including the board chairman, George Sloan, who found Bing socially acceptable, and David Sarnoff, the chairman of RCA, who gave Bing's business sense a passing grade.

But, once again, the major player was Mrs. Belmont. She made a trip to Europe in 1949 to learn what she could from her English friends. Lady Violet Bonham-Carter, chairman of the board of the Royal Opera at Covent Garden, gave Bing a rapturous recommendation, and Mrs. Belmont sent it on to the Met's executive committee.

The board, as usual, was divided into factions. The one that included the powerful Juilliard Foundation assumed that Mrs. Belmont had been sent to England to assess Rudolf Bing and had decided all by herself to give him the job. The head of the Juilliard Foundation made disparaging remarks about the ladies of the Opera Guild choosing the new general manager. Since Mrs. Belmont did not meet Bing while she was in London, the accusation was ridiculous, but it created a fortuitous bond between Bing and this powerful woman.

In the end, the board voted unanimously to engage Bing for a three-year period, beginning with Johnson's retirement in January 1950. His appointment was announced formally in June of 1949, and, from the beginning, his regime was controversial.

Bing had asked to come to New York a full year before he assumed the general manager's position in September 1950, in order to observe the

Met's operations, and the board agreed. Johnson resented the arrangement, and relations between him and his successor became strained. From
the start, Bing made clear what he didn't like about Johnson's Met. It may
not have been Johnson's fault that the theatrical and scenic aspects of the
company had deteriorated so much, but Bing understood the importance
of revitalizing this aspect.

The operatic repertory is relatively small; there is a core of popular,
often-performed works, surrounded by lesser-known works: contemporary operas, little-known operas by well-known composers, worthwhile
operas by little-known composers. But the musical scope of any opera
company is limited and most of these works are performed over and over
again. Thus, the lifeblood of any company becomes new productions: operas are rethought by stage directors, redesigned by set, costume, and
lighting designers, and cast with the best available singers. In this way, an
opera as familiar as *La Bohème* can become a revelation when produced
with acumen, perception, and imagination.

Bing knew that a continuous stream of new productions would keep
the Met not only artistically fresh but also firmly in the public's conscious-
ness. Not parenthetically, the more exciting the Met seemed, the more the
company would be talked about and written about, the more tickets would
be sold. Looking with disdain on what he considered the shabby displays
Johnson had been content to put onstage, Bing made plans to bring to the
company such theater and film directors as Alfred Lunt, Cyril Ritchard,
Tyrone Guthrie, Jean-Louis Barrault, José Quintero, Joseph L. Man-
kiewicz, Peter Brook, and Franco Zeffirelli. This emphasis on the theatrical was a new concept for the company.

Unlike Johnson, Bing had no fear of conflict. At his first press conference, in February 1950, Bing announced that Kirsten Flagstad would return. Himself a refugee from the Nazis, Bing believed himself to be in a
strong position to judge the accountability of artists who had performed
under the Third Reich.

Inevitably, there was a negative reaction to Flagstad's return, even
within the company. Lauritz Melchior, the heldentenor who had presided
over the Met's Wagnerian repertory during the Johnson years, publicly demanded that he be engaged again before any other artist, and he was out-

raged when Bing chose Flagstad for this honor. This was no oversight by Bing; he knew that Melchior hated to rehearse and showed no indication of changing his habits under the new regime. By allowing Melchior to resign, Bing let all the singers know that they were to follow his rules. No one, no matter how revered, was to be an exception.

Equally outraged was the American soprano Helen Traubel. A late-blooming dramatic soprano, Traubel had sung her first Wagner role at the Met in 1939, when she was forty. At the time, all the meatiest roles had gone to Flagstad, but when she returned to Norway, Traubel replaced her as the reigning Wagnerian, singing Isolde, Brünnhilde, Elsa, and Elisabeth for a decade. Unfortunately, she fit the classic unflattering image of a Wagnerian soprano: she was lethargic onstage and enormously fat. Bing had an instinctive dislike of some American singers whom he considered vulgar. Regina Resnik, for example, had been one of Johnson's busiest singers during the years of the American boom. But her down-to-earth, sturdy appearance did not fit with Bing's image of how a sultry temptress like Dalila or Carmen behaved or looked, and he balked at offering her glamorous roles. Similarly, he thought that Traubel, who loved to sing in nightclubs, in films, and on Broadway, cheapened the Met despite her popularity with the public.

When Bing brought back Flagstad, Traubel threatened to resign. So Bing, who did appreciate the magnificence of her voice, placated her by offering her the role of the Marschallin in *Der Rosenkavalier,* one she had long coveted, and she stayed for another couple of seasons. But in the end, Bing, the self-styled aristocrat, was too offended by her outside activities. He declared that singing in nightclubs was "slumming," and he fired her.

Bing was not, however, consistent in dealing with his singers. At the same time that he condemned Traubel for her commercial ventures, he tolerated similar behavior by the American mezzo Risë Stevens, who even went as far as appearing in cigarette advertisements. Unlike Traubel, Stevens was a slim, elegant woman who looked more like a film star than an opera singer, and her appearance made her behavior palatable to the image-conscious Bing.

Bing ran the Metropolitan Opera as a monarchy and he ruled over all aspects of the opera house. He planned every season, cast each role, engaged the conductors, stage directors, and designers, devised a healthy subscriber base, and chose the repertory. In all this, he was supported by two chief assistants, Robert Herman and Herman Krawitz. Herman assisted Bing with casting and artistic matters, and Krawitz dealt with the business and technical side of operations. Bing trusted them both and they were essential to the smooth running of the company.

Bing's whole life was devoted to the Met. He worked at the opera house from morning until the middle of the night six days a week. On the seventh day, Sunday, when there were no performances, he remained in his apartment in the Essex House on Central Park South with his wife, Nina, and his beloved dachshund, Pip. He considered artistic administration an art, and he honed his art as diligently as any of his singers and probably more than most. At some point, he had acquired a demeanor of immutable superiority, and he relied on it both as a weapon and a shield, often ridiculing or frightening an adversary into compliance. "Beneath that cold and icy exterior," Cyril Ritchard once declared, "beats a heart of stone."

Although he had never earned a university degree, Bing considered himself more refined and educated than any American. His being European, he felt, also made him more sensitive to opera as an art and more competent to decide what was good for the Met. When the board complained about the cost of the new productions that he insisted were so essential, he would retort, "My job is to spend money, not to raise it."

Paradoxically, Bing scorned class-consciousness at the Metropolitan. He began his campaign against it by removing opening night from the prestigious Monday-night subscription series and making it an evening open to anyone who could afford a ticket. This was a direct incursion into the world of social position that the directors still clung to—they wanted opening night on "their" series, the Monday-night series. Mondays never quite lost their status—until a few years ago, women in evening gowns and men in tails could still be seen in the audience on Mondays—and opening night is still considered the official start of New York City's social season. But Bing made sure that there were places available to the shabbiest standees, the kind of music lovers the early boxholders would never have thought worthy of consideration. As part of his campaign to round out his public image—and thereby the Met's—he was photographed taking the subway to work, although with his bowler hat and furled umbrella, he hardly looked like the usual commuter.

As the tenor Lauritz Melchior, whom most would have considered irreplaceable, discovered to his sorrow, Bing had little patience for the cavalier behavior of the leading singers. Under previous regimes, the Met had not insisted that "stars" show up for rehearsals, and most of the singers took major advantage of this tolerance. Bing prized professional behavior and made sure everyone knew he expected it. If there were infractions, the artists were dismissed.

Yet the atmosphere at the Metropolitan during the Bing years was suffused with secrecy and duplicity. Running an opera house is such a complex process that honesty can be a weakness; it is not always possible to tell everyone the truth about everything. Although the general manager was brutally sharp-tongued with the artists, even with members of the press, he was not always forthright. For example, Bing disliked and distrusted Francis Robinson, the assistant manager in charge of press relations, and Robinson, for his part, loathed Bing. Yet Bing was afraid of Robinson and his closeness to many members of the press, so the two men maintained an icy courtesy throughout Bing's entire tenure. Bing kept an eye on Robinson's activities and possible disloyalty through reports from other members of the staff.

Bing's accomplishments were substantial. He lengthened the New York season from eighteen weeks to thirty-one. He imaginatively restructured the subscription season by offering shorter series. When he arrived, there were six series to choose from; when he left, there were twenty-two. This quadrupled the number of subscribers from five thousand to twenty-one thousand, and, for many years, the solid subscription base guaranteed sold-out houses.

Though Bing styled himself as an aristocrat, his strong egalitarian instincts led to his courageous stand on civil rights. He broke the Met's color barrier by engaging the African-American ballerina Janet Collins, the first black artist to appear on the Met stage. And he encouraged other African-Americans to join the chorus and ballet before making his grand gesture, in 1954, of engaging Marian Anderson, thus opening major roles to black singers. Even more gallant was his insistence that the Metropolitan Opera

Company, on tour through the South, would brook no indignities toward its black members. The local sponsors in some parts of the South balked at inviting African-American company members to parties and private clubs, but Bing insisted on their inclusion, risking the loss of financially important tour engagements. His determination never faltered and, in the end, the black musicians, singers, and dancers on Met tours were welcomed everywhere.

A former Met administrator remembers watching Bing one night in Atlanta. He had made tickets available to a few black teenagers, and when they arrived at the theater, Bing noticed that they were treated rudely by some of the white ushers. He intervened immediately, and insisted that they be seated with the same courtesy displayed to white Atlantans.

Bing's self-assurance did not automatically help him in his dealings with the Metropolitan Opera's board. The directors—who thought of themselves as their own ruling class—had a great deal of collective self-assurance of their own. Bing arrived in New York knowing an enormous amount about opera administration, but almost nothing about the Metropolitan Opera and its hierarchy. His subsequent relationship with the board was rocky. His operating procedure was to outline expensive new projects, patiently hear the inevitable pleas of poverty from the directors, and then dictate fund-raising goals to pay for his plans.

Bing could be an imaginative fund-raiser when he wanted to be, or had to be. When the board flatly refused to consider more new productions, Bing came up with the idea of asking one or two wealthy people to fund individual productions. If he could not convince the directors that it was essential to redo the current production of *Don Carlo,* he would go to someone like Mrs. John D. Rockefeller and persuade her of the importance of a new version of the Verdi opera. The wealthy patron would then provide the funds necessary and Bing would not have to charge the expense to the general operating budget. This strategy was so successful that it is still in place today.

Still, the directors felt enormous frustration that Bing did not appreciate their fiscal problems. Bing, a stubborn man, refused to even pretend to understand. The tension between the directors and the general manager they had appointed was a hallmark of Bing's administration.

Bing also had titanic battles with many conductors and singers during his twenty-two-year regime, including George Szell, Giuseppe di Stefano, Franco Corelli, Renata Tebaldi, Birgit Nilsson, Beverly Sills, and Herbert von Karajan. Despite Sills's ascent to the unofficial title of the American prima donna, Bing refused to engage her, considering her vulgar. He hated George Szell so much that when someone once remarked that Szell was his own worst enemy, Bing muttered, "Not while I'm alive." He was impatient with Corelli's sensitive artistic temperament, which led to frequent cancellations, and considered Tebaldi's repertory requests unreasonable. But his most famous clash was with Maria Callas, a conflict that would define the operatic stereotypes of the temperamental diva and the autocratic intendant.

Callas, who was born in New York to a poor Greek immigrant family, was taken to Greece as a teenager to study in Athens. She began her career with the kind of dramatic soprano roles rarely associated with a young singer—Aïda, Turandot, Leonora in *Trovatore*, even Isolde and Brünnhilde. Then, in the late 1940s, she came under the musical spell of the great Italian conductor Tullio Serafin, who encouraged her to move into the bel canto roles that would define the rest of her career.

As a young woman, Callas had married a much older Italian businessman, Giovanni Battista Meneghini, who took charge of her career and her life, creating an environment in which the demands of the singer, rather than the woman, were paramount. Protected from everyday problems and worries, Callas developed an astonishing musical and dramatic persona. Her intelligence and intensity reinforced, even transcended, her vocal gifts.

In the early 1950s, Callas looked like a cartoon of an opera singer. She dressed badly, wore too much makeup, and was overweight, but her musical talent was so splendid that no one cared. There have been a few beautiful singers—Geraldine Farrar, Lily Pons, Risë Stevens, Mary Garden, and Maria Jeritza—but most were "big voices, which come in big people," in the words of Met assistant manager Francis Robinson.

In 1953, Callas began to lose weight and she told her friends that she had a tapeworm; some believed she had swallowed it on purpose. But she was a woman of awesome will and a determination that cannot be understated. Within two years, she had the figure of a fashion model and had learned how to dress and comport herself. The chubby prima donna had become a chic sophisticate.

At this point, Bing became interested in her. Previously, he had decided he had enough fat sopranos, and when her first contract fell through because of her husband's visa difficulties (he had belonged to the Italian Fascist Party), Bing did not try very hard to solve the problem. Callas made her American debut with the Chicago Opera.

When she finally came to the Met, in 1956–57, she did not even rate a new production, and she was unhappy with her conductors and fellow singers. But she and Bing discovered their mutual love of dogs; he even expressed sympathy when her toy poodle peed on one of the stage trees during a rehearsal of *Norma*. "Pip would probably have done the same," Bing told her, and a bond formed between the two. When Bing saw the excitement she generated with the Met audience and the sold-out performances that resulted, his fondness for her grew.

Bing offered Callas a new production of Verdi's *Macbeth* as part of the Met's seventy-fifth anniversary season in 1958–59. This was to be a lavish production, the most expensive in the company's history at over $100,000, and Callas was offered the Met's top fee of $3,000 per performance. She also signed a letter of intent promising to alternate performances of *La Traviata* with those of *Macbeth*, and, for the first time, she agreed to sing on the Met tour, again alternating both roles.

At some point between the signing of the agreement and the opening of the season, Callas and Meneghini began to have second thoughts about the Met contract. Violetta in *Traviata* is a lighter role than Lady Macbeth, and Callas decided she would not have enough time between performances to adjust her voice to the different parts. She suggested that the Violetta performances be given to another singer. Bing countered by offering her *Lucia di Lammermoor* or *Tosca* in place of *Traviata*, but Callas retorted, "My voice is not like an elevator going up and down." Bing, in return, suggested that eight days between operas was "a pretty long time for experienced artists to adjust their voices."

Bing suspected that all the "elevator" talk was a ruse for Callas to withdraw from the tour. Callas was already well known as a canceler, and, taking advantage of her reputation, Bing launched a preemptive strike by setting a deadline—10:00 A.M. on November 6, 1958—for her compliance with the letter of intent. When Callas did not sign by the date specified, Bing fired her. "Her reputation for projecting her undisputed histrionic talents into her business affairs is a matter of common knowledge," he said in a public statement. "Let us all be grateful that we have had the benefit of her artistry for two seasons. The Metropolitan is nevertheless grateful that the association is ended."

Even Bing was surprised by the uproar caused by the dismissal. On the day Bing fired her, Callas was singing in a new production of *Medea* with the Dallas Opera, and the front page of the *New York Daily News* shrieked, MARIA CALLAS BOOTED BY THE MET, with a picture of the distraught soprano in full costume and makeup. Callas continued to milk the controversy, stating, "I will do no more stinking performances. . . . I'm not supposed to make money for Mr. Bing, I'm supposed to do art." She told the *New York Post* about "those lousy *Traviata*s he wanted to make me do—and they're lousy, really they're lousy, everyone knows it."

Bing nevertheless made the best of a bad situation: he engaged the electrifying Austrian soprano Leonie Rysanek for *Macbeth*. On February 5, 1959, the night of the *Macbeth* premiere, many in the audience were still angry at the dismissal of their idol. When Rysanek made her first entrance, someone called out from the darkened auditorium, "Brava, Callas!" Rysanek froze for an instant, pulled herself together, and went on to give a mesmerizing performance. The ovation at the final curtain was in part an expression of sympathy for her but mostly a tribute to the performance she had just given. She immediately was transformed into one of the Met's most beloved artists, as she remained for nearly forty years until her death.

Ironically, Bing throughout his life expressed the greatest respect for Callas as an artist. But within a few years, she became a household name because of her affair with Aristotle Onassis. Through her time with Onassis, Callas let her career slide. Passionately in love for the first time in her life, she left Meneghini, the husband who had provided artistic security, for Onassis, who was bewitched by her glamour rather than her creativity. Her friends looked on in horror as she pursued, in the words of Franco Zeffirelli, one of her closest confidants and colleagues, "her stupid ambition of becoming a great lady of café society."

When Bing invited Callas back to the Met for two performances of

Tosca in 1964–65, she was no longer in a position to dictate terms; she did not even receive an orchestra rehearsal before her first performance. Nevertheless, the demand for the Callas *Tosca*s was enormous, and the performances instantly became Met legends. The Scarpia was Tito Gobbi, whose own dramatic intensity inspired Callas to transcendent acting and singing. But after two performances, Callas was gone. She never returned.

Chapter Six

RUDOLF BING AND ANTHONY BLISS;
THE BIRTH OF A NEW OPERA HOUSE

One of the first truths Bing learned is that more than one strong personality at the Metropolitan Opera leads to strife. He had been in New York only a few weeks when, one day in 1949, in the darkened auditorium, he met a young man with whom he would do battle for the next twenty years. Anthony Addison Bliss, the son of Cornelius N. Bliss, had recently joined the board, at thirty-five one of the youngest to serve as a director, and Edward Johnson was giving him a tour of the opera house. Although his late father had been president of the board, Bliss did not know enough about the actual workings of the theater to be the conscientious board member he intended to be.

When Bing walked by, Johnson stopped him and said, "Mr. Bing, here is one of your new board members. You'd better meet him." He gestured toward the confident young man. The contrast between the two men was remarkable; one was the self-styled European, the other, the embodiment of the American upper class. Bliss, tall, handsome, and well built, towered over Bing, and he immediately noted a coolness on Bing's part. "Rudolf did not look as if he were anxious to meet a new board member at all, but he was polite."

Years later, Bing remembered his chief feeling at this meeting as one of amazement that so young a man could be on the board. Had he known the history of the Bliss family and the Metropolitan, he might have understood better. Cornelius N. Bliss had died just before his son met Rudolf Bing; he had retired as board president in 1946, but had remained a director until his death.

Cornelius Bliss had often taken his son to performances; young Tony heard Caruso sing *Pagliacci*. But he was a sickly child, suffering from a twisted intestine, and spent most of his childhood at the family home on Long Island's North Shore. Intelligent but lonely, he became passionately involved in varied interests that, in addition to his dedication to the Met, would endure throughout his life. His love of the family dogs evolved into an avocation as a breeder, and at fifteen, he became the youngest president of the Chesapeake Bay Retriever Club of the American Kennel Club. Tony Bliss was incapable of getting only partially involved in anything.

But the Bliss family heritage was inescapable, and life as a gentleman dog breeder was not in his future. His idyllic, if solitary, childhood ended when he went off to the Groton School. After graduating from Harvard College, Bliss married Barbara Field, the daughter of the Chicago magnate Marshall Field, and entered law school at Columbia University. The marriage was not happy, although the young Blisses soon became the parents of a daughter, Barbara. Bliss's law school career seemed equally doomed; he was still more interested in his dogs than his law studies. When the canine population of the Bliss household exceeded thirty, Barbara Bliss told her husband to choose between her and the dogs. Apparently, the dogs won. The Blisses separated; Bliss flunked out of Columbia; and he and the dogs traveled south, where he enrolled in the University of Virginia Law School.

After graduation, Bliss returned to New York and joined Milbank, Tweed, Hadley and McCloy, the law firm where he remained in varied capacities until the end of his life. He served in the Pacific during World War II, and married the actress Jo Ann Sayres. The couple had three children, whom Bliss cheerfully referred to as his "second litter."

Bliss and his wife were a handsome couple, both slim and dark-haired, and they became fixtures in Manhattan society and the newspapers' social columns. On the surface, with his gracious demeanor and courtly voice, he appeared the personification of Edith Wharton's lost New York. But Bliss was never interested in social functions or frivolous publicity; he was far more concerned with exploring areas in which he could make a concrete contribution. He renewed his childhood interest in opera and frequently attended Met performances. Cornelius Bliss, however, a model of rectitude, had disapproved of nepotism on the Met board, so it was not until after his death that his son was asked to be a director.

Once on the board, Bliss approached his new responsibilities with his customary thoroughness. Despite his family's tradition of service to the Metropolitan, Bliss did not live in the past; he was secure enough to let go of tradition when it became burdensome. Even though he shortly became a full-time partner at Milbank, Tweed, he devoted far more time to the opera than any board member in history. He had not been a director for a month before he started going to the opera house almost every afternoon to sit in on rehearsals. Often, on his way home from the office in the evening, he would drop in again to be there for the opening curtain and watch the stage crew in operation. He quickly became friends with company members.

Bing regarded with suspicion any board member with this kind of curiosity. He didn't like board members roaming about backstage or sitting in the auditorium during rehearsals because he felt it upset the delicate balance between the authority he must have and the constant threat of encroachment from those who supported the institution financially.

But he realized that Bliss's legal expertise could be helpful in some of his crusades. Bing had been horrified when he first arrived at the Met to find that there was no health plan or pension provision for the full-time staff, including the orchestra, chorus, and stage crew. During his first years, he instituted a pension plan and some health benefits, and he worked closely with Bliss in setting these up. These were groundbreaking employment benefits for a nonprofit institution, but few company members remembered this when the Met's labor situation began to deteriorate.

Bing's social conscience did not extend to the labor unions. Coming from a different tradition in Europe, he lost patience with what he saw as the unions' unrelenting and unreasonable demands. Initially, he was relieved to pass this area of responsibility to Bliss, who was fascinated by it and who, as an American, had a more instinctive understanding of the situation.

Bliss became a member of the board's labor committee during his first month as a director, and he developed a lively interest in the labor struggles that peppered Met history. His earliest run-ins were with the stagehands. Having heard rumors that backstage was rife with nepotism, featherbedding, and kickbacks, Bliss, through the theater connections he had developed because of his second wife, brought in Herman Krawitz. Krawitz, the young man who would later become one of Bing's top two assistants, was experienced in dealing with stagehands on Broadway. He was a graduate of City College, and had a down-to-earth manner that, in the end, made him popular with the Met stage crew.

But when he first arrived, the stagehands promptly held a wildcat strike in hope of closing down the house. Undaunted, Bliss and members of the administration replaced the striking crew at a dress rehearsal of _Norma._ Bliss put Bing in charge of raising and lowering the gold curtain, an assignment that nearly resulted in the decapitation of Zinka Milanov. The stage crew came back to work.

After this crisis was resolved, Bliss, during the early 1950s, learned that many problems with the stage crew could be obviated if he frequently invited the president of the stagehands' union to lunch at the '21' Club. The board, clearly approving of his pragmatic approach to problem-solving, elected him president in 1956 at the age of forty-three.

His confidence in place, Bliss oversaw the negotiations for a new American Guild of Musical Artists (AGMA) contract in 1956. Although the orchestra and stage crew had already reached an agreement, AGMA failed to fall into line. Bliss dashed off a letter to the union's president, threatening to cancel the 1956–57 season.

This threat was repeated at every Met labor negotiation from 1961 to 1980. To the board, a threat to cancel the season made sense: to pay for rehearsals before each new season, the board authorized borrowing against the subscription funds that came in during the spring and were held in escrow. Bliss and the other directors thought it wiser to settle labor problems before borrowing money for rehearsals.

The unions, however, would put pressure on the board by choosing not to negotiate until the rehearsals were about to start. As a result, for decades the negotiations took place at the last possible moment. A kind of ritual developed: at the beginning of the summer in a contract year, the management would threaten to cancel the coming season unless the unions reduced their demands. The unions would not pay any attention until some rehearsals had been canceled. Constructive bargaining was impossible under this kind of time pressure, but neither side would change its tactics.

By 1961, the orchestra replaced the stagehands as the most intransigent union, and Bliss became almost nostalgic about his struggles with the stage crew. The stagehands trusted their union; the musicians did not. Symphony and opera musicians were a minority of Local 802, the New York City musicians' union. Groups like the Metropolitan Opera Orchestra and the New York Philharmonic felt they had no influence or representation in the union hierarchy. Instead of negotiating through their union, the Met musicians negotiated using a committee elected from the orchestra. Therefore, unlike the stagehands, who had the advantage of professional leadership from within their union, the musicians entrusted their fate to people who were trained as instrumentalists, not negotiators. There was no tradition of compromise for the orchestra members such as the stagehands had enjoyed, thanks to their president's lunches at '21' with Bliss.

Although the company contained twenty-two unions—from the box office treasurers to the ushers to the wardrobe, wig, and makeup departments—the stagehands, chorus and ballet, and the orchestra were the most important, because a strike by any one group could close down the house. The Met Orchestra began to assert itself during the labor dispute in 1961. The strife was a direct result of the Met's decision to build a new opera house.

$\mathcal{B}$liss had become fascinated by the idea of a new opera house right from the start of his term on the board. George Sloan, then the president of the board, had handed him two loose-leaf notebooks, one entitled "New House Project" and the other "Old House Project." The biggest issue before the board was to decide whether to raise funds to renovate the old, obsolete house, or to find a new location. Sloan, who wanted to stay in the old house, assumed that Bliss, the grandson and son of boxholders, would choose to save the old Met.

Bliss did his usual thorough research. After reading everything he could find and thoroughly exploring every corner of the old house, he decided to side with the new-house faction. He became determined to succeed in doing what Otto Kahn could not: build a new opera house.

The way had been paved by his father before his death. Cornelius Bliss had stepped down as board president in 1946 to make way for Charles M. Spofford, a lawyer and musician who had helped draft the agreement to buy the old Met from the boxholders. Spofford, with the elder Bliss's active support, had begun to press for a new house. In 1949, the two men seized on the passage of the Federal Housing Act, which made urban renewal a priority and provided federal funds for combining housing programs with educational ventures. Spofford and Bliss went to see Robert Moses, the head of New York City's redevelopment corporation. Moses was interested: an opera house in an undeveloped part of the city would be a magnet for the upper-middle class, just the people Moses wanted to attract to neighborhoods in need of invigoration. He suggested sites in Greenwich Village and at Columbus Circle, but, in the end, decided on the Lincoln Square neighborhood on the Upper West Side. Here, at the point where Broadway and Columbus Avenue crisscross, Moses undertook the largest urban renewal project he had ever tackled.

Lincoln Square, in 1953, was an ugly slum, and the Met's board, predictably, was appalled. Only Moses's threats to cut the company out of his funding persuaded some of the directors to stay with the project. Spofford approached the architect Wallace K. Harrison about creating a drawing that he could use to raise funds for the project.

Also in the mid-1950s, a real estate developer bought Carnegie Hall and announced that he would tear it down to erect an office building. Its resident orchestra, the New York Philharmonic, would be homeless. The Philharmonic's board approached Wallace Harrison, and the architect had the Met board and the Philharmonic officials meet and discuss their plans. Both institutions realized that there was strength in their acting together, and they approached John D. Rockefeller III with the idea of a new music center. Gradually, despite many unforeseen obstacles, difficulties, and disagreements, Lincoln Center took shape, and, with it, the new home for the Metropolitan Opera.

The decision to move to Lincoln Center was one of the few times Bing and Bliss saw eye to eye. Bing had been appalled by the physical condition of the old opera house: backstage was cramped and dirty, with so little room for storage that sets for each opera had to be carted back and forth from a warehouse for each performance. Often the scenery for one act would be moved offstage directly out onto Seventh Avenue to wait for the end of the opera, protected only by tarpaulins from rain and snow and other ravages of New York street life. Rehearsal space was so limited that the company regularly rehearsed in the restaurant and rest rooms. Bing heard constant complaints about the primitive dressing rooms, which he described as "a rabbit warren with worse plumbing than most rabbits are willing to tolerate."

When the move to Lincoln Center had been formalized, the directors also decided to tear down the decrepit old opera house and lease the land to a developer. Music lovers who had a sentimental attachment to all the great evenings of opera they had enjoyed at the house on Thirty-ninth Street were furious. The general impression was that Bing wanted the house destroyed so that no other opera company could rise up to inhabit it. The audience did not understand the financial value of the site, nor did they see the dangerous conditions backstage. The directors did not understand public sentiment and defeated a legal attempt to stop the destruction of the building. Just as they had planned, a developer leased the site, tore down the old Met, and built an office building. The lease brought in capital each year, and the board knew that if things became really urgent, they could always sell the site for even more money.

A conflict arose between Bing and Bliss about who would administer the move. Bliss had traveled abroad to inspect European opera houses and had met with architects and acousticians. As a board member and the son of a boxholder, he began to feel custodial about the new house and soon his feeling extended to the company as a whole. By the time of the projected move in 1966, Bing would have run the house for sixteen years; he felt equally entitled to be lord of the manor.

*D*own in the orchestra pit, the musicians didn't care who was in charge of the move. What mattered to them was the glamorous new surroundings in which they would be working. The amount of time they spent working was distinctly unglamorous. In 1961, every member of the orchestra played seven performances a week, a schedule both musically and physically exhausting. Most symphony orchestras during this period played only two or three concerts a week, and operas are much longer than symphony concerts.

During the early 1960s, the composition of the orchestra was undergoing an important change. For most of its history, it had been filled mostly by European musicians, but by 1961, there were more Americans, and the orchestra committee in particular was American-born and American-trained. These musicians were less intimidated by authority than their European predecessors.

Herman Krawitz, who by now had developed a close relationship with Bing, oversaw everything that went on in the opera house that was not directly artistic—business, technical, box office, administrative—and labor was one of his chief responsibilities. Krawitz, who had had considerable success with most of the labor problems in the company, found that the orchestra was different. He felt frustrated that he couldn't make the musicians understand that the Met had more complicated problems than a symphony orchestra, which has no chorus, no ballet, no singers, no scenery and costumes, and only one or two stagehands. At the Met, the orchestra is only about 10 percent of the company. But the musicians seemed to consider themselves more than equal to others in the company. In the end, the orchestra became negotiators for the entire company under a "most favored nations" policy: what they received through their tenacity was passed on to everyone else.

Bing became the orchestra's designated enemy; his hauteur did not go over well. In one famous episode, Bing was negotiating with the musicians' attorney, who finally snarled, "Mr. Bing, are you trying to show your contempt?"

"On the contrary," Bing replied. "I am trying very hard to hide it."

The major issue in 1961 was the orchestra's low pay, especially considering their tremendous workload. The average was about $245 a week, including overtime, rehearsal, and broadcast pay—this was for seven performances, often of operas lasting four or five hours. In addition, the musicians wanted some autonomy over the hiring and firing of the members. On the first issue, Bing was horrified that the salary demands would push the company over the edge into financial ruin; on the second, he was appalled that the musicians would have the gall to suggest they could evaluate each other's playing better than the Met's conductors.

In the spring of 1961, even a federal mediator from the Department of Labor failed to reach an agreement between the orchestra and management. He recommended closing the house and insisted that all the management principals leave New York to show that they meant what they threatened. Bing went to his usual vacation resort in Italy, and Bliss went to a family ranch in Montana. The closing of the house for the coming season was announced, and termination notices were given to the administrative staff. No one expected the Met to open again for at least a year.

But Bliss was not ready to give up; he had doubts about the mediator's advice. Bing, typically, had not trusted the mediator in the first place, but he assumed the situation was beyond repair, and passed the summer strolling in the Dolomites with Nina and Pip. Hearing of this, many singers canceled their contracts for the 1961–62 season.

Leontyne Price and Risë Stevens, however, two of the most renowned artists on the roster, were not about to give up, either. They got in touch with Bing and told him that they were ready to appeal to President John F. Kennedy, who, with his wife, Jacqueline, was reputed to be a patron of the arts. Bing replied that since most of the European artists had dropped out, he couldn't see what Kennedy could possibly do to help. "But the members of my board," he said later, "who were of course all American citizens, took a different view of the powers of the presidency."

Bliss was enjoying the kind of quintessential American vacation that would have reduced Bing to shudders. "I was about ten days into a month-long vacation on the ranch. . . . One morning I had rounded up twelve saddlehorses to drive thirteen miles over a mountain pass to a blacksmith [when] I had a telephone call."

It was from Arthur Goldberg, the secretary of labor. He told Bliss that President Kennedy had just come out of a meeting on the Cuban crisis and had asked him to see what he could do to straighten things out at the Met. Kennedy believed that the Met's closing would damage the country's prestige.

Bliss agreed to meet with Goldberg in Denver, so he delivered the horses to the blacksmith, consulted all the board members he could reach by phone, and left for Denver, no simple proposition. "In the early morning, I got into the jeep for a thirteen-mile ride to where I had to leave the car, walk over a mountain pass to a garage, and then drive to the airport in Billings, Montana." The jeep refused to start, so Bliss, dressed in city clothes, rolled up his sleeves and unclogged the gas line.

On reaching Denver, Bliss found three telegrams: two from New York Senator Jacob Javits and Representative John Lindsay, urging him to work with Goldberg, and one from Bing, who was horrified that Goldberg would give too much power to the musicians. "Don't reopen the house or you will kill the Metropolitan forever," he admonished. When Bliss met Goldberg, the first thing the labor secretary showed him was the headline in that morning's _Denver Post:_ SECRETARY GOLDBERG AND MET PRESIDENT MEET HERE TODAY. The subhead was "Bing Says They're Wasting Their Time."

Goldberg was chosen to arbitrate the dispute. The musicians were delighted: the secretary's brother was a cellist in the Chicago Symphony, traditionally the most hard-line orchestra on labor issues. They were certain that Goldberg, who had been a labor attorney, would take their side. A sullen Bing returned to New York, and Goldberg held meetings with both sides. After a few days, he announced his decision.

To the orchestra's stunned outrage, his decision was strongly on the side of management. Although Bing and Bliss were pleased, they feared the results of the orchestra's bitterness. "True to our predictions," Bing said years later, "relations with the orchestra moved from bad to impossible." And it wasn't just the Met musicians who were outraged: all over the country orchestra members who had been giving financial support to the Met musicians burned pictures of Goldberg.

The musicians described the settlement as "tea and sympathy."

Having achieved nothing, they shifted their attention to the negotiations due in 1966. Determined to win work reductions and pay increases, they decided not to target the 1964 negotiations. Instead, they maneuvered to get their contract extended to 1966, a season they knew could not be canceled. It was to be the first season in the new house.

Chapter Seven

THE NEW HOUSE

The Metropolitan Opera is a large family, and most families undergo problems at the time of a major event: a birth, a death, a marriage, a move to a new home. The Met's move twenty-five blocks up Broadway to Lincoln Center was traumatic.

The new house was far grander than the old, and its location more attractive and convenient. Instead of huddling on a frowsy midtown street, the new Met, with its five marble arches, rears ninety-six feet above Lincoln Center Plaza. The white marble façade is the perfect contrast for the jewel-like colors of the two vast murals by Marc Chagall, one mounted on each side of the soaring lobby area. The building extends the entire distance from the plaza on Broadway to Amsterdam Avenue: its depth is that of a forty-seven-story skyscraper lying on its side. The ten levels, which start deep underground, rise six stories above the bronze doors on street level. And behind the marble and bronze is a small city.

To a member of the audience, the vast auditorium, with its lashings of gold and yards of red velvet and the capacity to hold four thousand people, seems to dwarf the rest of the building. In fact, though it is the heart of the opera house, the auditorium is small in comparison to the rest of the theater. The Met is laced with rehearsal halls, dressing rooms, storage areas, and vast workshops where craftsmen build scenery, paint drops, construct electrical equipment, carve props, sew costumes, design makeup, and weave wigs.

There is an elegant, expensive restaurant for ticketholders and a reasonably priced company cafeteria. There are bars for drinks and snacks on each level, a photographer's studio and darkroom, a music library, extensive temperature-controlled archives, a ballet studio, an orchestra rehearsal room that replicates the acoustics of the orchestra pit, scores of offices, meeting rooms, and miles of echoing corridors, all of which look disconcertingly alike. There are hundreds of staircases and elevators, confusingly routed, since the ten levels are laid out in different configurations.

The quantities of materials used in construction and maintenance of the building are difficult to comprehend. There are eight thousand square yards of red carpet, two thousand in the auditorium alone. The 156 window panels are fitted into an exterior made of forty-two thousand cubic feet of travertine. The walls of the auditorium are covered with African rosewood, which was cut from one enormous tree and chosen to complement the garnet seats and carpet.

The main stage is huge, but it is dwarfed by the backstage area, which is two-thirds larger. There one finds a jumble of fifty-two trapdoors, seven elevators, hundreds of hanging lamps, four lighting bridges, and six sets of border lights. The heaviest operas require the most flexible stage equipment, and the Met stage can rise and fall, shift sideways on wheeled wagons, or revolve on a turntable designed not by theater technicians but by a company that builds revolving restaurants on the tops of skyscrapers.

Surrounding the main stage are three other stages of equal size that can be moved quickly out on top of the central stage, shifting enormous scenery silently and swiftly. Even the great gold curtain at the front of the stage is an engineering achievement: it can be deployed at various speeds to match the mood or the music of the scene just starting or concluding. Behind the main curtain is a second curtain, also gold, called the guillotine curtain; it drops straight to the floor instead of draping down.

The Metropolitan was the third of Lincoln Center's three big halls. Both Philharmonic Hall (now Avery Fisher Hall) and the New York State Theater were at first acoustical failures, and expectations were low for the new opera house. Wallace Harrison, however, understood that although he had control over other parts of the building, inside the auditorium it was the acousticians who had the final say. Cyril Harris was chosen to make the new Met sound as good as the old Met, and he succeeded brilliantly. The carved patterns in the auditorium's decor were designed to bounce the sound throughout the house, and the auditorium was constructed from plaster and wood, materials that conduct sound efficiently. When the new house opened, it sounded better than the old. In the old house, the stage was only partly visible from some seats, and great care was taken to make sure most of the seats in the new house have a good view of the stage.

Also to be considered, of course, were the boxholders. Harrison was told to provide the traditional setting for the company's wealthy patrons, and the new house held the same number of boxes as the old. The boxholders were to glitter on into the future.

What was to become the most beloved feature of the new house, however, was an innovation: the twenty-one starburst chandeliers made of Austrian crystal. Twelve of the chandeliers hang at the parterre box level during the half hour before the performance as the auditorium fills. Just before the lights dim and the curtain goes up, the stage manager pushes a button backstage, and these smaller chandeliers rise to the ceiling to join the huge central chandelier and its solar system of eight other lamps.

In April 1966, the Met held acoustical rehearsals in the new house. The first rehearsal was performed for the construction workers who had built the new building, but members of the press were also invited. The sound proved to be excellent. Bing was deeply relieved. "Well," he said, "I think we're out of the woods." He could not have been more wrong.

Bing and Bliss had sparred throughout the preparations for the move. Bing maintained an unswerving but parochial loyalty to the company he felt he had built. His belief that he alone was responsible for the company's artistic supremacy grew into an obsession. Bliss had a more realistic view of the Met's position in relation to the rest of the world. He also weighed every decision in terms of its long-term effect on the company as a whole.

Bing was furious when he discovered that there were plans for the New York City Opera to move into the New York State Theater next door to the Met, which had been built originally to accommodate the New York City Ballet. The City Opera move was mandated by New York State to secure state financing for Lincoln Center. Bing was particularly irate because he knew that George Balanchine had agreed to bring his New York City Ballet to Lincoln Center on the condition that no other ballet company could become a constituent. "I was under the impression that Lincoln Center aimed at the highest cultural achievements," he wrote to Bliss in a fury, "and the constituents . . . belonged to the highest class in their field. The City Center Opera has no place in that group." Bliss was more objective. "I had the happy delusion that more opera is the best thing for opera on the whole."

Bing lost this battle because of the finances involved, but for the rest of his time at the Met, he kept an eagle eye on the New York City Opera, waiting for his prophecy of cultural doom to come true.

Unlike Bing, Bliss saw clearly the changes happening in the contemporary world beyond the opera house, and he was determined to keep the Met in step with these changes. In the early 1960s, he became excited by the idea of forming a junior company at the Met, to be called the National Company. The new troupe would serve as a training ground for young singers, and would also reach out to new audiences—and new donors— through broad touring, which was impractical for the big company.

The Met's annual United States tour had been part of every season since the first in 1883. Originally undertaken by train and later by chartered airliner, the tour lasted about eight weeks, and the company played mostly weeklong engagements in large theaters in large cities: the longest-lived tour cities were Boston, Cleveland, Minneapolis, Dallas, Detroit, and Memphis, and, after the Kennedy Center Opera House was built, Washington. The National Company, on the other hand, would tour most of the season, except for a brief stop in New York, playing smaller cities and in smaller halls with smaller productions and orchestra. It would travel more flexibly and would extend the reach of the Met to places that had been unfeasible with the big company.

Cornelius Bliss had proved that the Met could be successful in national fund-raising, and under his son's board presidency, the company positioned itself as America's national opera company not only through its long tradition of touring the United States, but also via the weekly live radio broadcasts and an expanded presence on television. The

Metropolitan Opera National Council, established by Eleanor Belmont, reached out beyond New York City to attract supporters, and Anthony Bliss conceived the National Company as fulfilling a similar goal.

Bing hated the idea from the very beginning. When he felt threatened, he became even more European, looked down his aquiline nose at naive Americans. The National Company embodied everything he disdained. He defined it as "an expression of the American weakness for doing something—anything—for education and the young."

Bliss shot back, "Since you are not American by birth or adoption, it is only natural that your concern should be strictly for your own immediate job rather than the broad scene."

Bing had several reasons for fighting the National Company so determinedly in 1965. He knew that the move to the new opera house the following year would incur enormous expenses, and he believed this would be the wrong time to start another expensive venture. Although he knew that outreach projects do attract donors, he feared that the inexperienced young singers in the National Company would create an inferior image of the Met. For as long as the Metropolitan has existed, the declaration "This is _The Met_" has been used to justify not just artistic integrity and technical efficiency, but arrogance, capriciousness, and disdain, and Rudolf Bing exemplified this attitude. He ran the Met, and everything had to be the best. To Bing, the idea of the National Company was one of provincial mediocrity, and he fought it financially, artistically, and even through the labor unions he detested.

But Bliss would not be deterred from his vision of a more-accessible Metropolitan Opera, and he rallied the board around him. Most of the directors agreed that the new company would be a public relations triumph and, not incidentally, would position the Met for federal subsidies. In the 1960s and into the mid-1970s, arts leaders still expected that federal subsidies would help institutions bridge the widening gap between expenses and earnings. With the board against him, Bing was forced to accept the National Company.

The venture survived for two seasons from 1965 to 1967. To placate Bing, Bliss had promised that it would be financially independent from the big company, but this proved unworkable; the National Company, performing in small theaters around the country, could not generate enough income. Audiences, as Bing had predicted, were disappointed by the performance level. The critics agreed; as Winthrop Sargeant stated in the *New Yorker:* "The opera, if it is opera, is certainly *petit* rather than grand."

Bing was dedicated to the concept that opera was grand. When Lila Acheson Wallace of the *Reader's Digest* fortune offered $1 million to save the National Company in 1966, Bing, faced with the ruinous expense of moving into the new house, insisted that the money go into the Met's general operating fund. Mrs. Wallace threatened to withdraw her gift, and, this time, the board backed Bing, not Bliss. Mrs. Wallace took back her money, and the National Company collapsed. But Bing's bitterness toward Bliss endured and hardened.

*I*n 1963, Rudolf Bing realized how tired he was. His fatigue was so great that, for the first time, he began to think seriously of relinquishing his position. Of course, he did not consider leaving before the new house opened, but he thought there might be room for another major player.

Up to this point, Bing had been adamant that, while he was in power, there was no room for a music director. He made all the artistic decisions and he neither needed nor wanted help with them. The mounting difficulties of the move to the new house forced him to reconsider. And he was very fond of a young American conductor from the Midwest, Thomas Schippers, who was handsome and charming and possessed that indefinable ability to communicate with audiences. His career at the Met was already distinguished: when he made his debut in 1955, he was the youngest man ever to conduct there; he was the first American ever to conduct a Met opening night when he led *Nabucco* in 1960; and he conducted the American premiere of Gian Carlo Menotti's *The Last Savage* in 1963–64. In all, he would lead 341 Met performances, the largest number of any conductor at that time.

Schippers had another advantage: his agent, Ronald Wilford of Columbia Artists Management, who was in the midst of amassing a client list that eventually comprised most of the world's major conductors.

Wilford knew that Bing admired Schippers, who was an appealing package: he was attractive, personable, and young enough to appear malleable to Bing. Wilford set up a meeting to talk to Bing about Schippers's future at the Met.

Bing spent most of the summer of 1963 out of touch with Bliss, who was at his ranch, even though urgent negotiations were in progress for the move to the new house. "I enjoyed hearing that the [Bliss] phone line had been chewed off by bears," Bing wrote to an associate that summer. He did not mention Wilford's visit to Bliss until both returned to New York in the fall.

He then sent Bliss a memo outlining his discussions with Wilford and Schippers. Wilford had stressed that Schippers was one of the most sought-after young conductors in the world and that he was on the brink of being offered a major orchestra, as well as a deluge of guest appearances. But Schippers, Wilford reminded Bing, had his heart set on a career that included opera as well as symphonic work, and, in fact, "within four, five or six years . . . would hope to play a leading position in the management at an opera house. Whether or not he wishes to become general manager of the Met may be premature to discuss . . . but obviously his inclinations lead toward such a position."

Wilford explained that Schippers hoped for a three-year contract and was prepared to sacrifice large conducting fees with other orchestras and opera companies to "belong" to the Met. Schippers wanted to be called principal conductor. Bing, intrigued, countered with permanent conductor.

These negotiations between Bing and Wilford offer some insight into murky areas. Wilford's strategy is easily read between the lines. He was aware of Bing's affection for this beautiful young man, and, by suggesting that Schippers was so much in demand that he might stop conducting at the Met, he lured Bing into considering the previously unthinkable: a music director. Bing hoped that Schippers, as his protégé, would learn the operatic ropes quickly and work up to a position where he would be able to take over from Bing. Bing would have stayed in the picture even after his retirement as a mentor and consultant, thus adding one more advantage to his position vis-à-vis Anthony Bliss.

Bliss agreed to the Schippers arrangement, because in theory he was enthusiastic about the idea of a music director who would by definition dilute Bing's power. But he added some conditions. He was president of the board, he reminded Bing, and it was the board who appointed general managers, not general managers who designated their successors. "The agreement does not, in any way, signify that he [Schippers] is being trained as your successor. At this time there is no 'heir apparent' to the general manager."

Despite Bliss's tempered enthusiasm, Bing felt everything was in place to move ahead with Schippers. Wilford was delighted. The snag in the arrangement came from an unexpected source.

"Dear Tommy," Bing wrote on May 1, 1964. "I am a little worried that either you or I have not quite understood the idea behind the new arrangement." Bing told Schippers that he expected him to attend management and artistic meetings so he could begin to grasp the full picture of Met operations. But Schippers was not interested in going to meetings; instead, he suggested that Bing and his assistant manager for artistic matters, Bob Herman, prepare a list of questions for him.

Bing was furious. "Your suggestion," he wrote in reply, "is not only impractical but makes no sense, and it is to me a slightly upsetting indication that you either won't have enough time for us or really don't take it as seriously as I had hoped you would." The final straw came when Schippers did not bother to appear at orchestra auditions. The arrangement was canceled.

Schippers, however, was given the honor of conducting opening night in the new house in September 1966. To observe the occasion, the Metropolitan had commissioned the American composer Samuel Barber to write a new opera, *Antony and Cleopatra,* which would receive its world premiere on opening night. Franco Zeffirelli, the Italian producer, was chosen to direct and design the new production.

Bing had catastrophically jam-packed the first season in the new house: he had scheduled nine new productions, four in the first week alone. Originally, he had planned only four for the entire season, but then he heard that the Vienna State Opera had reopened its opera house that had been destroyed in World War II with a season featuring six new productions. He was too competitive to allow Vienna to outdo the Met, so he overscheduled.

The pressure on the company members was unrelenting. Stagehands slept on benches in the halls for five or six days at a stretch because they had no time to go home. The chorus and ballet frequently rehearsed until after midnight.

Watching the exhausted company, the management realized how ridiculously grandiose the plans for the new season were. Bing and his assistants began to retrench. The premiere of Strauss's *Die Frau ohne Schatten,* scheduled for the first week, was postponed to October. Days before opening night, new productions of Ponchielli's *La Gioconda* and Verdi's *La Traviata* were postponed. Bing took the blame upon himself. "It is all my fault," he said. "We simply bit off more than we could chew."

The most pressing problems involved the world premiere scheduled for opening night. When rehearsals began, Samuel Barber still had not finished the opera, and, as a result, Franco Zeffirelli, the stage director and designer, was also unprepared. Bing scheduled more and more rehearsal time for *Antony and Cleopatra,* and, in a domino effect, there was even less time for all the other operas in the repertory.

Zeffirelli was determined to make *Antony and Cleopatra* a grand spectacle, so he filled the stage with as many choristers, dancers, and supernumeraries—or extras—as it could hold. When the number reached four hundred, the new turntable stage, the pride of the technical department, gave out. The struts holding it bent, and the turntable jammed. This was a disaster for more than just *Antony and Cleopatra;* other designers working on that first season had also planned to use the turntable in their new productions.

To salvage opening night, the crew built Cleopatra's pyramid with wheels so that it could be turned manually by stagehands hidden inside. At the dress rehearsal, the crew wore their usual leather-soled shoes, but these slipped on the surface of the stage, and several stagehands fell down inside the pyramid as it turned with understandably jerky motion. Also inside was Leontyne Price, who was singing Cleopatra, waiting to make her entrance. At her musical cue, the door jammed and would not open. Describing her panic to Bliss later, Price said, "Man, that's when I lost my tan!"

At the same time, in the underground rehearsal rooms, members of the company began reporting unrelenting headaches that, they were convinced, came from lack of air. Wallace Harrison told Bliss that he had heard of similar problems in underground military installations during World War II and that they were psychological and had been solved by the clever use of interior design. So the big ducts that laced the underground rehearsal studios were painted different colors, the walls were decorated with murals, and comfortable couches, chairs, and tables were strewn strategically to relieve the utilitarian ambience. No one had time to sit down, but everything looked nice.

At one rehearsal, a leading soprano complained that the lack of air was affecting her ability to sing. "I'll fix that," Bing said, and pretended to move the controls on a nearby thermostat. He announced that everything would be fine in a few minutes. Ten minutes later, the soprano turned to him and said, "Oh, Mr. Bing, that's so much better."

Bing and Bliss were able to maintain some sense of humor about the technical glitches, but they also had to deal with another potential disaster. The orchestra had threatened to strike on opening night.

The musicians had remained bitter about the contract arbitrated five years earlier by Arthur Goldberg. They were still playing seven performances a week, and although they were among the best-paid musicians in the country, they worked so much harder than their symphony orchestra colleagues that they did not believe their salary level was sufficient compensation.

They also saw the huge amounts of money that had been raised for the new house and for Lincoln Center's construction, and this added to the sense they had been swindled. All this money was flowing everywhere except to them.

During the 1964 negotiations, rather than settling, the musicians had decided to extend their contract to 1966. Bliss and Bing knew the orchestra was setting up a crisis for the opening of the new house, but there was nothing they could do.

The time bomb went off in the weeks just before the house opened: the musicians announced their intention to strike immediately after opening night, September 16. Aware that the public might not be sympathetic to their disruption of the new Met's first night in the new house, they explained that they did not want to disappoint the audience coming from all over the world. They, however, had no qualms about interrupting the rest of the season.

Bliss became furious at the orchestra, blaming them for spoiling the evening he had worked so long to achieve. For him, opening night when it finally arrived was not the glorious celebration he had envisioned. Negotiations with the musicians went right to the moment the curtain went up.

Just before *Antony and Cleopatra* began, an agreement was hammered out. For the orchestra, the agreement was revenge for the wrongs of 1961. Each musician was given the right to refuse to play more than five performances per week. For the first time, the orchestra had adequate medical insurance; before, the musicians themselves had taken up collections to help incapacitated colleagues. Their pension plan was upgraded and they were given five weeks of vacation.

As the opening-night audience, regally gowned and bejeweled, filed into the new opera house, no one knew if the opening night would also be the only night of the new season. The musicians' strike threat had been well publicized, and all portents had been discouraging. So, once the orchestra had voted to accept the new agreement, Bliss decided to go out in front of the curtain and personally announce the settlement to the audience. There was a general sigh of relief, and the performance began as scheduled. But Bliss never forgave the orchestra for changing the night of triumph he had worked for years to achieve into a nerve-racking ordeal. Bliss, for so long proud of his friendships with company members, never forgot what he saw as the orchestra's worthless vindictiveness.

Opening night was not a decisive success. The acoustics were judged exceptional, the only hall at Lincoln Center where this had been achieved.

Despite the richness of the materials from which it had been constructed, the interior of the auditorium did not match the grandeur and elegance of the old Met's decor. Ada Louise Huxtable, chief architecture critic for the _New York Times,_ wrote, after opening night, "There is a strong temptation to close the eyes."

And the commissioned opera was proclaimed a garish failure. The excesses of Zeffirelli's production could not compensate for what critics cited as Barber's banal score. Sadly, the new opera, conducted by Thomas Schippers, America's most prominent young conductor, was a failure.

_B_y November 1966, complaints had lessened, productions were back on schedule, and the technical staff had learned how to operate the stage equipment. The artistic content of the new productions, however painfully achieved, was high, and attendance had never been so healthy. The company began to feel more at home in the new opera house.

But there were problems. By November, Bliss and Bing had to face a painful reality: the move to the new house had caused the most serious financial crisis the Met had faced since it was almost forced to close during the Depression.

As recently as September, the situation had not seemed so precarious. The company had an accumulated working capital deficit of almost $2 million, which the board had covered by authorizing borrowing of $2.8 million. There was the loss of $800,000 from Bing's bête noire, the National Company, but neither of these expenses was unexpected; the Met board was accustomed to living on the edge.

They also knew that Herman Krawitz, the trusted assistant manager whom Bing had put in charge of internal planning for the new house, had been realistic in planning for an anticipated operating deficit of $3.8 million for the first year. Judging by past experience, the board foresaw no problem in covering this amount by normal fund-raising.

There was, however, nothing normal about an unexpected additional overrun of $3 million. The cost of the 1966–67 season had been budgeted at $14 million, including operating deficits; the actual cost was $17 million. The old Met property was the only asset the company had. George S.

Moore, the board's treasurer and president of the First National City Bank, released a statement: "We grossly miscalculated the costs involved in the move to our new Lincoln Center home. We just made a mistake."

For the first time, ticket prices rose in midseason. The 20 percent increase added $1.5 million in revenues, since the box office was at an all-time high of 99.4 percent that season. But this further alienated a public already angry about the razing of the old house. And the lease income derived from the site of the old house could not help in such a dire emergency as existed in November 1966. So the board instituted a second, more conventional fund-raising tactic. They announced an Emergency Fund Drive for $3 million and, despite some negative feelings, the public responded and the sum was raised. No one on the board, however, wanted to deal with the underlying problem: the Met had no endowment to help it through bad times like this. The directors felt the present crisis was so acute that they couldn't risk trying to raise endowment funds at the same time.

The company was saved yet again, but the reserves of public goodwill were running thin. Bliss, Bing, and the directors were relieved, sure they were safe for a while. Past financial crises had come so far apart that the Met's reserves had been replenished between emergencies. Not this time. The next major crisis was much closer than anyone wanted to believe.

Chapter Eight

BING VS. BLISS REDUX

During his Glyndebourne days, Rudolf Bing had been friendly with the Earl of Harewood, a music-loving cousin of Queen Elizabeth II. Lord Harewood, who had been one of Bing's successors at the Edinburgh Festival, also served on the board of the Royal Opera at Covent Garden. When he came to New York for the opening of the new Met in 1966, Bing introduced him to Anthony Bliss, and the two men took to each other immediately. Harewood is a man of easy charm who, despite his startling resemblance to his grandfather King George V and his great-uncle Czar Nicholas II, is as down-to-earth as Tony Bliss.

At that time, Bliss had come up with another idea that Bing considered misguided. Bliss had suggested having ballet evenings interspersed among the opera performances during the Met season. Ballet was cheaper to produce than opera, and Bliss thought the evenings might relieve some financial strain. Bing argued that ticket prices would have to be reduced, which would wipe out any monetary advantage. He also thought that the Met's ballet company would be compared unfavorably with the New York City Ballet, across Lincoln Center Plaza. But what angered him most was that the early exploration of this idea had happened without his knowledge. "I somehow feel that we are now pulling in different directions," he wrote to Bliss. "This should not go on. It is unfortunate that the press and the ballet are given hints of great developments of which I am not even aware."

George Harewood began attending Met performances every night as Bliss's guest, and Bing watched the friendship grow with concern. Harewood was on the board of Covent Garden, where the Royal Ballet shared the stage each season with the Royal Opera. He was sure to agree with Bliss. To Bing, the earl, an experienced arts administrator, was beginning to look like a candidate for his own job.

Bing acted quickly. He knew very well that Bliss had fallen in love with Sally Brayley, a dancer in the Met Ballet. Brayley was a vivacious redhead who had joined the company in 1962. A Canadian, she had left high school to make a career as a dancer, and had been a member of the National Ballet of Canada and American Ballet Theatre. In 1964, Bliss had gone along on part of the Met's annual tour and that was when the romance had begun. Bliss and Brayley were not very discreet, Herman Krawitz remembered: "He sat in the ballet car on the train rather than the management car." Sally was twenty-six; Bliss was forty-nine. Despite an outgoing and cheerful temperament, she was a little in awe of her new boyfriend. "I used to walk down the street holding hands with him, and I still called him 'Mr. Bliss.' "

Unfortunately, both Bliss and Brayley were married. The Met tour has traditionally been a congenial and forgiving breeding ground for love affairs (including several of Bing's), but this one surprised people because it involved the president of the board and was carried on so openly. Bing, always discreet about his affairs, looked on in amazement.

In a letter to Bliss about the ballet plans, Bing slipped in a sentence that revealed how much dangerous information he had: "I hate to have to say [these disparaging things about the Met ballet's abilities] because I am keenly aware that this is a matter close to your heart and of deep concern to you." He certainly knew how the Met ballet dancers had heard about Bliss's plans for ballet evenings long before Bing himself.

By the spring of 1966, the press also knew about the relationship. Leonard Lyons wrote in his *New York Journal-American* column, " 'There is no separation and no divorce,' Mrs. Anthony Bliss told me emphatically when reached at their Oyster Bay estate. Maybe the former Jo Ann Sayres' studies at Columbia are keeping her too busy to attend the opera with her husband who heads the Metropolitan Opera Association. Let's hope so."

The morning after one particularly difficult evening in the new house, George Moore, the board treasurer, called a meeting of the executive committee in his office about the problems of the night before. Bing was talking about the previous evening's crisis when Bliss came in, late, and went directly over to Herman Krawitz, saying he had to talk to him immediately.

Krawitz went off into a corner and Bliss said, "You have to do something about the maintenance staff. They're just terrible. I went back to Sally's dressing room last night, and there was a lightbulb burned out on one of the mirrors."

"Did anyone call a maintenance man?" Krawitz asked.

"Well, Herman, I'm telling you to see that this doesn't happen again," Bliss said to the man responsible for the entire construction project of the new house. "You've got to take care of these things." The two men then rejoined the meeting. Bliss seemed unaware of the raised eyebrows among his conservative colleagues on the board.

Bing never missed anything, and he later asked Krawitz what he and Bliss had talked about. "So I told him," Krawitz said. "I thought he would have an apoplectic attack. This was the level of Bliss's thinking then. He was off base totally, and he lost Bing and Moore, and Mrs. Belmont and her ladies were not buying any of this." Bliss, previously the clear-sighted, decisive, and empathetic board president, seemed to have lost all judgment in the throes of this love affair.

Bing, sensing that Bliss had lost the board's support, felt he no longer had to endure Lord Harewood's constant presence, so he called a special meeting of the executive committee. "Mr. Bliss and I have had a happy marriage for ten years," he said to the assembled directors, including Bliss, "but now it is quite apparent that Mr. Bliss wants a new general manager and it seems he has found one." Bing then asked the committee to accept his resignation.

Bing knew this was a calculated risk; after all, he was in part responsible for the dire financial situation. But he also knew that Bliss's affair grated on the other directors. Bliss answered Bing by saying that he did not agree the general manager had any reason to resign nor did he have any intention of resigning as board president. But in the spring of 1967, as Bing coyly phrased it, "the strains of this desperate season became too much for Bliss, and soon, quite apart from the Harewood situation, he did resign as president."

On April 17, 1967, George Moore was elected to replace Bliss, following weeks of public speculation that Bliss was being forced out. Moore denied that the company's financial problems were a factor in the replacement of Bliss.

Bliss had many reasons for wanting to leave, aside from the strain of fiscal calamity and Bing's unrelenting animosity. He was divorced from Jo Ann Sayres and married Sally Brayley, and his need to finance a divorce and a new family persuaded him to return to full-time practice at his law firm. He had neglected his responsibilities at Milbank, Tweed to concentrate on the Met, but with a young wife eager for children, and with four children from his previous marriages, he needed to rejuvenate the old Bliss fortune. Within a year of the marriage to Sally, the first child of the "third litter" was born, a son, followed two years later by another boy. The Blisses settled down to family life on a beautiful shorefront estate on Long Island.

Bliss did remain on the Met board, however, and continued to serve as Bing's nemesis. In 1968, Bing was given an extension of his contract as general manager through the 1972 season. Although he complained constantly about the pressure of his job, and talked about retiring, he wanted to stay. The Metropolitan Opera was his life.

At the board meeting where Bing was granted his extension, Bliss was the only director to vote against him. He later wrote to Bing, "I feel that you have given everything that you have to the Metropolitan in terms of new directions and artistic achievement and that the job should now pass on to a young person (preferably in his forties) who can bring a fresh and vigorous approach."

Bing, undaunted, wrote back, "I am afraid I will have to disappoint you—I will accept the extension of my contract." He closed his letter with greetings to Sally and best wishes for the birth of the Blisses' new baby. Tony Bliss was no longer a threat, and the two men retreated to positions of mutual wariness.

George Moore had been chairman of the finance committee in addition to serving as treasurer before he replaced Bliss as president in 1967. Initially, he earned even Bing's admiration with his quick actions to revive the company's finances, raising ticket prices and galvanizing the association's fund-raising, which had been sadly neglected in the turmoil of the move to Lincoln Center.

But Bing soon realized that in divesting himself of Bliss, he had created new problems. Despite their disagreements, Bing saw that Bliss had a true vision for the company and respected it, even though this vision had produced the loathed National Company. Bliss was not a man to pinch pennies when the glory of the Metropolitan needed luster.

Moore was a banker with a conservative attitude toward money. He did not believe in spending money to raise money. Bing quickly found that he had to devote enormous energy to convince Moore that new productions were not a waste of money but an incentive for new donations. At the same time, Moore directed Bing to explore other ways for the Met to earn income, including recording and television projects. All this took even more time away from what Bing regarded as his real work: running the company. He considered Moore's enthusiasm for side projects, which he described as "mass communications gimmickry," ill conceived and unprofitable.

He was the most infuriated when Moore questioned practices that Bing considered immutable. The company traditionally spent a lot of money on costumes and scenery, which had to be sturdy enough to survive at least twenty years over the life of a production as well as the wear and tear of the eight-week tour. Moore insisted there had to be a cheaper way.

Moore and Bing did agree on one way to save money. For some time, Bing had worried about the tour. It had become more and more difficult to coax leading singers to travel to some of the less-appealing parts of the country; a disagreement about tour dates had caused his famous rift with Callas. Bing sketched out two seasons, 1968–69 and 1969–70, without the tour. Instead, he planned eight additional weeks in New York. With the Met operating at over 99 percent capacity, there seemed no reason to doubt his theory that eight more weeks in New York could sell just as well.

Chapter Nine

STAR POWER

In the fall of 1968, two extraordinary singers made their Metropolitan Opera debuts, only weeks apart. No one could have known then that Plácido Domingo and Luciano Pavarotti would go on to define opera for the next quarter-century.

The Metropolitan Opera has always been known as a "singers' house," a theater that relies on the strength of its operatic stars. At times, theatrical values seemed paramount, yet every Met era is defined in the public's mind by its singers.

Those Met singers who had influence on the administrative and musical policies of the theater had traits other than their superb voices. They were willing to try an unusual repertory and they projected a charismatic personality onstage. These talents directly influenced the box office. To this day, powerful singers know that they sell tickets and can affect the company's financial status by the great and loyal love of their audience, no matter what their human weaknesses.

Probably, the most famous opera singer of the twentieth century was Enrico Caruso. He was so central to the success of the Met that his illness could jeopardize a season's budget. In his seventeen seasons at the Met, from 1903 to 1920, he sang so many opening nights that it took Plácido Domingo thirty-one years with the Met to achieve the same number.

Caruso was an unlikely folk hero. He was not handsome; he was a short, rotund man with little acting ability. But there was an indefinable quality that emanated from him; his charm came from his everyman quality. Born in the slums of Naples, his parents' eighteenth child, he was the first to survive infancy. Throughout his life, he loved to sing, eat, drink, and smoke, and he did all with gusto. He also had a weakness for pretty women.

He began his career in provincial Italian companies, but after an audition for Giacomo Puccini, who became his mentor, his engagements improved. He made his La Scala debut in 1900, then Monte Carlo and Covent Garden. Maurice Grau signed him to his first Met contract for the 1903–4 season.

His debut, in *Rigoletto* on opening night in 1903, was also the first night of the Conried administration. The audience loved him at first sight; his most enthusiastic supporters were the opera lovers in ordinary seats who sensed his openness and warmth. They could not even wait for the curtain calls after each act to shout their approval, but interrupted the performance several times to acknowledge their new favorite.

Caruso loved them back and he also loved New York; he had found his musical home. Over the next five years, he became so beloved that tickets for his performances were unobtainable. People subscribed to the whole season to be sure of hearing Caruso sing, and from 1903 to 1921, he became one of the financial underpinnings of the entire company.

None of this success went to his head. He tackled life with a zest rarely found in modern opera singers, who often find maintaining their superstardom a tense and serious business. For Caruso, a performance was not an occasion for worrying about high notes, but a chance to plot new practical jokes. Once he switched places with a comprimario to sing Beppe's offstage serenade in *Pagliacci* to see if anyone recognized his voice; no one did. He kept a toy mouse in his pocket during the act 4 *Bohème* death scene with Nellie Melba and squeaked the toy in her ear as she expired. In the same scene with Frances Alda, he removed two of the wheels from the bed so it rocked back and forth throughout her death. Gatti finally became so exasperated that after one joke—Caruso for some reason wore a monocle through the same death scene—he fined the tenor $100.

But the public loved an opera singer who smoked four packs of cigarettes a day, gambled incessantly, and, most important, spent the entire season in New York, a member of the community. Later, he moved his family to New York, living in a hotel two blocks from the Met with his wife, baby, nursemaid, secretary, accompanist, and business manager.

Although he exhausted himself taking on every outside engagement he could for the huge fees, Caruso never held the Met hostage to financial demands. Even when he was receiving over $10,000 for each concert appearance, he sang at the Met for $2,500. After the boxholders became Caruso fans, he sang for the same amount at wealthy patrons' dinners and allowed the Met to keep any additional money that was raised.

The audience loved him so much that even a small scandal in 1906 only seemed to endear him more to the public. A week before opening night in 1906–7, Caruso was arrested in the monkey house of the Central Park Zoo for "annoying" a certain Mrs. Hannah Stanhope. The details were never specified, but contemporary reports allude to "improper advances" and "pinching." Caruso was convicted and fined, and the Met management was apprehensive about his next appearance. They need not have worried. "The theater rang with applause," reported the Met's historian, Irving Kolodin.

During World War I, when European artists could not get across the Atlantic, the Met made heavy demands on its resident singers, particularly idols like Farrar and Caruso. Farrar protected herself if she felt any harm to her voice, but Caruso loved to sing and did so as often as possible. This kind of artistic generosity can be costly for an artist.

On December 8, 1920, Caruso thought he had pulled a muscle in his side during a *Pagliacci* performance. The next week, he was still in pain but sang *L'Elisir d'Amore*. He coughed up blood during the performance, but wanted to continue. The stage manager came out in front of the curtain, told the audience that Caruso wanted to finish, and asked for their decision. The members of the audience, aware of what was happening, and many of them in tears, shouted "No!" Yet Caruso, his ribs tightly strapped, finished the performance and sang three more times in the next ten days. In the third week of December, he sang *La Juive*, his 607th performance in the opera house. Caruso was diagnosed with pleurisy on Christmas Day. He had to admit he was ill; when he developed a kidney infection, he went home to Italy to recuperate.

But Caruso had waited too long for medical attention, and although his wife sent the Met an optimistic report on his progress, he died in August 1921. He was forty-eight.

Caruso had achieved his goal for the Met. Because he worked himself so prodigiously, the Met closed the 1920–21 season with a small profit. Indeed, subscription sales had flourished during Caruso's illness, because the public saw this as a chance to get seats that were usually unavailable. What Caruso could not have foreseen was the effect of his long and busy career on future seasons. Because tickets for his performances were so desirable and difficult to get, New Yorkers had begun to buy subscription series rather than single tickets to be sure of hearing him. Even after his death, the habit of subscribing endured. His effect on the repertory was also strong. He sang thirty-seven roles in thirty-seven operas. Some, like *Lodoletta, Martha,* and *Julien,* are now forgotten, but most of the operas he sang became popular, establishing a place for the Puccini operas and the verismo repertory, operas concerned with common people and their preoccupations rather than the trials and passions of aristocrats. There would be artists with longer Met careers than Caruso, but few inspired the love that was felt for him.

Although there would be many box office draws after Caruso, from Leontyne Price to Franco Corelli to Joan Sutherland to Birgit Nilsson, two singers joined the Met roster in 1968 who, thirty years later, would still be singing, and selling out the theater. Luciano Pavarotti and Plácido Domingo are two of the rare opera singers who have become household names. Partly this was because their careers coincided with an unprecedented passion for celebrity in the United States, partly because of their own distinctive personalities.

Luciano Pavarotti sang Rodolfo in *La Bohème* at his professional debut on April 29, 1961, in Reggio-Emilia, Italy; he chose the same role for all his subsequent debuts in major opera houses, including the Met on November 23, 1968. He is a native of Modena, a city north of Rome, and for a while wanted a career as a professional soccer player. But he enjoyed one success after another as a singer; in the early years, he was a protégé of Joan Sutherland, with whom he sang *La Fille du Régiment* at the Met in 1972, a performance that started his ascent to world fame. Tossing off nine high Cs in the first-act aria, Pavarotti became the toast of the opera world overnight, only a few years after his debut.

In some ways, Pavarotti was an unlikely candidate for world fame. Domingo may have been a little heavy, but Pavarotti was downright fat. Like Caruso, however, he had a warmth and vulnerability that crossed the footlights effortlessly. Domingo, a more cerebral musician, lacked this essential appeal and he worked harder for his stardom. Domingo had been offered a contract with the National Company, but had turned it down. A Spaniard who had grown up in Mexico, he was the child of two zarzuela singers, and he had married another singer, Marta Ornelas, an older woman filled with enough ambition for both of them. He had sung major roles at the New York City Opera, not a credential that Bing respected, although the smaller company has always been an important source of singers for the Met. Domingo had to audition twice for Bing before he was offered a contract; he was scheduled to make his debut on October 2, 1968, singing opposite Renata Tebaldi in *Adriana Lecouvreur*.

On Saturday, September 28, Domingo rehearsed *Turandot* during the day, then went home to Teaneck, New Jersey, for dinner, before covering Franco Corelli's performance in *Adriana* during the evening. His dinner was interrupted by a call from Bing, who asked how he was feeling. "Very well," replied Domingo.

"That's good," Bing said, "because you are making your Metropolitan Opera debut this evening."

Domingo's reaction was furious. He was hardly in the rested condition ideal to make his debut after the day of rehearsing, and he was forced to warm up in the car as his father drove him back to the Met. He also had dark suspicions that Corelli had canceled at the last minute on purpose, knowing that Domingo had rehearsed all day and would be tired.

Tebaldi and the conductor, Fausto Cleva, were gracious to Domingo, but he had to face a public disappointed by Corelli's cancellation. Domingo at the time was overweight and had an awkward stage presence, unlike the svelte, glamorous Corelli. Actually, the fact that he had no chance to get nervous worked in Domingo's favor; he sang well, not having to worry about reviews. At the second performance, which the critics attended, he sang even better. And over the next few years, Domingo would slim down and cultivate his appearance to the point where he became one of opera's few sex symbols.

Domingo and Pavarotti were about the same age, and their careers would run parallel for a long time. Even beyond the opera world, their relationship would be scrutinized like a great love affair.

Chapter Ten

THE BING ERA ENDS

By the Metropolitan's third season at Lincoln Center, Bing, Moore, and the board had managed to stabilize the company. The sense of emergency subsided, and the 1968–69 annual report declared finances "under control." The number of new productions was reduced, the National Company was disbanded, and Bing made a real effort to cut production costs. As the situation improved, the board stopped worrying about establishing an endowment fund for future emergencies.

Earlier, in November 1967, the Met's fund-raisers did break new ground when the company announced that a new production of Wagner's *Der Ring des Nibelungen,* conceived and directed by the conductor Herbert von Karajan, would be underwritten by Eastern Airlines. In the past, new productions had been funded by individuals, foundations, or the Metropolitan Opera Guild. Now, for the first time, a large corporation stepped into the arena, joining Texaco, the longtime sponsor of radio broadcasts. A new realm of arts funding, corporate sponsorship, was born.

But the source of the money did not change either the artist's behavior or Bing's proprietary attitude. He had tried for years to lure Karajan to the Met and finally succeeded with the *Ring* by promising to re-create the conductor's Salzburg Festival production. Bing underestimated the factor that he was about to enter negotiations with a master.

When Bing respected conductors, he allowed them more leeway in casting their operas than he permitted ordinary human beings. He had taken advice when it was given by Pierre Monteux, Ernest Ansermet, or Karl Böhm, and he was prepared to offer Karajan the same respect. The only nonnegotiable casting was that of Birgit Nilsson in the role of Brünnhilde. Karajan had the reputation of casting eccentrically, but even he couldn't argue with Nilsson's reputation as the greatest Wagnerian soprano of the day.

She was also a special favorite of New York audiences. A farmer's daughter from Sweden, she had milked ten cows the night before her first professional audition. No amount of international fame had changed her direct and approachable manner. She also possessed an irrepressible sense of humor. When a jealous Franco Corelli nipped her neck while she held a high C longer than he could, Nilsson called Bing the next day to say she could not go on that night: "I have rabies," she announced.

Bing loved her spontaneity and wit as much as he respected her magnificent voice, and he and Nilsson enjoyed sparring over almost every aspect of her Met career. She fought him about the U.S. taxes deducted from her paychecks to the point where she named him as a dependent on her tax return. Close as they were, Bing forgot one important thing: she did not like Herbert von Karajan, whom she referred to as "Herbie."

Bing had his own misgivings about Karajan. His admiration for the conductor as a musician did not extend to him personally. Bing was suspicious of the conductor's well-publicized membership in the Nazi Party and dismissive of Karajan's pretensions as a stage director. After Bing went to see Karajan's *Ring* at Salzburg, the maestro proudly told him about the many lighting rehearsals he had demanded. "I could have got it that dark in one," Bing replied.

Somehow Bing and Karajan wove their way through the precarious preproduction negotiations, and when Karajan arrived in New York, Bing's misgivings shifted to a grudging respect when he listened to what the conductor achieved at rehearsals. But he and Karajan had trouble establishing a personal relationship; when Karajan was unhappy about something, he got in touch with Ronald Wilford, his manager, who would then call Bing. Bing's invitations to lunch or a drink were answered with a dismissive "I don't eat lunch" or "I don't drink." But Bing tolerated Karajan's iciness because he admired him artistically.

Nilsson was less easily won over. She suspected that she had been foisted on Karajan by the Met. She hated the darkness of Karajan's concept, at one point appearing onstage wearing a coal miner's helmet, complete with searchlight. "I told Mr. Bing that I could go out for coffee sometimes [when she was supposed to be onstage] and no one would know the difference."

Karajan and Nilsson continued to feud throughout the rehearsal period, so Bing was justifiably proud of his referee skill when _Die Walküre,_ the first _Ring_ opera produced, became a highlight of the 1967–68 season. The next year, Karajan returned for _Das Rheingold,_ in which Brünnhilde does not appear. The omens were good for similar success with _Siegfried_ and _Götterdämmerung,_ but by the 1969–70 season, the Met's labor problems were primary.

Moore had decided to take a hard stance, and instructed Bing to give the unions as little as possible, preferably nothing. But the musicians were still angry about 1961, the management and board were still furious about 1966, and the other unions were still jealous of the larger settlement given the musicians. Everyone was angry at everyone else, and distrust was pervasive. "Bing absolutely hated us," the chairman of the orchestra committee that season remembered. "Nineteen sixty-nine was 'get even' time. It was mostly attitude that created the 1969 strike—hatred on both sides."

When no progress had been made by the end of August 1969, Bing actually did what he had so often threatened: he postponed opening night indefinitely. Moore voiced his support, but his phrasing was unfortunate: "There was not enough time left to rehearse opening night," he explained to the press. "And not only that—people had dinner parties planned. We had to tell people."

Week by week, more of the 1969–70 season was canceled. Public opinion was divided: some saw the company members as greedy; others felt the board and management were patronizing, intent on teaching the uppity musicians a lesson. Bing did little to temper this impression. "In America," he observed, "even the sanitation men have temperament."

The strike lasted for three and a half months, during which nobody paid any attention to the Met's loyal subscribers. Few had ever questioned why they went to the opera: it was simply part of their lives. Now the Met had suddenly disappeared from these lives, and people discovered that life went

on anyway. This realization came at a time when the country was undergoing enormous social change. Going to the opera began to seem peripheral in
an era of assassinations, racial dissent, Vietnam, even Woodstock.

Bing assumed that his subscribers would be happy to forgo refunds for
canceled performances. He was wrong and the subscribers were angry at
his assumption: of $2.85 million in preseason subscription sales, almost
$2.3 million had to be refunded. To add insult to injury, refunding this
many tickets was an enormous and expensive job. The company was not
able to keep up with the demands for refunds, and the public became even
more offended.

The settlement itself was expensive, both in salaries and benefits.
Ticket prices were raised again, and attendance fell more. Ticket sales
plunged from 96 percent of capacity in 1968–69 to 89 percent the year after
the strike, and did not recover for ten years. Even then, the subscriber base
never returned to the levels preceding 1969; in the end, the Met preferred
this situation because more tickets were available to the general public,
who, before 1968, could never be sure of buying single tickets.

In January 1970, the Met did something unprecedented. The company
took out an ad in the Sunday *New York Times,* offering seats for all remaining performances that season. The days of small discreet ads inviting
people "to apply to subscribe" were over, as was the sense of gracious obligation on the part of subscribers that had cushioned the Metropolitan
Opera for eighty-five years. A year later, the box office for the first time accepted credit cards, because it had to.

At the end of 1970, after losing $3.8 million during the season, Moore
sent out a public cry for help. "The Metropolitan Opera is actively seeking
Government support for the first time in its history," the *New York Times*
reported in December. "We are not a Diamond Horseshoe anymore,"
Moore sadly admitted. "We hope to widen our public."

Moore realized he had to exert control over day-to-day operations,
and he decreed that financial accountability would now take priority over
artistic considerations. Previously, Bing had been ready to fight for his
artistic domain, but by 1970, he was worn down. In 1968, he had signed a
new contract that would terminate in 1972. The board launched a search
for his successor.

By 1970, as the Metropolitan Opera board looked for a new general manager, the opera world had changed. Over the course of a generation, the jet plane had altered the careers of major artists, allowing them to go quickly from city to city, from performance to performance, from one enormous fee to another. Enrico Caruso had taken an ocean liner to sing at the Met and stayed for most of the season; Plácido Domingo used the Concorde as regularly as most people take taxis.

Europe had recovered from World War II, and its state-supported opera houses easily matched and soon outdistanced the Met's top fees. European artists—and despite the burgeoning of American opera singers, most performers were still Europeans—preferred to live in Europe and fly to nearby well-paid engagements. The incentive to come and spend months in New York, far from family, friends, and lucrative concert dates, had disappeared along with the strength of the U.S. dollar. The fees demanded by singers went up; those offered by the Met did not; and fewer and fewer of the world's acclaimed artists found a Met engagement irresistible. The major singers, like the subscribers, learned to live without the Met.

The traumatic 1969–70 season had discouraged many prime candidates for Bing's position. In early 1970, Moore asked Bing to stay on for another season after his contract expired in 1972. Bing, dispirited, refused.

Although Bing's era was passing, his last years were marked by some memorable occasions: _Norma_ with Joan Sutherland and Marilyn Horne; a new _Tristan und Isolde_ produced by August Everding with Birgit Nilsson and Jess Thomas; and a new _Otello_, directed and designed by Franco Zeffirelli. And, during these last years, Bing did receive one treasured recognition. He had never given up the British passport he acquired during World War II, and in 1971, Queen Elizabeth II knighted him. To the public at large, he became Sir Rudolf; inside the opera house, he was still Mr. Bing, except for certain rattlebrained staffers who addressed him as Sir Bing.

Bing badly wanted one of his two assistants, Robert Herman or Herman Krawitz, to succeed him, and had lobbied hard to that end. Each had valuable talents and both possessed one asset not found in the other candidates: they had the specific knowledge of the unique way the Met operated. Either man would have made an excellent choice. But the board was determined to bring in the new general manager from outside, and when this was clear to Herman and Krawitz, they decided to leave with Bing.

On December 9, 1970, the announcement was made of the appointment of Goeran Gentele, intendant of the Royal Opera in Stockholm. His name was first put forth by Schuyler Chapin, vice president of programming at Lincoln Center, who had encountered Gentele while looking for opera productions to import to New York. George Moore investigated Gentele's credentials through his international banking connections and, impressed, urged his colleagues on the board to engage him.

Goeran Gentele was fifty-three years old, a ruddy, exuberant, and charming man who became an immediate success with the New York press and public. He presented a warm contrast to the austere Bing, and right from the start promised a change. He had no intention of being a dictator in the style of Bing and he hoped to relax the Met's traditional formality; he believed a company more firmly centered in America might attract the needed federal funding. "We must not forget that opera is a folk art, like bull-fighting and prize-fighting," he told the *New York Times*. "Music excites people. For four hundred years, opera has been in crisis. I think this is good. The ideal opera company never existed, and never will exist. When it does, it will be dead."

The press was thrilled by Gentele's spontaneity and accessibility. Only inside the opera house were dissenting voices heard. The word "provincial" was whispered, as was "lack of stature," but the comments never filtered to the outside world.

Gentele announced that he would spend much of the 1971–72 season observing the Met's operation, as Bing himself had done in 1949–50. Bing hated the idea. With an unforgiving eye, he scrutinized each of Gentele's decisions, and disapproval emanated from him like a toxin.

Bing decided to open his last season with a revival of Verdi's *Don Carlo*, the rarely performed opera that had opened his first season, in 1950. Despite Gentele's irritating presence, Bing was, as always, everywhere in the opera house during the weeks before the season. "Sir Rudolf rose to his feet [during a rehearsal] and surveyed the stage," the _New Yorker_ reported. "Summoning his master mechanic, Joseph Volpe, he pointed out that the pillars were crooked, the sky was wrinkled, and there seemed to be pleats in the tops of two arches. 'We'll fix everything,' Mr. Volpe said cheerfully." It was one of Joseph Volpe's first appearances in print.

And, in the midst of the clamor over Gentele's arrival, Bing quietly made a decision that would prove to have a far greater impact on the company. On November 12, 1970, he had signed an almost unknown young conductor for a series of _Tosca_ performances during his final season in 1971–72. James Levine had been recommended to him by Kurt Herbert Adler, the intendant of the San Francisco Opera, and on that basis, Bing invited Levine. Levine made his Met debut in 1971.

Gentele was also busy signing up people. He named Schuyler Chapin as his chief assistant, and he offered the position of music director to the Czech conductor Rafael Kubelik, a respected and beloved musician. Even the New York Philharmonic, famous for eviscerating guest conductors and restlessly unhappy under their strict music director, Pierre Boulez, revered Kubelik. A tall, ungainly man with a beatific smile, he would lope out onto the podium, and, in the way of great conductors, somehow instill in each musician the desire to play his or her best. Despite his gentle demeanor, Kubelik was capable of strong stands. When the Communists took over Czechoslovakia in 1948, Kubelik left the country and vowed not to return until the regime ended.

Kubelik told Gentele he would not take the music director's position unless he had equal artistic authority with the general manager. There was no precedent: Kubelik was the first official music director in the Met's history, despite Toscanini's ipso facto position and Bing's advances to Schippers. Gentele wanted Kubelik so badly that he agreed. He told Schuyler Chapin that he envisioned the Met run by a troika, with Gentele in charge of the stage, Kubelik in charge of the music, and Chapin running the administration. Chapin thought this was a wonderful plan. Bing shuddered. The one snag was that Kubelik could not assume his position until 1974–75.

Otherwise, Kubelik's appointment was greeted enthusiastically;

Chapin's less so. Chapin was one of the best-liked people in the music business, intelligent, charming, and well bred. But he did not inspire respect, perhaps because he was too circumspect and courteous. His career before his Met appointment consisted of number-two positions at Lincoln Center and with Leonard Bernstein's Amberson Productions. Chapin himself certainly had no illusions about his popularity with the board; he knew that Moore had expressed doubts about his appointment but had acquiesced to Gentele's wishes.

In place of Bing's two invaluable assistants, Krawitz and Herman, Gentele chose two young Met employees, Charles Riecker and Michael Bronson. Riecker was named artistic administrator, replacing Herman, and Bronson business administrator, Krawitz's position. Each was in his thirties, was loyal, and had been with the company for several years—but they lacked the expertise and experience of the Bing team. When Herman and Krawitz left, most of the Met's institutional memory went with them.

Kubelik planned to maintain his home base in Europe; he did not intend to move to New York. To ensure that his musical standards were maintained while he was away, he decided that the Met, also for the first time, should engage a principal conductor who would be in New York full-time. In consultation with Gentele, he chose a young man who had already made an indelible impression on the company at his 1971 debut conducting *Tosca*. He was the twenty-eight-year-old James Levine.

Chapter Eleven

THE YOUNG JIMMY

Someone once asked James Levine's mother what Jimmy had been like as a young child. "Old," she replied. "He was always very old."

Jimmy, the first child of Helen and Lawrence Levine, was born in Cincinnati in June 1943. In the years before World War II, his father had led big bands, under the name of Larry Lee. But after his marriage, Lawrence Levine gave up his musical career and went into his father's clothing business. Helen Goldstein Levine had a brief career as an actress on Broadway—she, too, performed under a stage name, Helen Golden—before she met and married Larry Levine. It was an impetuous romance; years later, James Levine, a man who never made an impulsive decision, would marvel that they had only seen each other about four times before they decided to marry.

Helen and Lawrence Levine settled in Cincinnati. Although the Levines felt part of a strong Jewish cultural tradition, particularly in regard to their love of the arts and education, they were thoroughly assimilated into American life and were not religiously observant. There were two more children: Tom, born two years after Jimmy, and Janet, five years later. Neither showed musical promise, although Tom became a painter.

James showed his love of music very early. When his parents tried to put him to sleep by singing him lullabies, he cheerfully sang along. His mother and father soon put this musicality to use. When they wanted to sleep in the mornings, "all we had to do was place a card table by his crib filled with his Victrola, records, and a stack of Graham crackers," his father said. "He used to reach through the bars and amuse himself for hours." He was taken to opera performances at the Cincinnati Opera from a young age; he usually brought along one of his grandmother's knitting needles so that he could conduct.

Levine never showed much interest in toys, absorbed as he was with his Victrola and collection of fifty records, but on a visit to FAO Schwarz, the famous toy shop, he spotted a miniature theater and begged his parents for it. He used the tiny stage to produce elaborate opera productions staged with dollhouse furniture. Family photographs show him, at the age of eight, curled up in an armchair, studying an orchestral score of Gounod's *Faust*. He wears the same bright smile now familiar to singers and orchestra players all over the world.

Levine's formal music studies began with piano lessons when he was four. Like most children, Levine hated practicing, but he loved his lessons so much that his father often enforced the practicing schedule by threatening, "No practice, no lesson."

He made his professional debut at the age of ten, playing the Mendelssohn Piano Concerto No. 1 with the Cincinnati Symphony. His father, thrilled, asked what he wanted as a reward, and Jimmy replied, "A week at the Met." So the Levines took their young son to New York. "The minute I got off the plane," he recalled, "I knew New York was where I belonged." He remembers the performances he heard that week: *Faust* with George London, *Così fan Tutte* with the original Bing cast, *Cavalleria Rusticana* and *Pagliacci* with Leonard Warren.

His parents arranged an audition at the Juilliard School to assess their child's talents. Although in awe of his drive and ability, Larry and Helen were determined to develop his talent without exploiting him. They turned down requests for him to appear as a child prodigy on television shows like *The $64,000 Question* and *The Sam Levenson Show*. After the Juilliard audition, they realized he needed more discipline and engaged the European-trained violinist, Walter Levin, to oversee their son's music studies.

Although Levin appreciated Levine's intelligence, he also saw a child who was "naively talented, undisciplined, slightly overbearing . . . in serious need of a teacher who could teach him what music was all about." He encouraged Levine not to coast by on his natural talent and never to skimp on the daily grind that goes into a professional musician's development: theory, harmony, solfège, and music history.

In the summer of 1956, Rudolf Serkin, having heard about Levine from Levin, invited the thirteen-year-old to spend the summer at the Marlboro Music Festival in Vermont. There Levine discovered a new joy in collaborative music-making, playing chamber music with people as talented as he, and living in a community of musicians. This was more appealing to him than the lonely life of a concert pianist who travels from city to city.

At Marlboro, Levine also made his first appearance as a conductor. He was asked to prepare and lead the choruses from Mozart's *Così fan Tutte* with an ensemble of festival instrumentalists. Among his choristers was the young Van Cliburn, just a couple of years before his triumph in the Tchaikovsky Competition.

Serkin arranged for Levine to audition for Rosina Lhevinne, the legendary piano teacher at Juilliard. She was impressed, and suggested that Levine enter Juilliard immediately, but his parents, concerned about his emotional and social development, decided he should stay in Cincinnati until he finished high school. Levine, however, was determined to study with Lhevinne. Finally, they came up with a compromise. Two weekends every month, he flew alone to New York on Friday afternoon, attended a performance at the Met in the evening, and on Saturday morning, he had a lesson with Lhevinne. On Saturday afternoon and evening, he would go to other performances. Sunday morning brought a second lesson with Lhevinne, followed by a concert, usually the New York Philharmonic. On Sunday evenings he flew back to Cincinnati.

Back in Cincinnati, Levine attended Walnut Hill High School, a public school for gifted children. Although his parents wanted him to have as normal a schedule as possible, he was excused early from school every day at 1:00 to practice. Although this arrangement set him apart from his schoolmates, he was so unpretentious that there was no resentment. He even made fun of himself in a school skit, playing the role of an obnoxious child prodigy.

Rosina Lhevinne taught at the Aspen Festival in the summers, so Levine, from the age of fourteen, spent thirteen consecutive summers in the mountains of Colorado. Here he was closer in age to the other musicians than he had been at Marlboro, and he formed friendships with other serious young students for the first time, relationships that flourished on his weekend trips to New York during the winter.

He was appointed to the Aspen faculty in 1965, appeared many times as a solo pianist and chamber musician and began serious conducting studies. He conducted his first full opera, Bizet's *The Pearl Fishers,* with the Aspen Music Festival Opera Theater and went on to *Così fan Tutte,* Strauss's *Ariadne auf Naxos,* Britten's *Albert Herring,* and many others. He was already exhibiting the broad range of style and period that has been characteristic of his whole career.

It was also at Aspen that he had his first professional disappointment. The festival was looking for a new music director, and Levine was one of the leading candidates. He organized a grassroots campaign among the musicians, spearheaded by a group of his closest friends, but the effort failed and another conductor was chosen. Levine tried, as always, to be positive. He had learned a lesson in institutional politics that he would use later.

He moved permanently to New York when he graduated from high school and entered Juilliard, where he continued lessons with Lhevinne and studied conducting with Jean Morel. He transferred almost immediately to the postgraduate curriculum, and he became the first student in the school's history to have a double major in piano and conducting.

At Juilliard, Levine, although he accepted some engagements as a solo pianist, decided on conducting as his lifework. During his third year, he auditioned for the American Conductors' Project, funded by the Ford Foundation. George Szell, the august music director of the Cleveland Orchestra, heard his performance and immediately offered him the post of assistant conductor in Cleveland. "You're a very good conductor," Szell told him. "Maybe we can make you a great one."

Levine dropped out of Juilliard and moved to Cleveland. His experience in conducting had not prepared him for the day-to-day relationship of a conductor and an orchestra; he sat in on all the rehearsals, recording sessions, and concerts, observing every interaction, and rehearsed the orchestra whenever Szell asked him to. He appeared as piano soloist at many concerts, and also conducted his own programs, which Szell attended. In addition, the older conductor spent hours at the piano with Levine analyzing scores.

Szell was renowned for an almost chamber-music quality in performances with his orchestra, which he achieved by establishing an unusually intimate musical relationship with his musicians. Yet, offstage, Szell was an austere figure, cold and remote, and many of the orchestra members were afraid of him. Much as Levine admired Szell, he did not want to emulate everything about him.

Levine was with Szell in Cleveland from 1964 to 1970, and became the focus of a tight group of young musicians who were soon nicknamed the Levanites. They were, for the most part, students at the Cleveland Institute of Music, where Levine had been appointed to the faculty. In 1966, he founded the University Circle Orchestra and began to explore symphonic repertory and also conducted opera in concert. By remaining in one city and not competing with the other "wunderkind" conductors who were flying all over the United States and Europe, Levine received a full musical education in an environment where he was comfortable and secure.

He also organized his personal life so that he could have the strong support he had experienced with his family. He was only in his early twenties and, like most people that age, did not spend all his time studying scores. The friends who surrounded him were perceived more as disciples than as friends, and the Levanites began to take on the aura of a cult, with Jimmy as the charismatic leader. There was malicious gossip, rumors of orgies and homosexuality and chamber music played in the nude. Thirty years later, the rumors persist, even in the absence of any evidence.

Perhaps the stories arose because Levine—then, as now—exudes friendliness and warmth, yet has an intense desire for personal privacy. "The members of the audience can come to a concert without sacrificing any of their privacy," he has said. "The performers should have the same right . . . when a musician becomes a celebrity, it takes something from his music."

Levine envies Szell and Szell's contemporaries—Serge Koussevitzky in Boston, Fritz Reiner in Chicago, and Eugene Ormandy in Philadelphia—who led private lives in their communities and whose wives were as obscure as the spouses of Soviet party chairmen. But this was before journalism became invasive. People like Levine, who choose to protect their personal lives, are suspected of having something to hide.

Many of Levine's contemporaries—Daniel Barenboim, Zubin Mehta, Seiji Ozawa—married women who were accustomed to the public eye. But Levine's friends are as private as he is, which is why they are his friends.

Levine spent more time with Szell than he did with conductors his own age. Although he wore bell-bottoms, had long hair, and used the vocabulary of the sixties, he identified with musicians of the generation before him. He had grown up in the age of conductors who were music directors of the old school. They stayed with their orchestras almost all season long, and they supervised everything.

In the early 1960s, that tradition changed. Conductors like Claudio Abbado, Barenboim, Mehta, Riccardo Muti, Ozawa, and Georg Solti discovered that the jet plane gave them freedom to be music directors of several organizations at the same time, often on different continents. Even the ascetic Pierre Boulez had orchestras in New York and London. This was not what Levine wanted. "My whole life," he said, "has been characterized by long cycles. Things grow and get better and evolve, and when they don't get better, you start to look for [other] things." Levine was determined to have a career that allowed him to stay in one place. He wanted a musical home.

Eventually, both Szell and Levine realized it was time for the young conductor to leave Cleveland. Before he died in 1970, Szell's final gift to Levine was his recommendation to Kurt Herbert Adler, head of the San Francisco Opera. Adler invited the unknown Levine to conduct *Tosca* in the fall of 1970, an engagement that led to Rudolf Bing and the Met.

Levine's first Met appearance was at a matinee on June 5, 1971, with Grace Bumbry as Tosca, Franco Corelli as Cavaradossi, and Peter Glossop as Scarpia. In the custom of the Met at the time—a custom Levine has dedicated himself to changing—he had had no stage rehearsal with the orchestra. After the first performance, one of the jaded Met musicians said, "He's an amateur. An amateur, but a brilliant amateur." More-generous players remarked on the excitement he had generated, the support he had given them, and his personal warmth.

Bing offered Levine multiple engagements, and, shortly afterward, Gentele appointed him principal conductor, beginning with the 1973–74 season. With so many Met engagements, Levine decided to move back to New York.

He did not come alone. While in Cleveland, Levine had met Suzanne Thomson, an oboist from Detroit who was studying with the principal in the Cleveland Orchestra. He was smitten both by her physical loveliness and her musicianship, and she came to New York with him in 1971. They have been together ever since. Their devotion to each other is obvious; thirty years after they met, Sue Thomson still attends every one of Levine's performances.

Levine and Thomson settled down in a roomy apartment on the Upper West Side of Manhattan. But it was at the Met that James Levine really found his home.

Chapter Twelve

TRAGEDY

The end of the 1971–72 season was also the final curtain on the Bing regime, which had opened twenty-two seasons earlier. The last night was a gala in his honor, featuring most of the major singers he had brought to the Met. "By inclination, I am given to understatement rather than the boastful trumpet," he said in his farewell speech, "yet I cannot suppress a certain pride when I look at tonight's program. This is not a concert of guests passing through the city. This is the roster of the Metropolitan Opera. One hears so much today about ensemble opera versus the star system. I feel that the Metropolitan Opera is an ensemble of stars."

When a reporter asked how he was feeling, Bing replied, "I feel no emotion. This is the only way I've survived my years here." And he added, "I've already seen everything but the phantom. Perhaps now that I shall be a kind of ghost myself, I'll see that, too." His last words were, "The company goes on."

Goeran Gentele, the man whom everyone expected to lead the company for long years into the future, was a realist. He knew that his first two seasons were largely Bing's because of the requisite advance planning. Bing had even scheduled the opening night of Gentele's regime—a revival of Wagner's *Tannhäuser*—and engaged two American artists who had never before sung Wagnerian roles at the Met, the mezzo-soprano Marilyn Horne and the tenor James McCracken.

To all this, Gentele was agreeable, until he discovered that *Tannhäuser* was one of the company's most bedraggled productions. When he heard jokes about this as "Bing's revenge," he canceled *Tannhäuser*. He looked at a repertory list to choose another opera in which the same singers could perform and decided on Bizet's *Carmen*. But the Met's *Carmen* production was also in bad shape.

Gentele knew that Bing's expenditures on new productions had been a primary cause of the board's disenchantment. But he also knew the importance of first impressions. He asked the directors for money for a new *Carmen*. The board, accustomed to Bing's patronizing air, were charmed by Gentele's geniality and granted the funds. He then announced he would direct the production himself.

Gentele also pulled off a miracle between April 1, 1972, and the beginning of his vacation in July. Union contracts were up for renewal, and the disaster of 1969 made everyone fearful. But Bing's view that he had been the scapegoat in union negotiations may have been valid. The presence of an approachable new general manager made considerable difference. The unions, particularly the musicians, judged Gentele to be a man who would be an ally, not an adversary. The settlement was reached a month to the day before the contract expired, the first time that the Met and its musicians had reached agreement before expiration.

Surprisingly, this took place under straitened finances and the board considered reducing the number of weekly performances to five. The money saved, however, would have been less than the costs of keeping the house dark. And Gentele suggested that the change might be bad for the Met's image, not to mention his own. The board decided to keep the usual number of performances, but they were not far from a state of panic.

The directors were therefore stunned to read in the *New York Times* that Gentele, as part of the Met's new image he was trying to construct, had decided to create an offshoot of the regular Met. This would be a kind of Mini-Met, which would perform in a smaller venue and produce works unsuitable to a four-thousand-seat auditorium. Gentele had gone and booked a season at the Forum, a small theater in the Vivian Beaumont

Theater next door to the Met. He had done so without consulting the board.

Acutely aware of the problems that the National Company had generated, the board summoned Gentele to an executive committee meeting. He explained that the _Times_ had published parts of an interview he believed to be off the record. He announced that he had procured an anonymous grant to underwrite the Mini-Met, and that the new company would cost the Big Met nothing. He was a very persuasive man, and, in the end, the board agreed to the small ensemble.

With that crisis over and the union negotiations completed, Gentele took his family to Sardinia for a vacation before his first season, which started in August. He left in charge Schuyler Chapin, the new assistant manager, in whom the board had little faith. But Gentele planned to be gone only four weeks.

On the evening of July 18, 1972, Chapin left the opera house a little after six. As he settled down to dinner in a restaurant across the street, he was called to the telephone. One of his staff members said, "Something's happened to Mr. Gentele."

Chapin raced back to the theater and learned that Gentele and his family had been in a head-on collision with a truck on a mountain road in Sardinia. His wife and daughter from a previous marriage had been severely injured; Gentele and his two teenage daughters were dead. He had held the Met's top position officially for eighteen days.

George Moore was on his way home from Spain for the July board meeting when Chapin reached him at Kennedy Airport as he stepped off the plane. Moore came directly into the city and took charge.

He had the board appoint Chapin acting general manager, but made clear to Chapin that this would be a dual authority. Moore himself planned to be just as much in charge as Chapin.

Chapin agreed, although the arrangement weakened his already shaky position. He had no experience in running an opera company, let alone the largest in the country. But the directors, who had noticed the extraordinary lift in company morale during Gentele's brief administration, hoped that loyalty would carry over to the assistant Gentele had chosen.

It did. Almost every member of the company went out of his or her way to express allegiance to Chapin. What astounded the board, after the years of enmity between Bing and the press, was that the journalists were also enthusiastic about Chapin. Buoyed by the goodwill Gentele had generated, Chapin rolled up his sleeves to tackle the problems the board felt he did not understand.

Kubelik, the new music director, came to New York after hearing of Gentele's death. When he saw the horrifying financial realities—the Met now had a large cash deficit and a net loss after contributions of $2.5 million—he spoke to Moore about his lack of confidence in Chapin. Having expressed his doubts, Kubelik flew back to Europe, and Moore told Chapin that unless the budget was balanced, he would be fired.

The board then formed a search committee for a permanent general manager. In interviews, Moore took credit for everything that was going on at the opera house, barely mentioning Chapin. His attitude undercut what little authority Chapin had with the other directors and eroded his self-confidence.

Rudolf Bing offered his services until a new man could be found and was devastated when the board turned him down. Instead, the directors turned to Herman Krawitz and asked him to help Chapin. Krawitz, still smarting from being denied the general manager position, refused to return if he had to report to anyone, particularly Chapin, whom he considered incompetent.

Chapin's most pressing problem was the new production of *Carmen*, scheduled for opening night, only weeks away. Leonard Bernstein was the conductor, and Josef Svoboda, the Czech designer, had created sets to match Gentele's concept. At one point, Bernstein offered to stage the opera, together with Svoboda, but Chapin instead appointed Bodo Igesz, a Met staff director who had been scheduled to assist Gentele, to do the staging. Gentele, who enjoyed collaborating, had discussed his production ideas with everyone: the singers; his wife, Marit, an actress who had worked with him in Sweden; Igesz; and Bernstein. Igesz created Gentele's concept.

And so the opera house began to function again. There was minor criticism about the austere settings, but otherwise *Carmen* was a success and it made clear the direction in which the theater would have moved under

Gentele, with a contemporary theatrical aesthetic. Chapin appointed Richard Dufallo, a young American conductor who specialized in contemporary music, to be music director of the Mini-Met, and initiated a series of children's performances called *Look-Ins,* hosted by Danny Kaye, conducted by Levine, and aired on national television by CBS. Kubelik scheduled the Met premiere of Berlioz's gigantic opera *Les Troyens* to celebrate the company's ninetieth anniversary in 1973–74.

But the financial mess was not so easy to fix. Moore demanded final authority on any decision and thus effectively took away Chapin's authority; Chapin mostly acceded.

But when Moore chose to save money by canceling the new productions Gentele and Kubelik had planned for the next three seasons, Chapin stood fast. He, like Bing, understood that new productions were essential; a company that relies on the past will not attract attention or contributions. Chapin, with his social contacts and beautiful manners, was a master fundraiser, and he saved the new productions by persuading wealthy patrons and foundations to underwrite five for 1973–74.

Moore, still angry about the gift to the Mini-Met that Gentele had procured on his own, insisted that this money go into the general operations budget and that the small company's season be canceled. But the anonymous donor refused, insisting that his money go to the Mini-Met, and Chapin backed him up. Infuriated, Moore stepped up his search for a new general manager.

He went in a most unexpected direction. Moore had long been Aristotle Onassis's personal banker and, as a result, knew Maria Callas well. He approached her about heading the Met; although she toyed with the idea, she did not consider it seriously. Moore then went to the head of La Scala, who expressed interest, and discussed this option with Kubelik behind Chapin's back. But the opera world is small, and Chapin soon heard the rumors.

When none of Moore's candidates worked out, he finally yielded on the matter of Chapin's title. On May 8, 1973, he and the board, with what even Chapin described as "great reluctance," appointed Chapin general manager. The contract was for three years.

Chapin did not have time to savor his victory. In meeting his first major responsibility—engaging artists for the coming seasons—he made a major miscalculation. To save money, he decided to have "house artists" replace expensive international stars. These house singers, largely Americans, usually functioned as comprimarios, character actor–singers in minor roles. These artists are the backbone of every opera house; they are in residence season after season and provide continuity and a sense of ensemble.

The press was intrigued by the experiment: the *New York Times* hailed it as "the Americanization of the Met," but the operagoing public hated it. Ticket sales plummeted.

This further undermined Chapin. Under Moore's incessant nagging, he canceled a new production of *Don Giovanni* that had been scheduled to celebrate the eightieth birthday of the conductor Karl Böhm. Böhm, furious, terminated all engagements with the company, acidly noting that the Met's cutbacks had not affected Kubelik's expensive new production of *Les Troyens*. In the end, when *Troyens* opened the ninetieth-anniversary season in 1973–74, the production was a musical success and a scenic and dramatic disaster. The Met's prestige had slipped to the point where United Press International noted that chances that the company would be around to celebrate its centennial seemed slim.

After *Troyens*, Kubelik spent most of his time in Europe. The large part of the Met's musical activity, therefore, was overseen by James Levine, described by the *Times* as "the Met's perky young principal conductor." Publicly, Levine supported Chapin, but privately he seemed appalled by what was happening. Schooled by Szell in impeccable musical preparation, he could not have been anything but dismayed by the reduced rehearsal schedule and the last-minute cast changes, which tossed unprepared and often inadequate artists into major roles. He sought Ronald Wilford's advice on how to disassociate himself from Chapin's policies without endangering his own position. Wilford counseled Levine to have patience and wait; he suspected that Kubelik would not have the forbearance to wait out the gathering crisis. Levine waited, although this stance became more difficult when Kubelik, planning the 1974–75 season, assigned Thomas Schippers more new productions than he gave Levine.

Moore and the board's tough new treasurer, James S. Smith, a vice president of Peat Marwick Mitchell, soon discovered that the Met's book-keeping was archaic and that each department maintained unreliable records. They brought in efficiency experts, a new controller, and gave the board an unequivocal appraisal of the situation. The working capital deficit had increased to over $5.6 million; a Met warehouse in the Bronx burned down in the winter of 1974, destroying the costumes and props for forty-one productions; the negligible endowment sank even lower, to $7.1 million; and selling the company's last tangible asset, the old house site that the board had held on to even through 1969 and that was estimated to be worth about $6 million, would barely keep the company from bankruptcy.

On November 15, 1973, Chapin called the company together. He froze salaries, reduced rehearsals, and cut the administrative staff by 20 percent. He canceled the June Festival, the free concerts in the parks, and the Mini-Met. The New York season was cut from thirty-one to twenty-seven weeks, and the tour reduced from eight weeks to five. Morale plunged and the crisis got regular press coverage, which increased the pressure and threatened to destroy the Met's reputation.

Meanwhile, relations between Chapin and Kubelik were deteriorating. Kubelik had been alarmed about the extent of the budgetary problems since Gentele's death and now he was frustrated by the cuts in rehearsals and changes in casting. But he remained in Europe.

Kubelik was away when the artistic problems reached the boiling point over a revival of *Tristan und Isolde*. Caterina Ligendza, the soprano who had been Gentele's choice as Isolde, canceled at the last minute, and Erich Leinsdorf, the conductor, refused to accept her cover. Jon Vickers, the Tristan, was six days late for rehearsals, and August Everding, the direc-tor, slipped on an icy sidewalk and cracked two ribs. He went home to Munich before the dress rehearsal.

Kubelik, from Europe, advised Chapin to drop *Tristan* and substitute *Tosca*. Levine was alerted to conduct *Tosca*, but then Chapin looked at the numbers. He estimated that the substitution would cost as much as $100,000 in overtime, additional fees, and ticket refunds. "I must take the final responsibility," Chapin said, and Kubelik reluctantly agreed to let *Tristan* go on.

Chapin engaged Klara Barlow, a little-known American soprano, to replace Ligendza. Although Barlow had sung widely in minor European houses, she had never sung Isolde with a major company. Vickers protested and, even though he had not shown up for early rehearsals, used a lack of rehearsal time as an excuse to withdraw.

This was the final blow for Leinsdorf. A vastly experienced musician and administrator, Leinsdorf had no patience with the never-ending crises at Chapin's Met. The people to whom he complained—Chapin and Charles Riecker, the new artistic administrator—reassured him, with little evidence, that the situation would be salvaged. Never a man to mince words, he wondered, publicly, at Kubelik's absence and Levine's low profile. "I'm a guest conductor here," Leinsdorf grumbled to the *New York Times*, "and the people who are supposed to be making these decisions all disappear. One deals only with Mr. Chapin. . . . They have these 'Commissars for Optimism' sitting around there." Leinsdorf resigned, though he later relented when the tenor Jess Thomas was persuaded to sing Tristan.

Tristan marked the end of Kubelik's patience, too. He resigned on February 13, 1974, effective immediately, citing as cause the company's financial problems, which had prevented him from "carrying out the artistic ideals to which I committed myself." But he was also humiliated by Leinsdorf's scorn for the Met's slipshod artistic operations.

Chapin, who had gone to Washington to give a speech, did not learn of his music director's resignation until he read it in the *Times*. No one had bothered to tell him.

At the annual meeting of the Metropolitan Opera Association in May 1974, the directors learned that the deficit had climbed to $9 million. George Moore, who could suggest no solution, resigned. He was replaced by William Rockefeller, a partner in the First National City Bank's law firm, Shearman & Sterling. Chapin's introductory call to the new president was to let him know that labor contract renewals were looming ahead in a year. Rockefeller told him not to start any negotiations. Chapin quickly began to loathe Rockefeller, whom he dismissed as "cousin to the 'other' Rockefellers, with very little imagination and lacking in leadership verve."

Rockefeller may have lacked ebullience, but he had initiative. He appointed an administrative committee of board members to supervise the day-to-day activities of the company in general and Chapin in particular. This had been tried before in the company's history, with varying degrees of success, but this time the head of the committee was to be Anthony Bliss, who would accept the position only as a full-time job.

Bliss had not campaigned for the post, and he knew it would entail some financial sacrifice for his new young family. But, as always, he took seriously his responsibility to the Met. The directors had confidence in his extensive knowledge of the company and his ability to make hard decisions.

Bliss resigned from his law practice and moved into an office in the opera house. Two years after the departure of Rudolf Bing and the death of Goeran Gentele, and only eight years after Bing had forced him out, Anthony Bliss was back.

Chapter Thirteen

THE DARK TUNNEL

In the fall of 1974, Anthony Bliss had a recurrence of a chronic heart condition, and his doctors were concerned about the stress caused by the problems at the Met. The job of running an opera company under any circumstances is daunting. Rehearsals begin at 11:00 A.M., and performances frequently run until midnight. Not only does the person running the company have to be in his office all day, he must also spend many evenings at the opera entertaining patrons, government officials, important visitors, and prospective donors.

In addition, Bliss faced intimidating institutional problems. The Met was close to bankruptcy; no one had confidence in Chapin, the general manager; union contracts were up for renewal; casting was in chaos; box office numbers were dwindling; and the country's economic picture was bleak. Bliss knew that only total reorganization could save the company, and despite his health problems, he knew he was the man to do it.

With William Rockefeller at his side, Bliss held a press conference on his first day back in the opera house in November 1974. It was not a success. The press, who liked Chapin, were confused by Bliss's new position and puzzled by its implications. "It seems like a complete sellout of the artistic wing," one reporter said angrily, "to the narrow business concerns of the board and its current management."

Rockefeller tried to clarify the situation: "To use a business analogy,

Mr. Bliss is the operating officer. Mr. Chapin reports to Mr. Bliss. Mr. Bliss reports to me."

Chapin, seething with resentment, saw little of Bliss, who characteristically went on long walks around the opera house to make personal assessments of what he saw. He and Chapin exchanged a series of painfully polite memos, and matters remained superficially cordial until Bliss ventured into an area Chapin regarded as inviolably his own.

Chapin was prepared to put up with Bliss's policy-making in the areas of finance and administration, but he expected to retain control of artistic policy. After Gentele's death, Chapin made a major decision when he engaged the English stage director, John Dexter, as head of production for the Met. Chapin, like Gentele before him, envisioned a triumvirate: Dexter in charge of the stage, Levine in charge of musical matters, and Chapin in charge of making administrative and financial decisions. Bliss had other ideas.

Despite the dire financial circumstances, Bliss was most worried about the Met's artistic situation. Since he had been away for several years, the deterioration was all the more evident to him than it was even to Dexter and Levine, who, having joined the company while he was away, were virtual strangers to him. He knew they were also strangers to each other. Bliss, accustomed to a close-knit company, thought the arrangement perilous.

Bliss knew a great deal about running an opera but little about singers and singing. Levine, under Wilford's guidance, quickly offered to fill this gap by suggesting that all artistic decisions be turned over to him. Bliss was willing to try this, since he believed that the music was the foundation of an opera house. This agreement delighted Wilford, who had fought unsuccessfully with Chapin to gain this power for Kubelik, whom he also represented. Wilford, Bliss, and Levine decided to bypass Chapin as they put together the Met's new artistic profile. Levine would have pleasant chats on the phone with Chapin, while, on another line, Bliss and Wilford would be negotiating Levine's new contract. When Chapin finally understood what was going on, he tried to lessen the breadth of artistic influence Bliss was promising Levine.

During the spring tour, Bliss and Chapin had dinner together in Atlanta. Bliss did not mince words.

"Look, the way you've been operating . . . does not fit in with my plans here. I don't want a general manager making the decisions and telling John Dexter and Jimmy what they are to do. Levine, in my book, is *the* conductor. He is *the* musician of the house. I want him to have complete authority."

Chapin replied that he had been making the artistic decisions for the last couple of years and thought they had been good ones. According to Bliss, Chapin said, "I cannot defer to Levine or anyone else." Soon afterward, the Met's attorney informed Chapin that he was no longer authorized to discuss Levine's contract.

Bliss also met with John Dexter to discuss the Met's stage operations. He had originally considered canceling all new productions for several years, but he changed his mind after talking with Dexter. The English director was an articulate champion of bare-bones productions; instead of being discouraged by the Met's financial problems, he found them inspiring.

John Dexter had come of age during the British theater's "Angry Young Men" period. Coming from a lower-working-class background, he also had a deep resentment of the wealthy and privileged. Yet his ideas for saving the Met coincided remarkably with Bliss's. He had been trained in the theater during the impoverished post–World War II period: "The tradition of putting less on stage and suggesting more is something we all grew up with. . . . Because materials were at a premium, we had to find simpler ways of doing things." He believed that removing extravagance from a production gave range to the intelligence and imagination of the director and designer. The more sparse the production, the more creativity was called upon, and the results were far more interesting than a more traditional stage set. Dexter looked forward to prodding the Met into the contemporary theater.

Bliss was enthusiastic. "In the future," he announced, "any new production will be smaller than the one it replaces." Now he turned his attention to the singers who would populate these productions: he hired Richard Rodzinski, from the San Francisco Opera, and told him to get casting back on track. Although Rodzinski was named co–artistic administrator with Charles Riecker, it was clear that Bliss intended Rodzinski to run the artistic administration.

On May 23, 1975, James Levine was named the Met's music director, beginning with the 1976–77 season. Levine announced that he would spend at least seven months a year in New York. "I will be in charge of all aspects of the music, including casting. I will work in conjunction with Dexter on the visual side, and the administration will carry out our artistic decisions."

Bliss's optimism was necessarily tempered by the hard fiscal facts. "Right now," he said in March 1975, "there doesn't seem to be much light at the end of a long, dark tunnel . . . I cannot see new sources of revenue [and] economizing can only go so far."

In February, Bliss called a meeting of the principal artists, chorus, orchestra, dancers, stage crew, and administrators, and asked everyone to accept a 10 percent pay cut and a shorter work year. "We must not let the opera house die," he said. "If it closes, I question whether it will ever open again." It was a stunning flashback to the days of Gatti-Casazza when, in the depths of the Depression, he had asked the company to take a similar pay cut.

Most company members agreed to Bliss's request. "Ninety percent of something is better than one hundred percent of nothing," one chorister told the *Times*. The exception to this cooperative response was, predictably, the orchestra. The musicians, who had been negotiating their new contract for about a month, immediately suspended talks. Bliss had hoped that the pay cut would impress upon the unions the gravity of the crisis, but, instead, the orchestra's stand hardened. When Bliss went home after the meeting, his wife Sally asked him how things had gone. "I did not receive a standing ovation," he replied.

Chapin's position was still not defined. In mid-April, Rockefeller told him that the company was now too complicated to be run by one man. The position of general manager was to be dropped. Bliss and the administrative committee would run the house, with Levine and Dexter reporting to Bliss. Rockefeller offered Chapin the position of development director and a cut in salary. Chapin was humiliated but decided to go on a tour of Japan with the company while he thought over the offer. In June, after the tour, the executive committee officially retired the title of general manager, and, almost as an afterthought, dismissed Chapin.

Chapin left the Met bitter and disappointed. "I think it is wrong on principle that a board member [Bliss] is going to administer the theater—a non-professional in a professional job." But he and Bliss both had the good manners of New York society. "You and Betty [are] invited to come and dine and sit with Sally and me on opening night," Bliss wrote to Chapin in September 1975, "but I understand that you might not wish to." Chapin declined, but added, "If you feel a brief talk between us could be helpful, just let me know if I can be of help." The politeness that ended the struggle between Bliss and Chapin was about to vanish forever, even from the Met.

With no performances scheduled, the company coasted through the summer of 1975. Desultory union negotiations took place, but nothing of substance was discussed; the general atmosphere was one of a wait-and-see pessimism. The only exception was Bliss. In the fall of 1975, he saw clearly that the company would run out of money by April 1976. He refused to be discouraged.

His office door was always open, and members of the company were invited to drop in. Many did. A few principal artists volunteered to cut their fees, and others offered to help with fund-raising and even made contributions of their own. Choristers, weekly artists, dancers, and stagehands also stopped by with their own ideas of how to cut costs. Bliss took every suggestion seriously. When he was told that the company was wasting money on the boots the costume shop bought, he consulted a friend in the shoe business and was reassured that the Met was getting the best quality for its money.

Word of his cost-saving inquiries spread, and the company began to see Bliss as an honest man searching for solutions. In September 1975, just before the season, the musicians' attorney offered an extension on the existing contract until the end of December. Bliss accepted.

The time was invaluable. Bliss decided to sell the Thirty-ninth Street site, but the real estate market was weak and the land went for only $5

In the late 1870s, the directors of New York's most elegant opera house, the Academy of Music, denied membership to many of the city's recently wealthy citizens, including the Vanderbilts, Morgans, Astors, and Goelets. They responded to the slight by building their own house; thus the Metropolitan Opera was born.

From the early part of the twentieth century to the onset of the Depression, Otto Kahn, a banker and president of the Met board, single-handedly saved the Met from financial demise. Ironically, because of his Jewish background, he was not eligible to own a box in the theater.

At the corner of Thirty-ninth Street and Broadway, the Met presented productions from 1883 to 1966, the year it moved uptown to its current Lincoln Center home.

During his seventeen seasons at the Met, the legendary tenor Enrico Caruso became opera's most famous singer. He was so crucial to the company's financial health that a cancellation could jeopardize a season's budget.

The year 1908 welcomed Giulio Gatti-Casazza *(right)* and Arturo Toscanini *(left)* from La Scala as general manager and chief conductor, respectively. Together, with Otto Kahn, they created an artistic alchemy that transformed the Metropolitan Opera into one of the world's leading companies.

This, however, would not alleviate Toscanini's insecurity about his inability to speak English. The famed conductor kept a notebook in which he practiced his remarks to the orchestra. But his brilliant command of music rendered English unnecessary; the musicians understood his directions perfectly.

Taking a break backstage, Gatti-Casazza *(seated)* listens to Toscanini *(left)* and leading soprano Geraldine Farrar *(right)*. It would soon become common knowledge that Farrar and Toscanini's ongoing relationship was not strictly professional.

Upon becoming general manager in 1950, Rudolf Bing ruled the company with an iron fist; but at home in the Essex House, Bing's gentler side would surface in the company of his supportive wife, Nina, and beloved dachshund, Pip.

By 1966 the company, having moved to its new home, was preparing Samuel Barber's *Antony and Cleopatra*; Bing *(right)* was overseeing the rehearsals of the Met Ballet, which included the dancer Sally Brayley *(center left)*. After a scandalous and very public affair with Met board president Anthony Bliss, Brayley married Bliss. But not before Bing ousted Bliss from his position, using the affair as the reason.

For the Met's opening night at Lincoln Center, *Antony and Cleopatra* was turned into a lavish production, complete with camels, to the delight of Bing, an avowed animal lover.

Meanwhile, during the sixties, a prodigy from the Midwest was coming into his own. James Levine's fascination for opera was apparent early on, as he designed tiny opera productions to stage for his parents, Lawrence and Helen.

Retiring in 1972, Rudolf Bing handed over the general manager's baton to Goeran Gentele. Well liked by all, Gentele's reign was tragically cut short when he and his daughters were killed in an auto accident while vacationing in Sardinia.

Subsequently, the board grudgingly appointed Schuyler Chapin *(right)* to succeed Gentele. Unbeknownst to Chapin at the time, Anthony Bliss *(left)* was reestablishing himself within the company, eventually forcing out Chapin and assuming the role of general manager himself only a few years after his own removal from the board by Bing.

Despite the waning support of the board, Chapin named the
creative genius John Dexter to the new post of director of
production. By the beginning of 1975, Dexter, Bliss, and
James Levine would guide the Met to a new artistic
renaissance in the midst of the company's dire
financial problems.

Chapin also named James Levine principal conductor in 1972.
Bing had signed the twenty-seven-year-old upon his
Met debut the year before. By 1975 Levine was
made music director and by 1983 artistic director.

The Met in the 1970s benefited from a new level of philanthropic giving from
Sybil Harrington *(seated)*, when, after the deaths of her husband and daughter,
she discovered a new family at the opera house. Funding many of the
company's new productions, including Puccini's *Tosca*, she avidly
watched her favorite stage director and designer, Franco Zeffirelli *(right)*,
and the late conductor Giuseppe Sinopoli *(center)* in rehearsals.

million. The need was too desperate to wait for a more favorable price. He also released some of the company's endowment fund, which, added to the sale of the site, enabled him to meet the payroll through the fall.

Bliss knew this could not go on. In the future, the Met was going to have to increase its contributed and earned income. He was convinced that economizing on artistic expenses would jeopardize the quality of the whole project. He also knew it was unrealistic to expect artists to reduce their fees; inflation was high, and opera houses in Europe had raised their fees beyond what the Met could afford. Bliss tried to establish a top fee that all the international companies would respect, but soon discovered that the European intendants had no intention of sticking to the agreement if they could get the top stars for more. The Met would have to find new ways to attract major singers.

Bliss also wanted to restructure the board to allow more flexible decision-making, to build a fund-raising department, create a marketing department, and develop earned income from summer presentations in the opera house while the regular company was on vacation.

Incredibly, the Metropolitan Opera had never had a marketing department. The few newspaper ads the company had placed via the ticket service office were ugly in appearance and patronizing in tone. Repertory was rarely announced in advance, and casting less often. "In the past, everything sold itself," Bliss said. "Once you lose an audience, you really have to work to get it back. We [had] to go out and aggressively find an audience."

Chapin had hired an aggressive young man named Patrick Veitch, but had not seemed to know what job to give him. Bliss put him in charge of creating the marketing department. Veitch's department immediately caught public attention with a bold advertising campaign. "You are cordially invited to strike a blow for civilization," the full-page newspaper ads trumpeted. "Subscribe to the Metropolitan Opera!" Five letters of complaint came in, but so did over three thousand new subscriptions, totaling over $500,000. Complete casting and repertory were listed for the entire coming season and there were options for shorter and more affordable series. The first package of short series sold out so quickly that another was quickly put up for sale. The Met's advertising budget when Bliss took over was $30,000 a year; during that first season, it went up to $400,000, but subscriptions also went up from 55 percent to 61 percent; nightly capacity rose to 95 percent, 10 percent higher than the previous season.

When Bliss had arrived, the Met's fund-raising operation consisted of two people, the director of development and his secretary. Bliss hired a well-regarded fund-raising consultant from Boston to build a new department. He also hired Marilyn Shapiro, an ambitious woman who had worked in city and federal government; she was to be a liaison with government officials. Through her, 180 members of Congress and New York State government came into the opera house to see performances and tour backstage. When Senator Lowell Weicker of Connecticut gave a cocktail party in the Senate Office Building for Bliss, nearly all the senators attended. Legislators who had never heard of the Metropolitan Opera learned of the company's existence. Within a few months, Shapiro was the Met's new development director.

Bliss also wanted to explore the earned income potential of presenting outside attractions when the house was dark or the company on vacation. In 1975, he had hired Jane Hermann, a staff member of the Joffrey Ballet, where Bliss had served on the board and Sally had run the training company. At that time, he was not sure what position she would fill but, as with Marilyn Shapiro, the right job emerged.

On Bliss's instructions, Hermann began to explore the possibility of turning the Metropolitan Opera Ballet into a company that would perform on its own, and her first job was to organize what became known as the Metropolitan Opera Ballet Ensemble. Inside the Met, the company became known as MOBE, or, waggishly, the Anthony Bliss Imperial Ballet. Remembering Bliss's fascination with the ballet after he became infatuated with Sally, people rolled their eyes even as Hermann pointed out that MOBE would provide more work for the dancers. But despite her best efforts, the Met Ballet, top-heavy with aging dancers, never shed its aura of mediocrity. Hermann endeared herself to the rest of the company by joining in the jokes about MOBE and quietly explored other ways to earn income.

Her opportunity came at the end of her first season at the Met. For years, Hurok Concerts, the company formed by the impresario Sol Hurok, had booked the opera house during the summer to present their own attractions. This arrangement supplied a small but steady income, so Bliss was concerned when Hurok Concerts began to deteriorate after Hurok's death. In July 1976, the organization allowed its exclusive summer lease with the Met to expire.

Bliss put Hermann in charge of restructuring the Met summers. The Met itself would present the programs, taking a chance on losses but also benefiting from profits if the attractions were successful. Hermann knew the dance world and started out by presenting mostly dance companies, but her curiosity soon led her into other fields.

She brokered a yearly arrangement with American Ballet Theatre to perform a spring season at the Met that is now a firmly established tradition. She brought *Einstein on the Beach,* the six-hour opera by Philip Glass, staged by Robert Wilson, to the opera house in 1976 and created an avant-garde sellout in this palace of cultural conservatism. She staged *Every Good Boy Deserves Favour,* a play by Tom Stoppard that was performed on the opera house stage by actors and a full symphony orchestra. She brought Japan's Kabuki Theater and the Peking Opera. Somehow, she even convinced the technical department that water could be frozen on the stage, and then presented the late skater-choreographer John Curry and his company. She sold out one-man shows by Yves Montand and Robin Williams; and she brought in all of the world's great dance companies whether they were ethnic, modern, or classical. Bliss and the board loved her, especially when they counted the profits from her presentations.

In December 1975, the company held an event that was quintessential Bliss. The opera house threw open its doors on a Sunday and presented an open house and a bazaar fashioned after the traditional church or school bazaar. Everyone was welcome; the entrance fee was $2. Sales booths sprouted on all public levels of the building, manned by choristers, dancers, musicians, administrators, and some of the major singers. They sold memorabilia culled from the Met archives, homemade food, Christmas gifts, records, librettos, and scores. Bazaar patrons could buy old costumes that had been donated by singers or deemed disposable by the Met archivist, including some that had been worn by Beverly Sills, Cesare Siepi, Nicolai Gedda, Franco Corelli, and Risë Stevens. The resident scenic designer made red and white streamers that flowed from the Grand Tier, and the co-principal trumpet player led orchestra members in fanfares. The soprano Lucine Amara served sandwiches in the elegant Grand Tier Restaurant, urging everyone to "Eat, eat. You're too thin!"

The staff had decorated most of the theater themselves. The Maillol nude sculpture on the Grand Tier wore a Met T-shirt and held an umbrella and shopping bag. Many of the young staff had spent all weekend getting ready for the bazaar and cleaning up afterward. The afternoon raised $100,000, but, more to the point, it raised company morale and let the public know that the Met was no longer an elite and haughty institution. The company was united in efforts to keep the Met going, and there was exuberance at the creativity beginning to flow from the new artistic team of Levine and Dexter.

Behind the scenes, the labor talks continued. New Year's Eve of 1975 was the deadline for settling the orchestra contract, and negotiations went to the wire. Minutes before the gala performance of *Tosca* that evening, a settlement was reached that guaranteed forty-four weeks of employment, supplemented by unemployment benefits. Now Bliss could turn his attention to the future, which, even with a new sense of company spirit, was still precarious.

Bliss's next move was to tighten his hold on the board. In May 1976, he announced the first reorganization of the directors in almost twenty years. To make the board more manageable, he established a group of twenty-five directors who would be called managing directors and would hold the real power in restoring the company. Forty other members of the board were named advisory directors: they were specialists in particular areas, like marketing and electronic media, and gave the board some racial and religious diversity; they were to meet only once or twice a year. Six venerable board members, including Eleanor Belmont and George Moore, were named honorary directors. This revolution passed almost unnoticed, exactly as Bliss hoped it would.

He also brought in a new board president, Frank E. Taplin, a longtime board member who had been one of the strong supporters of the National Company during the struggle between Bliss and Bing. Taplin was former board president at several cultural and educational institutions, including Sarah Lawrence College and the Marlboro Music Festival, and was experienced in board politics and financial management. Like Bliss, he was self-assured, friendly, and approachable. One of his conditions for accepting the job was that he be given an office in the development department. There he kept regular business hours and soon knew almost everyone in the house by name.

Taplin was a gifted pianist and frequently played chamber music at the Marlboro Festival, so he brought an important sensibility to his new position. When he learned that there was no cafeteria in the opera house, and thus no informal meeting place where people could form a sense of community, he and his wife gave the money to convert unused storage space into a cafeteria that served meals throughout the long day, from breakfast to the last intermission of the evening performance.

Just as Levine and Dexter set artistic priorities, Taplin and Bliss set institutional ones. They were determined to expand the base of support so that the Met would never depend on one wealthy patron, and, most of all, they wanted to build an endowment. The company's tiny endowment had been almost exhausted, its principal invaded with each successive crisis. Taplin decided to establish an endowment that could not be invaded and that would be substantial enough to provide a solid fiscal foundation.

Bliss, meanwhile, with the cooperation of the Metropolitan Opera Guild, explored merchandising. Over the next few years, he expanded the Metropolitan Opera Gift Shop and launched an ambitious mail order undertaking. There were a few raised eyebrows over the Metropolitan Opera tote bags and coffee mugs, but Bliss, by now accustomed to outrage, no longer wasted time defending his efforts.

By the beginning of the 1976–77 season, only months after the company seemed doomed, the *Times* carried an article titled "Met Opera's

Financial Outlook Is Brightening." But Bliss warned Dexter and Levine that the board was still considering reductions and that they might have to make some compromises in rehearsal and overtime. Even the musicians were aware of how dire things were, and during the 1977 negotiations, they backed off their demands for a reduction in their workload and signed a three-year contract that would expire in 1980.

Chapter Fourteen

JIMMY AND JOHN, AND JOE

John Dexter's attitude that cost-cutting freed creativity was contagious. Levine, working hard to improve the orchestra, was as enthusiastic as Dexter, and Bliss encouraged both men to use what resources were available as imaginatively as possible.

Both Levine and Dexter, however, were at critical junctures in their careers: Levine was giving up an embryonic international conducting schedule to run a precarious opera company, and Dexter was making the leap from straight theater to opera. Each man worried about being identified with a company on the verge of failure.

Together, they went to Bliss in the fall of 1975 and asked for an honest assessment of the Met's situation. Bliss knew there were no funds to meet the payroll as of April 1, 1976, and no resources to undertake the 1976–77 season. But he said to them, "Gentlemen, I cannot make any promises, but I would not have given up my law career if I did not feel that somehow the job could be done." Dexter and Levine considered this sufficient reassurance, and their collaboration began.

The two men had three joint artistic goals: to reinvigorate and restore the standard operas, to build the company's repertory of twentieth-century opera, and to explore the lesser-known operas by great composers. But they were an unlikely pair of collaborators.

Levine was the beloved son of a Jewish family securely assimilated into American culture. Dexter's early life had been perilous. He was born in Derby, England, on August 2, 1925, the son of a plumber. His formal education ended when he was fourteen and went to work in a factory. He, too, was Jewish, but he had suffered the English anti-Semitism of the mid-twentieth century, especially during his years of service in the British military. In addition, he had a slight limp resulting from a childhood attack of polio and he was self-conscious about it. And throughout his early life, he had tried to hide his homosexuality.

The theater, however, is a world where any background and almost any behavior is accepted, and Dexter turned to it gratefully after his term in the army. He began as an actor, then evolved into stage directing, at which he was quickly successful.

His rise was interrupted by a terrible ordeal. In the late 1950s, he was charged with abusing a minor, a young man who, in fact, was blackmailing him, and Dexter was sent to prison.

When he was released, the English theatrical community rallied around him, and his career resumed. In 1963, he was named one of Sir Laurence Olivier's associate directors at the National Theatre, and in the mid-1960s came to Broadway with Peter Shaffer's *Royal Hunt of the Sun*. His production of *Equus* by the same playwright was an enormous triumph both in London and New York.

But Dexter was not an easy man; his lined face was evidence of his hard times. His most compelling features were his eyes, black and cautious, and his gaze could scorch. He could be charming and witty, and knowledgeable and scholarly despite his lack of formal education. But Dexter could also be cruel. On one occasion, he walked into the office of a woman administrator at the Met who, he knew, feared him. He sniffed and said, "I smell stale milk. There must be a cow around here somewhere."

The fear he inspired interfered in his work with performers. Some singers were too angry to give their best, some too afraid. Yet others were inspired by his high expectations and vigorous demands.

But John was one of the company. Although Levine was friendly and supportive, with a warm smile and a kind word—"You look fabulous, sweetheart!"—for everyone from principal artist to cleaning lady, his friendliness was impersonal. He remained aloof in a way that Dexter, even with his cruel digs and quixotic moods, did not. At parties, Dexter would smoke dope, play word games, and discuss his love life. Levine, wineglass in hand, beamed at everyone, bestowed hugs and kisses, and still managed to remind everyone he was the music director.

One trait that endeared Dexter to the company was his openness about his personal life. Levine was far more circumspect; everyone knew he lived with Sue Thomson, but she rarely appeared with him at parties. Instead, he would flirt with one person or another, male or female, always charming, always evasive. Confused, his Met colleagues would gossip about what was really going on with Jimmy. No one knew. Dexter, on the other hand, would discuss his latest conquest in front of anyone.

Dexter had a partner, an actor and director named Riggs O'Hara, with whom he had lived in London for many years. Together with their four Saint Bernard dogs, the two men set up housekeeping in an apartment across the street from Lincoln Center and a weekend house in New Jersey. But their relationship was complicated.

When Dexter was working, he tended to stoke his creativity with hard drinking, which he handled well, and copious drug use, which he did not. And although he loved and depended on Riggs, he also used escort services to provide him with young men who served his sexual needs.

He worked hard, lived hard, played hard, and in the mid-1970s, Dexter was at the height of his powers, physically strong and impassioned about turning the Met from a Victorian behemoth into an efficient twentieth-century theater ensemble. "It's illegal to be as happy as I am at the moment," he told a reporter in 1977. "Perhaps one of these days a bus will creep up behind me and run me over as punishment."

He also maintained a frantic schedule, in part to avoid painful self-examination. When asked early on in his Met career what he had learned, he replied, "I don't know what I've learned, and if I did, I would stop working." Like many artists, he suspected that his career was the result of his ability to fool people into thinking he was talented. Unlike the supremely self-confident Levine, whose talent had been affirmed from early childhood, Dexter always feared being identified as a fraud. "My career," he wrote in his diary, "seems to have been, to a very large extent, a confidence trick executed by a very unconfident trickster whose aim was to be a magician."

His first duties at the Met needed little magic, but much ruthless en-

ergy. Dexter was appalled to discover that not a single member of the administrative technical staff could read a blueprint or had practical experience in judging what time, manpower, and space would be needed for any
given stage design. He urged Bliss to dismiss many of the technical staff,
from stage managers to department heads.

Meanwhile, even Levine the optimist was running into similar problems. The orchestra, affected by the chaos in the Met management, was in
such bad shape that he estimated it would take a minimum of five and possibly ten years to bring it up to his standards. Bing had fired one musician
and then hired him right back lest he leave the company on an unpleasant
note. Next, Gentele fired the same man, and after Gentele's death, Chapin
reinstated him. Bliss was determined to fire him again and make it unequivocal. But when Bliss tried to implement a policy to avoid such personnel imbroglios, he met massive resistance, especially from Levine, who
hoped to improve the orchestra without having to fire anyone. Dexter was
one of the few administrators willing to be brutal.

When Levine told Bliss that he planned to conduct the majority of
performances for at least five years, Bliss warned him that he might be accused of grandiosity. Levine, however, persisted in believing his presence
essential to achieving the proper standards for the orchestra. But the Met
Orchestra was barraged with criticism after almost every performance,
and Levine's dream, had he announced it, would have been ridiculed as
self-indulgent fantasy.

In the course of turning around the technical department, Dexter was
elated to find one man whose intelligence and talent met his lofty standards: Joseph Volpe. The master carpenter, who had been at the Met since
1964, had been born in Brooklyn in 1940 and raised on Long Island, not far
from the Bliss estate in Oyster Bay, although on a lower scale socially. His
Italian-American family spanned socioeconomic strata from construction
to government. His father was in the men's clothing business—as was
James Levine's father—and a cousin was John Volpe, the former gover-
nor of Massachusetts. While he was in high school, Joseph started his first
business, a car repair shop. After graduating, he horrified his upwardly

mobile family by deciding not to go to college, but to continue in the car repair business. Volpe did not, as he has said, "flourish in school." He was eager to get out into the world.

The father of his first wife was a member of Local 1, the stagehands' union, so Volpe indulged his love of the theater and became a stagehand. In 1964, he left his Broadway job and joined the Metropolitan as an apprentice stagehand.

The stage crew at the Met is an intensely close-knit group. Their union is a father-and-son organization; many members of the same family work on the Met stage. There are frequent arguments whether there are more Volpes, Diazes, or Hackers—three Local 1 dynasties—employed at any given moment. The situation becomes even more complicated when crew members marry other company members. When Volpe was divorced from his first wife, he married Nancy Sklenar, who danced in the Met Ballet. She, too, had been married before, and eventually both her daughter from her first marriage and her mother began working at the Met, as did several of Volpe's sons from his first marriage. Sander Hacker was head electrician; his sons were also electricians, and his wife, Millie, was wardrobe mistress. Steve Diaz, who was to succeed Volpe as master carpenter, was in turn succeeded by his son, Steve, Jr. His other sons also worked on the crew. These relationships are part of what makes the Metropolitan such a close and complicated community.

From his first days at the Met, Volpe attracted attention. Steve Diaz remembers being told after the young neophyte's arrival, "There's a guy there who thinks he owns the place." Volpe made little effort to hide his volatility, and in a theater where idiosyncratic behavior is admired, he rose quickly through the ranks onstage.

When the company moved to Lincoln Center in 1966, he was one of the first to work in the new building. Fascinated by the complex stage machinery, he took the manuals home at night so that he could study them. "When the Met moved to Lincoln Center," said a former resident designer, "technically it changed from being a carpenter's theater to an electrician's theater; Joe was one of the only people to realize this." He became so knowledgeable that when the stage turntable broke during *Antony and Cleopatra* rehearsals, he was the one Herman Krawitz sought for advice.

Franco Zeffirelli, a very hands-on designer, was always onstage when the crew was setting up. One day, during the frantic preparations, he asked Volpe what he was doing. Volpe, who had no idea who Zeffirelli was, explained that he was trying to fix the problems caused by "some wacko designer." Zeffirelli has always been delighted by bluntness, so he told Rudolf Bing about Volpe's remark, and a few days later, the general manager formally introduced the director-designer and the stagehand, beginning a close friendship.

During those first weeks in the new house, the head carpenter resigned, and Volpe was ready. He went to Krawitz and asked for the job. Krawitz checked with Bing, and Bing gave the position to Volpe. "I was discovered many times," Volpe says sardonically. "First by Krawitz, and then Bing, then John Dexter, then Bliss, and, finally, by Bruce Crawford." Volpe has never suffered from false modesty.

Dexter first spotted Volpe in 1975, and by the end of 1975–76, he had come to rely heavily on him. Dexter had found the Met a frustrating place to work not just because it was so big, traditional, and bureaucratic, but because of the intransigence of some of the people who had embedded themselves into the company over the years. He particularly disliked Michael Bronson, who had succeeded Krawitz as head of the Met's technical and business administration. Dexter felt Bronson did not have the expertise to oversee the stage, and he wrote memo after memo to Bliss complaining:

> The last time I tried to raise this subject with you . . . I was accused of creating a cabal. I feel that this . . . negated any further attempt to disperse the fog which continually surrounds all discussions concerning Michael. (Incidentally, this fog is made all the more dense by his staff, who are as out of touch with the present reality of the Met's goals as he is himself.) I need people of intelligence and imagination around me.

Through sheer persistence, he won Bliss's agreement. With Bliss's support, Dexter appointed Volpe to be the company's technical director. From then on, he referred to Volpe as "a technical director of international stature and the right arm of my work." Volpe kept tabs on the stage and technical departments for Dexter, sometimes questioning even Dexter's requests if they seemed too costly.

Volpe updated the stage operations and equipment as he raised the efficiency of the technical staff and stage management. The changes saved money even while garnering for the Met an enviable reputation for state-of-the-art stagecraft.

According to Volpe, Dexter worked in an unusual fashion for a stage director. He would devise an initial design for each production, rather than leaving it to the designers, and would give it to Bliss. When Bliss and the board asked the cost of turning the sketch into reality, Dexter would turn to Volpe and get a straight answer. Dexter would give the information to Bliss, and everyone would be happy. Dexter and Volpe literally collaborated on several productions. They also upgraded existing ones. Many of the old productions were classics of stage design, including the Eugene Berman *Don Giovanni,* the Nathaniel Merrill/Robert O'Hearn *Der Rosenkavalier,* and the Marc Chagall *Die Zauberflöte.* But they had been brutalized by years of neglect and overuse, and Dexter wanted to refurbish them. Not only would this save money, but it would establish another link to the Met's long history, one for which Dexter had great respect even as he tried to modernize operations.

*D*exter and Levine were also working well together. While Dexter improved the staging, Levine improved the orchestra through strict rehearsal. Each man appreciated the other's efforts. "It's not a maestro on the stage and one in the pit," Dexter said. "We share an aesthetic." They had first worked together on Verdi's *I Vespri Siciliani* during Chapin's regime, a production that had shocked the conservative Metropolitan Opera audience. Originally designed by Josef Svoboda for the adventuresome Hamburg State Opera, *Vespri*'s set comprised one immense staircase, almost no scenery or props, and harsh lighting against a black backdrop. Dexter hoped the lack of visual distraction would focus the audience's attention on the opera's drama, but the public thought the production cold.

In the winter of 1976, a new production of *Aïda* was scheduled.

Originally given to the French director-designer Jean-Pierre Ponnelle, his designs had proved far too expensive for the impoverished Metropolitan. Bliss turned to Dexter and asked him to put together a production literally on a few months' notice; Dexter agreed, although he hated working at the last minute. Levine was the conductor, so this production was the first joint effort of the new regime.

The idea Dexter came up with was one he had found suitable for many of the so-called "grand operas": "The collision of small, infinitely complex human beings with the gigantic political, religious disputes which seem only to destroy humanity." Dexter knew he had to work with two contradictory realities: the public's expectation of a massive production and the tiny budget available.

In the prepremiere publicity, Dexter and Levine tried to prepare their audience. In one interview after another, they attempted to articulate their joint concept. "It's an intimate opera," Dexter would begin, and Levine would interject, "It's traditionally been misunderstood. You don't create grandeur with lots of *papier mâché* icons. You put on stage a grandeur made of space and height." Then Dexter would explain that the problem was finding the right balance, a grandeur that wouldn't diminish the human scale of the characters.

There were several inventive ideas. The Triumphal Scene was conceived not as a joyful commemoration of victory, but as a barbaric celebration of death in battle. The priests were cynical political manipulators; the victory parade was staged as a neo-Fascist rally, set not in sunshine but on a torchlit night. The ballet was grimly violent.

The cast was superb: Leontyne Price in the title role, Marilyn Horne as Amneris, James McCracken as Radames, and Cornell MacNeil as Amonasro. In order to reinforce his view of the Egyptians as captives of ritual, Dexter directed the singers to move ceremonially, their arms forming gestures fashioned from hieroglyphics, even at moments of passion. The singers had a hard time with the arm choreography—Dexter abandoned it in later revivals—and sometimes looked as though they were sending semaphore signals to the audience. Despite this distraction, Levine's fiery conducting made *Aïda* a musical success.

The critical reaction was mixed. *Newsweek* called it *"Aïda* mummified." But the *New York Times,* so often critical of the Met, praised it as "a good augury" for the new triumvirate. "If future Metropolitan Opera productions under the new regime have this kind of probity and imagination," wrote Harold C. Schonberg, "this city and the entire world of opera will be fortunate."

It was a good augury. During the first years of the Dexter-Levine collaboration, one compelling production after another rolled onto the Met stage. In 1977, *Le Prophète* by Meyerbeer, a rarely performed five-act extravaganza, was envisioned by Dexter as a painting by Brueghel. The best news for Bliss was that the four-hour evening cost only $300,000, two-thirds of the allotted $500,000.

Two weeks later, *Dialogues of the Carmelites* by Francis Poulenc, had its premiere. Two new productions in such a short time was a dazzling display of the Met's new technical proficiency. It was, however, only John Dexter who wanted to produce *Carmelites;* a revival of Samuel Barber's *Vanessa* had been originally scheduled. When Dexter insisted on substituting the Poulenc piece, people were dubious: it is a twentieth-century work with a verbose libretto about Carmelite nuns during the French Revolution. Audiences will hate it, everyone warned Dexter. He replied that he could do the entire production for almost no money, and, once again, he used financial restrictions as the inspiration for inventiveness. He cannibalized old Met sets and costumes to produce the stark sets and concentrated on getting an intense performance out of the cast of mostly women singers. The production cost an incredibly low $68,000.

No one who was at the Saturday-matinee premiere of *Carmelites* or the millions listening on national radio will forget the occasion. At the end of the opera, as the last nun strode to the guillotine, most of the audience was in tears. Advance ticket sales had been poor, but as word of mouth spread after the premiere, all the performances sold out.

Dexter was overjoyed. But he was fighting a tough battle: even after *Carmelites* broke box office records, a board member remarked dismissively to Dexter that he was not really attracting a typical Met audience to such operas. Proudly, Dexter replied that he had not changed the audience: he had added a new one.

But even he was surprised at the success. *"Carmelites* worked!" Dexter crowed in his diary. "I think the struggle to achieve a tolerance in the public and the critics is over. Not exactly the right to fail, we have not earned that, but perhaps the right to make our own mistakes." Yet he quickly reminded himself of a failure earlier in the season. *"Rigoletto* did not work."

Dexter's efforts with standard operas were less successful than his productions of unconventional works. Part of the reason was that he often stepped in at the last minute to replace another director whose designs he and Volpe had judged too expensive. Bliss and Levine would then beg Dexter to take over the production. Dexter, well aware that standard opera was not his strong suit, would always give in out of loyalty to the company, and then bitterly regret his decision when the productions were not well received. *Rigoletto,* as an example, was an ugly design and functioned clumsily, and the singers floundered, sensing the director's uncertainty about the work. Also, Dexter was distracted during the *Rigoletto* rehearsals because of a prior obligation to direct a Broadway production of Arnold Wesker's play *The Merchant,* which was to have starred Zero Mostel. Mostel died during the Philadelphia tryouts, and Dexter's dreams for another success on Broadway like *Equus* were shattered.

Dexter's confidence with lesser-known works may have stemmed from his lack of musical knowledge. He feared that lack might be more apparent in operas the public knew and loved. In February 1979, Dexter came closest to success in the established repertory with Verdi's *Don Carlo.* After reluctantly accepting the assignment under the usual emergency conditions, Dexter insisted on doing the opera's huge five-act version; his gamble paid off, and, as usual, he brought the enormous production in under the $500,000 budget.

Chapter Fifteen

SYBIL AND JOHN

A few months before the opening of *Don Carlo*, Bliss told a delighted John Dexter that the new production had been underwritten. Mrs. Donald D. Harrington, soon to be known to everyone in the company as Sybil, was the widow of an oil magnate from Amarillo, Texas. In 1978, she was barely known in New York society, though she had made impressive contributions to medical, educational, and arts organizations.

Marilyn Shapiro's staff knew about generous donors who made frequent contributions but stayed out of the limelight. Sybil Harrington, although she had contributed to the company for years and had even been on the board, remained largely unknown. Shapiro, curious, invited her to some performances preceded by elegant dinners at the Grand Tier Restaurant. Mrs. Harrington accepted, and Shapiro struck gold.

The unassuming boxholders at the Academy of Music would have approved of Mrs. Harrington's lack of ostentation. Born Sybil Buckingham, she was the granddaughter of early settlers in the Texas Panhandle. After she married Donald Harrington in 1935, she and her husband gave scholarships to students at Texas Tech University, funded a cancer treatment center, and, in 1961, established a charitable foundation. In 1974, Donald Harrington and the couple's only child, Sally Harrington Goldwater, died within a few months of each other. Sybil sought comfort by throwing herself into the work of the Harrington Foundation.

She had not thought of financing an opera production until she met Marilyn Shapiro. Although Shapiro originally had approached Harrington in the quest for funding, she and the donor became fast friends. Harrington, a slender, petite woman, always exquisitely dressed, had a down-to-earth manner. Having committed the money to fund *Don Carlo*, she threw herself into life at the Met, attending all the *Don Carlo* rehearsals from the early staging in C-level rehearsal rooms to the dress rehearsal in the auditorium, and she learned everyone's name. When she went backstage, she greeted each of the stagehands by name. "Hi, Dennis," she would call out, and the reply would come back, "Hi, Sybil." Her manner endeared her even to the prickly John Dexter.

By the time *Don Carlo* opened, Sybil Harrington was considered a member of the company; she had found a new family. Delighted by her reception, she decided to fund one new production every year and spend much of the winter in New York.

Sybil Harrington's philosophy of charitable contribution was simple. She believed that private philanthropy was far better than government support of the arts. "We've got to have that free enterprise," she said. "It's important in charitable institutions as well as in business. Art has to have freedom." She certainly was generous when she believed in an institution. By 1980, she had become the largest individual donor in Metropolitan history, and she would go on to give an amount estimated at more than $30 million. When, in gratitude, the Metropolitan Opera Association named the auditorium Sybil Harrington Auditorium, Harrington professed discomfort at such recognition.

But at the Met, eventually everyone earns enemies, and Harrington was no exception. John Dexter liked her in the beginning, but his affections faded as he began to worry that her involvement might affect his artistic goals.

The first clash was over the opening scene of *Don Carlo*. Dexter had planned originally to have the soprano heroine, Elisabetta, make her entrance on a white stallion, accompanied by four enormous Irish wolfhounds. But decrying excess and dreading unnecessary expense, as rehearsals progressed, he decided to get rid of the animals. Harrington refused to hear of the change; she loved live animals onstage and wanted as many as possible. Since she was paying for the production, she won, but future conflict with Dexter was clearly inevitable.

*I*n the spring of 1979, the press began to speculate about Dexter's situation at the Met. Donal Henahan reported in the *New York Times* that Dexter was considering his resignation so that he could resume a full-time theater career. Bliss told Henahan that "we have known that Mr. Dexter might want to go back to his primary interest, the theater," even though there were two years remaining on his contract as director of production.

Dexter admitted that he had not realized how much of his time would be taken up by administrative duties, which he frankly hated; but he hoped that he could assume another post, one that demanded less administration. He did not want to leave the Metropolitan completely. Bliss said he had not yet made his decision, and, in an ominous note, declared that if Dexter were to leave, "I don't know at this point whether . . . I might or might not replace him." A few articles in other publications mentioned Dexter's possible resignation, and then public speculation died down.

In the fall, Dexter made his only attempt to mount a Mozart opera, *Die Entführung aus dem Serail (The Abduction from the Seraglio)*, which, to everyone's surprise, was a major success. Critics had always maintained that the Met was too large for one of Mozart's small-scale masterpieces. But one of Levine's priorities was to have new productions of the Mozart operas he loved most: *Entführung, Don Giovanni, Le Nozze di Figaro, Die Zauberflöte, Idomeneo,* and *La Clemenza di Tito.* "These are some of the greatest masterpieces, and it is baloney that the house is too big for them. People will say, 'Oh, but you can't see all the little details in a Mozart piece from up there.' You can't see all the little details in *anything* from up there."

Dexter figured out how to make the Met's vast space suitable to *Entführung*'s intimacies. Jocelyn Herbert designed simple, bright sets that extended out into the auditorium. The staging kept the singers near the front of the stage so that they were close to the Mozart-size orchestra in the pit and the audience.

The cast included a young singer who had joined the Met only two years earlier. "Kathleen Battle as Blonde," wrote Nicholas Kenyon in the *New Yorker,* "was perfect. . . . Miss Battle is one of those rare natural, instinctive singers that one would be happy listening to for the rest of one's life."

During this period, Dexter continued to rely on Joseph Volpe, whom he regarded as a loyal ally. By the 1980s, the Met's productions were so polished that they were considered as advanced as the most lavish shows on Broadway.

In 1977, Dexter brought on staff the Met's first real resident lighting designer; prior to his arrival, the productions had been lit by the master electrician. Gil Wechsler, a product of the Yale Drama School, where he had studied with Herman Krawitz, had designed the lighting for the Stratford Festival and the Lyric Opera of Chicago as well as several Broadway productions. Like everything at the Met, lighting the stage is a big and complicated process. The house has three hundred lights—in the ceiling, on four lighting bridges that are positioned far above the stage, on towers in the wings, and on the proscenium. Most of these lamps are used in all productions, and thirty-two or more stage electricians operate them in the course of an opera.

A charming and handsome man, Wechsler soon became a friend of Sybil Harrington's, and, in time, she paid for the installation of a computerized lighting board. Dexter, Volpe, Volpe's assistant Joseph Clark, and Wechsler formed the core of a revitalized technical staff and collaborated on a legendary series of contemporary opera productions: Benjamin Britten's *Billy Budd* in 1978–79; Kurt Weill and Bertolt Brecht's *The Rise and Fall of the City of Mahagonny* in 1979–80; the French triple bill *Parade* in 1980–81, the New York premiere of Alban Berg's complete *Lulu,* also in 1980–81, and a Stravinsky triple bill in 1981–82. Both of the triple bills were designed by the painter David Hockney; in the Stravinsky triple bill, the second section was the composer's ballet *Le Rossignol,* and the principal dancers at the premiere were Natalia Makarova and Anthony Dowell. Dexter longed to unite all the arts involved in opera—music, dance, drama, and painting—and raise them to the same level of excellence.

The years between 1976 and 1982 were distinguished by the excitement of changes at the Met and the camaraderie within the company.

Levine's work with the orchestra had developed an ensemble so good that it was praised as one of the best in the city. David Stivender, the demanding, uncompromising, and stern chorus master, was bringing the chorus up to a similar level. The theater was finally up-to-date technically.

When Dexter turned his energetic mind to the Met's educational role in the community, he drew up a proposal for the company to expand its education programs. He presented the plan to Bliss. "We must keep the old doors open, but open new doors as well," he wrote. " 'Come into our tent for a while, it may be risky, but it's never dull.' "

Starting in 1978–79, some of Dexter's rehearsals were open to students, whom he and the technical staff talked to afterward, and he led a series of new production previews. He envisioned a three-year plan in which, the first year, intermission features for the Met's television series, then called *Live from the Met*, would be coordinated with the educational program. For the second year, the program would encompass a touring unit; he also planned to commission musical theater works. By the third year, there would be student matinees specifically programmed for young people. The proposal, although detailed and carefully thought out, never happened. There were a few rehearsals opened to a small number of students and a few previews of new productions, but as they happened, Dexter was losing his footing in the Met hierarchy.

Michael Bronson, whom Dexter had displaced as head of the technical department, proved a tougher antagonist than Dexter expected. Bliss clearly saw Bronson's failings, yet he didn't want to fire him; he knew Bronson had the economic pressure of two young daughters just entering college. After taking the stage away from him, Bliss kept Bronson on as head of business and administrative services, and also left him in charge of labor negotiations. He was still capable of making life hard for Dexter.

Dexter also realized, three seasons into his post at the Met, that his relations with Levine were becoming tense. Dexter wrote in his notebook in the middle of the 1978–79 season, "The only creative work I have done this year was on *The Bartered Bride* . . . and that work was hampered by a lack of collaboration with James Levine, who attended only three staging rehearsals . . . James Levine: I cannot any longer make the compromises needed to run the Met with you, and I am not developing."

Levine was always drawn to people with strong personalities, and, initially, he had been very attracted to Dexter's energy. But, forceful himself, with little tolerance for those who disagreed with him, he soon tired of Dexter and his truculent, argumentative temperament. He began to think about adding control of the stage to his own job description.

In the winter of 1981, the problems crystallized over a new production of _La Bohème_. After Dexter's often-stated reluctance to work on the standard operas, Bliss and Levine sincerely believed that he would have no interest in doing _Bohème_. They offered the opera to Franco Zeffirelli, who had been absent from the Met for several years. His name had come up periodically as a possible director/designer, and Bliss, Levine, and Dexter all agreed that, because of his long and distinguished history at the Met, Zeffirelli should be invited back once every three years. Dexter, however, knew of Zeffirelli's tendency toward excess and insisted that his contract contain precise budgetary restrictions, "for him to ignore, but for our protection," as Dexter remarked sarcastically.

Zeffirelli accepted the new _Bohème,_ and to Bliss and Levine's astonishment, Dexter was furious. "The decision to ask Franco was reached without any consultation and presented to me _fait accompli,_ " he wrote in an angry memo. The production was underwritten by Sybil Harrington.

In a poignant aside, Dexter noted in his diary that _Bohème_ was an opera that he had wanted to do, because "it is really about keeping warm in the cold." By this point, as major decisions were made without him and as Sybil Harrington's wealth became more and more essential to the company, Dexter was beginning to feel very cold at the Met.

Chapter Sixteen

THE MET GETS ORGANIZED

Anthony Bliss enjoyed cordial relations with members of the press, but he did not seek attention from the public and the artists. He made few speeches and attended few performances. People at the Met were critical of what they saw as his indifference to the artists: he rarely went backstage the few times he attended the opera. But he was conserving his energy for work in the areas where he felt more qualified.

There was little he could do about the widening gulf between income and expenses. In fact, Bliss was a great believer in spending money to make money. He authorized a quadrupling of the marketing budget, and, as a result, subscription sales for one season rose from 51 percent to 61 percent. He correctly saw that there would be no increase in government support. Other artistic institutions were besieging state and federal sources for money. Instead, Bliss expanded the Met's fund-raising endeavors and explored the commercial potential in multiplying the Met's television and radio activities.

The Metropolitan already had a historic place in radio history, but long before Bliss became general manager, television had replaced radio as the dominant medium. As far back as 1950, when Bliss had been a young board member, he had been involved with the Met's television experiments. Knowing that the Met's annual United States tour would probably collapse from economic pressures, he hoped to have television replace it both as a revenue source and a means of a national presence. When the first Met telecast under the Bliss administration aired in March 1977, *La Bohème* with Renata Scotto and Luciano Pavarotti, and with James Levine conducting, more people watched that performance than had ever seen the opera onstage. Bliss's predictions about the income from television proved overly optimistic, but the *Bohème* telecast marked the first of the Met's yearly series of telecasts.

In the mid-1970s, Lincoln Center, Inc., was also exploring the possibilities of television as it inaugurated its *Live from Lincoln Center* series. Although the Lincoln Center administrators assumed that the Met would participate, Bliss stunned them by announcing that the Met was not interested. He felt strongly that the Met would attract major donors to its telecasts by maintaining its independent position, and he wanted to safeguard the company's long-term relationship with Texaco. Mutterings arose about the Met's legendary arrogance, but Bliss was unmoved.

The night of January 3, 1977, was expected to be a quiet one in the opera house. The week after New Year's is traditionally a slow time. Verdi's *Il Trovatore* was on the schedule, with the American soprano Martina Arroyo as Leonora and the Italian conductor Giuseppe Patané in the pit.

At every Met performance, representatives from the artistic, technical, and press departments are on hand. At 7:00 P.M. on January 3, Charles Riecker, the artistic administrator on duty, received a phone call from Martina Arroyo. She had slipped in the bathtub, dislocated her troublesome back, and would not be able to sing the performance.

This should not have been a major problem, except perhaps for those people who had bought tickets to hear Arroyo. The Met had a long-standing policy of having every role covered not by one but by two other singers who would have been rehearsed and prepared in the role.

Unfortunately, in the years since Bing, the artistic administration had acquired some sloppy habits. Even major roles occasionally went uncast until the performance dates were perilously close. For a matinee the previous December, a tenor had been hired so late that his name could not be printed in the program. Since paying two extra people to cover every role was expensive, no one had objected to the relaxation of the practice. On the night of January 3, there was not even one singer covering Martina Arroyo.

Riecker notified Bliss, who was still in his office, and then began calling every soprano in New York City who could conceivably sing *Trovatore*. Quite far down this list was Elinor Ross, a soprano formerly on the company roster who had not sung the role in five years. Although no one thought her a good choice, Bliss was desperate and called her husband, who also served as her manager. Bliss agreed that if Ross sang that night, he would bring her back to the Met the following season; her husband suggested the role of Aïda, and Bliss, watching the moments tick by, agreed.

No one thought to consult Giuseppe Patané, the conductor, who had also been the conductor for Ross's last Met performance in 1975. He had been so unhappy with her singing on that occasion that he had walked off the podium and out of the theater, and another conductor had to finish the performance.

Predictably, when Patané arrived on January 3, and was told who would be singing Leonora, he exploded and left the theater just as the curtain was about to go up.

There was no cover conductor. James Levine happened to be in the theater, and Bliss asked him to replace Patané. But Levine already had a heavy schedule, and felt he could not add *Trovatore* to the load. Nor was he a great fan of Elinor Ross.

Levine suggested David Stivender, the chorus master, who out of affection for Levine and loyalty to the company gamely agreed to make his Met conducting debut leading *Trovatore*.

By now, the performance was half an hour late, and the audience was restless. Bliss decided to explain the backstage drama, and he stepped out in front of the gold curtain as Ross, backstage, was hurriedly being dressed and made up. "Ladies and gentlemen," he began, and unfolded the tale of the missing soprano and conductor. He announced that David Stivender would be on the podium. "And in the role of Leonora, we are grateful for the kindness of . . ." He stopped in midsentence. He could not remember Ross's name.

Bliss ducked behind the curtain for a few seconds and then triumphantly returned to finish. The audience was not pleased, but a few minutes later, the performance began. It was, according to a member of the administration, "just about the worst _Trovatore_ I've ever seen."

Two seasons earlier, with high hopes of straightening out Chapin's artistic department structure, Bliss had brought Richard Rodzinski to be the artistic administrator. But Rodzinski, coming from a company that performed only part of the year, found the transition to the Met's frantic schedule difficult. He also had problems with Levine. The music director often thought of so many people for each role that he couldn't make up his mind whom to engage, and Rodzinski was too nice to hound Levine. Consequently, casting was perilously delayed.

Bliss was aware of the situation but hesitated to get deeply involved in artistic planning. The _Trovatore_ catastrophe changed his mind. In January 1978, Joan Ingpen, the former artistic administrator of the Royal Opera, Covent Garden, and the Paris Opera, arrived at the Metropolitan. Although Levine had had an opportunity to meet with her in London, she had been hired by Bliss to run the artistic department.

Ingpen was, at this juncture, well known throughout the music world as a no-nonsense and imperious administrator. She had begun her career as an artists' manager with the London firm of Ingpen and Williams (named after herself and her dog) after World War II. Among her clients were Joan Sutherland and Sir Georg Solti; it was Solti who persuaded her to join the Covent Garden administration when he was music director there. Ingpen, who regarded singers as slightly naughty and unpredictable, exercised a firm hand with them, and Bliss correctly felt that her brisk efficiency, in combination with Levine's imaginative but unfocused artistic planning, would stabilize the artistic administration at the Met.

Ingpen also had a good relationship with John Dexter. She had hired him to direct his first opera, _Benvenuto Cellini_, at Covent Garden. Although she made it clear from the start that the Met casting would be decided by her and Levine, she valued Dexter's opinions about whom to cast in operas he directed. She also took immediately to Joseph Volpe, whom she met at a small cocktail party Bliss gave to welcome her to the company. Her colleagues had already discovered that her English accent, combined with a habit of swallowing syllables, made her difficult to understand.

Volpe asked her how things were going, and she replied that after her experience in trying to adapt to the Paris Opera, the Met seemed relatively simple. "At least I don't have to learn a new language," she said.

"Well, sort of," Volpe replied. He won Ingpen's heart. Straightforward herself, she appreciated the quality in others.

Ingpen quickly learned how difficult her job would be. She arrived in winter 1978 to find that, although the 1978–79 repertory had been planned, the operas were only half cast. Her first task was to finish the casting, making sure that the cover contracts were as solid as those of the leading singers. Then she moved on to later seasons; she and Levine decided that 1980–81 would be the first season they could claim as their own.

The difficulties of planning a Met season were exacerbated by the complicated yet essential subscription system. As Bliss and his marketing department cut the subscription series into smaller and smaller units, the difficulties increased. No subscriber wanted the same opera two years in a row, or three contemporary operas, or a season without a superstar. Ingpen had to juggle the demands of the subscribers with the availability—three or four years in advance—of the singers, Levine's desire for a balanced repertory, the new productions that were planned even before casting, the number of times any singer could perform during the week, and nights off during the seven-performance week that were mandated by contract for the chorus and orchestra.

Ingpen and Levine generally agreed about everything. Her main problem was getting some moments alone with the hyperactive music director so that she could propel him to a decision. They saw eye to eye on most of the singers and repertory, but she became frustrated by Levine's refusal to engage any singer he had not personally auditioned. "I think you're absolutely right," she told Levine during her first season, "although I can't believe you've heard half the singers I've been hearing since I've been at the Met, because they're so dreadful." He backed down and began to take her word about singers he had not heard.

Ingpen shared Levine's intermittent frustration with Bliss when the executive director vetoed new productions on the basis of expense. Both she and Levine badly wanted to do a new production of *Les Troyens* to open the Met's Centennial season in 1983–84, because they thought

Kubelik's 1973 production ugly and clumsy. But Bliss refused; it was too much money to spend on a lengthy opera that could rarely be cast or performed.

*B*liss had reason to trust his financial instincts. In December 1977, he told the *New York Times* for its article "The Met Gets Its Finances in Tune" that he felt he and his staff had turned the company around. After eight years of operating deficits, Bliss felt confident enough in the company's fiscal health to announce that he would lengthen the New York season to thirty weeks in 1978–79.

He had secured three years of peace with the labor unions and his and Frank Taplin's fund-raising efforts had brought in nearly $13 million during 1976–77. A year earlier, Bliss had doubted there would be a 1976–77 season. At the end of that fiscal year, the Met had a surplus of $500,000.

Bliss was particularly proud that this turnaround had occurred at a time when the Met's artistic standards had risen under Levine and Dexter. Yet the artistic example Bliss gave the *Times* for the article on the company's new healthy finances was the new production of *Tannhäuser*, given its premiere in December 1977, and conducted by Levine. It was, however, directed by the Austrian producer Otto Schenk, not by John Dexter.

In fact, Dexter had done little at the Met during the 1977–78 season. The previous season had been a jubilant one for him, with *Carmelites*, his first major success, and an almost equally notable achievement with *Lulu*. But in 1977–78, partly because of his commitment to the doomed Broadway production of *The Merchant*, his only new production was *Rigoletto*, and it was a failure. *Tannhäuser*, on the other hand, was a triumph.

Schenk and his close associate, the designer Günther Schneider-Siemssen, created a production that followed the extensive staging directions of Wagner himself. The scenic designs created a Teutonic mythical world, with elaborate effects produced by Gil Wechsler's lighting and the projection of slides. The magical grotto inhabited by Venus in the first scene melted into the forest of the second scene, right before the audience's eyes. It was not a lavish production—it was brought in under budget for only $380,000—yet it created a luxurious sense that was far removed from Dexter's stark aesthetic. The audience loved it.

So did Levine. By now, he had the musicians playing the way he wanted them to, and the _Tannhäuser_ reviews singled out the orchestral playing as unusually beautiful. He reveled in the splendor of the production and especially in the audience's reaction. It was closer to his taste than much of Dexter's best work, and he began to discuss future productions with Schenk and Schneider-Siemssen. John Dexter did not come to these meetings.

Joan Ingpen's imperturbable demeanor seemed impervious to all the passionate confrontations that swirled around her. Most of the singers were in awe of her and her vast experience; some were afraid of her. All respected and valued her judgment even when they resented her candor. As a result, her evenings on duty always lent a sense of authority to the whole opera house.

But one snowy evening in January 1980, the season after she arrived, Ingpen was especially worried about the performance of _Un Ballo in Maschera_. Giuseppe Patané was conducting, and she knew just how carefully he had to be handled. He had caused the company great distress at the notorious _Trovatore_ performance and probably would not have been reengaged were it not that he was a favorite of the orchestra members, who revered his idiomatic understanding of the Italian repertory.

His behavior had become unnervingly eccentric during the run of _Ballo_ because of strain caused by his disintegrating marriage. He had recently been rumored to have begun a flamboyant affair with a soprano on the Met roster, and frequently appeared at his beloved's rehearsals with other conductors, much to those maestros' displeasure, particularly when he told them how each aria should be conducted.

Ingpen began her evening on duty that January night as she always did, with a quiet glass of red wine in her office. The new production of _Ballo_ had had its premiere a few days before. Directed by the young Elijah Moshinsky from Covent Garden, the opera had been done in a stark, modernistic style that had horrified Met audiences.

Luciano Pavarotti was singing the lead tenor role in *Ballo,* which complicated an already difficult situation. Although Pavarotti was at the height of his operatic success in the world at large, he felt underappreciated at the Met. He rarely sang with James Levine and believed he was treated less well than Plácido Domingo. Ingpen knew that with Pavarotti in the cast, a quiet evening was unlikely.

She was just finishing her wine and getting ready to make her backstage visits to the cast when Patané appeared in her doorway. "Good evening, Maestro," she said as calmly as she could at the sight of the dark expression on Patané's face.

"I have slipped on the ice," he said, speaking in German for some reason, although Ingpen understood Italian well.

Ingpen saw, indeed, his forehead was bruised and bleeding. But she sensed his problem was not physical; it was clear that he was extremely agitated. Using all the confidence her many years in opera houses had taught her, she coaxed the trembling Patané into the pit, and, to her relief, *Ballo* began on time and the performance seemed to go well.

The set for this production was built like a box of polished wood; the floor rose at a steep angle and was dangerously slippery. But the singers were accustomed to raked stages and had learned to accommodate them under most circumstances. But that night, during the masked ball scene that ends the opera, Pavarotti misjudged his footing, slipped, and skidded down the stage until he plummeted out of sight into the wings.

Ingpen was in her office, listening to the audio through a monitor on her desk. When she heard the audience gasp, she raced backstage. Pavarotti, having picked himself up, was standing shakily by the stage manager's console. He told Ingpen he would finish the performance, and gamely trooped back onstage to an ovation from the audience. Ingpen stayed in the wings as he sang his death scene, clutching the arms of the singers clustered around him.

To her relief, the final curtain came down with the conductor still in the pit and the tenor still onstage. Then, as the stage manager corralled the cast for curtain calls, everything erupted. Pavarotti, the shock of his fall wearing off, decided that he was gravely hurt. The house doctor set up a first-aid station just off stage right.

Now Patané, ashen and close to hysteria, arrived for his curtain call. "I'm having chest pains!" he announced, grabbing Ingpen's arm.

Ingpen tried to calm him, explaining that the doctor was with Pavarotti. The conductor exploded. "But *I* am having a heart attack!" He pushed Ingpen aside and ran toward the doctor. Pavarotti shoved the conductor away, and Patané shoved back. "I need the doctor first," each man shouted.

Eventually, Ingpen managed to calm everybody. Pavarotti's injury was judged minor, and Patané's heart attack was diagnosed as an anxiety attack.

Reassured that he wasn't dying, Patané poured out his story to Ingpen. He had not slipped on the ice. Instead, he said, he had been injured in a battle with his estranged wife.

Joan Ingpen decided that Patané's brilliance as a musician could no longer compensate for his unreliability and volatility. A few days after the *Ballo* performance, she told him that the 1982–83 season would be his last with the company.

Chapter Seventeen

THE SUMMER OF 1980:
MONEY AND MURDER AT THE MET

The 1980s began auspiciously. The crisis of the mid-1970s was long past, and the future looked full of hope. In December 1979, Frank Taplin announced that for the third consecutive season, the Metropolitan had met its expenses through revenues and contributions. Taplin and Bliss were buoyant; they could abandon the Met's old practice of fearing doom with every season. From now on, the Metropolitan would put forth a positive face; surely, potential donors would be happier to support a successful institution than a failing one.

On May 15, 1980, the company announced a $100 million Centennial Endowment Drive, a victory for Bliss, who had, with Taplin's help, convinced the board to solve the company's underlying financial insecurity: "We must have sufficient capital income," he said, "to survive cyclical ups and downs." For there were ominous signs of future trouble. The most serious was a slight but steady drop in attendance, from 96.3 percent in 1977–78, to 94.3 percent in 1978–79, to 90.6 percent in 1979–80. Frank Taplin attributed this to a "certain little resistance" to higher ticket prices, and pointed out that new subscriptions and subscription renewals were up.

The company launched the endowment drive with atypical fanfare. A public relations firm was hired to augment the company's press department, and Marilyn Shapiro enlarged the development department to take on the challenge.

On the day the drive was made public, the company announced that $33 million of the $100 million goal was already in the coffers. Much of it was from Sybil Harrington, but the press was not given a breakdown of the donors since it was hardly a good idea to let the public know the strength of a single contribution.

Bliss had been around the Met long enough to know that good news was frequently followed by bad. He kept a pillow prominently displayed in his office on which was embroidered, "Theater is a lunatic asylum, and the opera is a refuge for incurables."

The announcement of the Centennial Endowment ran in a front-page article in the *New York Times,* and it was noted with great interest by members of the Met Orchestra. Rightly, Bliss was troubled. "The popular impression that we are rolling in wealth is somewhat exaggerated," he told the *Times* two months later, and added that he expected the unions to overreact when contracts were up in September and ask for more money than the company could afford. "The timing of the announcement couldn't have been worse from that point of view," he admitted. "We may have a real confrontation as a result."

This interview with Bliss was published on July 23, 1980. That night, a hot evening in New York City, Helen Hagnes, a thirty-one-year-old violinist, did not return to her seat in the Metropolitan orchestra pit after intermission during a performance by the Berlin Ballet. The company, with guest star Rudolf Nureyev, was performing at the Met as part of Jane Hermann's presentation season.

Hagnes had left her violin on her seat, and when she did not return, the other musicians immediately suspected trouble. For a musician, especially a string player, leaving an instrument behind is like leaving a baby unattended outside a grocery store. Helen Hagnes had disappeared.

Everyone loved Helen Hagnes. She had come to New York from Canada to study at Juilliard and had stayed on to pursue a career as a freelance violinist. She was vivacious and attractive, with flowing blond hair, always ready with a humorous quip to lighten the atmosphere. The life of a freelance musician is not easy; they hurtle themselves from assignment to assignment. One day they may play a recording session; the next day a concert with a chamber orchestra. The lucrative "jingle" jigs are the most coveted: playing for commercials at high fees and, often, residuals.

But Hagnes never became discouraged; her career was well established. Because she was both personable and a good player, she was a favorite of the classical music contractors. And, besides, a fortune-teller whom she had visited in her early twenties had told her she would be famous by her thirtieth birthday.

After the performance on that Wednesday night, Hagnes's husband, Janis Mintiks, a sculptor, turned up at the stage door looking for her. He had spent the evening working on the new loft the couple had recently purchased in Chelsea. He often drove his van to meet her after performances and take her back to their Upper West Side apartment.

When he didn't see her, he called home to see whether she'd left early, and when he received a busy signal, he assumed she was there. The busy signal was in fact caused by other musicians frantically trying to reach her. Janis drove home to find an empty apartment. A little while later, several of the musicians arrived. By now it was 1:00 A.M. on Thursday, and Janis went back to the Met.

Backstage at the Metropolitan Opera House is the perfect environment for a disappearance. Even longtime employees do not know all the corridors, staircases, exits, and entrances in that vast expanse behind the gold curtain. At the insistence of orchestra members, the house staff realized that they would have to search the backstage area, an undertaking that might last all night.

A hasty preliminary search of backstage had revealed nothing, so the house manager called the police at Manhattan's Twentieth Precinct. The officers started a more extensive search of the long hallways, cluttered with large instrument cases and shipping boxes. At 3:00 A.M., having found nothing, the officers notified the Task Force, an elite division of detectives, two of whom immediately drove to the opera house.

Someone had given the shaken Mintiks a bottle of Jack Daniel's whiskey. By the time the detectives arrived and began to question Mintiks, he was so distraught that they quickly dismissed any suspicion of his involvement, and started to question the people who had seen Hagnes just before her disappearance.

The last musician to see Hagnes in the women's dressing room during intermission told the detectives that Helen had complained of not feeling well. Her friend had watched Helen walk the short distance to a backstage elevator, chat briefly with one of the Berlin dancers, then get on the elevator. Boarding the elevator at the same time was a man the friend did not recognize.

The detectives' most optimistic scenario was that Hagnes had become really ill and passed out somewhere in the building. But the more experienced officers feared this was not the case. Grimly, they began the job of mapping a room-by-room search of backstage.

Almost immediately they made two discoveries that limited the search. A wilted flower, surrounded by strewn bobby pins, was found on one staircase leading to the sixth floor; the detectives had been told that Helen was wearing a flower in her hair that night. Then, at 8:00 A.M., a Met maintenance man came to the detectives with a more ominous find: he had just been to the roof to do his daily inspection of the air-conditioning fans and on a ledge next to the fans, he had found a pair of women's shoes.

The detectives rushed to the roof. The entrance was in a part of the building almost unknown to most of the people who worked in the opera house. Around the side of each fan was a space about two feet wide that opened into a shaft three stories deep.

The police peered through the clammy spray spewed out by the fans' motors, down the three flights to the bottom of the shaft. There they saw Helen Hagnes. She was gagged, naked, and her hands were bound behind her. Obviously, she had been pushed to her death by her attacker.

It was now about 8:30. Within minutes, as word of the murder spread, the chief of detectives for Manhattan was on his way to the Met. Also en route was the chief medical examiner, who rarely went personally to crime scenes. Meanwhile, the press, having picked up the police transmissions on their scanners, crowded in hordes around the stage door.

The detectives had already concluded that the murder had been committed by someone familiar with the building. The traces of Hagnes's last moments were in widely separated parts of the building, areas that few Met employees entered as part of their normal day.

The stage crew became the main focus of the investigation, because the ropes binding Hagnes were tied with knots frequently used by the stagehands when working with ropes and lines backstage. Concentrating on the stage crew made the inquiry even more difficult. The stagehands as a group were so close-knit that they rivaled the police department in internal loyalty.

As the police delved deeper into life at the Met, they became intrigued by the long-standing animosity between the orchestra musicians and the stage crew. The musicians resented the stage crew's higher pay and generous overtime; they earned far more than most of the musicians even though they lacked the level of education enjoyed by the orchestra members. The stagehands retorted that they worked killer hours for their copious salaries, often reporting for work before 9:00 A.M. and rarely leaving before midnight. They considered the musicians overprivileged and lazy, smug and self-indulgent. The constant tension between the two groups and the steady exchange of biting remarks was an undertone to every rehearsal and performance where their paths crossed.

The detectives set up a control center in the atrium offices of the opera house, and the Met's midsummer camaraderie vanished. Everyone who worked there knew that the murder must have been committed by a fellow employee; no one else could have found his or her way to such an isolated part of the building. In addition, the police investigation revealed a seamy side of Met life that shocked almost everyone.

In searching the building for clues, the detectives had come across indications that several deserted parts of backstage had been used for sexual trysts. And there seemed to be a thriving backstage business in a variety of illegal drugs, purchased by employees from all over the theater. The roof where Hagnes's shoes had been found was a favorite place for stagehands to congregate and smoke pot. Met colleagues began looking at one another with frightened eyes.

The police circulated a sketch of the man who had been seen entering the elevator with Hagnes. To many, the face, although not immediately identifiable, was uncomfortably familiar.

Anthony Bliss was deeply shaken. In less than twelve hours, the opera house he loved had turned into a murder site, his employees were suspects, and packs of tabloid reporters were camped at the front gate.

On the afternoon of July 24, the day Hagnes's body was found, Bliss held a press conference and outlined the basic facts known by the police and the Met administration. He said there would be added security precautions at the opera house, and he expressed his condolences to Janis Mintiks and the Hagnes family. When he returned to his office, he called Mintiks and then phoned Hagnes's parents in Vancouver.

A few days later, Bliss attended the violinist's funeral. He took with him Joseph Volpe, who had been invaluable in holding the company together during the emergency. The church was crammed with members of New York's classical music community, many of the musicians carrying their instruments as they went to the service between freelance jobs around the city.

After the murder, all the people in the opera house became cautious. They avoided large areas of the building at night; never again would anyone take a shortcut through the eerie expanses of the set shops and storage areas. People who had used stairs instead of waiting for the elevators now exercised patience. The opera house had revealed itself to be mortally dangerous.

The police continued to concentrate on the stage crew as primary suspects, and eventually the code of silence among the stagehands began to break down. Five weeks after the murder, the detectives arrested Craig Crimmins, a twenty-one-year-old carpenter and a member of one of the Met's multigenerational stagehand families. Both his father and stepfather worked backstage. Crimmins had answered a questionnaire distributed to the entire crew and had been interviewed as a matter of course, along with everyone else. But the police took special notice of his nervous demeanor and the inconsistencies in his written statement. He maintained that he had not missed any of his cues the night of the murder, and, at first, no one contradicted him because stagehands always covered for one another. But the brutality of the act demanded the truth, and the detectives discovered that Crimmins had been missing for the entire second half of the July 23 performance.

The police interrogated him for several days, and at last, Crimmins broke down and confessed on videotape to murdering Hagnes. He was accused of second-degree murder and scheduled for trial the next summer. Surprisingly, in the months between his confession and trial, Crimmins continued to work as a stagehand at the Vivian Beaumont Theater, whose stage door is near the Met. In June 1981, he was tried and found guilty of felony murder, a murder committed during a rape. Since a felony murder is presumed to be unpremeditated, Crimmins was sentenced only to twenty years to life.

Joseph Volpe's role during the murder investigation changed many people's perception of him. He had taken charge from the moment the crime was discovered, and Bliss's sympathetic personal response to the tragedy was supplemented by Volpe's pragmatic approach. Backstage life at the Met was about to change forever. The press and public had been shocked by the stories of drug use, sexual activity, and alcohol consumption just steps from the opera house stage. Volpe made it clear that there would be no tolerance for such behavior. Anyone found intoxicated would be sent home; anyone selling drugs would be fired on the spot. The brisk business in recreational drugs dried up. Open drinking vanished; even on tour, where previously the backstage atmosphere had been especially relaxed, drinking was prohibited. Members of the stage crew began to police themselves, letting offenders know they'd better shape up. Most of the stagehands were dignified and decent men, with manners far more polished than many of the singers, and they were appalled at the damage done to their public image. Naturally, Volpe's enforcement of new discipline backstage made him unpopular with some of his former colleagues on the stage crew, but he was regarded with new respect. He would not tolerate sloppy work or illicit behavior, and amidst the grumbling, everyone began to function more efficiently.

Volpe and Bliss, meanwhile, had other concerns during the murder investigation. On the same weekend Craig Crimmins was arrested, the orchestra musicians rejected management's final offer on a new contract. In return, the board canceled several weeks of rehearsals, once again falling into the traditional cycle of Met labor conflict. But some sensed a new, tacit element in the impasse. Perhaps the musicians, having lost one of their own, were simply afraid to go back to work.

Chapter Eighteen

THE LAST STRIKE
AND THE PRICE OF PEACE

The labor dispute that followed the murder isn't a strike, the musicians kept saying through the long fall of 1980; it is a lockout. To most of the opera staff, still in shock over the murder, the terminology was irrelevant.

In July, Bliss had made Michael Bronson the chief management negotiator. Bronson, who had taken on many of Herman Krawitz's responsibilities, lacked Krawitz's affability and common touch. He came across to the unions as a calculating bureaucrat; anything he said sounded crafty and dishonest to them.

The dispute was kindled by the orchestra's unresolved complaints about working conditions, especially their demands for a four-performance week. Some musicians—wind and brass players—had already achieved this, and now the string players were determined to win the same conditions. Although they didn't play solos, many of them suffered from repetitive stress disorder as well as neck and back pain from the long operas.

The board, certain that having the whole orchestra change to a four-performance week would wreak financial disaster, proclaimed the demand outrageous. In the beginning, Bliss was in favor of the four-performance week and told the board that if the musicians would forgo a substantial increase in pay and benefits, the numbers could work. He also reminded the directors that one reason he had resigned as board president in 1967 was the accusation that he had been too sympathetic to the company members, including the musicians.

Bliss was in a complicated position. He considered himself to be part of the Met because of his family's involvement, and because he had married a company member. He certainly was no grandiose aristocrat; his wife, Sally, called him "the most unsophisticated man I've ever met. I could feed him Alpo."

But he had little understanding of the effects that the season cancellation the board was suggesting would have on his employees; his primary concern was the preservation of the Met's heritage and future. To him, a strike meant only that performances would stop for a while and then start again. He seemed not to understand the deprivation that the hiatus would inflict on the thousand or so employees who did not have family trust funds.

Perhaps more understandably, Bliss and the board could also not understand the musicians' unwillingness to see themselves as part of a company fighting for its existence; the orchestra, proud of its newly validated quality, felt it should be paid appropriately. "No one argues the fact that you have to raise the money," I. Philip Sipser, the musicians' attorney, said to the board in August. "Your job is to find the money."

The musicians, who had closely monitored the Met's return to financial health, noted the expensive new gold curtain, the new phone system, the new lighting board underwritten by Sybil Harrington. And they had read the front-page *New York Times* story about the successful launch of the endowment drive. The Met had been given $30 million, the orchestra committee pointed out, "yet you can't afford an increase for us. We're not laborers." The musicians truly believed that Bliss, Taplin, and the board considered them not trained artists, but mere workers.

The board declared that they needed to demonstrate fiscal firmness to the Met's donors and subscribers. And, with standard Met arrogance, the directors also invoked the company's role in holding the line against the musicians' demands as a role model for other American arts organizations. In an extensive article about the labor strife, the *New York Times* commented, "Class seems important to the struggle . . . [with] what is perceived as the American Anglo-Saxon elite on one side, and, on the other, men and women who see themselves as having to work their way up."

James Levine was in a delicate position, poised between the management and the musicians; he was, after all, a member of the musicians' union. He told the *New York Times*, "I can't mediate a family quarrel. I can only say I love them all." But he was clearly upset as the first three months of the season melted away; Sue Thomson would later say that she had never seen him so depressed.

On September 19, the Met board formally announced that "the 1980–81 season has been cancelled, for all practical purposes." The wording elicited some cynical amusement, but the dispute continued. Bliss stated, "Nothing will happen until the orchestra stops acting like lemmings."

"Like lemmings!" horn player Scott Brubaker said to a reporter. "That's no way to talk about musicians, no way to talk about *anybody.*"

The public showed little sympathy for the musicians, whom they perceived as people who worked only twenty hours a week and were well compensated. The musicians, convinced that they were involved in what amounted to class warfare, were stunned by the lack of empathy.

Near the end of October, the orchestra members let it be known that they would sacrifice certain benefits in return for the four-performance week. Now the management believed it had a chance to balance the budget while maintaining its pride. Negotiations began again, and a settlement was reached, although problems with the chorus contract held up the start of the new season until December.

Levine chose not to open the season with an opera. Instead, he conducted the orchestra and chorus in Mahler's Symphony no. 2, subtitled "Resurrection." The idea of starting the season with a symphonic work jolted the company and public alike; it was another bizarre turn. Opening night itself was understated. Hardly anyone was dressed up; the playing of the National Anthem was scrapped; and there were few celebrities or photographers present. "We're not treating this as a gala," Bliss said grimly. For the first time in his life, Bliss wore a dark suit to opening night instead of a dinner jacket.

There was no glittering after-performance party for major funders or cast; of course, there was no cast. Instead, Bliss gave a party for the whole company on the Grand Tier of the opera house, but it was a bleak affair, because feelings still ran high. Everyone had a glass of champagne on the house and went home.

Even the reviews were bitter. Instead of the usual paeans to the Met Orchestra's playing, there were snipes at the musicians. A semblance of normality returned on the second night, with the Met premiere of the three-act version of Berg's *Lulu,* which was an artistic success both musically for Levine and theatrically for John Dexter.

The four-performance week was now a reality, but the musicians had to give up being paid for some rehearsals. Philip Sipser predicted another dispute when the contract expired in 1984. "You can be sure that in four years our first demand will be the elimination of the 'free' four rehearsal hours."

After the season had started, Bliss called together the senior management and asked for their views, in writing, about what had gone wrong with the labor negotiations. Joseph Volpe submitted an assessment that Bliss found informed and honest. He did not spare Bliss's feelings. Rather, he wrote at length about the damage done by the management negotiators and about ways in which the union's trust could be restored.

On August 8, 1981, Bliss sent a memo to the president of every Met union. "In an effort to consolidate responsibilities within the Metropolitan Opera House for union negotiations, I am appointing Joe Volpe as the Metropolitan Opera union representative in dealing with you and all the other unions."

Immediately, there was a sense of optimism. The unions had intensely disliked the previous management representatives, but they trusted Volpe as one of their own. After all, he had worked his way up through the ranks. He understood their problems; he spoke their language. Volpe would never compare them to lemmings. Some people suggested this was because he didn't know what a lemming was, but others knew that he had grasped that insult in ways that Bliss and Taplin had been wholly unable to do.

It was true, however, that Bliss had felt early in the dispute that the Met negotiators were mishandling the situation. He had never been confident of Bronson; in fact, it appeared that he had moved Volpe into an office next to Bronson's so that he could keep watch on the situation, a maneuver that most people would not have expected of Bliss.

Within six weeks of Volpe's new appointment, in 1981, Bliss reported:

> The orchestra sent a delegation to see me, to thank me for what they said was probably a major contribution, and though they didn't agree with [Volpe] a lot of the time, they knew he was not a lawyer trying to trick them and that he knew what he was talking about. . . . They accepted that.

Joseph Volpe thus emerged from the labor dispute of 1980 as the strongest member of the Met's administration.

But for Bliss, the entire sequence of turmoil and negotiations was sad. "Tony lost all his zest after the strike," Frank Taplin said. Many members of the company now were convinced he was a cold man who regarded them as indentured servants. He had been vilified by the orchestra, whose members continued to scorn him; an orchestra party celebrating the return to work featured "lemming soup." Bliss was mystified by their attitude, because he saw himself in a fatherly role to all the members of the company; they saw him as paternalistic. The board believed that he had allowed himself to be misled by misguided advisers like Michael Bronson and the Met's labor attorney, Edward Silver. They were now no longer happy with his leadership.

After the labor settlement, there were moments when Taplin, Bliss, Levine, and Joan Ingpen wondered whether their efforts to save the 1980–81 season had been worth it. Taplin and the board put on an optimistic front; privately, they went back to pessimistic planning that again included reductions in the Met's season.

They ran feasibility studies of cutting the number of performances per week, of replacing opera performances with ballet performances, of placing a new emphasis on small-scale productions, and of a less-luminous artists' roster. The season itself was a patchwork; many of the artists who had been signed made other commitments during the months the Met was closed, and the new production of Tchaikovsky's _Pique Dame_ was shelved. For the first time in memory, some weeknights were dark, because there had not been sufficient rehearsal time or because the needed cast was not available.

In an oddly timed verification of its faith in Bliss, the board, on January 15, 1981, conferred on him the title of general manager. "General manager is a more appropriate description of Mr. Bliss's function," the press release read, "and in no way marks a return to the centralization of total responsibility and authority in a single individual," for which one was to read Rudolf Bing. For the first time since Bing, three assistant managers were also named at the same time: Joan Ingpen, Marilyn Shapiro, and Joseph Volpe.

The orchestra and chorus nourished their anger, especially after the announcement of Bliss's new position. But the season held some artistic high points despite the conflict: the new three-act _Lulu;_ Levine's first performance of _Tristan und Isolde;_ the premiere of John Dexter and David Hockney's _Parade_. The triumphant first night of the _Parade_ triple bill was marred for Dexter, however, when Bliss came to the curtain calls and abruptly informed him that the triple bill by Stravinsky for the following season had been canceled. As Dexter noted sardonically in his diaries, Bliss had second thoughts when he read the ecstatic reviews for _Parade;_ Stravinsky was reinstated.

Bliss, for all his kindness and gentility, had no idea how to handle the artistic temperament. From the beginning, he had made an effort to know the company's rank and file, but he had spent little time courting the principal artists. Most general managers enjoyed their relations with famous singers as one of the best parts of a difficult job, but Bliss wasn't interested. He was so secure socially that he had no need to make friends with famous people. And he was severely criticized because, after the labor dispute, he attended even fewer performances. He had to guard his physical strength because of his heart condition, and he minded spending time away from Sally and their young sons.

Although reserved by nature, he could be unstintingly honest and incapable of subtlety, traits in which he was matched by Ingpen, whose straightforward British manner also raised resentment in the artists.

In March 1981, Ingpen told the tenor Carlo Bergonzi, who was cele-brating his twenty-fifth anniversary with the company, that he would no longer be contracted by the Met because his singing was inadequate. Bergonzi and his wife did not go quietly; they called the newspapers to ex-press their anguish. "His heart is broken and he'll sing with tears in his eyes," Adele Bergonzi told the *Daily News*. The music press and public took Bergonzi's side, feeling he had not received the respect he deserved after his long career.

Erich Leinsdorf's on-and-off feud with the Met dated back to the 1974 *Tristan* revival, which had precipitated Kubelik's resignation as music di-rector. Leinsdorf was a master musician. Orchestras had great respect for him, though not great love, but he was not adept at dealing with people when he was not on the podium. He loved confrontation, and was frus-trated by Levine, who backed away from disputes as avidly as Leinsdorf sought them.

Bliss and Ingpen did not have the luxury of avoiding Leinsdorf. Leinsdorf had known Bliss for many years; indeed, Leinsdorf had known Cornelius Bliss in the "Eddie Johnson" years. But he made the mistake of assuming that Bliss, with his knowledge of Met tradition, would be willing to accept Leinsdorf's advice and listen to his endless complaints. He dis-liked the direction he saw the Met taking. "The Metropolitan Opera today is a corporation," Leinsdorf said in the early 1980s. "Like corporations that make . . . say, refrigerators. I am not criticizing," he added, "merely observing." No one was deceived.

He complained with special bitterness about Levine, grousing that the younger conductor led far too many operas and reminding Bliss about the many opera companies and orchestras that were seeking his, Leinsdorf's, services. Bliss, who had honed his letter-writing skills during his disputes with Bing, wrote back in defense of Levine: "I am probably responsible for insisting that James Levine conduct more operas in the first years . . . than I would want him to handle in later years. . . . After the first . . . years, I do not believe Jimmy will handle more than three or four operas a year." Bliss could not have been more wrong about Levine's intentions, but he acquiesced to Levine's desire to conduct as much as two-thirds of the repertory because, as he wrote to Leinsdorf, "I believe that Jimmy has the capacity to do the very difficult job [of] restoring the Metropolitan's artistic thrust."

The Met continued to offer Leinsdorf engagements, and after Joan Ingpen arrived, he negotiated with her. In the beginning, he loved her. He wrote to Bliss that her presence had made his contacts with the Met "pure joy" and "to work with such a professional is a privilege."

Bliss knew that this benevolent Leinsdorf was an aberration. And, in 1981, Leinsdorf and Ingpen clashed over rehearsal time and the casting of a _Ring_ cycle revival. He had been crushed when the 1980 labor problems had forced cancellation of the complete cycle; only three of the four operas could be scheduled, partly because of Leinsdorf's exacting rehearsal demands.

After Ingpen broke this news to him, he wrote back to her, enraged, in April 1981: "It might have been valuable to look into the past at the many instances of crisis from which I saved the Met and always with conspicuous success. . . . Mine has been a service which has put the opera house into long debt [to me]." He withdrew from the remaining _Ring_ performances.

In the winter of 1983, Leinsdorf did return to the Met to preside over a new production of Richard Strauss's _Arabella_. This time, even Leinsdorf could not complain about the cast: Kiri Te Kanawa sang the title role, Bernd Weikl was Mandryka, and Kathleen Battle was Zdenka. But no production involving Leinsdorf stayed calm.

First he announced that Te Kanawa's cover was inadequate. Since Te Kanawa rarely canceled, even Joan Ingpen had not been concerned about the cover's abilities. But Leinsdorf wanted preparation for every eventuality. Not all the trouble, however, stemmed from the conductor. From the earliest rehearsals, the two leading sopranos were at odds. Kiri Te Kanawa was an established star, and a woman who put up with no "diva" nonsense. Her young co-star, Kathleen Battle, was on the brink of stardom. Originally a friendly, cooperative colleague, she had recently become oddly remote, unreliable, and demanding. Te Kanawa had no patience with Battle's whims, and the two were soon in constant conflict. Te Kanawa left no doubt that unless Battle behaved professionally, one of them was going to leave the premiere, and she certainly didn't intend to.

But Leinsdorf is a strong man and a strong conductor can impose his discipline on an unruly cast. Both sopranos sang the premiere.

Leinsdorf was already under contract to conduct the revival of *Arabella* during the 1983–84 Centennial, a fitting gesture to a musician who had been such a large part of Met history. But Leinsdorf wanted assurances that *Arabella* would be telecast, and the Met, foreseeing an extremely expensive season with all the Centennial festivities, could not make the commitment. Leinsdorf withdrew and was not part of the Centennial; he would never again conduct at the opera house. His absence from the company during the last years of his life was everyone's loss.

*P*robably, Bliss's most publicized dispute with an artist was the brouhaha with Joan Sutherland in the late 1970s and early 1980s. The soprano had strong ideas about what she would and would not perform, and the Met had equally strong and opposing views on the same issue.

The falling out began over a production of Lehár's *The Merry Widow*, which Sutherland was eager to sing during her last seasons at the Met. She knew she would soon retire; always a homebody who loved gardening more than singing, she could hardly wait. But she had good years left onstage, and she was determined to enjoy them by singing what she wanted.

Sutherland was one of the few singers who could guarantee sold-out houses every time she set foot on the Met stage, and she knew it and did not hesitate to use her power. Among opera lovers, she was known as a warm and amiable woman, but this was not entirely true. With people in the company, she was friendly, but cool and often testy. Her husband, the conductor Richard Bonynge, was loved by everyone; a warm, outgoing, funny man who would occasionally, out of kindness, commit his wife to projects she had no interest in doing. On these occasions, everyone involved was subjected to Sutherland's annoyance.

In 1978, Sutherland had been singing at the Met for seventeen years. Only two years previously, the company had mounted Massenet's *Esclarmonde* for her, an opera that would never have entered the Met repertory without her insistence.

Sutherland and Bonynge came to opera companies as a team. No other conductor led performances in which Dame Joan sang, and she was the only major contemporary singer for whom James Levine had never conducted, at the Met or anywhere else. When the Bonynges announced in the late 1970s that they had decided to make *The Merry Widow* their next outing at the Met, Bliss first investigated the possibility of borrowing a production Dame Joan had done in Sydney and Vancouver. Although the worst of the Met's money problems were over for the time being, the board was not happy with the prospect of a new production for one singer. There was no definitive version of *The Merry Widow* that had been established by tradition, and Bonynge, a musicologist as well as conductor, had chosen one that John Dexter believed other sopranos would be reluctant to sing. In return, Dexter suggested a rendition more consistent in style with Lehár's period.

The New York City Opera had recently borrowed and produced the San Diego Opera's production of *The Merry Widow,* and the results had been disastrous. This convinced Bliss to write, in July 1978, "Dear Joan and Ricky, we are running into severe problems with *The Merry Widow.*" He told them that the City Opera's production had been savaged by the sophisticated New York audience and closed his letter by repeating the Met's philosophy of building new productions that would last for a generation and could be performed by a variety of artists. In other words, the Met had no interest in doing an expensive new production of an opera that no one wanted but Dame Joan.

Bliss had already written a memo to Levine and Dexter about the debate, putting himself on record as in support of the policy that the Met should not give in to individual demands that might affect its artistic standing. "I have never yet seen such concessions fail to produce unhappy results."

The Bonynges meanwhile sent off their reply. They were extremely disappointed, and they stipulated that "either we do the version we have prepared and performed with love (and not a little success) or we do not perform at all."

Negotiation was obviously not an option. So Bliss asked for a tape of the version the Bonynges favored, and on August 11, Bonynge sent it to New York.

Bliss was not alone in making the *Merry Widow* decision. He had had a tough time convincing the board to allow Dame Joan this diversion at all. But she had agreed that, in future seasons, she would sing new productions of Mozart's *Die Entführung aus dem Serail* and Rossini's *Semiramide*, two roles that she was better suited to than anyone else when she was in good voice.

Sutherland had always been intelligent about her career. Originally trained as a Wagnerian soprano, she and Bonynge had instead tailored her immense voice to the neglected bel canto operas and were instrumental in attracting new attention to this repertory. She was careful about what she sang and when she sang, and took such good care of her voice that it had endured for over thirty years. In the late 1970s, she realized her repertory had become limited by the physical restrictions of her age. Many singers describe themselves as athletes, with the same kind of reliance on physical health, and age takes an inevitable toll on endurance and range.

First she withdrew from the new production of *Semiramide;* then, in the fall of 1978, also withdrew from *Entführung.* At that point, the board saw no reason to mount *The Merry Widow*, which they believed to be an operetta and not suited to the Met. Here Dame Joan was refusing to sing two new productions that had been planned just for her. Bliss, with his usual bluntness, informed the Bonynges that, due to her withdrawals, "doing *Widow* is out the window."

Dame Joan, herself inclined to bluntness, wrote back to say that it was more ethical for her to pull out of uncomfortable roles in advance rather than to cancel at the last minute, "like some of my colleagues!" Bliss, relieved, thought the skirmish was over, and told Ingpen to find out what else Sutherland might like to sing.

But the Bonynges were angrier than Bliss knew and, in January 1979, went public with their disappointment. The dispute had gobbled up so much time that, given the long-term planning involved in opera casting, Sutherland and the Met suddenly realized that there would be a three-year hiatus before Dame Joan could appear again. With the paucity of artists who could sell out the theater, the Met certainly did not want this. And Sutherland, knowing she would soon retire from singing, wanted to appear in New York. But with the soprano's restricted repertory and Ingpen's ironclad advance casting, they were at an impasse. Ingpen had been hired to clear up the casting mess at the company, and she doggedly went on doing exactly that. Flexibility was not part of her strategy.

"I am not at war with the Metropolitan Opera," Sutherland stated, and Bliss said, "Everybody at the Met loves Joan and wants her here as much as we can have her." Both sides churned out baroque and self-serving explanations, but the press and public did not care. All they knew was that Dame Joan would be gone for three years.

But it was to be four years later, in November 1982, when Sutherland returned to the Met in the title role of _Lucia di Lammermoor,_ the role of her Met debut in 1961 and one of her great portrayals. Her husband conducted. Backstage everyone worked hard to soothe her ruffled feathers. The Met gave a rare press luncheon to welcome her back, and announced further plans for her, including a new production of _Il Trovatore_ and a gala concert performance with Luciano Pavarotti, who had once been her protégé.

The historical import of Sutherland's return was underscored when she announced that this would be her farewell to _Lucia._ The performances completely sold out, and would-be ticket buyers stationed themselves several blocks from every entrance to the opera house to plead for tickets. After Sutherland finished her first aria at the opening performance, a voice from standing room called out, "Welcome back!" and the audience roared their approval.

Five years later, Sutherland made her final appearances at the Met, leaving regally and with as much acclaim as she had when she first arrived. She was only sixty-one, but she knew the time had come. The great ones usually do.

Chapter Nineteen

THE DEFEAT OF JOHN DEXTER

In the winter of 1980, John Dexter came down with a severe case of shingles. This painful ailment is exacerbated by stress, and Dexter, already feeling shut out by Levine, was also feeling trapped by his administrative duties. He wrote in his diary, "The time has come to pull the chair away from the desk and float a little." It is hard to know whether his antennae were picking up changes in the air or whether he had just had enough of Met bureaucracy.

Even outside the company, rumblings about Dexter's position at the Met were being heard. In July, John Rockwell, the *Times* music critic who watched Met politics closely and perceptively, wrote, "For all practical purposes, responsibility for the Met's artistic affairs has shrunk to Mr. Levine and Mr. Bliss." Levine, Rockwell noted, was now the de facto artistic director, and he quoted Levine as taking credit for choosing directors and designers, formerly Dexter's domain. Dexter's position at the Met he described as "marginal."

In September, while Bliss and Levine were preoccupied by the labor situation, Dexter wrote them a long, ruminative memo about his unhappiness. "For the last year or so . . . I have become aware of a rift between James and myself," he wrote, "and that my authority has been undermined within the house. . . . Plans that you have discussed with Joan never reach me either verbally or on paper." He traced the source of his segregation to

Ingpen's arrival two years before. After she arrived, he pointed out, he and Levine had less and less contact.

He therefore proposed a new arrangement: he would relinquish his administrative duties and devote his energy to artistic concerns. "I do not wish or need power. . . . Nor do I wish to enhance my world reputation. That seems to have reached a point which would have satisfied even my own father!" He had begun to see Bliss and Levine as the "grown-ups" and himself as the child preoccupied with imagination and creativity while his two colleagues were raising funds (Bliss) and gathering power (Levine). Bliss and Levine postponed a decision on this memo until the 1980 strike was resolved.

When the labor dispute ended in December, the board saw the necessity of administrative changes. It was clear that the management under Bliss had failed to recognize the gravity of the musicians' discontent. The executive committee, encouraged by Frank Taplin, discussed the change in Bliss's title and in the structure of the management that took place in the winter of 1981. With the appointment of the three assistant managers, Bliss had more control of his time.

When, in December 1981, Franco Zeffirelli's new *La Bohème* was savaged by the critics but adored by the public, Bliss realized that there was a solution other than Dexter's to the dearth of superstars. While Dexter wanted to concentrate on theatrical productions peopled by singing actors who were not necessarily the most famous singers, the vast scale of Zeffirelli's productions dwarfed the singers so completely that it hardly mattered who was onstage. The sets were enormous and the number of supers onstage often numbered in the hundreds. At an early rehearsal that Bliss attended, Zeffirelli ran down the aisle during the second act, which utilized more than two hundred supers, screaming, "No, no, that's all wrong!" Bliss turned to the person next to him and said, "How can he tell?"

In January 1982, Bliss relayed to the executive committee Dexter's wish to become production adviser, relieving him of administrative duties and enabling him to accept more outside engagements. This change, Bliss pointed out, was possible only because Dexter had put in place a first-rate technical department. The board agreed, and Dexter officially became production adviser.

It was also possible because Bliss realized that lavish productions attracted almost as many ticket buyers as performances by Sutherland or Pavarotti. Zeffirelli's *Bohème,* followed by his *Tosca, Turandot,* and *Traviata,* became huge box office attractions. The credit "Production by Franco Zeffirelli" ensured a healthy box office, no matter who was singing. And Mrs. Harrington was delighted to provide the funds; she remembered the problems about *Don Carlo* and, in any case, her own taste clearly did not run to the starkness and severity that characterized Dexter's staging. Dexter, angry at what he saw as Bliss's abandonment of their creative quest, was bitter: "Bliss, having created the [Harrington] monster, can no longer control it."

Meanwhile, Levine, who had been spending his summers at the Salzburg Festival, developed the idea, together with the French producer Jean-Pierre Ponnelle, to do a series of Mozart operas. Dexter's success with *Entführung* was brushed aside, and Ponnelle was contracted to direct and design *Idomeneo, La Clemenza di Tito,* and *Le Nozze di Figaro.* Zeffirelli was hired to do a new *Don Giovanni.*

Levine also was swept up in the planning of his first *Ring* cycle. Günther Schneider-Siemssen, who had designed the Karajan *Ring,* was chosen to design this one as well, and the director was to be Otto Schenk, whose production of *Tannhäuser* had been so successful. Schenk and Schneider-Siemssen developed an idea of a *Ring* that could have been Wagner's own: a fairy tale straight from the Bavarian woods, with monsters, dragons, giants, disappearing and appearing sets, stage elevators ascending and descending, and an apocalyptic final scene of carnage. They would use every trick of which the Met stage was capable and would present a pictorial vision of the Wagner mythology. Those who felt stage direction had gone too far in conceptualization were thrilled; others felt the Met had taken a giant step backward from Dexter's innovative vision. Levine was blamed for the new conservatism: "Jimmy's musical taste was formed by Callas and Toscanini," said one disapproving critic, "but his visual taste is straight from the Cincinnati Zoo Opera."

Dexter, watching the frequent planning meetings with Schenk and Zeffirelli, knew that his days at the Met, even as production adviser, were numbered. He also blamed Levine. "I could not work with JL in any creative way and I do not enjoy the 'political atmosphere' he creates and the relentless pursuit of popularity in which he drowns himself like a child with a sweets' trolley."

Dexter had been disillusioned with Levine for some time, but in the early 1980s, he uncovered something going on that hurt him far more deeply. "The question is whether or not to point the finger . . . in the direction of the guilty parties, especially when at least one of the persons to be accused is, as one should have known, the last to be suspected and had until recently always been regarded as a valued associate." He meant Joseph Volpe.

From his first days at the Met, Dexter had admired and relied on Volpe, and his respect had helped Volpe make his rapid ascent to the position of assistant manager. Now it was apparent to Dexter that Volpe, having seen the power commanded by Levine and secure in Bliss's approval, was cutting his ties with his mentor. Dexter understood that the new triumvirate in power was Bliss, Levine, and Volpe. He was out.

In his notebook, Dexter summarized the situation as he saw it: Sybil Harrington had given the Met an enormous endowment; she liked nineteenth-century opera; Bliss chose her money over Dexter's taste, which had seen the company through the lean times; Levine had also chosen money over art; and, finally, "This hurt. My own discovery, someone I took from the floor and trained and promoted, betrayed me. Joe Volpe chose money over loyalty."

Crushed by what he considered Volpe's betrayal, Dexter characteristically cloaked himself in sarcasm. He began referring to Bliss as "Miss Blisskins," and to Levine as the "chubby maestro." He declared that trying to get Levine to make a decision was "like expecting Clytemnestra to fry you an egg."

"I learnt about betrayal at the Met. Betrayed on all levels—personal, professional, political, you name it," he wrote after calling from England to ask if he was expected back to direct a revival of *Parade* in 1985. ". . . Volpe called at last. He understood that I was not coming—eventually I had to ask if I was being asked not to come. Volpe said 'he'd have to work on it.' Bet your ass, Joe, you bet your ass you will."

Volpe was philosophical about the end of his close relationship with Dexter. He said:

In the early days, we collaborated. But when I moved up from technical director to operations director, I was in a position where I could tell John what to do. John, meanwhile, had become disenchanted with the Met because of Jimmy, Joan, and Sybil, and he began to care less and less about how much his productions cost. He'd tell me right to my face that I was a son of a bitch, and I'd tell him the same thing right back.

The ultimate battle was fought over a production whose costs far exceeded what was expected. Sir Peter Hall, the British stage director, had been scheduled to do *Simon Boccanegra,* but after his first two productions at the Met failed, Levine convinced Bliss that he should not be engaged again. As usual, Bliss turned to Dexter, and this time, Dexter wanted to do the production. But when he turned in his plans, they were, to use Volpe's word, "huge." Volpe said flatly no; the Met could not afford to present Dexter's production. Instead, he borrowed a *Boccanegra* from another opera house. "In his eyes," Volpe said, "I became a traitor."

As the Met approached its Centennial season, 1983–84, Bliss more and more sided with Levine when there were difficulties with Dexter. "It's a musical house," Bliss repeated many times. Dexter's acerbic manner did not help. Levine, although somewhat elusive, remained affable. He began to campaign hard for the title of artistic director and, since he was already filling that role, Bliss gave the idea favorable consideration.

When the Centennial season opened in September 1983, Dexter's name still appeared as production adviser. But just before the season opened with a lavish revival of *Les Troyens,* Levine achieved what he had wanted: at the age of forty, he was named artistic director of the Metropolitan Opera, thereby gaining greater control over artistic decisions than anyone had had, except the general managers.

In the second month of the Centennial season, Bliss also saw the fulfillment of a dream. On the morning of October 22, the company's one hundredth birthday and the day of the company's Centennial Gala, the Met and its orchestra announced their agreement on a new three-year contract, nine months before the current contract expired. For the first time in years, the company had been able to avoid confrontation and arrive at an amiable compromise. Bliss accorded all the credit to Joseph Volpe.

Five months later, in March 1984, Bliss, his health suffering from accumulated stress, announced his intention to resign from the post of general manager, and the board formed a search committee to find his successor. A year later, Frank Taplin suffered a major heart attack and resigned as president of the Met. With these two stalwarts receding in importance, Levine's position became even stronger.

John Dexter's name disappeared from the roster by 1984. Over the next few years, he appeared from time to time to direct revivals of his past triumphs, but his was a fleeting presence. And he had changed: he was pale, thin, and listless. Dexter had, however, a major success on Broadway in 1988 with _M. Butterfly,_ the play by David Henry Hwang, and, for a brief period, his life was joyful again. In June, he won a Tony Award as best director and the play was awarded the prize as best play. But, a year later, his production of _The Threepenny Opera_ with the rock singer Sting failed miserably; it opened on November 4, 1989, and closed in less than two months. An ill-conceived production of _Gigi_ in London suffered the same fate.

After that, Dexter's health deteriorated; his diabetes worsened, and in February 1990, he had a heart attack. His long history of drug use and illness had taken its toll and his recovery was slow. When he was better, his doctor recommended heart surgery. On Friday, March 23, 1990, in a London hospital, John Dexter died during the operation. He was sixty-four. "Fury for perfection makes me difficult to work with," he had said. "[People] have no right to stand next to me unless they are insured against fire." His anger toward the Met, especially toward Levine and Volpe, was fierce to the end. "Jimmy and Joe killed John," Riggs O'Hara said.

Chapter Twenty

THE HOUSE SOPRANO

Anyone who observed the Italian soprano Renata Scotto at the outset of her career in the early 1960s would have had difficulty imagining the imperious and controversial diva she would become twenty years later when she had become the Met's leading soprano. The young Renata Scotto was a pretty woman, tiny yet plump; she was described by Andrew Porter, the *New Yorker*'s music critic, as "a dear, bright little bundle."

Scotto may have been young, but she had no intention of remaining anyone's bundle. Her career began just as Maria Callas and Renata Tebaldi were fading. Even as a young singer, Scotto had many characteristics similar to those of Callas, and the Greek soprano was her heroine; she particularly admired the dramatic intensity Callas brought to her roles. What Scotto underestimated was the passion Callas inspired in her admirers.

When Scotto did her first *Vespri Siciliani* at La Scala, Callas was in the audience, and the audience applauded her, not Scotto. Scotto may have admired Callas, but she was also a true diva and the public's tribute to the older singer infuriated her. She told the *New York Times*, "I said, 'Callas, if you want to sing, please come to me and I'll let you sing, *if you can* . . . I am the one who is singing *Vespri.'* It's fine to have respect for her, but she *was*. She is past. Now you have to go with me."

With this gesture, Scotto turned the Callas lovers into Scotto haters. Those who should most have admired her performances became her enemies.

But Scotto refused to disavow her truculent attitude, even as the Callas fans launched a campaign of booing and catcalls against her. She became renowned for her interpretation of Cio-Cio-San in *Madama Butterfly,* but she hated the fact that this was the role every opera house wanted her to sing. She had, after all, little in common with the frail Puccini heroine who was the victim of an unfeeling American. Scotto was not a victim.

Eventually, the Metropolitan wanted her, and of course they asked her to sing *Butterfly,* the role in which she would make her debut. But what she wanted was not another *Butterfly* production. She wanted opening night, new productions. She announced that she would not sing at the Met again until they gave her what she wanted.

Finally, she was offered a role she considered challenging, the 1975 *Vespri Siciliani,* with John Dexter directing and James Levine conducting. In 1975–76, the Met gave her everything she wanted, both opening night and a new production; in 1976–77, they also gave her something she didn't know she wanted, the first Met live telecast, *La Bohème,* with Luciano Pavarotti, and suddenly she was a true American opera star. Her Met contracts stretched years into the future, so accompanied by her husband, the former concertmaster of La Scala who was now her manager, Scotto moved to New York to become the Met's reigning diva.

Dexter admired her as an actress and loved her fighting spirit. Levine loved her even more. His propensity has always been for singers who bring passion to their roles, even at the occasional expense of vocal perfection. Montserrat Caballé, Kiri Te Kanawa, Mirella Freni, were rare visitors to New York during the Scotto years: Caballé, at the time Scotto's chief rival in the Italian repertory, antagonized Levine by showing up unprepared for several operas; Freni avoided the United States for years because of income tax problems. Their many admirers resented their absence. But Levine was in love with Scotto as a performer. "She is a direct descendant of the great, expressive Italian sopranos," he told the *Times.* Scotto's hold on the role of house soprano tightened, and soon it seemed that she was singing everything at the Met.

Scotto's appearance in the 1977 *La Bohème* had been a revelation to opera lovers all across the United States who discovered a soprano who could act. It was a different revelation for Scotto herself, however. Until she saw herself on television, she had no idea how fat she had become.

The subject of eating and singers has given rise to countless theories. Francis Robinson, who dealt with many singers during his years as a Met assistant manager, said, "They're larger than life. They have to be. You're not going to pay our prices to see somebody who's just like the girl next door. . . . They stand out. Thank God."

Singers travel constantly, from city to city, country to country, continent to continent, as they fulfill their contracts. As a result, many are often alone much of the time. "People don't realize it," Marilyn Horne, who also struggled with her weight, said, "but ours is a very lonely profession. Eating is company."

Essential to every singer's vocal production and stamina is the phenomenon known as "support," the singer's ability to control the muscles of the diaphragm that enable him or her to sing and breathe. When a singer loses weight, those muscles may sag, and unsupported singers wobble, scoop, shriek, and sing off-pitch. The one area of agreement among throat doctors is that the worst way for a singer to lose weight is quickly, as Scotto had. Crash diets weaken the support muscles just as a long illness does. They can also affect moods in already volatile artistic temperaments.

Scotto dieted with the same fervor she brought to every aspect of her life, and when she returned to the Met in the fall of 1977, she was unrecognizable. Singers and conductors who had known her for years walked right by her backstage. The dear little bundle had been replaced by a slender, elegant woman. Her glamour was certified when she was photographed for one of the Blackglama mink advertisements, "What Becomes a Legend Most."

Unfortunately, Scotto adopted an imperious manner to match her figure; she stalked through the Met corridors like a small tigress in spike heels, rarely smiling or granting a nod of recognition. The comparisons to Callas, who had also lost much weight midway through her career, only angered her.

And if it is true that extreme dieting can degenerate the artistic temperament, Scotto was a prime example. She developed an intense jealousy of her *Bohème* co-star, Pavarotti. In 1979, the two collaborated in a televised performance of *La Gioconda* at the San Francisco Opera. Before Scotto even arrived in San Francisco, her husband sent a telegram to the intendant, Kurt Herbert Adler, demanding that Scotto be guaranteed the same amount of time on camera as Pavarotti. Otherwise, he warned, she would walk out.

When Scotto arrived, she found the usual hate mail from Callas devotees, but this time she became convinced that Pavarotti was behind the letters. She was so angry that when, in the televised opera performance, Pavarotti took a solo curtain call at the end of act 4, the act that contained her great aria, "Suicidio," she lost control. She refused to take her own curtain call, stormed back to her dressing room, threw Adler out of the room, and screamed curses at Pavarotti. What she forgot was that this was a telecast, and one that featured extensive coverage of life backstage. Every single thing she did was recorded and, since it made wonderful television, was shown around the world when *Gioconda* was aired. Her unpopularity exploded.

As it happened, Scotto's erratic behavior coincided with a perceptible decline in her voice. Whether the vocal deterioration precipitated her tantrums is a valid question; an insecure singer is usually an irritable colleague. She was far too intelligent not to know that she was squandering vocal capital as she moved into heavier repertory. Levine, although knowledgeable about vocal technique, was hungry to do the operas containing the great dramatic roles so suited to Scotto's temperament, if not her voice. He acquiesced in her ventures into ultimately damaging repertory.

For opening night of the 1981–82 season, Levine fulfilled Scotto's long-held desire to sing the title role of Bellini's *Norma*. Scotto was forty-seven, and that this had been one of Callas's most acclaimed parts only whetted Scotto's appetite to sing it.

The atmosphere was festive for the opening of the first season after the 1980 labor problems. More than seven hundred people came to the dinner before the performance, and the box office receipts of $365,000 were the highest of any opening except the debut of the new house. Fund-raising had held up remarkably well during the truncated season the year before, and the endowment campaign was thriving.

The trouble began after dinner, when the curtain went up on *Norma*. When Scotto, singing the role for the first time anywhere, made her entrance, someone screamed out, "Brava, Callas!"

As the Met's security staff removed the shouter from the auditorium,

Scotto bravely attempted to continue. But when she concluded the opera's most famous aria, "Casta diva," booing erupted throughout the theater. As the evening progressed, the booing alternated with outright laughter. Most singers would probably have walked off and refused to continue, but Scotto kept going. The customary curtain calls after act 1 were dropped, and James Levine was booed when he entered the pit to begin act 2. At the final curtain calls, Scotto's appearance provoked a mixture of catcalls and bravos. Scotto, however, took her final bow and then thrust her arm upward in a clear gesture of her scorn toward the audience.

The next day, the Associated Press called it "the Met's most unruly opening night," and the reviews were devastating. The _Daily News_ called the audience's behavior "execrable," but _Newsday_ said, "Renata Scotto essayed the role of Norma and failed terribly."

That Scotto was able to finish the performance was amazing; her most distinctive characteristic, her iron will, kept her going. Despite having been gored at the _Norma_ opening night, three months later, she gave brilliant performances in all three roles of Puccini's triptych _Il Trittico_. Scotto had been acclaimed for her interpretation of this opera, and she enjoyed the chance to exhibit her acting skill in three contrasting roles, showing sexual frustration, religious obsession, and innocence in one three-opera evening.

Reassured by the success, she and Levine scored triumphs: her terrifying interpretation of Lady Macbeth in an otherwise scorned new production by Sir Peter Hall of the Verdi opera; the title role of Zandonai's almost unknown _Francesca da Rimini;_ and she even survived another booing incident during a live telecast of _Luisa Miller._ In 1983, _New York_ magazine praised Scotto as "a more confident singer than she was a year ago." Her extraordinary determination had pulled her through a disaster that would have ended the careers of most singers.

Finally, however, the vocal damage from singing the heavy roles could not be denied, just when a new generation of young sopranos like Carol Vaness, Aprile Millo, and Renée Fleming with healthy, beautiful voices was emerging. These sopranos easily sang the roles that Scotto performed only by steely determination. Levine could not help noticing, and Scotto found herself cast less and less often. Her mentor had deserted her.

The end of her Met career was a personal as well as professional heartbreak. "She was truly in love with Jimmy," a member of the Met's music staff said, "not just musically, but as a man, too." The wounded soprano sang her final role on the Met stage; ironically, it was *Madama Butterfly*.

WHITHER THE MET?

In the mid-1980s, the United States was enjoying bountiful times, a period of lavish entertaining and spectacle, and the emergence of a new breed of wealthy people following the boom of mergers, acquisitions, and takeovers. Names such as Steinberg, Milken, Kravis, and Pomerantz began to jostle the Rockefellers, Blisses, Vanderbilts, Astors, and Goelets on lists of Met donors. The new rich attended the opera, and as in the company's early days, attention often shifted from the stage to the boxes. Opera was a favorite beneficiary of the nouveau riche because they became part of the show. On opening night, there were three opera performances: the jewels and lavish gowns on the Grand Staircase before the curtain, the opera itself, and the parties afterward.

Once more, the Met could not afford to turn a cold shoulder to the newly rich because, despite the public stance celebrating its financial security, the company was still struggling. The "New Met" needed major repairs after only sixteen years; it was structurally sound but in dire need of refurbishment and heavy-duty cleaning. The massive rear-stage sound curtain collapsed in December 1981, and it was a miracle no one was killed. The offices had become so crowded with expanded marketing and development staff that Bliss moved the scenic and carpentry shops to a warehouse the Met purchased in Weehawken, New Jersey. This was interpreted by company members as an indication of Bliss's corporate mentality; there was room in the opera house for "all those people with clipboards," as one chorister said, but not for the scenic artists and carpenters who created what was seen onstage.

The 1982–83 season opened in late September. During the earlier rehearsal weeks, Jane Hermann presented Yves Montand's one-man show, which was a success financially—all seven performances sold out—and artistically. If the Met was to experiment with pop culture, Yves Montand had the elegance to make the crossover.

The first new production of the season, however, was a disaster of classic proportions. "The quicker said the better," the *Times* review began. "Peter Hall's *Macbeth* is the worst new production to struggle onto the Metropolitan Opera's stage in modern history." This may have been hyperbole, but no one in the theater was happy about *Macbeth*. Levine had publicly stated, that with the departure of John Dexter, he hoped never again to have to conduct a production he disliked, so he maintained a brave front throughout the initial run, but his feelings did not bode well for Sir Peter's future at the Met.

Theater people believe that to speak aloud the title *Macbeth* is bad luck, and it is usually referred to as "the Scottish play." The Met's production bore out this superstition. At the premiere, the audience laughed out loud at the opening scene and its depiction of the witches. Although Verdi specified only eighteen in three covens of six, there seemed to be hundreds of them on the Met stage, swooping around on broomsticks, clutching stuffed black cats, and surrounded by rubber bats. Later on, large polyester apparitions loomed out of the witches' cauldron, Banquo's ghost popped up and down through a visible trapdoor, a corps de ballet costumed as the Wilis from *Giselle* appeared out of nowhere, and Hecate arrived onstage completely naked, except for an illuminated crown.

During the 1983 tour, *Macbeth* went on the road, and although the witches were toned down considerably, the nude Hecate was retained for the tour. When the company arrived for a three-day visit to Memphis, Tennessee, scandal again made front-page headlines. The city fathers of Memphis had recently banned performances by strippers in local nightclubs, a restriction that had provoked much controversy. When the strippers learned that the Metropolitan Opera, that national cultural pinnacle, was about to display frontal nudity, they announced that they would picket the Met performances to protest unequal treatment.

Soon the controversy was picked up by the wire services and became national news. Paparazzi roamed Memphis trying to find the actress who portrayed Hecate while she hid in her hotel room to avoid any more excitement. The night of the performance, *Time* and *Newsweek* were among the unlikely national publications covering a Met tour performance, and the protesting strippers did not disappoint the reporters. When the Hecate scene began, the strippers, who had bought tickets and were seated in the balcony, took off their blouses and shone flashlights on their bare breasts. Somehow, complete bedlam was avoided, but the refined reputation of the Met's annual visit to Memphis was tarnished.

Macbeth was revived several times, even with its unlucky aura, and in January 1988, it was brought back for several performances, culminating in a national broadcast of the matinee on Saturday, January 23.

Everything was going well that afternoon when the curtain came down for intermission at about 3:20 P.M. In List Hall, the broadcast Opera Quiz began, and audience members began filing out of the auditorium for a coffee or a drink in the lobby. Backstage, the singers, chorus, and orchestra took a break in the company cafeteria. A few minutes into the intermission, the usual buzz that was transmitted to the backstage audio speakers was replaced by blood-chilling screams.

An elderly man had plunged from the Family Circle tier, which is on a level with the chandeliers. Falling the equivalent of five stories, the man struck and broke a rail of the balcony before landing in an aisle on the orchestra level. He narrowly missed hitting several people. Witnesses later said that they had seen the man, impeccably dressed in a dark blue pinstriped suit, with a pocket watch on a chain, climb onto the railing around the Family Circle and rock back and forth. An usher ran down the steps to stop him, but the man jumped from the guardrail.

The scene on the orchestra level was horrible, since the man had been decapitated when he hit the seats. The police arrived, the auditorium was closed, and, backstage, administrators tried to figure out what to do. Met performances do not stop in midstream, particularly during a broadcast. The intermission Opera Quiz ended, and the Met's unflappable announcer, Peter Allen, began an unrehearsed discussion of Verdi, *Macbeth*, the afternoon's singers, and anything else he could think of. Finally, a taped singers' round-table discussion from a past broadcast was found and put on the air. Allen informed the radio audience only that there had been an accident, which was delaying the performance.

The Met's phones were jammed by calls from curious listeners as well as from frightened people whose friends and family were at the opera and who wanted to know what the "accident" was. The Met press office was well aware, after the Hagnes murder, that when the police arrive, the press is not far behind, so it issued statements. An NBC newsman who had been listening to the broadcast heard Allen's vague reports even as the AP wire into the newsroom was carrying details of the fall. In the end, the remainder of the performance was canceled.

The fall had been a suicide. The victim had been a devoted Met standee, someone known to everyone in the opera house because of his nightly presence and his courtly manners. Bantcho Bantchevsky had been a Bulgarian vocal coach, and, now retired, his attendance at the Met had become his whole life. When illness and old age made that life unbearable, there was only one place he wanted to die.

The incident evoked memories of the Hagnes murder, but when the New York City medical examiner promptly ruled Bantchevsky's death a suicide, the story faded. So did the Peter Hall production of *Macbeth* and the presentation of the opera. *Macbeth* has not been seen on the Met stage since that Saturday afternoon.

*I*n the early 1980s, the group of tenors singing the Italian repertory at the Met were hard to tell apart. All were in their early forties, not particularly handsome, but endowed with voices easily capable of filling the Met's auditorium. They sang adequately but without much individuality and even the artistic administrators had trouble sorting them out. Their names are not familiar to most operagoers: Giorgio Merighi, Giorgio Lamberti, Giuliano Ciannella, Bruno Beccaria, Amadeo Zambon, Vasile Moldoveanu. A board member was heard to observe that he believed they were all actually the same person.

Carlo Bini, although Italian and a tenor, was not as interchangeable as the others. Young, handsome, and personable, he joined the Met in 1978, and soon became popular with everyone. His English was limited, but he had a quick, friendly smile. When he walked into the press office or the rehearsal department, he was not greeted with the stifled groans or barely concealed impatience that other singers often encountered; people were glad to see him.

Many of the interchangeable tenors had omnipresent wives, women who tended not to speak English and appeared sullen and suspicious, vigilant to any threat to their husband's virtue. Carlo Bini also had a hovering wife, Margaret, an Englishwoman nicknamed Bunny. But though Bunny Bini was around the theater more than seemed necessary, she was pleasant and communicative.

Carlo Bini was a hard worker and a quick study. When José Carreras canceled an engagement of *Luisa Miller* during Bini's first year, the new tenor learned the role in four days. The Met rewards this kind of dedication and ability; Bini became a regular with the company, serving as cover to major artists and singing his own principal roles. Frequently, he had to step into a part at the last minute, and he always did a creditable job.

In the autumn of 1982, Bini's contract included covering Plácido Domingo as Enzo in Ponchielli's *La Gioconda* on the night of October 13. Bini had arrived in New York only two days earlier, so he spent part of the day of his arrival with the *Gioconda* staff director learning part of the staging. No one was concerned about his preparation; he had proven himself as a competent cover several times. The Met had confidence in him even though the evening's conductor was Giuseppe Patané, who was not flexible with last-minute cast changes.

The artistic administration was reassured that among the cast members that night were several experienced Met singers, including Mignon Dunn as Laura and John Cheek as Alvise. In addition, Matteo Manuguerra, the Barnaba, was an Italian baritone of the old school who could have sung the role in his sleep.

But the woman singing the leading soprano role was something of a problem. Eva Marton, a tall, smoldering Hungarian dramatic soprano, had accumulated a devoted and vociferous Met following since her triumph in

Die Frau ohne Schatten in 1981–82. She was not a particularly intense singer: the drama in her performances was vocal, not visceral. She sang roles that had not been satisfactorily cast for years: the Empress in _Frau,_ the title role of _Turandot,_ and Ortrud in _Lohengrin._ Tall and imposing, Marton was a striking woman from a distance. Up close, however, one saw her coarse features, dominated by a pair of ice-cold blue eyes. She did not waste her dramatic energy on courtesy to her colleagues or to the Met staff, and often was heard to ask someone to leave her dressing room with a shout of "You! Get out!" Her softer side emerged at parties, when she might end the evening by singing her favorite pop song from the musical _Cats,_ "Memory," or, as she pronounced it, " 'Mammaries' from 'Katz.' " She was physically strong and reliable in performance, and her outbursts of displeasure could be very loud.

Plácido Domingo, usually professional and thoughtful of his colleagues' feelings and his own responsibility to the audience, was suffering from a bad cold. He alerted the artistic department that he intended to start the performance but that it would be wise to have his cover nearby.

On the nights when they are under contract, Met covers must be within a phone call's reach and able to reach the opera house in twenty minutes. In the past, disasters had struck when sudden indisposition overcame a singer and the cover was nowhere to be found. If a scheduled principal alerts the company that he or she is unwell, the cover must be in the opera house during the performance, and the costume shop has his or her cover costume clean, ironed, and waiting.

Bini was happy to sit in the audience that evening, because he had two scheduled performances of _Gioconda_ the following week, and he wanted to study the staging and familiarize himself with Patané's interpretation. He had already had two staging rehearsals, but not his musical run-through with Patané. He settled into his seat; he knew Domingo was not one who canceled, and he had seen the tenor arrive backstage on schedule even though he was unwell. Everything seemed in order.

The theater was sold out; the audience enthusiastically awaited the performance. Just before act 1, the stage manager emerged from behind the gold curtain, and a huge collective moan arose. Quickly, the stage manager reassured the public that, although Mr. Domingo was not feeling well, he intended to perform. The Met, as it has traditionally and quaintly done under such circumstances, "begged the audience's indulgence." The audience clapped and seemed happy to comply.

Domingo did sing the first act, in which the tenor role is brief and not too demanding. But by the time the curtain fell on that act, he realized that he was much sicker than he had thought. He went to Charlie Riecker, the artistic administrator on duty, and, with regret, said he could not continue.

Within seconds, Bini was summoned backstage. While Domingo undressed in the first tenor dressing room, Bini was rushed into an empty room. Immediately, he was surrounded by the dressers, pulling his arms and legs into Enzo's costume; the makeup artist, daubing at his face; and nervous assistant conductors and coaches, showering him with advice. Everyone, especially the tenor, knew that he had had no musical rehearsal for the role.

The makeup man was smudging some color onto Bini's pale features when, over the backstage speakers, he heard the stage manager's announcement. "As you know, Mr. Domingo this evening has been attempting to sing through a heavy cold. Although he wanted to finish the performance, he has determined that he will be unable to do so." Bini heard the disappointed groans from the audience.

"We are pleased to announce that Carlo Bini will step into the role of Enzo so that the performance can continue." There was a spattering of unenthusiastic applause.

The stage manager returned to his desk backstage. "Maestro to the pit," he called. "Act Two principals onstage. Curtain going up."

Led by an assistant manager, Bini made his way through the darkened backstage, clambering over cables. Now he was in the wings, and then, with a push, he was onstage, blinking in the strong lights. Directly ahead lay the most famous tenor aria in the opera, "Cielo e mar," sung by Enzo at the very beginning of the act. As Bini took his position, he remembered the one thing that had been left out of his frantic preparations. He had not warmed up.

"Cielo e mar" is technically difficult, and its familiarity makes any vocal misstep instantly apparent. Bini, under enormous pressure, nervous, unprepared, sang the aria badly.

The audience reacted with prolonged booing. Perhaps they were angry at Domingo for disappointing them; perhaps they were truly outraged at Bini's performance. Normally, the Met audience rarely boos during an act; they save their most intense demonstrations for curtain calls. There are exceptions; certain famous singers seem to attract as high a level of hatred as of affection. Carlo Bini was not one of these famous singers; to the audience, he was unknown.

As the booing died away, Mignon Dunn made her entrance, sailing out from the wings in a boat. A warm and sympathetic woman, she reached out to Bini and embraced him. Her gesture was meant as a sign of support, but she had an ulterior motive. Dunn was afraid that unless she held Bini, he would run off the stage.

Patané kept beating time, and the performance went on. Every time Bini opened his mouth, the booing began again. Other audience members tried to shut up the hecklers by screaming back. Up in the Family Circle, the Met's top balcony, where the fans are the most avid, fistfights started and people on opposite sides slapped each other with programs.

Finally, Patané had had enough. He stopped the orchestra and turned to the audience. "Have at least some respect for Ponchielli!" he shouted. "If you don't like it, don't clap!"

He turned back to the orchestra and began conducting again, and Bini continued to struggle through the act, the audience howling at every error. He was so upset that in the intermission after act 2, he sat in his dressing room, sobbing. The Met's artistic administration went into high gear and cajoled him back onstage.

But the conductor's fragile nerves could bear no more. He collapsed on the podium as the third-act curtain came down and had to be carried from the pit by two orchestra members. The house doctor was summoned to the conductor's dressing room on A-level, and the diagnosis was made: fluctuating blood pressure. Patané could not complete the performance.

Just as every singer at the Met is protected by a cover, so is the conductor. The artistic administrator summoned Eugene Kohn, a young staff conductor, and told him that he would have to go on for the fourth and, thankfully, final act.

In Eva Marton's dressing room, Riecker apprehensively told her the latest development. "I only want to ask one question," she said. "Has the orchestra gone home?"

Assured that the orchestra had not deserted, she said imperiously, "Then I will stay!" and headed for the stage. The fact that her big aria, "Suicidio," is in the fourth act probably influenced her decision. Somehow, she, the orchestra, the new conductor, the tearful Bini, and the rest of the cast managed to finish the opera.

Anthony Bliss was a man to whom courtesy under pressure was second nature, and he was horrified the next morning when he read about the audience's behavior in the performance report. He told the Associated Press, "Bini is a highly respected international artist. . . . This booing is new and I hope it doesn't spread. The only alternative is to have the curtain stay closed. I hope we're not coming to that."

With that official support, the amiable Bini tried to make the best of what had happened. He bravely dismissed the evening as "a funny performance," and then asked for a thorough musical rehearsal.

Patané, on the other hand, canceled the rehearsal scheduled for the next morning for _Un Ballo in Maschera_ and issued ominous warnings about the state of his health.

The New York press, of course, pounced on the story. The Associated Press sent a lengthy report over the wire that ran throughout the country. The _Times_, which had always relished backstage intrigue at the Met, ran several stories dissecting the _Gioconda_ catastrophe.

When the _Times_ realized that Bini was scheduled to sing the next _Gioconda_ performance on Tuesday, October 19, the editors decided on full-scale coverage. They assigned not one but three reporters to cover Bini's second Enzo: one critic to review the performance, one reporter backstage to observe Carlo and Bunny, and one in the Family Circle to mingle with the more rabid fans.

Although many other performing arts organizations would have been delighted with a _New York Times_ presence of this size, the Met was worried. Bini himself had publicly dismissed the night of booing to the AP as "everything is making a big casserole," but people in the company saw how traumatized he had been. The _Times_ coverage guaranteed that the Bini episode would become Met legend. The Met's press staff spent the evening of October 19 chasing *New York Times* reporters all over the opera house, while the artistic administration tried to keep things calm in the dressing rooms.

Bini's prosaic activities before the performance were noted in numbing detail. What distressed him most, he revealed, were the dramatic reports of his misfortune that were appearing in the Italian press. He felt even more pressure to outdo himself in New York and restore his reputation in his country.

But, as the *Times* sadly noted, there was no fairy-tale ending. Bini sang as respectably as he had in innumerable other performances during his career, and received the same polite, unenthusiastic reviews. The *Gioconda* fiasco became one of those Met nights that people boast about having witnessed. The opera world loves such evenings; they reflect the high drama, broad comedy, and suspense of the best opera plots. The Metropolitan had received amused yet affectionate coverage, and Domingo was reassured once more that he was irreplaceable.

It is easy to ignore the darker side, to forget that these evenings when the drama onstage merges with the drama backstage often exact a high human cost. Patané never returned to the Met; he died of a heart attack during a performance in Europe several years later.

As for the genial Carlo Bini, "I feel I'm a little bit unhappy," he told the *Times* that night, "but I love the Met and the American audience. We say, in Italian, time cures all things."

Time was not to cure this thing. In effect, Carlo Bini's career ended the night of *Gioconda*. He never returned to the Metropolitan, and his name gradually disappeared from casts in Europe and South America.

JAMES LEVINE IN ASCENDANCE

From James Levine's first weeks at the Met, he had stated that he wanted to widen the company's repertory by exploring lesser-known operas by great composers and reaching into twentieth-century opera, an area that had been virtually untouched by Bing. In those days, Bing had limited his experimentation because he believed the public would not support new operas. "That may have been true in the 1950s," Levine said in 1981. He and Joan Ingpen decided the gamble on low box office sales was worthwhile, and he pressed Bliss to plan seasons that were more adventurous.

But while Levine wanted to be musically bold, theatrically he was a conservative. When Jean-Pierre Ponnelle did his trio of Mozart operas between 1982 and 1985, he joined Franco Zeffirelli and Otto Schenk on Levine's elite producer list. For several years, these three men directed nearly everything done at the Met. They were responsible for enormous, literal productions that exactly suited Levine and also Sybil Harrington, who cheerfully wrote checks to subsidize many of them. Only Joan Ingpen, accustomed to the more daring European stagings, quibbled with this reliance on "safe" directors. "Why are the rich so unadventurous?" she asked rhetorically in a *Times* interview. Sybil Harrington took her question personally and was hurt.

The new productions pleased the Met audience. Levine, who was planning a new production of Schoenberg's *Moses und Aron* with Ponnelle for the Salzburg Festival, let it be known that he would like to do the work in New York. Bliss agreed, and for three seasons, Levine tried to fit it into the Met schedule, but the piece required marathon rehearsals for the chorus and orchestra. He finally had to admit that the company was not ready to do *Moses und Aron* up to his standards, and he reluctantly shelved the work. Even when the much-smaller New York City Opera put on a production, Levine bided his time. He was determined to do the piece, but only when he judged his company was ready to do it right.

All of Levine's plans were subject to Bliss's veto on financial grounds, and Bliss used this power, as he did in refusing a new production of *Les Troyens*. Levine chafed under Bliss's restrictions, and he began to drop hints that perhaps time had come for a change at the top.

Levine's career outside the Met was expanding. He still made a point of limiting his guest appearances so that he could spend most of his time in New York, but that seemed only to make orchestras and opera companies want him more. He had his choice of all the major American orchestras, but believing that every musician needed experience in Europe, Levine concentrated on the German-speaking countries. He was a frequent guest with both the Vienna and Berlin Philharmonics, and made records on an ambitious scale with Vienna. His summers were spent commuting between the festivals in Salzburg and Bayreuth. He became only the third American to conduct at Bayreuth, the festival conceived by Richard Wagner and still controlled by the Wagner family.

In 1982, Levine was chosen personally by Wolfgang Wagner, the composer's grandson, to conduct the centennial production of *Parsifal* at Bayreuth. This opera was already one of Levine's signature pieces; when Leonard Bernstein heard him conduct it in 1979, he wept; it was, he said, the most beautiful *Parsifal* he had ever heard. Bernstein would have understood why Levine ignored the outrage of other Jews over his engagements at Bayreuth, Hitler's chosen music festival, and Salzburg, another of Hitler's favorite musical centers. Bernstein himself often conducted at Salzburg, and especially enjoyed bringing the Israel Philharmonic there to perform.

Levine is a thoroughly secular Jew who has frequently conducted on the Jewish High Holy Days. His parents were Reform Jews, and, although his grandfather was a cantor, he never had a bar mitzvah. When asked by *Time* magazine about conducting at Bayreuth, his answer was curiously remote. "I wanted to go to Bayreuth," he replied, "because the only way I know to solve the enigma of Wagner's being a genius and an anti-Semite is to get as close to it as possible."

In January 1983, *Time* magazine gave its cover to James Levine, accompanied by an article titled, "Making Opera Grand: James Levine, America's Top Maestro." The cover photo showed Levine happily conducting while cradling a dollhouse-sized Metropolitan Opera House in his left arm.

The extent of Levine's power at the Met had been an issue for a long time. For many years, with Bliss's blessing, he had conducted at least 70 of the annual 210 New York performances. Everyone could hear the beneficial effect of Levine's regular and consistent discipline on the orchestra and chorus. Other supporters pointed out that one of his predecessors, Gustav Mahler, had conducted almost every performance when he was running the Vienna State Opera. "Yes, but Levine is not Mahler," the dissenters replied.

Despite his success in shaping the orchestra, he was criticized for not inviting other conductors of his stature to work with the company. "Where are Abbado, Bernstein, Mehta, Ozawa, Muti, Colin Davis, Solti, Haitink, Maazel, and others?" the press and public asked. "That was *most* unfair," Joan Ingpen said long after she had left. "Both Jimmy and I tried very hard to get all these people. The trouble with visiting conductors is that most of the people you want have other positions and can't take the time. And if they come to the Met, they want new productions, which take even more time than standard repertoire. Jim asked Zubin [Mehta], partly because he knew I didn't want him," she said with a chuckle, "but Zubin said no, because when he wasn't in New York [with the New York Philharmonic, where he was music director], he wanted to be in Europe."

Pierre Boulez's specialized repertory often overlapped pieces that Levine wanted to do himself. Riccardo Muti, who agreed to do a work from the Italian repertory, suddenly left the Philadelphia Orchestra (where he had been music director) and took the entire cast with him to do the same work at La Scala. Abbado was never asked, but, after all, he had the

Vienna State Opera and the London Symphony at the same time. Kurt Masur, who succeeded Mehta at the New York Philharmonic, was asked many times for standard repertory. Ingpen admitted that some of the lesser conductors who cropped up on the Met roster were her choices, "but they were much better musicians than some of the young conductors who were better known," she said. Scheduling difficulties were eventually worked out with many conductors: Andrew Davis came several times, as did Leonard Slatkin; Seiji Ozawa came for a revival of *Eugene Onegin*, Bernard Haitink for *Fidelio*, and Klaus Tennstedt, also for *Fidelio*. Before his death, Karl Böhm was a fixture at the house. The Met even succeeded where almost everyone else had failed when it lured the elusive Carlos Kleiber for performances of *La Bohème*, *Der Rosenkavalier*, *La Traviata*, and *Otello*, over several seasons before he vanished again from performing in public anywhere. "You name them," Levine said, increasingly irritated over the years by the conductor question. "I keep asking [them], and I'll continue to keep asking."

Some conductors began their careers at the Met and, by the time they were well known, were too busy to come very often. James Conlon's early career was full of engagements at the Met, but only after achieving major success in Europe was he boosted in the public's mind to top rank. Ironically, after becoming music director of the Paris Opera, Conlon had little time to accept the many Met contracts he was offered.

Levine was also accused of grabbing all the best operas for himself, casting them with the best singers, and taking most of the rehearsal time, leaving little for everyone else. But, in general, he enjoyed a lasting honeymoon with the music press; he rarely received a bad review, even if the same piece panned his singers and production. Levine himself made the best case for his domination of the conducting roster. "At every period of time in musical history where the level of performance was what it should be, the reason was that the music director was giving time to the organization. That is what gave us the Reiner Chicago Symphony, the Koussevitzky Boston, the Szell Cleveland."

His orchestra members realized exactly what Levine was creating. "Levine trains an orchestra better than anyone," said one longtime orchestra member. "This takes enormous energy. He has the patience for measure-by-measure rehearsal when other conductors are more involved in their relationship to the cosmos. He will rehearse the accompaniment to the Tchaikovsky Violin Concerto for six hours, a single chord for half the rehearsal. Anyone else would die of boredom."

The orchestra personnel changed almost completely during the Levine years. Some critics have pointed out that it is easy for a conductor to improve an orchestra if he can pick all the musicians, but Levine, in fact, has chosen few of the new musicians. The new musicians are selected after blind auditions attended by the principal players. "I couldn't believe it when I came out from behind the screen after my audition," said one of the co-principal string players, "and Jimmy wasn't there." Only rarely does Levine attend auditions, and even more rarely does he have a say when, for example, a concertmaster or associate concertmaster position is available. Some of the musicians claim that "everyone he has picked has been terrible," and on occasion these new musicians leave quickly or are demoted back into the section. The musicians chosen by the orchestra's own members have had the highest rate of success. Most impressively, Levine has brought the Met Orchestra up from mediocrity to superiority without firing one musician; he has moved people around inside their sections, in some cases to expedite retirement, but he is too kind to end a musician's career.

Levine rarely loses his temper; incidents that would cause most conductors to have a tantrum hardly faze him. At a rehearsal of the Brahms Symphony no. 1, for one of the Met Orchestra's symphonic concerts, the musicians were playing the piece together for the first time. The trombone section was missing at the start of the fourth movement, the first time these instruments play in the symphony. Opera musicians are accustomed to leaving the pit when they have long breaks, and they develop a sixth sense of when to return, often disappearing as if by magic in the middle of an offstage conversation or snack. Levine began the fourth movement of the Brahms First with no trombones, and although he kept glancing at the empty seats, he seemed confident that the musicians would appear on time. He stopped only when it was obvious they would not. "Where are the trombones?" he asked mildly, stopping the orchestra. He looked incredulous rather than angry, and dispatched the orchestra personnel manager to hunt down the missing brass. While the search was in progress, he exhibited only slight irritation to the rest of the orchestra, sitting idle in the rehearsal hall. "That's symphony orchestra behavior," he said, clearly considering an opera orchestra a more disciplined group. Then, he chatted casually with the other musicians about some concerts he had seen recently on television. When, finally, the trombonists appeared, he did not rebuke them but merely lifted his baton and started where he had left off.

Levine talks constantly during rehearsals, and this running commentary is one of the musicians' few complaints. Most orchestras lose respect and affection for their music directors over time, but the Met Orchestra personnel manager, Robert Sirinek, says this orchestra's "just grows." There is little of the usual orchestral carping, when every break is a chance to complain about the temperature, the lighting onstage, the length of the concert the night before, the overtime for the rehearsal the next day, and, especially, the conductor. One mild complaint heard around the Met Orchestra is that occasionally Jimmy, as all the musicians call him, sight-reads the score at first rehearsals for operas he has never done before. After the first rehearsal for one Met premiere, he praised the orchestra. "That was very good for a first run-through," he said, and one of the musicians replied, under his breath, "We could say the same to you."

Levine's great gift is bringing out the best in his players: he emphasizes their strengths and plays down their weaknesses. He also creates a sense of collaboration with his musicians. "If he knows that allowing you artistic freedom is going to elicit your best playing," said Julie Landsman, the Met's co-principal horn player, "he'll give you room. If you need guidance, he'll give it to you. I know what he wants, and he knows what I need."

As Levine's relationship with the orchestra became better and better, his cordial affiliation with Bliss after six years was beginning to fray. In addition to the constant frustration Levine felt at the financial restraints on his programming, he was losing Bliss's previously dependable support. Bliss wrote stern memos during the 1981–82 season expressing his dismay that artistic planning was spiraling out of control.

> I want it to be clearly understood that there is no authority at the present time to do more than four telecasts in any one season. . . . I

continue to be greatly concerned at the idea of bringing [Ezio] Frigerio in the house. . . . I find that we are moving away from the initial concepts shared . . . when our tenure began in 1975.

In August of 1982, Bliss wrote a formal letter to Levine, who was conducting at Bayreuth, insisting that a telecast of _Don Carlo_ be broadcast live to Europe but, contrary to Levine's wishes, aired on tape in the United States. "Texaco is extremely unhappy with our selections for telecasts in future seasons," he wrote, not mentioning that all the selections had been made by Levine, "and the relations with [Plácido] Domingo will not be helped if we do not telecast the _Don Carlo._ "

Levine considered this an intrusion into his territory. Bliss was also beginning to fuss about Levine's personal expense account. When he was on tour, Levine stayed at the most expensive hotel in each city, while Bliss, "to set an example for the staff," stayed at a more moderately priced one. He found it necessary to remind Levine that the Met had to watch its expenses. He had read and approved Levine's latest expense statement, "but I do want to point out that Lutèce is perhaps an expense center that does not necessarily fit with a not-for-profit center. I suggest that in the future you might omit such extravagances."

Now Levine felt it was time for a new general manager. He called one of the board members and asked him to lunch. The subject of the lunch was "What can we do about Bliss?"

Bruce Crawford, a member of the executive committee, was the president and chief executive officer of the advertising company BBDO International. He had joined the Met board in 1967, just as Bliss initiated the development of the marketing and fund-raising areas. Crawford's experience in advertising proved invaluable, and he was named chairman of the board's new electronics committee. He soon became instrumental in the company's exploration of possibilities in the growing fields of television and home video, as well as direct mail and telemarketing.

Crawford was markedly different from most of the Met board members up to this time. First of all, he worked in advertising, quite a different profession from those of the lawyers, bankers, and stockbrokers who predominated. He had been born in West Bridgewater, Massachusetts, on March 16, 1929, but disclosed little else about his early life. He had received a degree in economics from the Wharton School in 1952 and stayed on at the University of Pennsylvania to put together its development department. While there, he was active in the university's theater department and perhaps his acting pursuits explained his patrician voice, dotted only occasionally with a trace of his New England origins. He came to New York in 1956 to work in advertising, and joined BBDO in 1963.

A fastidious and elegant man, he nevertheless wore his white hair a little longer than the average Rockefeller and his suits fit much better. There was nothing remotely flashy about Crawford; he came from a town outside Boston, and his loyal support for the Red Sox matched his understated style. He had made a great deal of money, but his only obvious extravagances were a beautiful apartment and a car and driver. His refined wife, Chris, was as soft-spoken and reserved as her husband; she worked as an interior designer. The Crawfords were so aloof that little was known about their personal lives; they chose to preserve their privacy.

Crawford was an astute observer of human behavior and his comments on people were to the point and often scathing. He had dealt with artists before; he had worked with Michael Jackson on a campaign for Pepsi, so he was familiar with some aspects of the artistic temperament, although not particularly sympathetic to the childlike behavior that so often accompanies talent. He was well aware that Bliss's position needed attention. He knew how tired Bliss was, how the labor problems had worn him out and hurt him. He also believed that Bliss had already made his major contributions and believed that, after ten years in the job, it was probably time for Bliss to leave.

In March 1983, Bliss announced his resignation, to be effective at the end of the 1984–85 season. With his usual pragmatism, he wanted to give the board a healthy amount of time to find a new general manager. He suspected that the search would be difficult.

In June, the *Times* ran an article speculating that Levine was about to assume artistic control of the company, in name as well as in practice. LEVINE SAID TO SEEK ARTISTIC CONTROL OF THE MET ran the headline of the article by Harold C. Schonberg. The critic went on to predict that Levine's ambition would hamper the search for the new general manager; the Met would have to find someone willing to serve as an administrator without attempting to impose his artistic taste.

Levine, with the backing of Ronald Wilford, began to press for a new contract, although the contract he was working under would not expire for three years. Apparently, he wanted his position clarified and in place before a new general manager was named.

William Rockefeller acknowledged that "if we did not have Mr. Levine, we would be looking in a different direction." He pointed out that the board now was convinced that one man could not run the entire Met operation. "It's no longer as it was in 1950, when a Rudolf Bing could come in and take over every aspect. Today we have [an] operation that is too much for any one man to handle."

There were many possible candidates, including, once again, Lord Harewood, and the intendants of the Chicago, San Francisco, and Royal Operas. But the board openly worried that no one accustomed to having artistic control at another company, and therefore the necessary experience, would choose to come to a theater where Levine had already taken charge.

The front page of the *New York Times* carried the news on September 16, 1983, just before the opening of the Centennial. "The Metropolitan Opera yesterday announced James Levine as artistic director of the company, a position that gives him greater artistic control than anyone in the company's history except for its general manager." The change was to take place in September 1986, and Levine's official new responsibilities were listed, among them the casting and repertory and selection of stage directors and designers. Day-to-day authority on all artistic matters rested with him. The announcement was careful to stress that this was merely a formalization of Levine's de facto status at the theater. "I want to be a musician," Levine said somewhat unpersuasively, adding that had he not been given the new title, he would have reduced his commitment to the Met. The threat of his leaving was implied.

Taplin and Bliss emphasized that the general manager and the board still had the last say about financing. "The line goes from Levine to the general manager to the board," said Taplin, but Bliss, after his ten battering years at the opera house, was more realistic. "These things work in terms of personalities. . . . If a real clash came up, it would have to be resolved by the board." Taplin blithely added, "We'd just have to get a new team."

As James Levine walked into the Met pit to open the company's Centennial season, he was a happy man. His situation at the Met had been secured. At the age of forty, he was the most powerful musician in the United States and one of the mightiest in the world. Herbert von Karajan was arguably the world's leading conductor, but he was ill. Most of the music world now began to assume that Levine would replace Karajan at the helm of either the Salzburg Festival or the Berlin Philharmonic, possibly both. Both men were managed by Ronald Wilford, and, more important, beloved by him, another of the most powerful men in music. The future for Levine could not have been brighter.

Chapter Twenty-three

THE MET'S ONE HUNDREDTH BIRTHDAY
AND THE YEARS OF TRANSITION

On the night of September 25, 1983, two weeks after James Levine was appointed artistic director, the Metropolitan Opera's Centennial season opened. The opera was the expensive and extravagantly cast revival of the unpopular 1973 production of Berlioz's *Les Troyens*. Opening night featured Plácido Domingo, Tatiana Troyanos, and Jessye Norman, making her belated Met debut. In addition, the company was planning an eight-hour concert for the actual anniversary on October 22.

The preseason period was crammed with publicity: retrospectives of the Met's hundred-year history, museum exhibits, coffee-table books, a postage stamp, a poster by the artist Jim Dine, and the usual centenary presidential, senatorial, gubernatorial, and mayoral proclamations. Even the Empire State Building changed its tower lighting to red and gold, the Met colors, for the anniversary.

All the puffery was somewhat displaced by a series of articles on Domingo's role in *Troyens*. Music critics writing Centennial stories had been allowed to attend rehearsals, and they had noticed that the tenor was having difficulty with Aeneas's high tessitura. DOMINGO'S OPENING AT MET IN DOUBT was the *Times* headline on September 17; four days later, the paper reported the nonnews that Domingo had shown up for the dress rehearsal. Anyone who knew Domingo's determination never doubted that the tenor would sing opening night, and he did, as well as at a subsequent live telecast. He withdrew from later, less celebratory performances the following spring.

*O*n October 22, 1983, the company celebrated all day, not with an opera, but with a gala concert that began at two in the afternoon, was interrupted for a two-hour dinner, and ended after midnight. There were over seventy singers and conductors, some of the most famous musicians in the opera world. At the end of the evening, there was an onstage tribute to twenty-five of the company's former singers, including Zinka Milanov, Jarmila Novotna, Eleanor Steber, and Bidú Sayão. The entire day was televised across the United States and by satellite to Europe.

But during the Centennial year, while the Met garnered international attention and acclaim, it was faced with a deficit of $4 million. None of the new productions that season—Handel's *Rinaldo,* Verdi's *Ernani,* and Zandonai's verismo opera *Francesca da Rimini*—were received with much enthusiasm by the public. The best productions from the past ten years, including *Entführung, Arabella,* and five twentieth-century operas, were mounted, but box office income dropped as expenses increased. Another financial crisis loomed.

A major problem was the Centennial Endowment itself. Donors to that fund did not increase or, in some cases, maintain their usual annual contributions, so annual giving dropped off. This was what the board had always feared would happen with an aggressive endowment campaign.

Bliss took action. He closed the warehouse in Weehawken, moved the sets to containers at a nearby rented site, and had new Met sets constructed at Broadway shops. These moves alone saved $2 million a year.

He also took a strong stand on artists' fees. For years, he had gone to meetings where the heads of all major opera houses would agree on a top fee for all singers. Bliss would return to New York and decree that the top fee would be the one decided at the intendants' meeting. The other intendants would go right on giving the artists as high a fee as it took to secure them. Bliss decided that he would at least exercise control in his own house. He sent a memo to the artistic administration stating that no artist could be moved into the top fee category without his approval.

The Met also took the offensive public by announcing the loss, rather than allowing a leak; Bliss stressed the economies he was instituting and referred optimistically to "manageable deficits," which would be eliminated by the following season.

In May 1984, at the annual meeting of the Metropolitan Opera Association, Bruce Crawford was elected to be the new president, replacing the ailing Frank Taplin. In an interview with the *Times* the day he was voted in, Crawford announced that he planned to change the president's focus. Taplin had been concerned primarily with fund-raising, but Crawford planned to concentrate on running the opera house because of Bliss's impending retirement.

The search for a new general manager continued, not helped by the bad financial news. In June, August Everding, the genial intendant of the Bayerischer Staatsoper in Munich, asked to have his name withdrawn from consideration. Everding, long rumored to be the front runner, was beloved at the Met as much for his habit of gnawing on his necktie when in a creative rapture and drinking coffee cups of Scotch at rehearsals as for the popular productions he had created for the house, including *Lohengrin*, *Khovanshchina*, and *Boris Godunov*.

Why did Everding turn down the job? The New York press repeatedly posed the question, hoping some official would articulate the long-held belief that no qualified candidate would take the job as long as Levine held so much artistic power. Everding would only say that he was withdrawing because of "timing and other problems." When pressed about these problems, he said, "I don't see the value of a discussion of the other problems . . . I look forward to continuing my work at the Met."

Joan Ingpen announced that she would return to England at the end of the 1983–84 season. She had been with the Met ten years. "I told Jim [Levine] I wanted to leave because I was getting old and tired, but he kept saying, no, no, you must stay." Bliss and Crawford felt differently; they believed that, although she had resurrected the Met's casting system, her rigid operating style had now become counterproductive. She worked five seasons ahead, which meant that the company was helpless when a young singer suddenly exploded into the opera world. The Met could not engage him or her for at least five years, and then might not have the suitable repertory. The Met had missed out on the best years of some singers.

When Bliss realized that Ingpen was serious about leaving, he brought in a young man he liked to work with her. Ingpen, a caustic judge of character, knew instantly the newcomer's personality was not going to mix with Levine's. When the combination proved so bad that the young man could not even get an appointment with Levine, Ingpen helped him find another job. Then she took over the search for her own replacement.

Jonathan Friend had come to the Met from London in 1981 to work in the rehearsal department. Levine had been unhappy for some time with the man then heading rehearsal; it was a more complex job than the name would suggest, and involved not only the thirty-odd rehearsals scheduled every day, but also coachings, studio assignments, and chorus and orchestra schedules. At the time, the head of the rehearsal department was also head of the music staff: the assistant conductors, rehearsal pianists, and coaches—all vital to the work of the artistic director.

When Ingpen interviewed Friend in England, she was not overwhelmed, but she could see that he was bright and enthusiastic, so she hired him to work in the rehearsal department. Friend learned quickly, and soon the head of rehearsal was fired and Friend put in his place. When the dismissed man went to Levine to get his job back, Levine told him that the decision had been made by Bliss, and there was nothing he could do.

Two years later, Levine and Bliss asked Ingpen if she thought Friend would be a good replacement for her—he had become close to Levine in the interim. She was dubious. She told Bliss and Levine that "Jonathan can't quite do what I do . . . but I think he'd work very hard and be very loyal, so if you can't find anyone else, maybe you could try him." She was particularly concerned because she thought Friend, only thirty years old, would have trouble dealing with the delicate feelings of the singers. But Levine, who prizes loyalty, had taken to Friend, and he was given the job of artistic administrator.

The 1983–84 season, which had begun with a celebration of the company's past, ended as a season of transition to the future. With the impending departure of Bliss and Ingpen, the power shift to Levine, and Crawford as new president, the company was launched into another period of evolution.

The most conspicuous item on Anthony Bliss's desk during his eleven years as general manager was a can of Alpo dog food. Jane Hermann had given it to him after the interview in which Sally Bliss had claimed she could feed her husband Alpo without his noticing. He had received more elaborate offerings over the years—plaques, framed tributes, floral displays by the hundreds—but the can of dog food was Bliss's favorite. The next general manager was unlikely to have a sense of humor about himself.

The company had started to wonder if there would ever be a new general manager. After August Everding had withdrawn from consideration, the search committee had approached Bruce Crawford, even though he was a member of the search committee. Crawford had turned the offer down.

But, after becoming board president in May 1984, he began to spend more time at the opera house and quickly realized that the position was not as daunting as it might seem to someone not in the theater on a daily basis. He enjoyed the time he spent at the Met, gradually lessened his obligations at BBDO, and reconsidered the committee's request.

On September 29, 1984, it was announced that Bruce Crawford would become the new general manager. He would not assume the position until January 1, 1986, fifteen months later. Until then, he would remain president of the board, a job he had accepted only the previous May.

Bliss was to leave in July 1985, so there would be an interim when no one would serve as official general manager, but Crawford assured his colleagues that he could handle both Met jobs as he completed his commitment to BBDO International.

Crawford was the perfect solution to the problems created when Levine had taken over the artistic direction. He intended to concentrate on the practical aspects of managing the opera company, whose budget was rising rapidly and would reach $100 million by 1986–87.

Levine, who had courted Crawford's support for several years before he became board president, was delighted; he even expressed his pleasure at what some saw as Crawford's woeful lack of theatrical experience. Levine made a point of saying that the very lack was "in the very area of expertise in which they've already hired me. Our way of connecting is deep and efficient and buoyant and balanced."

Bliss was publicly enthusiastic; he said that Crawford had been his choice for the job. In private, he was concerned because he considered Crawford cold.

Advertising is known to some as a world of killers; anyone who rises to the top has a finely honed sense of a dangerous corporate environment and an ability to manipulate internecine politics. Crawford's courteous yet chilly demeanor inspired immediate respect and, often, fear in subordinates. A story quickly circulated among his new Met colleagues about Crawford's office at BBDO, which had been decorated in shades of white by his wife. Any visitor was offered only Perrier or white wine, liquids unlikely to leave behind untoward stains. Although devoted to his Siamese cats, Crawford was not a man who would have a can of dog food on his desk.

Crawford had been going to the Met since 1948. "I was hooked but had no money, so I would sneak into the last act or two in the Family Circle. One of the reasons Mozart and Wagner became my favorite composers was that I learned quickly that loads of people came out at intermission and gave away their tickets. It took me years to catch up with the front ends of these operas." His finances had improved over the past twenty-five years, as had his seats. During his years at BBDO International, Crawford had traveled widely, and everywhere he went he attended as many opera performances as he could squeeze in. Crawford never remained an amateur in anything that absorbed him, and he was soon highly knowledgeable about opera. "Bruce has the best ear of anyone running a major opera house," declared the late soprano Leonie Rysanek, not known to deliver unwarranted compliments.

Crawford was made chairman of the television and radio committee, an area in which he had obvious expertise, a year after he joined the board in 1976. In this role, he had been instrumental in developing the Met's electronic activities: the telecasts, a few cable television ventures, and the relatively unsuccessful venture into the home video market.

Although his new position carried enormous prestige, it also entailed a considerable drop in salary. At BBDO, his compensation had been around $750,000; in the 1970s and early 1980s, the Met general manager was paid in the range of $200,000. But Crawford had been a wily investor, and money, at least for the time being, would not be a problem.

Crawford quickly acquainted himself with every part of the opera house and was appalled at what he considered overstaffing and poorly used resources. The lack of promptness in making decisions, a well-known fault of Levine's, had infected the rest of the company as well. Crawford asked to see every piece of advertising before it ran and perused the complete repertory and casting before it was set in stone.

He directed the artistic administration to leave some spaces open in casting for new singers and never be swayed by sentimentality in the hiring of singers. Aware of the dearth of great singers, he was determined to improve the Met's program for young artists. His theory was simple: if the Met achieved a higher degree of excellence in opera, people would give it more money. And they would buy more tickets.

He explained his idea of the "tight ticket." If tickets are "tight" or "hot" for a majority of performances, sales for less-popular operas would go up. From then on, he decided the Met would draw up realistic budgets, setting lower goals for the *Wozzeck*s and *Pelléas*es. But he was also determined to have more nights with big names; he believed Pavarotti had not appeared often enough, and he set out to clear up certain misunderstandings with the tenor. Pavarotti had long felt that Levine preferred to work with Plácido Domingo. Bliss had not spent much time making the singers feel wanted; he thought they should feel honored just to be at the opera house. Crawford, to the contrary, wanted the singers to feel appreciated by the Met, which could never pay them the fees they commanded in Europe. By June 1985, UPI wires carried the story "Pavarotti and the Met Make Up," describing the pleasure of both the Met and Pavarotti that the tenor was to open the 1985–86 season with a gala *Tosca;* that the contract specifying this agreement had been signed years in advance was secondary. The article let the public know that Pavarotti was once again happy at the Met.

Crawford differed from Bliss in another important way: even before he became general manager designate, he went to the opera at least fifty times a season, and eagerly anticipated attending several performances a week, as well as all the dress rehearsals. Soon company members became accustomed to Crawford's punctual arrival at rehearsals; he would take a seat right in front of the stage director's desk and stay until the very end.

During Bliss's last season, there was a sense of discontent about the Met, both inside and outside. All the Centennial celebrations had momentarily stopped the public and press questioning why so many artists were *not* singing at the Met. But in 1984–85, a spate of artist cancellations upset ticket-buyers, and when the German conductor Klaus Tennstedt canceled his scheduled performances of *Elektra* because of illness, Levine took them over, upping his already healthy percentage of performances to an average of four a week. The Met was aware of the resentment about Levine's seeming omnipresence, but the board considered Levine so valuable they were willing to happily tolerate the wave of displeasure.

February brought the Metropolitan Opera premiere of George Gershwin's complete *Porgy and Bess.* The expensive venture was undertaken to celebrate the fiftieth anniversary of the work, for which Gershwin's estate specified that all chorus members were to be African-American. The Met hired an extra chorus to sing the *Porgy* performances but, because the company was racially integrated, had to hire very few outside singers to fill the large cast. Levine shrugged away protests that *Porgy* is not an opera: "It is a great opera and it has everything great opera has—great music, great drama and a psychological and social milieu that is as involving as the milieu of *Don Giovanni* or *Boris Godunov.*"

The public was ready to accept Gershwin at the Met, and all sixteen performances sold out, fully justifying the added expense. The critical response was almost unanimously positive, with particular praise for Levine's energy and thoroughly American sensibility.

Performances of Berg's *Wozzeck* and Mozart's *La Clemenza di Tito* did not do as well. But Levine insisted that he would continue to schedule challenging works. His theory was that the more often they were heard, the less difficult they would be. He promised to bring back *Lulu, Wozzeck, Clemenza,* and *Pelléas et Mélisande* as often as there were casts available. He was certain the audience would grow. Crawford backed him up completely.

The last new production of the season was Franco Zeffirelli's staging of *Tosca.* Advance publicity hinted that the cost surpassed $1 million, and after the public success of *La Bohème,* critics lay in wait for this new extravaganza, ready to pounce. Also popular as a target was Levine's choice for the title role. Hildegard Behrens was his favorite singer for the German dramatic soprano repertory. She had contributed memorable performances of Leonore in *Fidelio,* Elettra in *Idomeneo,* Marie in *Wozzeck,* and Isolde, but she was not known for singing Italian roles. Her being cast as Tosca was hailed by optimists as imaginative and by pessimists as potentially disastrous. There was additional pressure, because Zeffirelli had not directed *Tosca* since the seminal production for Maria Callas at Covent Garden twenty-one years previously. Comparisons between the two sopranos were inevitable.

Ironically, Behrens had made her Met debut singing an Italian role in Puccini's *Il Tabarro* during the mid-1970s and she had made an excellent impression through her stage presence and intelligence. A former law student in Germany, she had turned to singing at the late age of twenty-six and begun her operatic career in the early 1970s. Her successful career was marked more by her dramatic acting than by her voice, which was on the small side and not beautiful. But, most of the time, she made audiences forget her vocal limitations. Offstage she was not particularly beautiful, but people were attracted by her vibrancy and her powerful sex appeal. She was riveting, onstage and off.

Behrens made no secret of her unconventional life. She had two children by two different men. In her dress and manner, she was the antithesis of a diva. Many of her clothes were made of leather and suede; she never feared wearing tight skirts, and her choice of footwear was usually high boots. Her most frequent traveling companion was her faith healer. She was literate, intense, and more interested in intelligent discourse than in partying after performances. "I live very intensively, both on stage and off," she said. "I am liberated. When I do something, I do it. Either I do it all or I don't do it." James Levine loved her.

Levine had previously decided not to conduct *Tosca.* The late Giuseppe Sinopoli, who did conduct, like Behrens had started on a career far removed from music; he had been a psychiatrist. But because of an extensive contract offered to him by the august recording company Deutsche Grammophon, he went straight from his medical practice to a major conducting career. An eccentric, with long, dark hair and a full beard, he was usually garbed in a long black cape and wide-brimmed black hat. It was rumored that he was successful with women all over Europe, but he was assuredly not popular with the Met Orchestra. Oddly, for a former psychiatrist, he committed the worst sin there is for a conductor: he criticized individual musicians during rehearsals. He was rewarded with a sullen, unresponsive orchestra.

In the meantime, Zeffirelli was busy rehearsing and doing his usual publicity barrage. When one magazine canceled an interview because so many had already run, he raced to the press office, screaming that his career was ruined; the scene ended with tears on all sides.

In fact, his career at the Met was blooming. Sybil Harrington had underwritten the new *Tosca*, and the opening became, as always with any of her productions, a big social occasion. Music critics, for some reason, tended to be more caustic when surrounded by ostentatiously dressed rich people, and the *Tosca* premiere was a perfect target. The sets were beautiful, realistic, and gargantuan; the stage was filled with hundreds of supers in elaborate costumes. "I wonder if there is any singer today who could possibly compete successfully with such garish opulence," speculated *New York* magazine.

During the third act, Zeffirelli produced an effect that the critics loathed and the audiences adored. During the changeover from Cavaradossi's prison cell to the parapet on which he was to be executed, the entire Met stage moved, as the prison disappeared beneath the stage and the moonlit parapet rose into view.

Although the critics fussed about *Tosca*'s extravagance, Behrens was so popular with the music press that, even while they could not wholeheartedly commend her style, they could lavish praise on her acting. But she never again ventured into Italian opera at the Met. Sinopoli was dismissed as inept; he canceled his Met contracts and did not appear again with the company. Plácido Domingo was a bit overlooked because of the fuss over the production, as was the great Verdi baritone Cornell MacNeil, who was making one of his final appearances at the Met. But the performance was a financial triumph: single tickets sold at $250 and boxes at $2,400, huge amounts in 1985. At the party after the performance, as he celebrated his last new production at the head of the company, Bliss toasted Harrington, calling her kind of support "vital to the survival of opera in this country."

*A*nthony Bliss was in his last months as general manager, but Bruce Crawford was gradually assuming his new role. And on June 20, 1985, an announcement made by Crawford, not Bliss, indicated vividly just how completely Crawford was now in charge.

The Metropolitan Opera was canceling its annual United States tour, a part of every season since the very first, in 1883. The tour had been important; it accounted for a fifth of the Met season and a fourth of the total audience. But the tour had fallen on hard times. The big stars, with a few exceptions, had long stopped going on the tours as part of their commitment to the Met. The Met's success on television had also damaged the tour. Since 1976, the whole country had been able to watch the best of the Met from home: great singers and conductors adorned by fabulous sets and costumes, and subtitles that made the most convoluted plots manageable. When these same Met lovers went to see the company on tour, they were disappointed. Special sets built for the tour were smaller and less ornate than those in New York, because theaters of most cities could not handle the technical demands. Often, the acoustics were dreadful and, in some cases, the orchestra pits were so small that the orchestra had to be sharply reduced. In addition, regional opera had grown over the past years at a furious clip, and the tour sponsors now had to compete with their local companies in fund-raising.

Dragging a company the size of a small town around the United States was very expensive. One tour city after another found it impossible to raise the Met's vast fee; well over $1 million a week, it did not come close to covering the company's basic expenses, only those directly related to the tour.

In May 1985, the Detroit sponsors told the Met that they could not afford to pay the company, and canceled their participation in the 1986 tour. This was the death blow; Memphis, Dallas, Washington, and Boston had already cut back or canceled.

Crawford expressed his reluctance at taking such a step but said, "Touring the way the Met has always toured is a little out of date."

The cancellation of the tour was a shock to everyone, but especially to the company members who had come to see their two-month excursion as an immutable part of their lives. All of a sudden, inside the company, the realization hit that there was a new man in charge. Crawford was not someone who had grown up in the opera world, like Bing and his predecessors, or someone who had been born into the company, like Bliss. He was a realist, with a determination forged in the tough world of commercial advertising. There had been many complaints that, under Bliss and his large staff, the Met had turned into a large corporation. That was exactly what Crawford was accustomed to, and he had no blind allegiance to the beloved traditions of the company.

He quickly made clear, however, that he was not simply making negative decisions; he intended to replace the national tour with activities that would not drain the Met's resources but, indeed, would expand them. The Met and Deutsche Grammophon announced a joint project to produce recordings for the first time in almost twenty years, starting with the massive *Ring* cycle, and serendipitously providing employment for the Met Orchestra during the weeks made vacant by the tour cancellation. Levine, who hated touring and loved making records, was happy.

But Crawford wanted to initiate a series of international tours that would reap the company more money and prestige. For the first such tour, the company would travel to Japan in the spring of 1988 for three weeks of opera and concert performances. Japan, in the midst of an economic boom, was one of the few places that could afford to bring the entire company, along with singers like Kathleen Battle and Plácido Domingo.

One month after the announcement of the tour cancellation, Anthony Bliss emptied his office at the Met and the Manhattan pied-à-terre he had used while running the Met. He and his family were headed for a two-month vacation at their home on Prince Edward Island in Canada. After that, he planned to return to his old firm, Milbank, Tweed. Although the official date of Crawford's assuming the title was January 1, 1986, the office would be Crawford's; his wife already had her decorating plans in place.

In his final interview for the *Times,* Bliss expressed his pride in what he had brought about: the endowment fund, Levine's artistic leadership, the Met's television series, and, going back to his years as board president, the construction of the new house.

July 29, his last day, happened to be the day when the Met Chorus returned from vacation to start rehearsing for the new season in September. Always gracious, Bliss welcomed them back, one of his last acts as general manager. Then he went down to his car parked under Lincoln Center and drove off to Canada. He was seventy-two years old and had spent more than half his life at the Met.

Chapter Twenty-four

BRUCE CRAWFORD TAKES COMMAND

Opening night of the 1985–86 season marked a striking change in the Met's alliance with New York society, a change forged by Bruce Crawford. Crawford himself had no interest in climbing the social ladder, but he knew the company needed the kind of money represented by people eager to be bold-type names on the society pages. The columnists Suzy and Liz Smith, *Women's Wear Daily,* and the social writers at the *Post, News, Times,* and *Newsday* suddenly became recipients of seats for Met premieres.

The 1985–86 opening was the first underwritten by a commercial sponsor—a high-end sponsor but still commercial. The fashion house of Chanel used the occasion to launch its new fragrance, Coco. Chanel not only underwrote the dinner following the performance of *Tosca* but also donated $750,000 to the Met and presented a fashion show on the Grand Tier during the dinner.

As if by magic, glamour returned on a grand scale to the opera house. The lobby and balconies were filled with flowers; trumpet fanfares greeted the audience; and the grandiosities of Zeffirelli's production of *Tosca* fit perfectly. With Luciano Pavarotti onstage, accompanied by the equally robust Montserrat Caballé, the music, of course, could not be completely overlooked. James Levine took the night off, leaving conducting honors to Carlo Felice Cillario.

After the curtain came down, the candlelit dinner on the Grand Tier was the setting for the Chanel models, who glided down a specially constructed ramp around a giant facsimile of a Coco perfume bottle. Among those attending the dinner were Madame Claude Pompidou, Henry Kissinger, Oscar de la Renta, the French ambassador, and the secretary general of the United Nations. "There is a new feeling about the Met," said Schuyler Chapin, clearly delighted that Bliss, his nemesis, was gone. "This is what grand opera is all about."

Inevitably, some people were aghast. There were quiet murmurs about the "rag trade" infiltrating the Met, but Crawford was unruffled. "Chanel," he pointed out, "has a wonderful image. There is no business more elegant." And he promised more glamour and elegance.

The Met staff, meanwhile, was somewhat leery of Crawford. Unlike Bliss, who had wandered through the house with his jacket off and his tie loosened, Crawford rarely left his office. Reassuringly, he had his eccentricities; most days when he did not have a business lunch, he walked the fifteen blocks to Zabar's to buy eggs, because he considered these the best eggs in New York.

Bliss had had an open-door policy; Crawford had the opposite. A true believer in the delegation of authority, he chose to see only those department heads who reported directly to him. No longer would stagehands, orchestra musicians, and ballet dancers feel free to drop by and say hello to the general manager. But the door was always open to Cecile Zilkha, Crawford's cohort in corralling the glamour and elegance that had been missing from the Met.

A petite and immaculately chic woman who had been a board member since 1978, Cecile Zilkha, wife of the banker Ezra Zilkha, had thorough experience in fund-raising for hospitals. Crawford appointed her chairman of special events, and sent out word that any request for cooperation from Zilkha was to be treated like a direct request from him.

Despite her small and fragile appearance, Cecile Zilkha gave one the immediate impression that she could quite efficiently run IBM. She was an Iranian who had married into the Zilkha Egyptian banking family; despite their Egyptian heritage, the Zilkhas were Jewish. Her primary goal as chairman of the special events department—which, she said sweetly, "was a little asleep"—was to "maximize the revenues," by understanding how and where money could be raised. "You work just as hard making $60,000 as you do making $1 million."

Her first venture, carried out at the end of the 1983–84 season, was a Centennial Presentations Gala, nominally to celebrate the Met's summer season, but largely an excuse to have another big party that would raise lots of money. Mrs. Zilkha was determined that her gala would be elegant, fun, and, of course, lucrative. She priced the center parterre boxes at $50,000 each. "Everyone told me no one would come," she said, "but they sold out. One box even sold twice: once to Texaco and then again to a desperate donor."

For $150,000, she rented a huge tent in which to hold the party after the performance. It was erected over Lincoln Center Plaza, and was the site of a delicious after-performance supper. There was no reason for people to eat badly just because this was a charity function, she believed. In the end, the gala raised over $3 million, and every penny Zilkha spent on the party was underwritten by the corporate sponsors she had enticed to the project. No one had ever had the courage or the connections to do this.

She also established a corporate commitment to annual giving. With the important exception of Texaco, the Met had had little such support. She started holding corporate dinners on the Met stage, eliciting howls of outrage from the technical department, but raising close to $1 million each season. She set rules about her galas: no tickets would ever be given away, although most charities had a standard practice of providing free seats to celebrities in hope of attracting press coverage; she was determined that not every gala should be for the rich and resolved that at least one a year would be priced moderately to attract new people and out-of-town visitors. Much as she wanted to raise money, she also knew that to preserve the éclat of the Metropolitan name, she had to set strict limits on the evenings like the Chanel opening night. There has not been another commercially sponsored gala since opening night in 1985. Overall, Mrs. Zilkha's enterprise has enriched the Met by about $5 million per year.

Cecile Zilkha was one of the three powerful women who rose to prominence at the Met during the 1980s, continuing the tradition that had begun with Eleanor Belmont. Sybil Harrington had given enormous gifts and continued to underwrite new productions by her favorite directors and designers. Interestingly, neither Zilkha nor Harrington came from backgrounds usually associated with patronage of the Metropolitan Opera.

By contrast, Louise Ireland Humphrey had an impeccable social pedigree. In January 1986, she was elected the first woman president of the Metropolitan Opera Association. She was a member of one of the primary mining families in the United States—the Hannas, who had amassed a huge fortune when this country became industrialized—and married Gilbert W. Humphrey, a member of a prominent family of Ohio philanthropists.

Louise Humphrey's own love of music had been nurtured by her attendance at Boston Symphony concerts under Serge Koussevitzky when she attended boarding school in Massachusetts and, after her marriage, at concerts by the great Cleveland Orchestra under George Szell. She soon became a trustee of the orchestra, and also was active in the organization that sponsored the Met's visit to Cleveland each spring.

After she became president of the Northern Ohio Opera Association, she joined the Met board as one of the tour presenters, but when she became a managing director in 1974, she moved into the inner circle. She and Bruce Crawford became close, and after he resigned as board president to become general manager, she replaced him. Humphrey had seen how her fellow Clevelander, Frank Taplin, had enhanced the board president's position by keeping an office in the opera house, and she did the same. She also added a new social role to the job of president, and often gave parties in her New York apartment after first nights.

Devoted as she was to the Met, the opera was not Humphrey's whole life. She owned a five-thousand-acre plantation in northern Florida, where she lived the life of a gentlewoman farmer. Supervising a large staff, she grew corn, soybeans, peanuts, and timber, and leased much of the land to contract farmers. She also raised shooting ponies, beagles, pointers, and black Labradors, and although an avid hunter was also a protector of wildlife. Often, when Met administrators called her in Florida, they were told, "Oh, she's out beagling." She kept a close eye on the running of the plantation. "There's no fertilizer," she has said, "like the boss's foot."

Louise Humphrey, known to friends as Lulu, had the same demeanor as Anthony Bliss. Like him, she had been taught that "from those to whom much has been given, much is required." Her parents, particularly her unconventional father, who had shocked Cleveland by his swearing, brought her up to despise snobbishness and to contribute to society. As a result, her patrician manners extended to everyone in the company, although in some moments of testiness, she was heard to snap, under her breath, "N.O.C.D." ("Not our class, dear") about someone she considered vulgar. She became particularly devoted to Marilyn Shapiro, who in turn responded to her motherly manner.

Since Bliss had left, Shapiro and Joseph Volpe had unleashed their intense personal ambitions and had grown to dislike each other intensely. Crawford admired them both and, in time, made Volpe his top assistant.

But he also recognized in Shapiro a mind as sharp as his own. In July 1986, he merged the marketing department with development, and put Shapiro in charge of both.

Over the years, the company had grown accustomed to a general manager who ruled as a paternalistic autocrat. Crawford, with his background in the profit-making sector, had no interest in perpetuating this tradition. People quickly understood that if they didn't produce, they were out. The artists took notice of the new general manager's standards, as well, when Crawford fired the soprano Mara Zampieri after a disastrous dress rehearsal of *Macbeth*. Levine had been away, and Crawford made the decision unilaterally. "It was the start of the period," said one leading Met singer, "when the management [in addition to the artistic director] wanted to make the point that you can't show up at the Met and sing badly."

In the fall of 1986, William Rockefeller, who was now board chairman, was seriously injured in a riding accident, and never fully recovered. With the departure of Bliss, Taplin, and Rockefeller, by the winter of 1986 a completely new regime was in place.

The box office at this point was disastrous; 1985–86 was one of the worst years in the company's history. The repertory had been overbalanced with unfamiliar works, and the public had been frightened away.

Crawford was not discouraged; he was challenged. "I've never been terrified by business problems," he said. "When you're in a creative enterprise, it's always somewhat messy." And while he was trying to get the theater back to box office vitality, James Levine was wrestling with some very messy problems in the artistic area.

Chapter Twenty-five

Divas in Distress

In December 1985, the Met presented *Le Nozze di Figaro,* the third in its series of Mozart operas directed and designed by Jean-Pierre Ponnelle and conducted by James Levine. The cast was first-rate: the distinguished bass Ruggero Raimondi in the title role, Thomas Allen as the Count, the up-and-coming young soprano Carol Vaness as the Countess, the beloved Frederica von Stade in her signature portrayal of Cherubino, and Kathleen Battle, the woman about to become the brightest star of this operatic generation, as Susanna.

Levine admired the production of *Figaro* that Ponnelle had done for the Salzburg Festival, but, as he later conceded, even he felt some trepidation when he saw the gigantic sets looming on the Met stage. It was not that he didn't like big sets in some cases, but he had a shrewd sense of the theater's acoustics after his years there, and he saw instantly that these sets would hinder the projection of voices into the house.

From the beginning, the production was filled with tension. Kathleen Battle had become a full-fledged star in the eight years since her Met debut as the Shepherd in *Tannhäuser.* Back in 1977, she was a cheerful, unaffected young woman who came to rehearsals in blue jeans and giggled loudly. The debut was in a tiny role, but she made her way through the lyric soprano repertory with the gently guiding hand of James Levine at her back. He understood that her voice was a small and delicate instrument, and he taught her to nurture it with care.

Battle was a small-town girl, the seventh child of an Ohio steelworker. She had begun singing in the local church choir and started her professional career teaching music in a Cincinnati inner-city school. An exemplary role model for young black women entering a white environment, she succeeded without repudiating her background, and remained close to her family and her roots.

But around 1980, people began to see a different Kathleen Battle. No longer outgoing and affable, she was withdrawing from the other singers; she would arrive at rehearsals at the last minute and would not join the cast table in the cafeteria. Her collegiate wardrobe disappeared and she became a fashion plate offstage as well as on; all her concert gowns were designed for her by Rouben Ter-Arutunian. When she went on tour with the company, she insisted on her own car, often refusing to ride with other singers. As she turned herself into what she apparently thought was the quintessential diva, she became cold and unapproachable. Meanwhile, her reviews went from enthusiastic to worshipful. One critic even called her Sophie in *Der Rosenkavalier* the finest portrayal of the role in the opera's history. Even the pictures on her record album covers were perfect enough to run in *Vogue*.

By the time of the *Figaro* premiere, she was the finished product. What few people outside the music business knew was that Battle was quickly becoming the leading contender for the title of most-loathed performing artist. A few kind souls spoke of her with sympathy, suggesting that her manner and actions were probably manifestations of psychological problems rather than a venomous nature. "I think she is frightened to death," Beverly Sills said.

In *Figaro*, both Battle and Carol Vaness were singing their demanding roles for the first time. Susanna is the longest and among the most-strenuous roles in the soprano repertory, but the leading soprano in this opera is generally considered to be the Countess. According to Metropolitan Opera tradition, dressing rooms are allotted by role, and the leading soprano receives the principal soprano dressing room. When Battle arrived for the *Figaro* rehearsals that November morning, she was stunned to find Vaness in that dressing room. Vaness, ten years younger than Battle, was on the verge of a major career; Battle was incensed. Not one to waste emotional energy on negotiation and compromise, she scooped up Vaness's belongings, tossed them into the corridor, and commandeered Dressing Room 1 for herself.

Vaness was wise enough not to engage in open warfare. With great dignity, she took her possessions into the second dressing room and spoke courteously to Battle. When she wasn't onstage during rehearsals, she sat in the darkened auditorium, her white Countess costumes billowing around her, and twisted and untwisted the ribbons and lace. Over and over, she reminded herself that Battle was playing the role of her maid in *Figaro* and that she was the Countess; she repeated a mantra: "She's only the maid, she's only the maid." Not once during those long rehearsal weeks did she confront Battle; the time was not yet right.

Battle's malicious behavior was directed not only toward Vaness. She was continuously rude to the wardrobe ladies, who are a vital component of the backstage support staff. She would ask them to fetch food and drinks for her, which was not part of their jobs, and then castigate them. Like Carol Vaness, the wardrobe ladies said nothing; they, too, waited.

Levine seemed to regard the situation with his usual nonchalance. When anyone complained about Battle's behavior, he would shake his head and say, "The list of people who won't work with Kathy Battle is as long as my arm." But he let Battle stay in the dressing room she coveted.

Several of the critics were aware of the tension on opening night. "Kathleen Battle is the one thing I thought this irresistible singer could never be—irritating," wrote Peter Davis in *New York* magazine. In the fourth act at the final performance of the *Figaro* run, Battle came out to sing "Deh vieni," one of the most moving moments in opera. Alone in the center of the stage, she stepped forward toward Levine's supportive beat, expecting to be bathed in light from her follow spot. For some reason, the spotlight never came on, and Battle sang the entire aria while standing in the dark. Everyone backstage was doubled up with laughter. The master electrician, who controlled lighting onstage, was married to the wardrobe mistress.

Two seasons later, the Metropolitan took this same *Figaro* production, including most of the cast from the 1985 premiere, to Japan. Vaness was again the Countess, Battle was Susanna, and Levine was conducting.

Throughout the tour, Battle stayed in a different hotel from the rest of the company; she provided the hotel switchboard with a list of the few Met people from whom she would accept phone calls.

The Japanese presenters treated Battle with special deference. She had filmed a series of TV commercials for a popular whiskey that had made her famous throughout the country, and they arranged a press conference for her, Domingo, and James Levine to publicize the Met tour. On the day of the final run-through before the *Figaro* dress rehearsal, Battle did not show up; she was having her hair and makeup done for the press conference.

The other singers seethed with resentment as Battle continued to treat rehearsals as interruptions to her schedule, arriving late and leaving early. Carol Vaness, as she had for the past two years, watched in silence.

On the night of the final performance in Tokyo, the cast gathered on-stage for the curtain calls. When the applause died away and the curtain came down for the last time, the singers hugged one another, tired yet exuberant after the ovation they had received. Levine stood talking to Battle as Vaness approached. "Kathy," she said in a cold, firm voice, "I want you to know that I've instructed my manager that I will never sing with you again. You are the most horrible colleague I've encountered in my whole career." Vaness is close to six feet tall in high heels, and as she turned away with her customary stateliness, everyone's eyes were riveted on her.

Battle turned to Levine, who put his arm around her shoulders and began guiding her offstage. Her pretty face twisted in astonishment, Battle cried, over and over, "What did I do? I've never done anything to her!" Levine patted her shoulder, and everyone else looked away. Vaness had just become the company heroine; the story of her spunk passed into Met legend.

*I*n the spring of 1986, Levine conducted another new production that centered on one of his favorite protégées. Maria Ewing, a mezzo-soprano from Detroit, had had Levine's support from the very beginning of her career. She sang often at the Met during the early Levine years, as Cherubino in *Figaro,* the Composer in *Ariadne auf Naxos,* Blanche in *Dialogues of the Carmelites,* and, even though she was pregnant, in the 1982 new production of *Così fan Tutte*. Her appearances had become less frequent since she married the English director Sir Peter Hall.

Although Peter Hall had been director of the disastrous 1982 production of *Macbeth,* he had already signed a contract to produce Bizet's *Carmen,* with his wife in the title role. There were questions about Ewing's vocal suitability for the part, but she was ideal physically for the sultry temptress. Slim and lithe, she moved well onstage, and, like many of Levine's favorite singers, was a committed actress.

But some worried about the repertory she was now undertaking. She had begun her career as a light lyric mezzo-soprano, singing such roles as Rosina in *Il Barbiere di Siviglia*. Her recent contracts were for dramatic soprano roles, like Salome and Tosca, which previously would have been both too high and too heavy for her voice. Hall encouraged her to move into the heavier roles; he often directed her, drawing forth intense, melodramatic performances.

Offstage, Ewing had always been elusive. Although she was African-American, she never associated with the other black singers, who, however different, seemed to feel a kinship for one another. Kathleen Battle and Jessye Norman, for example, gave joint recitals, even though they did not socialize. Ewing became even more remote and regal after she married Peter Hall.

When the rehearsals for *Carmen* began, no one at the Met liked the new sets. The previous production, which Goeran Gentele had planned, was large and awkward; the sets covered with carpeting gobbled up sound, even from singers as powerful as Marilyn Horne and James McCracken. The Hall *Carmen* was also big and, unfortunately, had the same gray quality as its Gentele predecessor. But Ewing and Hall had received praise for the *Carmen* they did at Glyndebourne the previous year, so Levine and the rest of the Met crossed their fingers. Perhaps Ewing's strong acting would make the dreary sets come alive.

The opening night was another gala, with paparazzi clustered on the Grand Staircase, New York society in designer gowns much in evidence, a formal dinner in the opera house before the performance, and an exclusive party after it at La Côte Basque. Only the performance put a pall on the evening. Liz Smith, the usually relentlessly enthusiastic society columnist, wrote, "Never dreamed I'd go to _Carmen,_ one of my all-time favorites, and consider that the . . . dinner beforehand was the best part of the evening. But the opera itself—deliver us. Turgid, long, boring, silly, badly sung on almost every count, and the leading role by Maria Ewing . . . like Jimmy Dean trying out a night club act."

Luis Lima, the handsome Argentine tenor singing Don José, fought a losing battle against tracheitis throughout the opera; his performance of the "Flower Song" was moving because of his courage in attempting it. At the party afterward, Bruce Crawford offered a special toast to Lima, who was too sick to attend.

But the most startling element was Ewing's Carmen. She seemed to interpret the seductive Gypsy as a woman in the grip of catatonic depression, standing stunned onstage or throwing herself wildly about, her eyes huge with dementia. One review said, "Carmen Goes Crazy," while another declared, "The Lady Is a Klutz." She might have survived her interpretation had she been able to sing the role, but she couldn't. Her voice was shredded, with obvious register breaks and frequent off-pitch passages. It was obvious that the heavy dramatic roles had severely damaged her voice.

Levine often resents any of his favorite singers turning to someone else for advice, and he blamed Peter Hall for what had happened to Ewing. He could not deny that Ewing was in bad shape, and he chose the Greek mezzo-soprano Agnes Baltsa to sing a telecast of _Carmen_ the following season.

Maria Ewing's reaction to Baltsa's casting surprised everyone, including her former mentor. She withdrew from all her future engagements at the Met as well as other concerts she had been signed to sing under Levine's direction. And then she did the unthinkable: she went to the press.

In an article in the _Times,_ Ewing was quoted as saying that Levine had assured her that she would sing the _Carmen_ telecast, and though the conductor vigorously denied having made that promise, Ewing's accusations stirred up criticism about Levine that had gone unspoken for years. With his great desire to be kind to singers and, in return, to be loved by them, he frequently had offered roles he knew they wanted. In the beginning, the singers believed him; in some cases, they turned down other engagements. But in many instances, no contracts were offered. Mystified agents would call the artistic department at the Met to say that Levine had said their clients would be singing certain roles but that no contracts had been offered. A famous mezzo-soprano who had every reason to believe that she was one of Levine's favorites once told Bruce Crawford that Levine had offered her a prized role, "but I won't believe it until I hear it from you."

Levine has always maintained that his enthusiasm was sincere. Perhaps singers found it hard to believe that the man who was artistic director of a powerful theater could not have everything he wanted. But Levine was the first to point out that he was not a miracle worker. "If I've said I want something and it hasn't happened, it has only been the case that we really did want it, and we really could not."

When Agnes Baltsa sang the role of Carmen in the telecast, with José Carreras as Don José, both were so savaged by the music critics that they swore never again to sing at the Met. Maria Ewing, on the other hand, did return. Her marriage to Peter Hall ended in a bitter divorce, and she and Levine mended their friendship. She appeared in a revival of *Les Troyens*, in which she sang badly, did two new productions, and participated in the Levine twenty-fifth anniversary gala, singing Gershwin's "My Man's Gone Now." Once again, she was singled out for ridicule; one publication nicknamed her "the artist formerly known as Maria Ewing." Her name has not recently appeared on the Met's roster, and she sings only rarely in other theaters.

JAMES LEVINE, ARTISTIC DIRECTOR

James Levine's first official season as artistic director of the Metropolitan Opera began in September 1986. The shiny new season began under a shadow, however. Manuela Hoelterhoff, the *Wall Street Journal*'s Pulitzer prize–winning critic, wrote a summary of the 1985–86 season that roundly condemned Levine for everything wrong with the company. Bliss, she declared, had conceded all artistic decisions to Levine, which had led to old-fashioned productions with mediocre singers and a poor box office. She unearthed the old complaints about the lack of great conductors and even the "peeling ceilings, worn-out cheap carpeting, the tacky coat rooms."

Her article concluded: "At the same time Mr. Levine's power is growing, the company's reputation is dwindling. . . . Perhaps now is the moment for Mr. Levine to . . . spend a little less time at the Met." There was a sense around the opera house that Bruce Crawford had enjoyed the article.

Levine was learning some of the hazards of reaching the top. During the summer, a controversy arose about his continuing to conduct at the Salzburg Festival despite the election of Kurt Waldheim as president of Austria. Anthony Lewis wrote, in the *New York Times:*

> Private citizens . . . who think there is an eternal obligation to
> remember what Nazism meant are free to express our moral revul-

sion at the Austrians' choice. The opportunity to do so, and the responsibility, lie especially with those in the public eye. . . . One such opportunity is at hand. It rests with the brilliant young music director of the Metropolitan Opera, James Levine. . . . If Mr. Levine . . . were now to drop out of the festival he would send an unmistakable message about the obligation to remember.

Levine has always taken the position that he is a musician, not a politician. One of his musical idols, however, put his priorities in a different order. Arturo Toscanini refused to return to the Bayreuth Festival after Hitler came to power; he declined to conduct Wagner at an engagement in Palestine after Kristallnacht; and he not only refused to conduct in Mussolini's Italy, but he also left the country to come to the United States. Of course, he also had resigned his position at the Met when he felt his musical ideals were being compromised. Levine over the years has adopted an attitude of patience. If there is a situation at the Met that displeases him, he does not resign. He waits.

A brief controversy raged over the view expressed in the *Times*, but Levine remained silent. He could have pointed out that he was not the only Jewish musician performing at Salzburg that summer. The violinist Pinchas Zukerman, an Israeli, gave a recital (although he made the symbolic gesture of wearing a yarmulke), and Leonard Bernstein not only conducted several performances, he also brought along the entire Israel Philharmonic. None of these musicians would have been allowed to perform in Salzburg during the period when Waldheim fought for the Nazis; their presence itself was a powerful statement of how much had changed.

Ironically, the 1986–87 season opened with the first opera from the Met's new production of Wagner's *Der Ring des Nibelungen*, a work Hitler believed symbolized the Third Reich. Levine, ignoring the subtext, was confident that the new *Die Walküre* would serve as a symbol of his intentions as artistic director. The new production was to be modeled on the 1977 *Tannhäuser* of Otto Schenk and Günther Schneider-Siemssen, a romantic interpretation that nevertheless relied on state-of-the-art stage technology.

It would be an important artistic statement, the first opera in the first *Ring* at the Met in a decade. The remaining three operas would appear over the next two seasons, with three complete cycles planned for the spring of 1989.

Die Walküre was a triumph for Levine and his orchestra. Although the orchestra had been amply praised for several seasons, it was now welcomed into the elite circle of great orchestras. Levine's favorite dramatic soprano, Hildegard Behrens, sang Brünnhilde with her usual dramatic flair and pushed her vocal resources to the limit. The American bass James Morris was acclaimed as the leading Wagner baritone of the day. Others in the cast were considered acceptable. The real controversy surrounding the premiere was the physical production.

The Levine *Ring* was a measure of his visual taste. Schneider-Siemssen's sets were a direct rebuttal to the avant-garde interpretations of the *Ring* in Europe. His were realistic interpretations of the forests and mountains of Wagner's Germany, although he admitted that he was inspired by the scenery of the western United States.

This was the first time Otto Schenk had directed the *Ring*. A famous actor in his native Austria, he wanted to turn the fairy-tale legend into human drama. He tried to avoid the Wagnerian clichés: the Valkyries would not have horses, Fricka would not arrive on a ram, and there was not to be a single horned helmet in sight. He and his designer used every component of the Met's stage machinery to create their atmosphere of romantic realism. The fire that surrounds Brünnhilde at the end of the opera was real, even to the cinders that floated down. The dragon in *Siegfried* was so realistic that the *New York Times* did an entire article on him. At the end of *Götterdämmerung*, not only did Valhalla collapse, it was flooded by the Rhine. The critics called the production hopelessly old-fashioned; audiences loved it. Many Europeans, accustomed to the avant-garde interpretations, came to New York for every revival of the *Ring*.

For this new season, and in his new position, Levine would conduct sixty performances instead of the ninety he had been doing. In interviews just before opening night, he explained why he had chosen the post of artistic director. Initially, working with John Dexter, he had concentrated on improving the orchestra and chorus, planning the future repertory, and organizing a development program for young singers. But he had become frustrated by the lack of one coherent aesthetic standard for both the musical and the visual elements. "Finally," he said, "I told the board . . . either engage me as a guest conductor . . . or put me in charge."

Whatever anyone else thought of the new *Ring*, Levine made it clear that it was much to his liking. He felt at home in this style of staging—big, romantic, and factually representational. All the stage directors he admired created such productions—Schenk, Jean-Pierre Ponnelle, and Franco Zeffirelli. During the next few seasons, these men would design almost every new Met production.

At the beginning of October, the Met revived Zeffirelli's *Tosca;* once again, this director's work had all the performances sold out. Eva Marton sang the title role for the first time. Although Marton had won her adoring Met public by singing Wagner and Richard Strauss, she brought a strapping dramatic presence to the Italian repertory, as she had done in the tumultuous revival of *Gioconda* several years previously.

The conductor for the revival was in his second season at the Met. Joan Ingpen had engaged Luis Antonio Garcia Navarro, a handsome Spaniard who had had successful engagements at the San Francisco and Chicago operas, for several of the Italian operas in the 1985–86 and 1986–87 seasons. This repertory had been unclaimed since Patané's dismissal, and Ingpen hoped she had found a reliable man to replace the quixotic Patané.

In Navarro's first season, however, it was immediately clear that he came from the same tradition as the tempestuous Italian, although he had something of a provincial quality. Often he clashed with singers; he made noisy and time-consuming demands on the busy opera house staff; and he had such a flashy conducting technique that he was known to the orchestra as The Slasher. But he lacked Patané's brilliance. During the spring tour, he had infuriated the legendary mezzo-soprano Grace Bumbry, no temperamental slouch herself, by ignoring her preferred tempos and dynamics, sending the diva flying into the wings after act 1 of *Carmen*.

"What's happened to the maestro?" she cried. "Has he had a stroke or something?" By the end of his first season, his temperamental outbursts had convinced Jonathan Friend that this was a man with no future in the house.

In this _Tosca_ run, Plácido Domingo sang Cavaradossi. He and Navarro, both Spanish, were old colleagues and got along well, despite Navarro's simmering resentment of Domingo's international career. Domingo and Marton, however, kept up a nasty feud. Their mutual dislike, as is the case with sopranos and tenors, began with a disagreement in a previous production over how long to hold a certain high note. Marton was considered the winner.

The villainous Scarpia was sung by Juan Pons, a stolid, portly Spaniard whom Marton and Domingo ignored and Navarro patronized. Pons came to the Met well prepared, rehearsed diligently, sang his performances solidly, and cheerfully collected his fees. He was respected and liked, and his occasional flirtations with chorus ladies and pretty comprimarios were, in the usual Met tradition, regarded affectionately. Since Marton and Navarro had a strange compatibility, two major sources of tension were neutralized. And since Marton regarded herself as the star of the show, choosing not to see that the performances had sold out largely because of Domingo's presence and Zeffirelli's production, she behaved with a magisterial graciousness. Rehearsals went smoothly, which pleasantly surprised the artistic administration, given Marton's habit of steamrollering colleagues.

At last it was opening night, when the opera house was filled with the special anticipatory hum that precedes certain performances. Marton had never sung _Tosca_ in New York and her adoring fans were there in great numbers. All the major New York critics turned up, a rare happening at a standard repertory revival, even with Domingo singing.

The first act went well. The orchestra followed Navarro, in spite of his self-congratulatory manner and his habit of dousing himself with so much Yves St. Laurent cologne that some women musicians had allergic reactions. Pons made a striking, if hardly a dynamic, figure on stage, and his large, dark voice easily rose above the clamor from the orchestra. Domingo was Domingo. But Marton was the evening's sensation. Offstage, she embodied Tosca's egomania. Onstage, her presence was larger than life and her voice just as theatrical. After all, she also sang Brünnhilde.

In the second act, the duet between Scarpia and Tosca took fire. Pons did not attempt the sadistic sexual charm some baritones bring to the role, but his firm presence did take on a sinister quality. Marton played Tosca with a statuesque passion. The effect was heightened by the singers' size: Marton was a solid five-nine, and Pons a heavy six-five.

Just before "Vissi d'arte," the staging calls for a struggle between Scarpia and Tosca. Somehow, during the scuffle, the baritone's elbow connected with the soprano's prominent jaw. "When I was hit, I knew something happened—I heard a crack," Marton later said. "'Oh my goodness,' I said to myself, 'I can't even open or close my mouth.'" And her big aria was coming up. As directed, Marton sank to the ground to sing "Vissi d'arte" stretched out on the stage. "I shaped the vowels with my tongue. I suddenly had to invent a whole new way of singing."

As the curtain came down on act 2, the artistic administrator on duty heard the stage manager frantically summoning him over the backstage intercom to go to Marton's dressing room. As he was hurrying through the maze of backstage halls, he bumped into the house doctor springing in the same direction. They reached Marton's dressing room simultaneously to find the soprano sprawled on the couch, her husband, Zoltan, a surgeon, bending over her. "What happened?" the administrator asked, his voice instinctively switching to the soothing mode developed over years of coping with real and imagined backstage emergencies.

Marton reared up on the couch, in obvious pain, and sobbed that her jaw was broken. "Can you continue?" the Met administrator asked, thankful that Marton's cover was in the theater. "I don't know, I don't know," she managed to croak out, and the house doctor began to examine her. Zoltan thought a small bone in her face had been broken.

Navarro arrived on the scene, full of sympathy. Two years earlier, he had been struck in the face by his garage door, and his broken jaw had been wired shut for two months. Zoltan advised his wife to withdraw, but she was determined, upholding the long-held belief that the show must go on.

Theatrical tradition aside, Marton's decision that night was a serious one. If a bone was broken or a ligament torn, she could have incurred irreparable damage. The final act of _Tosca_ is challenging, including a high C and high drama requiring a clarion delivery. But Marton told Navarro she would continue. "If I stop singing, keep going anyway."

The Met administration, meanwhile, had swung into its emergency procedure; the artistic administrator warned wardrobe that the cover costume should be prepared; he told the house manager that intermission would be longer than usual; and he briefed the press representative who had to deal with the critics attending the performance. Preparations for the huge and complex third act proceeded on schedule. The stage would be ready long before the singers.

When Marton decided to finish the performance, the artistic and press representatives raced to send the news to their constituencies, and the stage manager began composing his speech begging the audience's indulgence for the injured soprano. Juan Pons, in the safety of his dressing room, was heartily relieved that he had been killed in act 2 and had no more scenes to sing with Marton.

Marton finished the performance. The next day, reviews were excellent, but her injury received much more attention than her Tosca portrayal. Although X rays revealed no broken bones, the doctors postulated that her jaw had been dislocated, and had returned to its normal position as she sang the third act.

At first, Juan Pons felt bad for Marton, but his sympathy turned to outrage as the publicity about the incident swelled out of proportion. The scene between Tosca and Scarpia was always staged as a physical struggle; he had only been doing his job, and he was quite sure he had not injured Marton in any way. But as the public curiosity continued, he wisely decided to step back. Soon his name was no longer associated with the episode, and he escaped the Carlo Bini curse of too much publicity under the wrong circumstances. His Met career flourished. Garcia Navarro's did not; he never returned to the Met.

Eva Marton nursed her pain and her publicity. Sissy Strauss, one of the artistic liaisons and always a warm-hearted hostess to the artists, called her a day or two after the _Tosca_ premiere to invite her to a quiet, consoling dinner. "I'll make you something easy to chew and swallow," Sissy promised. "Some soup, a soufflé, maybe."

Marton gave the matter some thought. "Very nice," she said. "Some soup. A puree." She paused. "And, you know what else might be nice? Filet mignon is a very soft meat, I believe."

Marton's future at the Met seemed secure, with contracts signed for the coming seasons in such roles as Turandot, Salome, and Brünnhilde. With that kind of insurance, she saw no need to be patient with anyone who irked her. Finally, even the kindhearted stagehands plotted revenge. On the evening of her last *Tosca,* the crew substituted a new mattress for her to land on after plunging to her death. This mattress, filled with feathers, exploded when Marton crashed down, and small white feathers filled the dusty air backstage. Marton took her curtain calls in a rage, bedecked in tufts of feathers in her wig, costume, and heavy stage makeup.

But only a few years later, Marton would suffer a much more severe blow. With no explanation, the Met unceremoniously canceled her contract to sing Brünnhilde in the second complete *Ring* cycle with Levine. Levine had been so impressed by Hildegard Behrens's performance in the 1989 cycle that he had decided to give the role to her, even with her fragile vocal resources. Her theatrical credibility, the combination of bravery and vulnerability in an unusually nuanced interpretation, convinced him that she should sing the second cycle. It was the one that would be taped for television—and therefore for posterity.

Marton's voice was more suited to the role, but Levine had never admired the singer's artistry. She might well have sung a finer Brünnhilde vocally, but she would never have attained Behrens's understanding of the part.

Marton, as she had a right to be, was outraged by Levine's decision. She had had signed contracts for these performances for several years, and although she was now paid for them, the money did nothing to heal her injured pride. As Maria Ewing had done before her, Marton turned to the *New York Times* and blasted the Met's tactics. What was interesting was that the person who approached Marton and asked her to give up the *Ring* performances was Joseph Volpe; this was his first foray into the artistic area. According to Zoltan Marton, it was not carried out very successfully. He accused Volpe of behaving in "a tactless and abrupt fashion" at the beginning of rehearsals for a new production of _Salome_ during the 1988–89 season, and declared that his wife "will never sing Brünnhilde in New York, or at least not in this production!"

Marton also canceled every one of her other Met contracts in a gesture as understandable as it was futile. By the time her wounded feelings had recovered and she was ready to return to the Met, she was beyond the best years of her career. Young dramatic sopranos like Jane Eaglen and Deborah Voigt had appeared and claimed the roles in Marton's repertory.

Chapter Twenty-seven

THE IMPERIAL MET

The Metropolitan's age of excess reached its giddy height in the winter of 1986–87, along with the social frenzy accompanying the stock market boom. The Met's latest patrons, the newly wealthy masters of arbitrage and acquisitions, and their trophy wives, clad in Christian La Croix's puffed skirts, clamored to see the new Met productions, laden with their own grandiosity.

For Johann Strauss's operetta *Die Fledermaus*, Otto Schenk and Günther Schneider-Siemssen came indoors from the Bavarian mountains and river Rhine to a lush, Belle Époque Vienna. In their Wagnerian expeditions, the Austrian director and designer had learned a great deal, about both the Met stage and the Met audience. For the frothy *Fledermaus*, their sets were lavish and danced along with the waltzes of the opera. While the chorus and ballet gyrated through a raucous conga line, shrieking at the top of their lungs, the stage turntable rotated. Schenk himself played the drunken jailer Frosch. And in a strange linguistic schizophrenia, the copious spoken dialogue was in English and the sung sections were in German. No wonder Kiri Te Kanawa's Rosalinda was judged somewhat stodgy, and no wonder that Jeffrey Tate, an English conductor brilliant in Berg, Schoenberg, and Wagner, seemed unable to capture the Straussian lilt. The overdone scenery and heavy-handed slapstick sank the lighthearted operetta. And there was more to come—before Black Monday sank the financial community.

Jean-Pierre Ponnelle, number two in the favored trio of Met directors, made his contribution with a lumbering production of Massenet's *Manon*. Catherine Malfitano, an intelligent and serious actress, was miscast in a role where charm is an essential ingredient. Ponnelle, who was devoting much of his energy to fulminating against the New York press, did little to help her maneuver through the elephantine sets. Neil Shicoff, the American tenor considered most likely to achieve the status of a Domingo, was beset with personal problems and spent most of the production struggling against tracheitis.

Shicoff was a troubling example of the young singers Levine shepherded toward stardom. In his late thirties, blessed with a truly beautiful voice and an ardent presence onstage, he was tortured by his own insecurity. The Met boasted of its nurturing attitude toward young singers and yet at times seemed unable to provide psychological support. His marriage foundering, his health fragile, Shicoff began to manifest personal eccentricities, canceling an exorbitant number of performances. His sweet disposition, however, and his sense of the absurdity of the opera world left him still popular with the company. But when he became embroiled in an extramarital affair and messy divorce, he fled to Europe, where his career thrived.

For the last new production of the season, Puccini's *Turandot*, Franco Zeffirelli took up residence at the Met. The weary technical crew began to erect the entire city of Peking on the revolving main stage as Sybil Harrington's ninth new production started rehearsals.

Eva Marton was cast in the title role, one that suited her perfectly. Turandot was the princess of ice, a woman who delighted in beheading prospective suitors and torturing disobedient slave girls. Plácido Domingo was Calaf. The tenor, dealing with Calaf's higher-than-comfortable tessitura (or voice range) and a leading lady who, although unsubtle, could blow almost any singer off the stage with her vocal power, was tense throughout the rehearsal period.

Zeffirelli raced around the opera house, giving extensive interviews about his innovative use of plastics and fiberglass in building the production. The chorus complained to their union about their precarious footing on the steeply slanted stage for act 1. The staging demands of this *Turandot* were so complex that Joseph Clark, the technical director, decreed that absolutely no one could go backstage during the performance, not even the elegantly dressed wealthy patrons who savored their intermission trips behind the scenes to glimpse the crew hard at work. Meanwhile, the stagehands who were struggling with the huge *Turandot* sets were working on three other enormous productions: *Die Walküre*, *Manon*, and *Carmen*. There was barely room backstage to store all the scenery.

As their contribution to the stress, Marton and Domingo, who had barely tolerated each other during *Tosca*, now engaged in open warfare. One of them would stalk out of rehearsals, accusing the other of holding a note too long or too loudly; Marton was trying to sing while encased in heavy, cumbersome costumes; Domingo complained about the slow pace of rehearsals. The only person who seemed to be having a great time was the French tenor Hughes Cuénod, making his Metropolitan debut as the Emperor at the age of eighty-five.

Despite the chaos, opening night was a triumph. Zeffirelli had found in *Turandot* the perfect vehicle for his talents. Needless to say, the premiere was a gala benefit. This time, the society press was as pleased with the production as with the celebrity-packed audience. The music critics gave as much attention to the opulence of the production as to an apparent shoving match that took place between Marton and Domingo during the curtain calls. The combination of star temperament and extravagance made tickets for *Turandot* the hottest in town. Bruce Crawford had certainly achieved one of his goals.

Only days after the premiere, the zenith of the social season occurred when First Lady Nancy Reagan attended Cecile Zilkha's second onstage corporate dinner. Mrs. Reagan was regal in pearls and diamonds and a dark green velvet dress by Carolina Herrera, herself a member of New York society. The stage was decorated with Chagall's *Magic Flute* sets, and Cecile Zilkha, dressed in white silk Chanel, presented Mrs. Reagan with the Met's Centennial medallion. The evening was also made notable by Louise Humphrey's announcement that the auditorium of the opera house would be known as Sybil Harrington Auditorium, in honor of the woman who had contributed more money to the Met than any other person. Harrington, clad in a black-and-white Galanos, gave a tender speech, thanking her late husband, Donald D. Harrington, who had made all this possible.

The First Lady's presence ensured copious social coverage of the dinner. The guest list was sprinkled with such names as Kissinger, Mosbacher, Rockefeller, Perelman, Schlumberger, and a small turnout of minor royalty. Relegated to the last paragraph in the *New York Times*'s lengthy article was the "entertainment": Marilyn Horne, accompanied by James Levine, sang selections by Rossini, Bizet, and Copland in a briefly tolerated reminder of why everyone was eating dinner on the Met stage in the first place.

The closing night of the *Turandot* run was so glamorous that it was featured on the front page of the *Times,* together with a group picture of Birgit Nilsson, who was the most renowned Turandot in operatic history, Franco Zeffirelli, Eva Marton, Plácido Domingo, James Levine, and, quite unexpectedly, Elizabeth Taylor. Taylor, who had been greeted with cheers by the audience, was about to start working with Zeffirelli on a film about the young Arturo Toscanini, a movie that has never been released for public distribution. Even the usually imperturbable Eva Marton was impressed by Nilsson's presence, and confided to the *Times* that "it was Birgit who encouraged me to sing the role."

James Levine, who normally eschews the glamour of café society, looked happy as he led his gigantic forces to the end of the performance. Onstage on that frenetic night, sequins drifted down from the flies, silken banners exploded with riotous color, crowds of supers moved to the thunderous sounds of the Met Orchestra, and the curtain fell on the final *Turandot* of the season.

Shortly after that performance, *New York* magazine published a long article by Peter G. Davis, its classical music critic, entitled "Jimmy's Met." In it, Levine was quoted on the joys and frustrations of his job.

> Sure I get discouraged. Everyday I walk in here, it's the same. This singer is sick. This singer has just cancelled a contract. . . . This one just never showed up. What should I do? Throw in the towel and play chamber music? I will eventually. But in the meantime, I really do believe something good is happening.

Davis also chatted with Bruce Crawford, whom he praised for his involvement in all aspects of the opera house. During his first season as general manager, Crawford had taken an active interest in the artistic planning, traveling to Europe frequently so he could hear the latest young singers who, in previous eras, would have been ignored by the Met. He insisted that some of them come to the Met; a few were successful; a few vanished overnight. Crawford's greatest coup, however, was having the elusive conductor Carlos Kleiber accept the invitation to make his Met debut during the 1987–88 season. Bing and Bliss had both done their best to lure Kleiber, a legendary eccentric, to New York, but only Crawford had succeeded.

The perceived significance of this event was that the company had finally, under Crawford, lured a truly great conductor to the theater. When Kleiber's engagement was announced, there was general rejoicing. No one believed that Levine had been involved—which he had been, as had Ronald Wilford, both his and Kleiber's agent—but Crawford received most of the credit.

Kleiber, according to those who know him—he has never given an interview—is witty, intelligent, shy, demanding, volatile, sophisticated, childish, and deeply insecure. He rarely agrees to engagements in advance and, when he does, quite often does not show up. If he actually arrives and begins rehearsing, the slightest event can trigger his fury and an immediate departure. He walked out of a Vienna Philharmonic rehearsal because he thought the musicians were making fun of him. This is hard to imagine, because orchestral musicians regard him with unparalleled awe. They treasure the small notes containing suggestions that he leaves on their music stands, which they call "Kleibergrams." Kleiber, they say, knows his scores better than any other conductor they have ever encountered, but his performances are always unpredictable. He is the only conductor that James Levine praises without qualification; he is proud that Kleiber comes to Met Orchestra performances when the ensemble is in Europe.

Kleiber came to the Met to conduct *La Bohème* with a cast that included Mirella Freni and Luciano Pavarotti. Incongruously, he is a close friend of Franco Zeffirelli, and they have done several productions together in Europe. Kleiber arrived on time, rehearsed the orchestra assiduously, and pronounced it an exceptional ensemble. This feeling was reciprocated by the musicians, who still call the Kleiber performances one of the highlights of their career.

The atmosphere at the Met outside rehearsals seemed peculiar to Kleiber. Everyone in the opera house had been instructed not to speak to him unless spoken to first, because Crawford and Levine were so worried that he would take offense at an offhand remark and bolt. The conductor wandered the halls, smiling cheerfully at everyone he encountered, all of whom nodded silently in return. "I can't understand it," he finally said to one of the stage managers. "Everyone in New York is so friendly except in the opera house."

His performances were rapturously received and Kleiber decided he loved being at the Met. He accepted contracts for *Der Rosenkavalier,* *Traviata,* and *Otello* in the next few seasons. The one oddness was that he refused to specify the dates when he would conduct. The company went out of its way to accommodate his idiosyncracies. Only one of his requests was unfulfilled. He liked to arrive for performances several hours in advance, and one Saturday afternoon, he arrived at the theater to get ready for an evening performance. To his horror, a matinee was in progress, and there was another conductor in his dressing room. He asked that the next time he was booked for a Saturday evening, the matinee be canceled. But even for Kleiber, the Saturday broadcasts are inviolable, and he was turned down.

Kleiber came to the Met several seasons and then, just as unexpectedly as he arrived, he went away. But Levine has not given up; Kleiber receives regular invitations to return.

Levine frequently talked about his unrealized hopes over the past decade of reviving the Mini-Met. He had enlisted the avant-garde director Peter Sellars to establish a smaller company in a smaller house, and, with the big deficits in the past, Crawford agreed to the project because it was one of Levine's priorities. "If it ever became clear to me that such a small house will be an impossibility, I will just have to leave the Met," he said. "After this contract period is up in 1991, I would see the future here as just more of the same."

James Levine had more reasons to be frustrated than just the burdens of running a major opera company. For over ten years, he had been the object of scurrilous gossip. No one knew the source of the rumors, though certain disenfranchised Met singers and administrators were suspected, and the persistence of the vulgar stories was troubling to the company. In time, they filtered beyond the Met community.

The gist of the stories was that Levine was guilty of criminal behavior, which the Met board had condoned by paying off the aggrieved parties. One tale had Levine soliciting a child in Pittsburgh on an evening when, as it happened, he was in Boston conducting a Met tour performance. In fact, he conducted on the entire tour that season, and the idea of his going to Pittsburgh on one of his few nights off was ludicrous. Another tale with the same theme had the New York City subway as its location. This provoked particular hilarity because no one who knew Levine could imagine him taking the subway under any circumstances, ever. Inside the company, the stories were dismissed as preposterous.

One rumor, however, was particularly persistent. Levine, it was said, had had a relationship with a boy whose parents had gone to the Met board, threatening to expose the situation. Supposedly the board had then authorized a major payoff to the family. But Anthony Bliss, during whose tenure this reportedly took place, consistently and adamantly denied it, as did other board members. According to other gossip, Levine was asked about the incident at a relaxed social gathering, and his response was that he would consider a relationship only with "someone who was old enough to order a drink."

Starting in the spring of 1979, these stories came to the surface at more or less regular intervals. Each time, the Met press office would tirelessly point out the cyclical nature of the gossip and the complete lack of substance. Investigative reporters from the *New York Times, Newsday, New York* magazine, and the *New Yorker* had probed police reports and Met financial statements and had turned up nothing. And "you can't hide police reports," one *Times* reporter said.

In the summer of 1987, the "rumors," as they became known in the company, cropped up again, this time with a virulence that the *Times* found impossible to ignore, even in light of its earlier investigation. Crawford, alarmed, decided to meet with John Rockwell from the _Times_'s cultural staff; he urged Levine to talk to Rockwell, too. Levine, who was in Salzburg, agreed to a telephone interview. The resulting article appeared on July 23, 1987, and was headed "Met Opera Changes Managerial Balance."

Until this time, Levine had not addressed the "rumors"; in fact, no one had questioned him about them. To Rockwell, he denied the accusations as total fabrication.

> This is nothing new for me. Ten years ago, Tony Bliss called me about reports of a morals charge in Pittsburgh or Hawaii or Dallas. Both my friends and my enemies checked it out, and to this day, I don't have the faintest idea where those rumors came from or what purpose they served. Ron Wilford says it's because people can't believe the real story, that I'm too good to be true. . . . Look, I'm not a doctor married with three children living in the suburbs. I live my life openly; I don't make pretenses of this or that. What there is is completely apparent, so if people want to damage me, they have to invent things that are lurid and vicious.

In the years following, this statement was interpreted as Levine's saying he was gay. He did not say anything like that.

Rockwell's reluctance to deal with the entire subject was obvious in the finished article, and, in fact, the first and longer part of the piece dealt with much the same subject Peter Davis had written of in April 1987.

> The Metropolitan Opera is evolving a new managerial structure [Rockwell wrote at the beginning of the article] in which Bruce Crawford, the general manager, will assume more of the artistic authority previously vested in James Levine, the artistic director.

Levine is quoted about his need for more time away from the Met, fewer administrative burdens, and more opportunity to work on musical matters. He also talked about doing more work away from the Met and said he could envision a day when he would relinquish the title of artistic director.

Crawford pointed out that he had already taken over some artistic decisions, and gave as an example his cancellation of a Zeffirelli *Aida*, which had been too expensive. Both Levine and Crawford agreed that they did not foresee a formal restructuring of the administration, but, rather, a readjustment, based on the growing familiarity each felt with the other. But perhaps there were other factors, too.

During the fall, Levine had taken the Berlin Philharmonic Orchestra on a tour of the United States. Originally, the tour was to have been led by Herbert von Karajan, the orchestra's music director, but ill health had forced him to cancel. Levine conducted all the performances he could, and Seiji Ozawa took over on the dates that conflicted with Levine's Met responsibilities.

Karajan had been in poor health for some time. His audiences had seen him grope his way painfully to the podium at the start of a concert and then conduct with obvious difficulty. Indomitable as he was, it was clear that he could not continue to conduct much longer. Articles about his possible successor were published all over the world, and among the five or six names always mentioned was that of James Levine. The Berlin Philharmonic is a self-governing orchestra; the players choose their music director in secret balloting. When Levine was chosen to replace Karajan on the American tour, many believed him to be the orchestra's choice.

But if Levine was chosen, what would happen to his Met commitment? Karajan, who admired Levine, had engaged him for every season at Salzburg, and Levine had been so revered in Austria that he was selected to conduct the memorial service for Karl Böhm. "You don't understand what you have with Levine," said an admiring member of the Vienna Philharmonic to an American visitor. In both Germany and Austria, Levine was considered one of the world's great conductors.

Levine, with Ronald Wilford's counsel and advice, had planned his European career this way. He rarely conducted in other than German-speaking countries. All his time away from the Met in Europe was spent conducting in Vienna and Berlin, Salzburg and Bayreuth.

The Vienna Philharmonic does not have a music director; it is primarily the orchestra of the Vienna State Opera, and it presents few concerts as a separate ensemble. Levine often spoke of needing a European component to his career because of the musical tradition in that part of the world, so the obvious position would have been the Berlin Philharmonic.

Levine said nothing about this to Rockwell in July 1987; Karajan was still alive. But it could have explained his ruminations on reducing his Met commitment, when only a year or two earlier he had fought hard to win the title he now held.

Crawford's instincts had been correct; the Rockwell article quashed the 1987 outbreak of gossip. Levine's apparent concession of some artistic power to Crawford was generally accepted without much comment. Crawford's remark that the company could not undertake the financial risk of experimentation in either productions or repertory was the statement of a _fait accompli_. He had become head of the company by accruing power on the board, and the board has always been a moderating artistic force.

In September 1987, the _Times_ saluted the opening of the 1987–88 season with a feature article entitled "Crawford's Met." Only five months earlier, _New York_ magazine had run "Jimmy's Met."

Chapter Twenty-eight

THE PHANTOM OF THE OPERA

By the late 1980s, Sir Rudolf Bing, who had once mused about becoming the Phantom of the Opera after his retirement, had largely disappeared from public sight. The last decade had been difficult for him. Bitterly disappointed when the board did not turn to him after Gentele's death, he worked at Columbia Artists Management, though no one was quite sure what he did, and, for a while, he taught arts management at Brooklyn College. This was hardly a satisfying life for a man who had once run a great opera house.

His life had been seriously disrupted in 1978 when Nina Bing suffered a stroke. Her doctors and Bing's friends urged him to have Nina go to a nursing home after her hospital treatment, but Bing would not hear of it. Instead, he hired round-the-clock nurses and oversaw her medical care himself in their apartment at the Essex House.

The strain quickly became overwhelming. Nina, on whom Bing had long been dependent emotionally, although he had been constantly unfaithful, was so ill that he plummeted into depression. He could not eat; he wept for hours. During this terrible period, he found himself thinking of his old nemesis Maria Callas, alone in Paris with no one by her side when she died.

Nina Bing died in 1983, and Sir Rudolf gave in to his exhaustion. His friends noticed that, although well physically, he was failing mentally.

People saw him in the lobby of the Essex House, asking everyone he came across, "Where am I?" Then, at some point that year, he met Carroll Douglass, a tall, forty-seven-year-old blonde from a wealthy family, who had for many years suffered mental problems.

Douglass had a dubious history of romantic attachments that even stretched to an obsession with Pope John Paul II. She had dedicated herself, she told her friends, to the "plight of the Polish people," and had tried to send the pope a check for $70,000 payable to "His Holiness for the Polish Project." She had been negotiating to buy a helicopter so that she could take flying lessons and serve as the pope's pilot when her family had her declared incompetent. In 1982, her brother and sisters were named her conservators.

Now she became fascinated with Rudolf Bing. She started to show up at his favorite restaurants and to send him bouquets of orchids and roses. Soon, they were seen together, often at Fontana di Trevi, a restaurant on Fifty-seventh Street that Bing had long enjoyed. Once, they were seen quarreling at La Côte Basque, one of Manhattan's most exclusive restaurants.

They also went to the Met. Bing would show up at the front gate with Douglass and demand to be seated for the performance. He never had a ticket nor had he called anyone in advance. He just appeared.

Long ago, Bliss had instructed his office to give tickets to Bing whenever he asked, preferably in the general manager's box. Crawford had continued the practice, but he was stymied by the unexpected appearances. No one in the opera house wanted to embarrass Sir Rudolf.

In January 1987, a gossip column in the *Daily News* reported that Rudolf Bing had started appearing at the Met "with his flashy new female escort." The article implied that Bing's privilege of seats at any performance he wished to attend was retracted when he was with his new lady, "leading to the appalling spectacle of the eighty-four-year-old former manager in Standing Room while his friend goes on reconnaissance for empty seats."

At about the same time, Paul Guth, Bing's lawyer and friend for many years, noticed that his client was giving Douglass checks for large sums; he went to court to have Bing declared incompetent. In response, Bing and

Douglass traveled to Arlington, Virginia, where they were married on January 9. Two days later, they returned to New York and tried to file a will. Then they attended the competency hearing.

The judge found that Bing was suffering from Alzheimer's disease. Guth was appointed his conservator. Since Bing had an estate of close to $1 million, the judge ordered Bing's assets frozen and ruled that Douglass was to make her new husband available to his doctors and lawyer.

Her rebuttal was to set off with Bing on a bizarre journey that was to take them from the West Indies to the Caribbean to Great Britain. Once ensconced on Anguilla, Douglass, who now referred to herself as Lady Bing, gave a series of lurid interviews about the couple's affair. Bing, haggard and unshaven, sat by her side while she met the reporters.

When asked about the money she had supposedly embezzled from Bing since moving into his Essex House apartment, she explained, "I took Sir Rudolf to dinner at the Plaza, the Pierre. I took him to places that Eisenhower, Jackie Kennedy, and the pope have eaten. I wanted to keep him in the lifestyle he is accustomed to. He is royalty."

When a reporter asked Bing whether he wanted to go back to New York, Bing said, "Where are we now?"

"We're on our honeymoon," Lady Bing reminded him.

In an attempt to elude Guth, she took Bing next to England, where the couple's behavior became more bizarre. They adopted several stray dogs, and Bing was often found by the police wandering in a daze. Douglass ignored a court order that she bring Sir Rudolf to New York, and the judge allowed Guth to begin annulment proceedings.

When the couple's money ran out, they did return and again lived in Bing's apartment. They went to the Met—Bruce Crawford made sure that Douglass also received a ticket—and arranged to be photographed for a newspaper on the Met stage. Crawford allowed this as well.

In 1989, the New York State Supreme Court annulled the marriage after less than a year, ruling that Bing was mentally incompetent. Guth arranged for him to be moved to the Hebrew Home for the Aged, in the Bronx. The Metropolitan Opera, under orders from Crawford, paid his nursing home fees; his nest egg had long ago been depleted by his former wife and his own lawyers. Bing had few visitors; only the soprano Teresa

Stratas came to see him on a regular basis. Bing's longtime fears about dying penniless had come true.

Carroll Douglass was taken to the psychiatric unit at Bellevue Hospital. When she recovered from the breakdown, she continued to live in New York, wandering around the city and often going to the Met.

Rudolf Bing died on September 2, 1997, at St. Joseph's Hospital in New York. Although Bing's death merited mention on the front page of the _Times_, few noticed his passing; Diana, Princess of Wales, had been killed in a car accident only three days earlier. After a friend called to tell Douglass about Sir Rudolf's death, she had her nails done at the Essex House salon in the color Bing had liked, and then went to the British Consulate. There she wrote in the book of condolences for Princess Diana, "You shall live in our hearts forever—Sir Rudolf and Lady Bing."

Chapter Twenty-nine

THE THREE TENORS

During the first week of the 1988–89 season, James Levine fulfilled one of his dreams when he conducted a performance of *Das Rheingold;* on that evening, he exceeded Artur Bodanzky's hitherto unsurpassed record of 1,081 performances conducted at the Met. Whatever his ambitions concerning the Berlin Philharmonic, he had become the most important musical figure in the company's history.

Before the beginning of the season, Levine had given an onstage recital at the Met with Luciano Pavarotti. Only a few years earlier, Pavarotti had felt like an outcast, especially from performances with Levine. Domingo had had the larger share of new productions that the artistic director conducted, and he also recorded frequently with Levine.

But the situation had changed recently. Crawford paid a great deal of attention to Pavarotti, aware that he was one of those few singers who could guarantee the "hot ticket." And Levine had become more interested in Pavarotti since the tenor had courageously tackled *Idomeneo* in 1982, a work far from his usual Italian repertory.

Likewise, outside the Met, Domingo had never felt secure about his position vis-à-vis Pavarotti. By the early 1980s, he had developed an obsession that Pavarotti was more famous, more recognized, more celebrated than he was. Domingo felt that he had built his career with a painstaking care that Pavarotti had not. He had learned repertory by spending five years with the Hebrew National Opera in Tel Aviv, where he sometimes sang as many as twelve performances a month. He gave his early New York years to the New York City Opera; after serving that probation, he moved on to the Met in 1968. At the Met, he was a faithful company member, singing in revivals as well as the new productions. Pavarotti lived in Italy; Domingo and his family, for many years, lived in suburban New Jersey.

When Domingo's extraordinary talents began to receive notice, he set up a meeting with Herbert Breslin, one of the best press agents in the classical music world. Breslin had made his name when he promoted Alicia de Larrocha, a petite, unassuming Spanish pianist, into a major international success. Brash and self-confident, Breslin believed that if he admired an artist, the whole world only needed to know about this person to feel the same way. He had a good ear, and he knew that Domingo was on his way to an enormous career. The two men worked together, and, for a while, everything was fine.

Then Breslin took on Pavarotti, and Domingo was incensed. Most press agents represent only one major artist in each category, and Domingo had assumed that he was Breslin's tenor. He demanded that Breslin give up Pavarotti; the press agent refused, telling the tenor that if he didn't like the situation, he could go to another publicist. Domingo did exactly that. But the relationship between an artist and a press agent is complex, and it took Domingo several years to find another good fit.

The ensuing years showed that Pavarotti and Breslin, both uninhibited and down-to-earth, were made for each other in a way that Breslin and Domingo were not. Domingo, despite his affability, is a reserved man; he does not come across as simple and extroverted. Pavarotti, on the other hand, was willing to do whatever hard work was entailed in gaining valuable publicity. He saw nothing wrong with feature articles about his struggles with his weight; he loved serving as grand marshal of New York City's Columbus Day Parade, riding in front on a tall chestnut horse; he kissed and hugged every pretty woman in sight; he attended opening-night parties wearing his costume from the performance instead of a tuxedo. In short, he was great copy, and the media gobbled him up.

As Domingo's relationship with Levine grew, he sang more new productions, and between 1971 and 1983, he opened the Met season six times, more than any other contemporary singer. But, meanwhile, Pavarotti was discovering television: he sang in the first *Live from the Met* telecast; the following year, he sang a live telecast of a solo recital from the Met stage, an event that garnered New York's public television channel three times its normal audience. Not only was this the first time an opera singer had performed a completely live recital on national television in the United States, it was also the first done at the Metropolitan Opera House. The *New Yorker* proclaimed Pavarotti *primo tenore*. Domingo seethed.

Domingo was usually kind and friendly to everyone who worked at the Met; he would drop by the offices to chat with administrators, especially if they were young women or had pretty secretaries, and he regularly ate in the company cafeteria. Except for his secretary, he had no entourage.

Pavarotti was temperamental, irritable, and childlike. He would arrive at the Met with his secretary, nutritionist, and at least two press agents, and go directly to his dressing room, from which he emerged only to sing or sign autographs. He would cancel performances. The Met stage managers' most horrible memories were to have to go before an audience to announce a Pavarotti cancellation. "What am I supposed to say?" asked one in despair when Pavarotti canceled a Christmastime performance: "The good news is that Mr. Pavarotti asked me to send you all his holiday wishes. The bad news is that he sends his wishes from Modena." When Anthony Bliss himself had to announce a Pavarotti cancellation, he would stand in front of the curtain carrying a prop Valkyrie shield.

Pavarotti was not very respectful of his colleagues. If a photographer came to a rehearsal to shoot one of the other singers in a Pavarotti production, the tenor would reflexively clown around on the other side of the set, inevitably upstaging his colleague. Once, in the middle of a love duet, he became thirsty, and walked offstage to get a glass of water, leaving the soprano to stare after him in bewildered panic.

But somehow Pavarotti was always forgiven. When he was unhappy, he sulked or shouted. When he was happy, his smile lit up the entire theater.

Domingo also had a ready smile, if not quite so radiant, and a cheerful wave. And he never behaved like a temperamental superstar—until his obsession with Pavarotti took hold. Then the charming Domingo vanished. He no longer visited management offices to flirt; he was there to complain. "So many pictures in the _New York Times_ this Sunday," he whined to a member of the press department, "and none of me!"

In September 1979, Pavarotti had appeared on the covers of both _Time_ and _Newsweek_. The _Time_ article, "The World's Greatest Tenor," aroused Domingo to such fury that Pavarotti was easily able to play the injured victim. The feud between the two tenors caught fire.

Shortly thereafter, Domingo hired Edgar Vincent, another high-powered press agent, and went to war. Pavarotti may have given a live television recital from the Met stage, but Domingo teamed up with Zubin Mehta, music director of the New York Philharmonic, to present a televised tribute to Caruso. Pavarotti was not impressed. In a _Playboy_ interview, he sorrowfully said, "That was not the way to celebrate Caruso. . . . It was very embarrassing. It was really the festival of bad taste, like many other things Plácido does." When asked to comment on this, Domingo took the high road: "I don't talk about Pavarotti; he only talks about me."

Pavarotti himself was beginning to stretch the limits of good taste. He made a dreadful movie called _Yes, Giorgio_ about a tenor who loses his voice and falls in love with his throat doctor. He virtually stopped giving recitals in concert halls and mainly sang, using amplification, in sports arenas and casinos. He booked and sold out Madison Square Garden for a nationally televised recital. When Domingo did the same thing a year later with less success, he was criticized for bringing along a Mexican zarzuela troop, which so dominated the concert that the tenor was only onstage for fifteen minutes.

When Francis Robinson, the host of the Met telecasts, referred to Pavarotti as the most famous singer since Caruso, Domingo raced to his office and shouted in fury at the frail old man. When an advertisement for Pavarotti recordings appeared in a Met program for one of Domingo's performances, he refused to go onstage until he was promised that the ad would be pulled from future programs. The Spaniard, formerly admired for his courtly behavior, was acting like a man possessed.

With the help of his new press agent, Domingo positioned himself as "the thinking man's tenor," a logical rejoinder to the adulation Pavarotti inspired in his audiences. No one denied that Domingo was the better musician; he was an able pianist and would soon become a regular conductor at opera houses where he sang. Pavarotti could not read music, but he had flawless intonation and diction and a beautiful lyric sound. Domingo, who had begun his career as a baritone, had a darker, more stentorian tone.

As both men aged, they struggled with their weight. Pavarotti's zoomed up and down the scale. Domingo, after subsisting on starvation diets whenever he had to appear on television, finally accepted middle-age spread and let his costumers deal with it.

When Domingo's conducting ambitions were bolstered by a contract to lead *La Bohème* at the Met, Pavarotti fans said that Domingo had threatened not to sing in any opera house where he didn't conduct. At about the same time, Pavarotti made a major musical step in the *Idomeneo* he sang under Levine's supportive direction. But he appeared terrified; his eyes were frozen on the prompter, his body seemingly cemented to the front of the stage. The beauty of his singing could not override the panic on his face.

Neither man was a great actor. Domingo had one, querulous facial expression for despair, hope, love, and anger. Both musically and dramatically, he conveyed intelligence but not the impassioned core so essential to many operatic roles, and this kept the audience at arm's length. Pavarotti, who moved well despite his size until his knees and hips began to fail, rarely feigned any emotion. But he exuded the need for love, and that may be what evoked the audience's response. They respected Domingo but they loved Pavarotti.

Then circumstances changed for both men. Domingo continued to boldly experiment. After claiming for his own most of the dramatic tenor roles like Radames, Alvaro, Don Carlo, and, especially, Otello, he moved on to Wagner. His first Lohengrin at the Met in 1984 was revelatory; his lyric sound lent the heldentenor repertory a new dimension. Audiences accustomed to the "Bayreuth bark," which characterized most Wagner singers, melted at the beauty of Domingo's voice. Emboldened, he went from Lohengrin to Siegmund to Tristan. In 1999, at almost sixty, he took his first role in Russian as Ghermann in a Met production of _Pique Dame_. Learning Russian was a struggle for him, but his photographic memory and instinctive musicianship again rewarded him with success. He had no need to take on this challenge; he chose to take on the new role because, even after thirty years at the top of his profession, he still yearned to grow as an artist.

But the pleasure in these new successes was crippled by a family tragedy. In 1985, Mexico City was devastated by an earthquake and Domingo lost his aunt, uncle, and two cousins. Photographs in newspapers showed him frantically digging through the ruins in the search for his family. Although some made cynical remarks about the publicity value, Domingo was in mourning. And, soon after, his parents died. He canceled many of his engagements for the following year and spent time producing and singing in concerts to raise money for the Mexican people who had been left homeless.

Around the same time, Pavarotti was making tentative advances into a heavier repertory, but with little success. As he aged, his sweet voice did not darken as much as Domingo's had, and his attempts at roles like Otello were neither comfortable for him nor successful. Then Pavarotti's young daughter was diagnosed with myasthenia gravis, a potentially fatal disease, and the tenor was in misery.

Both men seemed to mellow; when their schedules overlapped at the Met, they were often seen deep in conversation. Everyone soon knew that mentioning one's name to the other was no longer a dangerous slip. Then, in 1987, another potential tragedy brought them close to real friendship, and put professional life into true perspective.

The young Spanish tenor José Carreras came to the opera stage several years after Domingo and Pavarotti. He had a far sweeter disposition than either of his colleagues and happily made friends with both.

When Carreras made his debut at the New York City Opera in 1972, the opera world was enchanted. Not only did he possess a beautiful lyric tenor voice but he was strikingly handsome, with an appearance more often seen on a movie screen than an opera stage.

Within two years, he was at the Met. All the staff members, accustomed to the usual singer mixture of egocentricity and dense stubbornness, were astonished to meet a singer who was intelligent, soft-spoken, modest, and blessed with a sense of humor, even about himself. He was also uninterested in publicity. Photographers found him an excellent subject because he was photogenic and polite, but he sometimes canceled interviews and photo sessions, not thinking them important. He was not immune, of course, to all the failings of famous tenors. Although he had a wife and child in Barcelona, he was soon swept up in a torrid romance with the Italian soprano, Katia Ricciarelli, a glamorous blonde. Neither one indulged in fey denials about their relationship; instead, they booked themselves as a couple in opera houses around the world, and filled in any gaps with joint recitals and television appearances.

In 1976, Carreras's wife, Mercedes, became pregnant. Ricciarelli, who apparently had believed that Carreras, although officially married, had remained faithful to her, was desolate, and their relationship gradually waned. Within a year or two, the tenor began an affair with Jutte Jaeger, a flight attendant with Austrian Airlines. Mercedes remained in Barcelona with the two children.

In 1980, when he was thirty-three, Carreras sang Radames in *Aïda* at Herbert von Karajan's invitation. It was a heavy role for his voice, but few young singers would turn down Karajan. Carreras soon added Don José in *Carmen* to his spinto repertory, and, within a few years, his voice had lost much of its silken quality and freshness. He still sang beautifully, however, and remained a favorite with major opera houses because of the passion he brought to the new roles.

In 1987, Carreras sang Don José in the Met telecast of Peter Hall's *Carmen* production, and the reviews were so terrible that he told friends he would never return to New York. His career in Europe was unaffected. Also in 1987, he agreed to sing Rodolfo in a film of *La Bohème*. The role had been his debut at the New York City Opera, and he had starred in the premiere of the legendary Zeffirelli production at the Met. In July, he flew to Paris to begin the filming, but after the first day, he canceled the next sessions. He was exhausted, and sought medical advice.

Carreras was far more worried than he let anyone see. His mother had died of leukemia at the age of fifty, so there were grounds for his fears. His blood tests showed that he had an extremely low platelet count, and two days after the _Bohème_ filming was to have begun, his doctors confirmed that Carreras did have acute lymphocytic leukemia. The prognosis was bleak.

Carreras canceled _Bohème_ and went home to Barcelona for chemotherapy. He underwent treatment for four months—his hair fell out, his weight plummeted, and he was constantly nauseated. His manager at Columbia Artists told the press only that "José Carreras . . . was hospitalized for a toxicity in his blood system . . . the result of dental problems and an adverse reaction to antibiotics."

But by December he had undergone a bone-marrow transplant at the Fred Hutchinson Cancer Research Center in Seattle, and his condition became public knowledge. Over 100,000 cards and letters poured into the hospital, friends and colleagues were in constant touch, and both Jutte Jaeger and Mercedes Carreras went to Seattle. Somehow, Carreras maintained the inner strength necessary to cope with the cure as much as with the disease. After the successful transplant procedure, he received radiation therapy, and within four months, he was well enough to return to Barcelona. But neither he nor anyone else knew whether he would ever return to the stage.

Carreras consulted European throat doctors to assess the damage to his vocal cords from the radiation and chemotherapy. They were optimistic, so he began to vocalize cautiously, and to use his suddenly acquired free time to become acquainted with his two children.

But the marriage was irretrievable. He and Mercedes divorced and Jutte Jaeger eventually left him. In 1988, he established the José Carreras Leukemia Foundation, and traveled widely to raise funds. Finally, in 1989, he was well enough to sing, and he gave his first concert in Barcelona for an audience of 150,000. "It was better than any medicine," he said. "It was good for my spirit."

Both Pavarotti and Domingo had been deeply affected by Carreras's illness. When Carreras presented the idea of the three of them giving a benefit concert for his foundation at the Italian World Cup, they agreed immediately. All three were avid soccer fans, and they relished a chance to sing together and raise money for such a good cause.

Zubin Mehta conducted the concert at the Baths of Caracalla in Rome; it coincided with the World Cup finals, and was filmed for TV and video distribution. For lack of a better title, it was called "The Three Tenors." And so a phenomenon of classical music was born.

Chapter Thirty

More Change

The first new production of the 1988–89 season was Handel's *Giulio Cesare*, at which the conductor Trevor Pinnock was to make his Met debut. He was exactly the kind of conductor the Met had been chided for not engaging—he was a highly respected early music specialist, young, photogenic, with excellent recordings. If it seemed paradoxical for him to appear in one of the world's largest theaters conducting a Baroque opera, he himself regarded it as an interesting experiment.

James Levine's favorite singers headed the cast, with Tatiana Troyanos in the title role and Kathleen Battle as Cleopatra. Troyanos, a tall, statuesque Greek-American mezzo, was one of Levine's closest friends and possessed his most-prized artistic quality: she imbued her performances with an intensity that mirrored the passion with which she lived her life. But she suffered so severely from stage fright that it was agony for her to walk out on stage at all. During one performance of *Parsifal*, when she was singing Kundry, she became so upset during the second act that she started to walk offstage. Only the stage manager's firm grasp propelled her back on.

Trevor Pinnock's friendly disposition was comforting to Troyanos. Like many conductors, he was short in stature but tall in self-confidence, and his sense of security pleasantly affected the entire production—with one exception.

Pinnock had heard all the Kathy Battle stories, but he wasn't worried about working with her. He was the expert in the field of Handel opera, after all, and felt certain he could handle any difficulties.

But Pinnock was used to the affable world of early music, where artists are supportive of one another, and he had never encountered a singer as insolent as Battle. She frequently stopped rehearsals, running to the stage edge to lean over the orchestra pit and demonstrate to Pinnock how he should conduct. It is true that singers and conductors often disagree about tempos and dynamics, but they discuss these matters privately. Battle, however, upbraided the conductor in front of the other singers, the stage crew, and, worst of all, the full orchestra. Pinnock tried to make light of the situation, but he was so disconcerted that he consulted a former boyfriend of Battle's, a member of the Met Orchestra, about how to handle her. The tension, meanwhile, reduced Troyanos to tears.

In the end, unfair as it seems, _Giulio Cesare_ was a triumph for Battle. She looked wonderful, and the music suited her elegant musicianship. But her successes no longer silenced her demons; her antics became more and more bizarre. When her role, Zerbinetta, in Strauss's _Ariadne auf Naxos_ was sung by another soprano a few months after she had done it, she accused the woman, who had been her cover, of shrinking her costume. When she sang with the Boston Symphony, she changed hotels because she thought the bellmen were looking at her strangely and that room service was slipping peas and other strange substances into her pasta. She delayed for months some of the albums she had recorded for Deutsche Grammophon because she couldn't decide on a cover photo; she would arrive for a photo session with racks of evening gowns and insist on being photographed in each one. Traveling to engagements, she would refuse to board a plane because she had a "bad feeling." When she performed with orchestra and opera companies, minor staffers were instructed not to talk to her. She stopped taking phone calls and insisted on being contacted through her manager, who would then send her messages to her in writing.

The most famous episode took place during a recital tour. Riding in her limousine, she used the phone in the backseat to call her manager in New York. She wanted her to call the driver in the front seat and ask him to turn down the air-conditioning in the car.

Battle was out of control. Levine was far too canny not to realize that. On the same Japanese tour where she had been confronted by Carol Vaness, Battle, along with Levine and Domingo, had been assigned their own interpreter because they had more press and public appearances than the rest of the artists. One morning, Levine's interpreter called to say she was sick. Since he had a television interview that day, his assistant called a member of the Met management and asked her to arrange for Levine to borrow Battle's interpreter for the afternoon.

The administrator called the hotel where Battle was staying so that the soprano could approve the switch. Unfortunately, Battle had made up a list of people approved to be put through to her room and the administrator was not on it. When someone on the list had been located, he called and reached the interpreter. She said she'd be delighted to work with Levine, but, of course, would have to ask Battle's permission. But Kathy was still asleep. The Met caller convinced her to slide a note with Levine's request under the diva's door. Several hours passed.

Shortly before the TV crew was to arrive at Levine's hotel—he was staying at the same hotel with the rest of the company, unlike Battle— Battle's interpreter called to say that Kathy had told her she could not translate for Levine.

Levine told close associates that he had reached the end of his patience and would no longer schedule appearances with Battle. But he apparently sidestepped breaking the news to Battle herself. He continued to give recitals with her, and she sang at the Met for another six seasons under other conductors.

Trevor Pinnock never returned to the Met.

When Bruce Crawford was named general manager in 1985, he told an interviewer, "I think you should remain in a job as long as you're passionate about it, and when that feeling passes, you've got to turn to another arena." By 1988, the beginning of his third season as general manager, he was beginning to feel restless at the Met.

"It's more different from a business than I originally perceived," he told the *Times*. "In enterprise, rewards are financial. Here, associations are long-term and people get psychic rewards. You count on a support system of people doing something for the love of it."

Although an opera house filled with people who work there because they love opera would seem admirable, Crawford found drawbacks. In the corporate world, people constantly look ahead to the next position, to the next rung on the ladder. In the opera house, he found, people were content to stay where they were. This did not lead to dynamic decision-making. Since people planned to stay where they were, the only evidence of their authority was the number of people who worked for them. All the department heads reported directly to the general manager, and therefore tended to fight among themselves. Crawford had appointed two assistant managers—Joseph Volpe and Marilyn Shapiro—and delegated to them most departments, with the exception of press and finance. As a result, Crawford frequently found himself in an empty office with his capable assistants solving all but the most intractable problems.

From his office at Milbank, Tweed, Anthony Bliss expressed disapproval. "I knew the people who worked at the theater much better than Bruce could," he said, "because my door was always open. I talked with everyone." But Crawford didn't want to talk to everyone. He found the petty squabbling ridiculous and enervating. The board irritated him by constantly suggesting how he should run the Met as a business. He put a stop to that by icily suggesting that any board member who second-guessed him could leave; no one did. The endless labor problems were maddening and frustrating, so he left those in Volpe's capable hands.

The artistic area was one that continued to fascinate him. With the skills he had honed in advertising, he made the box office more secure than it had been in years; he wasn't afraid of huge sums invested in new productions because he had produced thirty-second TV spots that cost as much. And he enjoyed negotiating with the artists and directors even while he was amazed by their lack of business sense. "It helps that I've run a big business. . . . If Franco Zeffirelli is doing a new production, you know he'll spend more than you tell him to spend. You pay for it out of the cushion somewhere else in the budget."

At the Met, Crawford saw people who behaved like small children, throwing tantrums, canceling performances, walking out of negotiations, yelling at each other. There was screaming, there were tears, even at the top level of management. He was a disciplined, intellectual man with a lively curiosity about the undisciplined environment of the opera house, but the truth is that, in the end, he lost patience.

In November 1988, Crawford resigned suddenly from the Met and took a position as CEO of the Omnicom Group, the second-largest advertising agency in the world.

The announcement stunned the music world. Louise Humphrey, his successor as board president, barely managed a civil public expression of regret at his decision. Privately, she was incensed that he would leave so abruptly and with absolutely no backup plan in place.

Theories abounded about why he was leaving, and since few knew how bored he had become, almost everyone assumed that he had financial motives. He had taken a huge cut in income to become general manager, and though the trappings of wealth did not interest him, the cerebral rigor required to earn a great deal of money did. For two and a half years, he had sat on the edge of the giant sandbox that is the Metropolitan Opera, and now he was ready to go back to the grown-up world, with grown-up compensation. His salary at Omnicom was estimated to be in seven figures.

James Marcus, the board chairman, and Louise Humphrey discussed their search strategy. They knew they still had the old problem in finding a new general manager: with Levine in place, the new intendant would have all the difficult parts of an administrator's job with none of the fun parts. The same cast of characters who hadn't been interested in the position when Bliss had resigned were still not interested. So Marcus and Humphrey turned to an executive search firm, and set September 1989 as the deadline for finding a new chief executive.

Then another factor was added. Herbert von Karajan, music director for life of the Berlin Philharmonic, resigned after a series of disputes with his musicians. The greatest orchestra in Europe was looking for a new music director.

Herbert von Karajan was a giant even among the colossal figures of history's great conductors. He conducted more orchestras, made more records, earned more money, made more enemies than practically any other maestro. His only rival as the greatest conductor of the late twentieth century was Leonard Bernstein, another outsized personality.

His early career was shadowed by his membership in the Nazi Party and the admiration bestowed on him by his fellow Austrian Adolf Hitler. But in 1955, after some of the scars of World War II were a little less tender, he became the fifth music director of the hundred-year-old Berlin Philharmonic. He set out to rebuild the orchestra. To attend a Karajan performance with his orchestra was to see an entire orchestra playing with the passion of a solo musician. The musicians moved as one, the tips of the string players' bows rising and falling with a miraculous exactitude. Technically, the musicians were close to perfection. In later years, Karajan conducted with his eyes closed. Since a conductor's eyes are his foremost means of communicating with his musicians—more important than the beating of time—it was as if Karajan wanted to show how completely his orchestra was in his thrall.

But if there is such a thing as a prima donna among orchestras, the Berlin Philharmonic was just that. The musicians would not let even Karajan forget they were self-governing. Five years before his resignation, he had a confrontation with his musicians when he asked them to hire a young woman as principal clarinetist. The orchestra members believed she was too much of a soloist to integrate herself into the orchestra. In the Berlin Philharmonic, integration of the individual into the whole is one reason the orchestra is so great. The orchestra refused Karajan's request to engage the clarinetist.

There were further disputes over recordings and tour fees, all complicated by Berlin City politics, which, since the city supported the orchestra, affected every aspect of the Philharmonic. The situation deteriorated to the point where Karajan, in Salzburg, sent a telegram to the orchestra offices saying, "Looking forward to our concerts together in Salzburg." The orchestra replied, "Orchestra not looking forward to them at all."

The final straw, as it happened, was a misstep committed by Karajan's manager, the president of Columbia Artists Management, Inc. (CAMI), Ronald Wilford.

Much has been written about Ronald Wilford's influence on the world of classical music. *Who Killed Classical Music?*, by the English music critic Norman Lebrecht, essentially blames Wilford, and the greed he encouraged in his artists, as the cause of the imminent destruction of the classical music industry. Wilford, in addition to running Columbia Artists, acts as the personal manager for most of the world's principal conductors. To be accepted as one of Wilford's clients is a badge of honor among young and not-so-young conductors, even though many of them are assigned to his assistants. The theory is that he who controls conductors controls everything. Wilford is James Levine's manager; therefore, it must be he who decides who sings and doesn't sing at the Met. Wilford manages the music directors of most of the world's big orchestras, and thus can stipulate who appears or doesn't appear with them—or so the theory goes. His domination of professional conducting, however, is awesome.

The first person to express incredulity at this formulation of his power is Ronald Wilford himself. A soft-spoken, slender man in his early seventies with silver hair and sharp features, he is known in the industry as the Silver Fox. For years, he has cultivated an image of obsessive secrecy. He is never photographed if he can help it, and he gives press interviews on the average of once a decade. His list of clients is impressive: James Levine, Seiji Ozawa, Valery Gergiev, André Previn, and James Conlon are but a few. And among these are the music directors of four of the leading opera companies in the world.

With his artists, he is gentle, unless they are considering choices he thinks are wrong. With young conductors, he is fatherly; they respond almost in gratitude, relieved after the hours of commanding orchestras to have someone else make decisions.

The only man Wilford ever called his protégé is Peter Gelb, a controversial figure even before he went to work for Wilford. The son of a managing editor of the *New York Times*, Gelb rose from a job as an usher at the Met to a public relations associate to assistant manager of the Boston Symphony. He accomplished this, some say, with the help of his powerful father, Arthur Gelb. But Peter Gelb is endowed with personal charm and a rare ability to get along with such difficult artists as the late Vladimir Horowitz, Jessye Norman, and Kathleen Battle. Of course, no one rises as fast as Gelb did without making enemies, and he brought them along with him when he left the Boston Symphony to work with Wilford at CAMI.

While he was there, Gelb also forged a partnership between CAMI Video and the Metropolitan Opera. As president of CAMI Video, he became the producer of the Met telecasts, a highly unusual arrangement between a profit-making and nonprofit institution. It came to an abrupt halt with Joseph Volpe's rise to power. Indeed, it was reported that Volpe, who got along well with Wilford, threatened to throw the brash young Gelb across Lincoln Center Plaza.

Gelb's way of working also infuriated the members of the Berlin Philharmonic. If Wilford had a prime client, it was Herbert von Karajan, and he put Gelb to work selling the Berlin Philharmonic—on tour and on television all over the world. In 1987, Gelb booked a tour of the Far East for Karajan and the Philharmonic. He charged a fee of DM 600,000, which was astronomical in classical music, and demanded that the presenters in Taiwan also buy ten Karajan telecasts at an additional cost of $350,000. The Taiwanese refused. When the tour fell through, and the Berlin musicians quickly learned why, the affair became a scandal in Berlin. The musicians' anger was clearly directed at Wilford and his associate as much as at Karajan, whom they saw as selfish and greedy.

Karajan was eighty years old and in poor health. He had no strength to continue fighting with his orchestra, and in 1989, he submitted his resignation. The orchestra accepted his resignation and began the search for a successor.

In no time, lists of all the leading contenders were being circulated. James Levine headed every list, followed by Lorin Maazel, Seiji Ozawa, Daniel Barenboim, Bernard Haitink, and Riccardo Muti. "I don't think the orchestra itself knows what it's going to do," Levine told the *Times*, and Wilford agreed.

These events in Berlin had immediate repercussions in New York at the Met, because Levine seemed poised to take the Berlin position. As the 1988–89 season drew to a close, the company had lost its general manager and the continuous presence of its artistic director seemed uncertain. Levine, however, has always denied that he was ever interested in Berlin. "I never agreed even to be thought of," he said. "That never had the slightest validity."

Herbert von Karajan went to his home in Salzburg, where he maintained iron control of the Salzburg Festival. There, on Sunday, July 16, only a few weeks after his last concert with the Berlin Philharmonic, he died.

In September 1989, ten months after Bruce Crawford's abrupt resignation, the search for his successor was in such disarray that the *Times* described the institution as a large and rudderless ship. Louise Humphrey and her search committee were not about to consider Joseph Volpe, who had been Crawford's primary deputy. It was said that one board member had declared in horror, "He wouldn't even know what fork to use." Later, Volpe would speak with rare bitterness about Humphrey: "Louise has a tendency to forget that her father was pretty crude." Her father, the venerable Cleveland blue blood J. Livingstone Ireland, was one of the Met's main patrons in that tour city. Often, at dinner parties before performances, he would stand up, pull out a bullhorn, and bellow, "Get your asses into your seats!" But Volpe didn't stay bitter very long; he tried to understand the board members' reluctance to give him the top job. "They needed someone they could talk to," he said.

Other than the board, people at the Met could not have cared less about Volpe's social skills. All those who dealt with him knew that he was a tough manager, with a strong sense of fairness and compassion toward everyone, from the stagehands to the principal artists. Those people hoped he would be given the position, and Bruce Crawford recommended him to the other directors. When his advice was rejected, Crawford withdrew from the search committee. He seemed uninterested in a process that judged people by their table manners.

Volpe, in fact, knew exactly which fork to use. Because Crawford as general manager had delegated authority, Volpe had gained experience in all areas where a general manager functions. He knew the board well; he knew the company inside out; he had stabilized labor relations; he was sensitive to the smallest nuance of company politics. On the 1988 tour to Japan, Volpe had taken over the seating of every party, making sure that people who needed to sit next to each other did and people who disliked each other were at opposite ends of the room. He kept the superstars like Kathleen Battle happy, as well as the singers who resented being overlooked by the Japanese sponsors. He was everywhere on that tour, a tall, imposing figure who always had a funny remark to reduce tension or a diplomatically worded rebuke for company members who slipped up. Crawford and Levine, although they stayed at the same hotel everyone else did, kept more or less out of sight, except at performances. But Volpe was an authoritative presence. And he was always on the scene, no matter how late at night or how early the next morning.

Somehow, on that same tour, he had found the time to fall in love. Jean Anderson was one of the dancers in the Met Ballet. In becoming involved with her, Joe Volpe was following in the tradition that went back to Gatti-Casazza, to Rudolf Bing, to Anthony Bliss. The problem was that Volpe was already married, as was Jean. Volpe's second wife, Nancy, had also been a member of the ballet. He and Jean were relatively discreet about their relationship, but nothing is secret in an opera company, especially during a tour. Neither Crawford nor Levine seemed to care; many of the board members, however, had a less-enlightened attitude.

When the tour was over, Volpe and Jean both separated from their spouses, and a year later, in September 1999, they were married. The guests at their wedding were Met dancers, administrators, orchestra musicians, labor lawyers, and, of course, the stage crew.

Volpe faced other vital decisions that fall. His reputation as a gifted administrator had spread beyond the classical music world, and he was constantly approached about major positions, including one as the commissioner of a major sport. Twenty years earlier, under similar circumstances when Bing's regime ended, Herman Krawitz left because he was not named as the new general manager. That was probably the wrong decision, as the board itself realized when they tried to lure Krawitz back during the difficult Chapin era; the company endured several traumatic years of fiscal and labor crises as a result. But Volpe decided to stay.

Eventually, the board's search committee, in consultation with an executive search firm, selected as general manager a man who was possibly the most unlikely choice in the arts world. Hugh Southern had spent most of his professional life in the theater and had most recently been the deputy director of the National Endowment for the Arts in Washington. He was well liked in cultural circles, but lacked the experience and the stature necessary for his new position. Anthony Bliss, who had consistently avoided involvement in Met business since he had stepped down, was so alarmed when he heard about Southern that he went to the board and told the members they were about to make a terrible mistake. Levine was not consulted; he had only one brief meeting with the new general manager before he was appointed. Southern, however, was charming and refined and he had an English accent and had gone to Oxford. Soon he was going off on quail hunts with Louise Humphrey at her Florida estate, and cutting an elegant figure in black tie at gala openings. He did not get around to much else at the opera house.

Seven months later, Southern was unceremoniously fired by the board on June 22, 1990. The board had given him a job for which he was not prepared or qualified. It was almost as if he had never been there.

_C_hanges at the Berlin Philharmonic, meanwhile, were happening more rapidly than Wilford or Levine had expected. In October, just before the orchestra met to elect its new music director, Levine's German agent, an associate of Wilford's, began to negotiate a European tour for Levine and the Philharmonic. She asked for a fee of DM 250,000, approximately twice as much as the orchestra had charged with Karajan. When the presenters in London balked at the expense and canceled a concert at the Royal Festival Hall, the orchestra wanted to know why, and were told that the problem was the fee Wilford's associate demanded. This was only a short time after Peter Gelb had lost the orchestra several engagements by asking too much. Wilford had also been Karajan's trusted manager, and the musicians had become leery of his influence.

When the musicians met to elect their new music director, Levine was not under consideration because the orchestra associated him with

Wilford. After several votes, the musicians found themselves deadlocked between two prominent European conductors; they decided to compromise on Claudio Abbado, the music director of the Vienna State Opera. He had been just about to sign a contract as the new music director of the New York Philharmonic, but he accepted the Berlin offer instead, leaving the New York Philharmonic with no music director designate.

So, Levine remained at the Met. Now he was ready to face what was going on in his opera company. With no new general manager, he once again had to assert the power he had ceded to Bruce Crawford only a year earlier.

The 1989–90 season ended with another run of *Ring* cycles. Even this production, which had brought so much acclaim to Levine and the company, turned into disaster when Hildegard Behrens was injured by falling scenery during the last scene of *Götterdämmerung*. But the *Ring* was telecast nationally on four successive evenings. It was a critical and popular success, so the season finally ended on a positive note.

The capital fund drive to refurbish the opera house had also been successful, and workers throughout the theater were hard at work during the summer of 1990: resealing the windows, replacing the worn carpeting in the lobbies, painting the columns and arches, fixing the stage floor, replacing the house curtain, and updating the radio booth and other equipment. Spring cleaning was in full swing when, at the annual meeting of the Metropolitan Opera Association in May, Bruce Crawford was elected chairman of the executive committee. By this time, Southern was on his way out; his failure had weakened Louise Humphrey; Crawford was back in control.

And on August 1, 1990, the board named Joseph Volpe to the newly created position of general director, the principal administrative officer in the company. Marilyn Shapiro, who had had ambitions toward the general manager's office, was named to another new position, executive director of external affairs, in charge of all fund-raising and marketing. Humphrey had been an opponent of Volpe and a strong supporter of Shapiro, but she was appeased by Shapiro's new title.

Immediately, the mood at the opera house brightened. Volpe faced considerable challenges: he had enemies on the board; he had an artistic director hungry for domination; and he knew that the two previous years of uncertainty and weak administration had weakened the company. But he was exactly where he wanted to be.

Years earlier, when Rudolf Bing had announced his retirement, Volpe was at his father's house for Sunday dinner, and noticed the family Ouija board. He picked up the board, and disingenuously asked, "Will I be general manager one day?" And the board had answered, "Yes." Volpe preserved the intuition that someday, probably in the not-too-distant future, he could be the man at the top. He had reached that top in under twenty years.

Chapter Thirty-one

JOSEPH VOLPE TAKES OVER

When Volpe was named to the top administrative post, the board still had so little faith in his capability, and his social graces, that they changed the title from general manager to general director. But Volpe had not spent his years at the Met without cultivating some wily skills of his own. The first thing he did was turn his relatively rough exterior to his advantage. He was not, after all, as working-class as he pretended to be. His family roots were solidly middle-class. When Volpe had elected not to attend college, he had seemed to be turning away from his background; now he enhanced his social status immeasurably.

The respect he felt from most of his Met colleagues helped Volpe curtail his bitterness at his initial rejection by the board. It also helped him deal with his first major crisis, which struck when he had been in office only two days.

A new production of *Die Zauberflöte*, scheduled years earlier for the 1990–91 season, was to be produced by the film director Werner Herzog. But when Volpe looked at the plans, he quickly saw technical complications that would make the production impossible. He canceled it immediately, only four months before the premiere, and substituted a borrowed production by David Hockney. This swift action brought a rush of publicity about the new general director's style, but this did not worry Volpe; he knew a quick decision had been required. For Volpe, this would be the first of many such crises and his method of coping with them would quickly evolve into his distinctive way of operating.

Joseph Clark, the technical director, soon became the man Volpe relied on, much as Dexter had once relied on him. Intelligent and well educated, with a solid technical background from the Yale Drama School and years of working in German opera houses, Clark worked harder than anyone else. Some of the resident designers, however, found his perfectionism intolerable, particularly after Volpe's trust in him became obvious and several of them left after confrontations with him. "He had a certain prim and proper taste but he didn't know how to implement it," one said. "He loved to push people around. Joe Volpe used Joe Clark to do all his dirty work. Joe Clark would tell people they couldn't do such and such, and Joe Volpe would still be the good guy." Clark also had little patience with activities in the opera house that were not directly related to rehearsals or performances. He was particularly irritated by the onstage dinners. "Why don't we just stop doing opera and give parties?" he asked, horrified.

When Volpe became general director, Clark was considered the second-most-powerful person in the opera house. Some worried that he was running things behind the scenes. But Clark loved opera; he loved the mechanics of getting a production onstage and he loved the music. Although he could be extremely charming, he had no patience for stroking the egos of board members or star singers, and certainly none for fund-raising.

Volpe and Clark soon learned of a clear differentiation between the various works in the repertory. "Every production that has an Italian composer becomes complicated and develops a long history," Volpe pointed out. "We've had much better luck with the non-Italian repertory." The statistics bear him out. During the Volpe years, many of the Italian operas have changed directors and designers multiple times. The producers themselves tend to have as volatile personalities as opera singers are believed to possess. There were innumerable transmutations with Piero Faggioni, Zeffirelli, Ezio Frigerio, and Gian Carlo del Monaco—cancellations, reinstatements, and substitutions. Meanwhile, the other new productions proceeded onstage with few delays or problems, among them *Parsifal, Katya Kabanová, The Ghosts of Versailles, Elektra, Die Meistersinger von Nürnberg,* and *Ariadne auf Naxos.* They were not all successful, but the toll they took on the Met company was less debilitating.

James Levine, who on New Year's Eve 1990 described the previous year as the worst of his life, rebounded from his disappointments to bring his orchestra to new prominence. In the spring of 1991, the Met Orchestra made its first solo tour, and then performed at Carnegie Hall as part of a festival celebrating Carnegie's Centennial season. Other orchestras participating in the festival were four of the American "big five": the Boston Symphony, the New York Philharmonic, the Philadelphia Orchestra, and the Cleveland Orchestra. The Met Orchestra proudly took its place in this elite company, and the consensus was that it was an equal among equals.

In May 1991, at about the same time that the Met Orchestra was having a triumph at Carnegie Hall, Bruce Crawford traded his position as chairman of the executive committee for that of president of the board, making formal the power structure that had Crawford above both Volpe and Levine. "It's great to have a board president who once ran the company," Volpe said. "He knows how everything works, and he doesn't want my job, because he's already had it." There was some discussion about just how much time Crawford would devote to administration, but Volpe maintained an effective public image as the chief executive. Crawford occasionally stepped in to make decisions, but, in actuality, Volpe was running the Met.

At some point during his second season, Volpe changed from the man who had become so familiar to the company; he began to show his formidable temper. He shouted at people, often in front of others. Some in the company became afraid of him. His inconsistency was the most frightening: no one knew what might set him off, and this heightened the apprehension. As assistant manager, Volpe had been fatherly. Now, apparently, he had decided to rule by fear. He did not exactly interpret his attitude this way: "I consider it an honor to work here," he said, "and I have no patience with people who behave as though it is not an honor."

In August, Anthony Bliss was seriously injured while driving his jeep on Prince Edward Island. The local hospital, not equipped to handle grave injuries, transferred him to Huntington Hospital on Long Island.

Bliss had been alone in Canada because Sally was teaching dance in New Brunswick. She had maintained her career while married to Bliss, and had run the second company of the Joffrey Ballet. Bliss admired her determination; he had always liked strong women and had hired many of them at the Met. When she heard about her husband's accident, she was in Washington attending a meeting of the National Endowment for the Arts. She was concerned, however, and stayed closely in touch with her husband by phone.

His eldest daughter, Barbara, was convinced that the accident had been the result of a small stroke, but the Long Island hospital sent him home after only three days. When she spent the evening with him a day or so later, she found him exhausted; all he wanted, he told Barbara, was to spend the rest of the summer in one place. He had dinner with her and two of his sons, and left the next morning to return to Prince Edward Island.

When he arrived there, the only other person with him was Timmy, one of his two sons by Sally, who watched in horror as his father's strength ebbed. On August 10, Bliss had a brain hemorrhage, and died shortly after Sally arrived at his side.

Bliss left his entire estate to Sally, but, in actuality, there was little money left from the Bliss fortune. He had suffered financially by taking the general manager's job, and his two divorces had been costly.

After Anthony Bliss died, there was no member of the Bliss family associated with the Metropolitan for the first time in its history. There is a plaque in the boardroom, commemorating Cornelius Bliss's contributions to the company, and a large portrait of Anthony Bliss hangs in Founders' Hall. Elegant and imposing, he is clad in an opera cape, something no one remembers him wearing while he was general manager.

In 1992, the Met and its orchestra had announced agreement on a new three-year contract, to take effect in 1993–94, the fourth time the musicians and the Met had reached an early agreement. The long chronology of labor strife retreated farther and farther back into history.

A year later, in 1993, Joseph Volpe finally received the title of general manager. As Bruce Crawford said, the traditional title now "represent[ed] his responsibility and authority with the company."

No one now doubted Volpe's ability. Everything was going wonderfully well. The company had for the first time in twenty-five years presented the world premiere of an opera—John Corigliano's *The Ghosts of Versailles*—followed the next season by another world premiere, *The Voyage*, by Philip Glass. There had been tours to Europe and Japan, and recordings by both the full company and the orchestra alone; the original contract with Deutsche Grammophon had been supplemented by an agreement with Sony Classical.

Volpe had also introduced Met Titles, a creative solution to the problem of supertitles. For years, the company had been criticized for its refusal to join the growing trend to provide audiences with simultaneous translation of the opera's libretto. The Met's proscenium was too high for the usual supertitles, went the company's argument, and Levine was quoted as saying that there would be supertitles only over his dead body. But Volpe believed that supertitles were an irreplaceable asset in making opera more accessible to the general public. So he and Joseph Clark devised a way of projecting an English translation of opera texts onto the back of every seat in the house. The positive results were immediate. Levine proclaimed himself ecstatic; even the orchestra musicians felt the audiences' new responsiveness, as they now understood what was happening onstage; the box office receipts improved. Met Titles are a prime example of Met innovations; while the company often introduces something years after every other opera house has done so, in the end, it does the project better than anyone else.

JAMES LEVINE IN HIS MIDDLE YEARS

In June 1993, James Levine turned fifty. After almost a quarter-century at the Met, he looked much younger than his age, his hair still a halo of curls, his face ruddy. But behind the wire-rimmed aviator glasses he always wore, regardless of fashion, his eyes were more wary. Perhaps this was because of "the rumors," since the rest of his life had a charmed quality. His parents had been supportive, he had had extraordinarily early success, he had been running one of the world's great opera companies while still in his thirties. If he had any personal problems, he kept them well hidden. Sue Thomson continued to attend every performance, as did his brother, Tom, and his assistant Ken Hunt. Thomson and Levine had never married, but they had formed a household, despite rumors that each had other relationships from time to time.

In some ways, Levine's relations with his brother were more intriguing than his living arrangements with Thomson. Tom Levine, two years younger than James, is a painter. But, in addition, Levine pays Tom a salary for handling his finances and the coordinating of his schedule, which still leaves Tom freedom to pursue his own career. The younger brother nurtures the older. If James needs a fresh drink or a plate of food at a party, Tom will get it. When James developed a tremor in his arm in the late 1990s, Tom, with utter discretion, helped cut his brother's food.

And while most of the business between Levine and the rest of the company is conducted by Ken Hunt, when Levine travels or is on tour with the Met, Tom Levine is omnipresent. He makes appointments with people James wants to see and discourages those he doesn't want to see. When, on the eve of a Three Tenors concert in Spain, Levine was stricken with an ear infection, which meant he could not fly to Europe, he dispatched Tom overseas to explain the illness to the tenors, men with fragile egos.

Tom Levine, in general, lacks his brother's considerate manner, and is not always popular with people at the Met. "Tom can be a big problem for Jim," Volpe has said. A record company executive once wondered whether Tom represents the dark side of James; she called him "the evil twin." The brothers do look so much alike that they could be twins, especially as they have grown older. But Tom's hair is less unruly, and he does not wear aviator glasses.

When Tom is not around, his duties fall to Ken Hunt. Hunt, a tall, slender man with pale blond hair, left his studies at Harvard College to work for Levine. He presides over his many duties in a first-floor office at the opera house, piled from floor to ceiling with correspondence and scores. No one can reach Levine without being cleared by Hunt, and since so many people need to talk to Levine so often, Hunt has to make difficult decisions.

He is also in charge of Levine's travel, and, again, this is no small job. Levine, who hates to be pinned down, may make several reservations for each trip so that he can choose his flight at the last moment. Hunt takes care of Levine's car and drives him almost everywhere. At one time, Levine always drove or was driven in a large Cadillac. But after working in Germany and Austria, he switched to a Mercedes-Benz. Several years ago, at the bustling corner of Broadway and Seventy-second Street in New York City, a man approached Levine's car, pulled a gun, forced Levine and Hunt out of the car, and drove off in the Mercedes. Levine was most concerned about the music that was in the trunk.

Music lovers are accustomed to the image of a conductor who wears arrogance as naturally as white tie and tails. Leonard Bernstein, also an American, swept into concert halls wearing a black opera cape; Karajan flew his own jet and dressed only in black. Riccardo Muti, the director of La Scala, is almost as renowned for his profile and flowing dark hair as for his performances.

Levine fits no one's image of a conductor. He wears the same outfit every day, except at performances: a white golf shirt, blue polyester pants, and the black sneakers that replaced his desert boots a couple of years ago. The only thing that changes from day to day is the color of the towel swathed across his left shoulder. And he pays careful attention to that color. He once paused to compliment a staff member on the tint of her dress and informed her that he had a towel in just that color. At one rehearsal, he arrived in the pit to find the entire orchestra waiting attentively, each musician adorned with a towel. Levine loved it.

"People forget he is from Cincinnati," pointed out Richard Dyer, a writer for the _Boston Globe_ who has been Levine's friend for many years and who also grew up in the Midwest. "He's defined by this. Total friendliness as a way of guarding yourself is a Midwestern trait." Everyone speaks of him with affection—the press, the public, his orchestra, the singers, the Met staff—and refers to him as Jimmy. But no one knows him. What is baffling is that he has such a friendly and uncomplicated demeanor. Levine has maintained this benevolent detachment throughout his Metropolitan Opera life. But in every opera house, the conductor is treated with an awe that would not be inappropriate for the sovereign of a small nation, and Levine is no exception. Despite his informal manner and appearance, Levine simply is not like everyone else.

Levine has always given Christmas gifts to the people he works with. In the past, he gave different presents to different people, and maybe he would have been surprised to know that his Met colleagues tried to gauge their place in Levine's esteem by their gifts. Did a bottle of champagne mean he liked you less than someone to whom he gave a set of his CDs? For some reason, boxes of cookies were considered the most prestigious, possibly because Levine loves cookies. He finally made the process easier for himself by making charitable contributions in everyone's name. The comparisons stopped.

Friendliness may seem an unlikely irritant, but when it is experienced in juxtaposition with Levine's inherent aloofness, it can be perplexing. Like all charismatic people, he homes in on the person to whom he is talking. "He makes you feel that you and he are the only ones standing against the end of Western civilization as we know it," one friend said. Anyone who has experienced that sense of privileged intimacy is disappointed to

Luciano Pavarotti quickly became an audience favorite who always guaranteed a sold-out house. When the tenor unexpectedly canceled a performance, Bliss anticipated the crowd's fury with a shield that he borrowed from the prop department as he announced the news.

In 1977 the entire nation got a glimpse of the charismatic Pavarotti when he appeared in Puccini's *La Bohème* with soprano Renata Scotto in the company's first live telecast, the precursor to the Met's renowned series.

Rivaling Pavarotti's increasing popularity, however, was another talented tenor, the handsome and brilliant musician Plácido Domingo, shown here as the Duke in *Rigoletto*.

Meanwhile, more creative approaches to stage productions sometimes were met with disapproval and even outright laughter, as with Sir Peter Hall's 1982 production of Verdi's *Macbeth*.

After an absence of several years, Joan Sutherland returned in 1982 to sing the title role of Donizetti's *Lucia di Lammermoor*—a repeat of her 1961 debut performance—and retired five years later.

Backstage, however, the company was shaken by the highly publicized murder of violinist Helen Hagnes by stage crew member Craig Crimmins at the opera house in 1980. The tragedy also uncovered a miasma of more lurid activities, forcing the rising administrator Joseph Volpe to introduce stronger discipline measures.

During Bruce Crawford's *(left)* tenure as both general manager and board president, director Otto Schenk *(right)* was a favorite of James Levine and, during the 1980s, frequently was invited to stage productions from the German repertory.

Two months after the murder, the Metropolitan Opera orchestra went on strike, the last major labor disruption in recent Met history.

The Met's image became more glamorous during the mid-1980s economic boom, as reflected in the backstage gathering after a performance of Zeffirelli's production of Puccini's *Turandot,* which included *(left to right)* the Wagnerian soprano Birgit Nilsson, Zeffirelli, Levine, Eva Marton, who had sung Turandot that evening, Zeffirelli's close friend Elizabeth Taylor, and Plácido Domingo, who had sung the role of Calaf.

Nineteen-ninety ushered in a new era under the direction of Joseph Volpe; he became the first person ever to work his way up through the company ranks to become general manager.

A few weeks after the highly publicized dismissal of the soprano Kathleen Battle, one of Levine's favorite protégées, the conductor's own rapport with the singer was fragile as he joined Battle in a recital at Carnegie Hall.

On the company's roster today is one of its most prominent singers, soprano
Renée Fleming. The beauty of her voice and her personal warmth easily shine
through in such roles as her celebrated portrayal of the Marschallin in
Strauss's *Der Rosenkavalier*.

Other leading singers include Ben Heppner and
Karita Mattila. Heppner is highly regarded for
his musicality and strength as a heldentenor,
which has enabled Wagnerian productions that
previously were considered uncastable;
Mattila's versatility in a broad spectrum of
roles, combined with her beauty, have made
her, along with Fleming, one of the most
sought-after sopranos in the world. In 1995
these two rising stars appeared in the new
production of Tchaikovsky's *Pique Dame*.

In the meantime, Cecilia Bartoli has become one
of Levine's favorite young singers; he respects
her hard work and musicianship and often defends
her against accusations that she frivolously cancels
performances.

The famed conductor Herbert von Karajan was a mentor to Levine.
Karajan often engaged him at the summer Salzburg Festival; when Karajan died,
Levine conducted his memorial concert and was erroneously predicted to
succeed him at the Berlin Philharmonic.

Tension between cast members and directors was common throughout the company's
history; the mid-1990s production of *Carmen* with Domingo and Waltraud Meier was no
different. The choice of Meier—a mezzo renowned in the German repertory—for the
lead role was met with fierce resistance from Zeffirelli.

In 1997 the position of principal guest conductor was established and given to Valery Gergiev, the charismatic Russian conductor; this spurred rumors that he was being positioned to replace Levine as artistic director at some time in the future.

In the late 1990s, an enigmatic Cuban-American philanthropist, Alberto Vilar, arrived on the scene, stunning the music world with his record-breaking gifts to the most distinguished artistic organizations worldwide, including $25 million to the Metropolitan Opera.

By the time the Met celebrated the millennium, Levine's *(left)* and Volpe's *(right)* personal differences had melted into affection.

discover that the busy conductor has little time for personal friendships. "First you get the private phone number, then the private private phone number, then the beeper number," remembered a former Met administrator. "And then, one day, he just walks past you in the hall."

Although the musicians in the orchestra appreciate Levine's clear respect for them and reluctance to lose his temper—"I am not a 'lose-my-temper' kind of person," Levine has said. "I don't like to say something terrible to someone and try to clean up afterward"—and greatly admire him as a musician, they are still wary of him and of what may lie behind the compliments he strews about. One maxim of the Met Orchestra musicians is: "Beware the Three *F*'s: you're fantastic, you're fabulous, you're fired!"

The Met musicians do worry about Levine's health. For several years, Levine has coped with a muscle tremor in his left arm and leg for which he receives physical therapy and medication. He attributes the tremor to a pinched nerve that has resulted from the effort of keeping his ubiquitous towel on his shoulder, but others are concerned that the cause may be less benign. In any case, his recovery has been patchy. He also suffers from attacks of sciatica, an occupational hazard of standing up through so many long performances. "I don't have a twenty-five-year-old body anymore," he said, "and I can't keep up a twenty-five-year-old's schedule."

Often during rehearsals, Levine appears to be having a conversation with the orchestra—except that he is the only one talking. He enjoys talk. His running commentary is one of his musicians' few complaints, and members of the administration refer to him, when he is at his most voluble, as James Levine, Guest Lecturer. His comments, although always anchored in music, range over philosophy, nature, psychology, literature, and contemporary culture—or the lack of it. He grew up at a time when classical music and all the arts were a more prominent part of American life than they now are, and he feels a lack of cultural connection to most of the population in this country. "One thing that has happened in the last half of this century is that, little by little, people gave up on really having a society that is connected to itself." His complex, circuitous sentences can make his meaning hard to unravel, but his passion is evident.

On occasion, the orchestra members' doubts about his sincerity have been borne out by Levine's dealings with singers. According to one story, Levine ran into a singer who had made his debut the previous evening, and congratulated the singer on his performance. The singer, flushed by the praise, went on to his meeting with one of the artistic administrators, expecting to be offered future contracts. Instead, he was summarily fired; it was done on Levine's direct orders. "His greatest single problem," one manager of prominent singers groused, "is that, in front of a singer, he'll promise the world. Then, when the singer's not around, he'll renege."

Another singer, who has been very successful at the Met, said, with some bitterness, "Jimmy is famous for getting rid of singers who don't sing what he thinks they should. Joe [Volpe] sees artistic planning as part of a larger picture than Jimmy does. Joe looks at everything from the point of view of the good of the house, the interest of the audience, the good of the company."

But, in general, singers truly admire Levine. Most of the world's great singers appear at the Met largely because they want to work with Levine. "Jimmy is so quick," said Cecilia Bartoli. "Besides, it's wonderful to see a conductor enjoying himself during a performance."

"He always said, 'Take your breath, I can wait,'" reported Leonie Rysanek. "I always have the feeling Jimmy loves voices."

"He loves with a capital *L* what he is doing," Plácido Domingo reflected. "And when he is happy, his face can say 'bravo' long before the audience has a chance to shout it."

"They're doing the best they can," Levine said about the singers. "They're looking at me to lead, inspire, organize. I have a real horror of pointless criticism." Talking of his press coverage, one of his least favorite subjects, he said, "Remember the long phase when every article talked about how I'm too nice?"

Because of his gentle manner, it is easy to forget that Levine is a powerful man. His approval or disapproval can create or destroy careers. "He's adorable," said an associate, "but he's the most powerful man in the music world today, so who's not going to say he's adorable?"

There are some aspects of being powerful that Levine clearly does not cherish. One of these is publicity, and Ken Hunt runs endless interference between his boss and the press, whom Levine seems to see, collectively, as a pack of vultures. "He really has not tended to his image," observed a *New York Times* reporter. Perhaps this is a reaction to the gossip about him, but it may be that he is naturally a private person. There has been much speculation about how Levine's dislike of the press has cast the Met in the image of, in the words of a critic, "an impregnable fortress." Even the English director Jonathan Miller, who has done several new productions with the company, says the Met is "just like the Vatican."

Many believe that Levine has a responsibility both to himself and the institution he heads to be more approachable, and to make himself more available to the press. He does not share this belief: "In order for me to do my work, I've had to keep from being distracted." Interviews are distractions, but he will grant them if the subject is the music he is performing and not himself. "Suppose somebody says, 'Tell me about your life, everything which isn't about music.' I resent the implication that there is a sharp distinction between the parts of life. Someone who thinks I'm reclusive doesn't know me. But, for me, socializing with a big group of people is noisy and tiring."

Levine has said, "If I worried about the noise about me, I couldn't get anything done."

Much of the noise around him for years had to do with his sexual preferences; these rumors were probably started by a hostile board member or disaffected company member, but they have been perpetuated by some members of the press. Levine has obviously been hurt. "This guy came to interview me and he brought a pile of stuff he'd gotten off the Internet. He didn't know I'd been on the cover of *Time* magazine, but he did have to ask me if I had an arrest record. I've never even had a parking ticket!" He continued: "A journalist once asked me if I were having an affair with So-and-so, and answering 'That's none of your business' doesn't begin to express my outrage. I have two questions. How much of myself is not enough, and how good do I have to be?"

Leonie Rysanek, who worked with Levine often, made an astonishing comparison:

> He reminds me sometimes—only nicer, more modest—of Karajan. With Karajan it was the same. I knew he loved my voice, he

was a great admirer of mine, but you never, ever could come so near that you could give him a hug. Jimmy hugs you at least. But there is a similarity between him and Karajan. It's a great talent, it's the same talent . . . he's a wonderful, brilliant musician, a wonderful, clear conductor. But there is also with Jimmy the feeling that "I don't want to have people look into me . . ."

I hope, really, for Jimmy that he will have a wonderful second part of his career. For a conductor, he's still young. I hope there will be more easiness in his life. A sad bird doesn't sing. Jimmy doesn't trust anyone; he doesn't even trust himself.

[After my first rehearsal with Jimmy] I said to [my husband], "At last there is another conductor who makes me feel loved." He always makes me feel wonderful, even when I'm not. He lifts me up, and that is a rare gift.

BACKSTAGE WITH PLÁCIDO DOMINGO

Plácido Domingo, who, in 1993, celebrated the twenty-fifth anniversary of his Met debut, has become a man the public feels comfortable with. Even in middle age, he is considered an avuncular sex symbol, and he has a reputation for geniality, a contrast to the temperamental tenors who have a temper tantrum at the drop of a soprano's high C. In reality, he is someone whose public image is different from the private person.

Domingo certainly has his assets. Around the opera house, he can be an understanding colleague, at least until he feels that another singer—not necessarily a tenor—is being given the attention and publicity he feels belong to him.

Probably the low point of this kind of behavior was at a dress rehearsal for *Don Carlo* in the winter of 1983, a production that marked the return to the Met of the beloved soprano Mirella Freni, after an absence of seventeen years. Domingo was tired during the rehearsals; he always packed his calendar as full as possible. He was under contract to the Met during *Don Carlo* rehearsals, and was not supposed to leave New York without informing the artistic department. Yet he did not tell anyone when, the day before the dress rehearsal, he flew to Paris for the opening of Franco Zeffirelli's film *La Traviata*, in which he had a starring role. The next morning, he returned to New York on the Concorde and went directly to the opera house for the dress rehearsal, scheduled to start at 11:00.

It was 10:45 when he walked through the stage door, and, on his way to his dressing room, Domingo glanced inside the Green Room.

Always alert for the sight of a camera, he spotted a *New York Times* photographer setting up to photograph Mirella Freni. The pictures were to accompany an article on her return to the Met. Freni, elegantly clad in her act 1 costume, clasped the leads of the four Russian wolfhounds she was to lead onstage at her entrance. The room was hot with the extra lights, and filled with the smell of large, warm dogs. Domingo took a long look at the four huge, panting animals, went into his dressing room, and commanded his secretary, "Get me the press office."

When the representative arrived, the tenor shut the door, turned to her with his usual suave smile, and said, "Tell me, can those dogs sing Don Carlo?"

Silence.

Domingo's smile vanished. "Well, they'd better be able to, because I'm the one singing the title role of this opera, and you've chosen to photograph the dogs, not me!"

The press representative tried to explain about the Mirella Freni article, but Domingo did not listen. Instead, he picked up the phone and called James Levine's dressing room. "I'm leaving," he told the conductor, "and if you want to know why, ask your press department." With that, he stormed out of the dressing room and out of the theater.

It takes more than a display of temperament to discombobulate Levine. When he climbed on the podium at 11:00, he said, "Mr. Domingo has chosen not to sing the rehearsal, so you'll have to put up with me singing Don Carlo today," and then gave the downbeat. Until Domingo's cover was found, Levine sang the title role from the podium.

Mirella Freni graciously overlooked Domingo's absence—he did sing the premiere and apologized profusely for his behavior—and the *Don Carlo* revival met with the success of most Domingo performances. And Levine continued to admire Domingo as an artist and perform with him as often as possible.

One of Domingo's appealing characteristics is his occasional refreshing frankness about himself. After he had trouble with the high tessitura of *Les Troyens* in 1983, he told an interviewer, "There's always the risk of an unknown part. You cannot know it until you actually do it." Perhaps he was mollified by finally getting his own _Newsweek_ cover and watching his crossover album with the pop singer John Denver hit the best-seller charts. He also published _My First Forty Years,_ an autobiography that some thought a little premature.

Shortly afterward, Domingo took up conducting. He had always been a fine musician, and, with an eye toward the future, he informed opera houses around the world that he was now available in the pit as well as on-stage. He was engaged everywhere; no intendant wanted to take the chance that forgoing the maestro Domingo might also mean losing the tenor Domingo.

Adding a conducting career to his already frantic schedule brought Domingo more of the public attention he craved, but in one area, he was experiencing some trouble with his public image. Domingo had long cast himself as the faithful husband and family man, a stance that produced much merriment in opera houses. Like Pavarotti, Domingo had long en-joyed the sexual perks that come with world fame. Pavarotti had managed to keep his philandering relatively discreet, because he usually had one principal girlfriend at a time, and because his girlfriend also filled a role in his entourage. He did make lewd remarks to women in his dressing room and was known to grab any female within arm's length, but most of this was clearly an act, meant as a compliment to the woman.

Domingo would never grab a woman's breast in public, and, when asked about rumors of his womanizing, always assumed a saintly expres-sion and waxed poetic about his love for Marta, his wife of many years. Reporters who dared to voice suspicions about the truth of this image risked being immediately barred from future interviews. Domingo even suggested he allowed women to be attracted to him for their own good. "Women follow me to many, many places," he said. "It is beautiful, you know, beautiful that they have something in life to look forward to."

On at least one occasion, a woman he may have spurned got even. Marcia Lewis, a California gossip columnist, wrote _The Private Lives of the Three Tenors,_ a book filled with false anecdotes and factual errors. In the preface, she hinted that she had had an affair with Domingo, a claim she repeated during her tour to publicize the book. Domingo, outraged, issued a denial. The book sold few copies, and Ms. Lewis retired as an author. She would later become much better known as the mother of Monica Lewinsky.

But everyone in the opera world knew of Domingo's womanizing. None of his affairs seemed particularly serious, but almost no female in any opera house was safe from his advances—singers, coaches, secretaries, stage managers, and stage directors.

Domingo's age has always been in question, but the general consensus is that he hovered around sixty toward the late 1990s. Like several of his colleagues, including Pavarotti, he reacted to this birthday by entering an uncharacteristically serious involvement with a much-younger music student. He became so infatuated that he decided to leave his wife. When he called various friends to tell them of his plans, the general reaction was that the great lover had finally been snared.

Marta Domingo had lived through many of her husband's affairs. Friends say she had threatened divorce in the 1980s, when photos of her husband embracing a young woman in an airport appeared in the Spanish papers, and when his liaisons with a famous movie star and the wife of a world leader were spread across the tabloids. Even though this time it was her husband who wanted to separate, Marta did not flinch. And Domingo, who, despite his philandering, is devoted to his extended family, if not exclusively to his wife, may have realized that leaving Marta would fatally disrupt his world. His frenetic schedule, combining operatic roles, concerts, conducting engagements, and the recent addition of running two opera companies, depended on a secure foundation at home. He stayed with Marta. "Life is complicated, you know," he has said, somewhat obliquely. "If you have something to admit once in life, if somebody makes a mistake and admits it, she might understand. The only thing she will say is 'Plácido, don't forget it is an eye for an eye. For one tooth, the whole mouth.'"

Marta, however, wanted a career. She decided to expand her earlier experiments in stage directing.

Domingo is an intelligent man, and he has planned intelligently for his life after singing. He had hoped conducting would replace his singing, but his musical gifts did not transfer so easily to the podium. When he realized that his conducting career was relatively limited, he turned to administration, and by 1998 was artistic director of the Los Angeles Opera and the Washington Opera. In both jobs, he has proved to be an energetic and effective fund-raiser.

In both Washington and Los Angeles, Domingo engaged Marta as a stage director; she is now the resident stage director in Washington. He would often sit in the auditorium during Marta's rehearsals, whispering in her ear as she plotted the action for the next scene. "They're like the Macbeths," marveled an opera director after observing Marta's rehearsals. Met company members were stunned by the recent news that Marta Domingo will soon make her Met debut directing the opera *Sly* by Ermanno Wolf-Ferrari, which will star her husband.

Domingo's schedule takes on a compulsive quality as he juggles his three careers, sometimes crossing the Atlantic or continents two or three times a week—and perhaps squeezing in romantic assignations. His thirst for attention and reassurance has somehow compromised his copious gifts, and, throughout the opera world, there is sadness that his musical artistry has not been enough for him.

Is It a Power Struggle?

Jonathan Miller has compared the Metropolitan Opera to the Vatican; others find the Kremlin a more appropriate analogy. Possibly only a Kremlinologist would have noticed the minute but far-reaching changes charted in the Met's house program during the winter of 1992.

When Joseph Volpe was appointed general director in 1990, the program listings had his name on the same line as Levine, the artistic director, and Marilyn Shapiro, the director of external affairs. By March 1992, Shapiro's name had been relegated to the page listing the board of directors, but Volpe and Levine remained at the top.

By September of 1992, Volpe alone inhabited that line; James Levine was listed directly beneath him. By 1993, when Volpe was at last named general manager, the Met publicity also underwent a change, generally unremarked at the time. Instead of bearing just the name of the Metropolitan Opera, it appeared now as the Metropolitan Opera; Joseph Volpe, General Manager; and, on the line below, James Levine, Artistic Director.

Levine reportedly was upset that Volpe's name appeared above his, but he was reassured that no mere listing could change his place in Met history. His tenure would always be remembered as the Levine Years. Anyone who knew Volpe well, however, realized that the new general manager would concede nothing to future historians. He wanted to be remembered as the primary power during his years at the top, and he was determined to ensure that.

Vanquishing Marilyn Shapiro had been easy, in the end, despite her influence with certain board members. With Crawford's confidence and support, Volpe created the public perception that he was in control.

The 1993–94 season was a pivotal time. For Levine, it began tragically when Tatiana Troyanos died of breast cancer in her mid-fifties.

But on September 27, despite his personal sadness, the Met opened its season with a gala performance celebrating the twenty-fifth anniversaries of the debuts of both Plácido Domingo and Luciano Pavarotti. Domingo sang the role of Siegmund in act 1 of *Die Walküre*, a role Pavarotti would never attempt; Pavarotti sang one act of *Otello*, one of Domingo's most famous roles; and they shared a performance of Manrico in one act from *Il Trovatore*, which both had sung to great acclaim. The two tenors, no longer feuding, were now fast friends.

*D*espite the gala opening, the 1993–94 season was difficult for Volpe and the entire company. New York City underwent one of the most severe winters in decades, with seventeen snowstorms, and box office revenue plummeted. The country's economic growth was slow, and, as always, the Met's finances reflected the national situation. Volpe, having decided to institute a cost-reduction program, carefully reviewed season planning, especially in respect to repertory balance. He also took a long, cold look at the company's marketing strategy and decided to strengthen it with some long-range changes. He began to develop a new structural hierarchy for the administrative staff.

In March 1994, the first new staff member was announced, one who promised direct challenge to Levine. Sarah Billinghurst, a top administrator with the San Francisco Opera, was hired as Volpe's assistant manager. Billinghurst had been in charge of casting in San Francisco and this was her major area of expertise. Her hiring was a major step for Volpe into artistic territory since one of the people closest to Levine was Jonathan Friend, who had been in sole charge of casting up to this point. The Met press announcement was clear: Friend would report to Billinghurst, and Billinghurst would report to Volpe.

By coincidence, at about this time, one of Billinghurst's favorite artists made his Met debut. The Russian conductor Valery Gergiev, artistic director of the Kirov Mariinsky Theater in St. Petersburg, had made his United States debut with the San Francisco Opera. In March 1994, he arrived at the Metropolitan to conduct a new production of *Otello*, with Domingo in the title role. When Gergiev had first begun conducting outside the former Soviet Union, he had led a Spanish production of *Otello*, also with Domingo, who suggested Gergiev as conductor for the new production he wanted at the Met. Levine respected Domingo's musical judgment, and the Met enjoyed pleasing singers who guaranteed sold-out houses. So Gergiev was engaged, even though *Otello* had always been Levine territory. Incidentally, Gergiev's manager was Ronald Wilford.

From his first days at the Met, Gergiev imparted that ineffable quality of charisma possessed by most of the great conductors, back to the days of Arthur Nikisch and Arturo Toscanini. He projects an intensity and passion, even with his back turned to the audience. The consensus has always been that Levine lacks this kind of magnetism, for all his energy, charm, and drive.

Gergiev also has a talent for making important friends. Domingo is a prime example, and the tenor was soon announced as president of the Friends of the Mariinsky, an international organization dedicated to raising money for the impoverished opera and ballet in St. Petersburg.

Meanwhile, Volpe became prouder of his ability to bond with artists than with wealthy donors. He formed close friendships with several of the major artists, something that never happened during the Bliss and Crawford eras. Volpe and Pavarotti forged a particularly close bond; Volpe became one of the few people who could talk Pavarotti onstage when he wasn't feeling well. He and Domingo were also friends. And when Gergiev began appearing at the Met, he and Volpe developed a mutual appreciation.

Volpe could not avoid comparing Gergiev's outgoing personality with the more reclusive Levine. For example, when he and Gergiev lunched at one of Volpe's favorite restaurants, San Domenico on Central Park South, they ate at a table in the middle of the room. When he and Levine went there, they sat in a corner where no one could see them. In fact, this was Levine's special table; he always sat there during his frequent lunches at San Domenico.

Soon Volpe and Gergiev were discussing ways in which the mighty Met could help Gergiev's struggling company. The Mariinsky was richly endowed with productions of the Russian repertory, which was not an area in which the Met had ever concentrated. But the Met was replacing its productions of the Italian repertory, and Volpe suggested lending or even giving the old productions to the Mariinsky. In return, the Met would borrow elements of the Mariinsky's Russian productions. Clearly, in addition to his charitable impulses, Volpe was intrigued by Gergiev and his dramatic struggle to keep the Mariinsky alive. That Gergiev understood the value of publicity and his own charisma also did not escape Volpe. For years, the Met had been regarded by the press as secretive, a characterization reinforced by Levine's avoidance of reporters and critics. Gergiev, on the other hand, loved to give interviews.

Meanwhile, at the end of the 1992–93 season, James Levine had given up his position as music director of the Ravinia Festival in Chicago, where he had spent his springs for the past twenty-three years. His unvarying pattern had been to spend winters at the Met, spring with the Chicago Symphony at Ravinia, and summers divided between the Salzburg and Bayreuth Festivals.

During the summer of 1994, he conducted the premiere of a new *Ring* cycle at Bayreuth; it was the culmination of his years there, and he became the first American ever to conduct the *Ring* at this Wagnerian shrine. But Gerard Mortier, who had become the new head of the Salzburg Festival after Karajan's death, was determined to cut as many links as possible to the Karajan years, and Levine no longer appeared there. At the end of the summer, he returned to the Met, unsure what effect the new assistant manager would have on the running of the company.

By now, Kathleen Battle no longer was engaged by any opera company. Her conduct had alienated everyone who had worked with her—administrators of the major opera companies and orchestras, recital presenters, and almost every conductor with whom she had worked. One of the few exceptions was still Levine. Battle was considered capable of driving Mother Teresa to homicide, and Levine's continuing, although diminished, loyalty to her was a mystery to everyone who knew them both.

One of Levine's favorite orchestras is the Vienna Philharmonic. He was the conductor when Battle announced she was indisposed and pulled out of a performance of Mozart's Mass in C minor at five o'clock on the evening of the concert, causing the venerable orchestra to cancel for the first time in its history. Already disliked by the Philharmonic musicians, who had nicknamed her "the singing mosquito" because of her tiny voice, she was never engaged again.

In the winter of 1993, Battle arrived at the Met to rehearse for a revival of *Der Rosenkavalier,* in which she was to sing Sophie, one of her signature roles. She had sung the part often under Levine, but this revival was conducted by a gifted young German, Christian Thielemann. At one of the final rehearsals, she attempted to correct his conducting, just as she had with Trevor Pinnock during *Giulio Cesare.* But Thielemann did not have Pinnock's forgiving nature. He refused to speed up his tempos to satisfy Battle's whims.

Battle stormed off the stage, and from her dressing room placed a call to Volpe's office, demanding that he come see her immediately. Volpe at that very moment was on the phone with Luciano Pavarotti. Told that Battle had summoned him, Volpe went right on talking to Pavarotti. If Battle wanted to see him, she was welcome to come to *his* office. Her response was succinct. She walked out of the opera house and out of the *Rosenkavalier* production.

Volpe was furious. He called Battle's manager, the ubiquitous Ronald Wilford, and told him, "Everyone is entitled to one mistake, but no one gets more than one."

Volpe did not have to wait long for the next Battle confrontation. For the following season, 1993–94, she was contracted to sing the title role of Donizetti's opera *La Fille du Régiment.* She arrived for rehearsals well prepared, having just sung the role in San Francisco during her final appearances there. Levine was away, vacationing in Florida.

The problems started almost immediately. Battle repeatedly asked for changes in the rehearsal schedule; she was frequently late; she walked out when she felt like going home; and, occasionally, she did not show up at all. She accused the other singers of staring at her mouth and demanded that none of them look at her while she was singing.

Certainly, there have been other artists with temperamental quirks, but she alone brought her bad manners onstage at rehearsals. Even the most difficult singers who scream and storm backstage behave with respect toward each other onstage. Not Battle.

One of the cast members of *La Fille du Régiment* was Rosalind Elias, a mezzo-soprano who had been with the Met for nearly forty years, a warm, affectionate, hardworking woman who was beloved at the Met. Elias played the role of the Marquise of Berkenfeld, who in the second act plays the piano while coaching Marie, Kathleen Battle's role, in a song. During a rehearsal, Battle began to upbraid Elias, accusing her of playing the piano so badly that she was throwing off Battle's timing. She became more and more abusive, and finally walked out. Even Battle veterans were aghast at her attack on an older colleague.

This time she had picked the wrong fight. Volpe and Elias were old friends. He had warned Battle that she could not get away with any more misbehavior. He called Ronald Wilford.

Wilford tried to smooth over the situation. Battle's problem, he told Volpe, was not insolence but perfectionism. She had a higher musical standard than most singers, and this made her difficult to work with.

Volpe was not impressed. He called Levine in Florida the next day to tell him that he had decided to fire Battle. He knew of Levine's loyalty to Battle, but he also knew the time had come to take a stand. Levine told Volpe that he disagreed with his decision, and urged the general manager to do what he himself would have done had he been in New York: nurse Battle through the few performances. In the future, Levine said, Volpe could veto future contracts with Battle.

Although artistic decisions, according to his contract, were Levine's domain, he could be overruled by Volpe under extraordinary circumstances. Levine suspected that the present circumstances could be considered extraordinary, so, even though he thought Battle should not be fired, he covered himself. "Joe, you're the one sitting in that chair," he said. "My job is to tell you what I think. I'm telling you."

Two days later, Ronald Wilford went to Volpe's office and spent an hour trying to persuade him to change his mind. Even as the men were talking, the press office on the fifth floor was preparing a release announcing the dismissal.

The Metropolitan has often clashed with its major singers, but the company usually presents the disputes in polite press announcements that Miss So-and-so or Maestro X has withdrawn from scheduled performances due to "artistic differences" or, more frequently, "indispositions." Met insiders know that if someone is "ill," then the cancellation is valid. But "indisposed" covers a variety of situations: the artist involved hates the stage director, conductor, or the other singers; the artistic administration realizes that a singer, booked years in advance, is no longer able to sing the contracted role; the artist has not been considered for future performances and withdraws in a fit of pique from current contracts; or the artist has received another offer, usually more lucrative and geographically convenient. The last usually provokes the Met into legal action. One thing "indisposed" rarely means is illness.

Despite arguments from Wilford and Levine, Volpe was determined. His patience with Battle had run out, and he was also eager to establish himself as the general manager who would not put up with bad behavior. Volpe had come to the Met during the iron-fisted regime of Rudolf Bing, the man who had become a household name by firing Maria Callas. The lesson had not been lost on Volpe.

Perhaps what was more important was that he was ready to take a public stand on artistic matters. None of the previous general managers had dared dispute Levine's policies unless they had clear financial implications. Volpe had now held the top administrative position for four years, and it was time for him to challenge Levine.

"Kathleen Battle's unprofessional actions . . . were profoundly detrimental to artistic collaborations between cast members," read Volpe's quote in the Met's press release. These strong words were being faxed to the major cultural press even as Battle made a last-minute phone call to Volpe, asking for one final chance. "What can I do to make you change your mind?" she asked, but it was too late. Within minutes, telephone lines all over New York City were buzzing with the news that someone had at last dealt with the spoiled superstar.

Battle sent out her own release, complaining that no one had warned her that she was acting unprofessionally, and Wilford defended her as "a perfectionist." There was no statement from James Levine, who was on his way to see his ailing father in Cincinnati. His father died the day after Battle was fired.

The reaction of the music world to Volpe's decision was one of jubilation. At one of Battle's record companies, the staff threw an impromptu celebration party. At the Met, company members broke into spontaneous applause. Joseph Volpe was hailed as a hero by other opera companies where Battle had misbehaved, and Volpe basked openly in the acclaim.

Levine said privately that he could not understand Battle's behavior, but, publicly, he continued to support her. In April, while she was making a recording of Mozart arias with him and the Met Orchestra, she decided that the musicians were acting disrespectfully toward her, and left the session. The recording was never finished.

Later that same month, Levine accompanied her at a long-scheduled recital in Carnegie Hall. Battle refused to rehearse with him, saying she had just performed the same program with another pianist and knew her music. Levine, who actually is the perfectionist Battle claims to be, went through with the recital, but his unhappiness was clear. The two have not collaborated since.

Kathleen Battle's career did not end after her Met debacle. She went on making best-selling recordings, appearing with symphony orchestras at astronomical fees, and giving recitals, which were reviewed with less and less enthusiasm. But her opera career was over. No one expressed much regret.

Levine's position as the artistic director of the Met was unchanged in the aftermath of the Battle episode. But there had been a nearly imperceptible shift. Volpe had dismissed one of Levine's favorite singers, and the artistic director had been unsuccessful in trying to dissuade him. For twenty years, Levine had allowed no one to encroach on his territory; after only four seasons, Volpe appeared to have done so.

Rarely have two men achieved equal status at the Met at the same time.

The dismissal of Kathleen Battle is not just the story of a temperamental diva. The lasting importance of her downfall is its effect on the relations between Levine and Volpe. Both men deny this, but Battle's firing clearly seemed to be the first major victory for Volpe in the undeclared war for control of the world's largest opera company.

THE LONG CAREER
OF LUCIANO PAVAROTTI

Joseph Volpe was far more understanding of a singer like Luciano Pavarotti. And Pavarotti, who, like many famous people, was overwhelmed by sycophants, appreciated Volpe's directness. When the tenor canceled his appearance at Levine's twenty-fifth anniversary gala at the last minute, Volpe called his hotel and insisted he come and at least put in an appearance. Pavarotti refused, insulted that Volpe would tell him what to do. But the quarrel was quickly mended, and the two men were back on good terms, sparring occasionally but mostly enjoying mutual respect and affection.

In 1996, when Pavarotti was learning the role of Don Alvaro in *La Forza del Destino* for performances in the winter of 1997, he was beset by personal and health problems and decided that he could not learn the role in time. Volpe, though sympathetic, did not want to lose the valuable Pavarotti appearances, which guaranteed sold-out houses. He offered a compromise.

In the fall of 1996, the Met announced that the previously announced ten performances of *Forza* would be replaced by the same number of performances of *Un Ballo in Maschera*, a role Pavarotti knew well. The soprano Deborah Voigt and the baritone Juan Pons, who had been scheduled to appear in *Forza*, switched to roles in *Ballo*. "Changing the Met's schedule is an extremely rare occurrence and one we do not undertake lightly,"

Volpe said in the press release about the change. And he made excuses for his star singer. "Luciano would very much like to sing *Forza,*" he told the *Times,* "but last season, respiratory difficulties forced him to cancel quite a few performances and . . . he never had a chance to learn *Forza.*" A recording of *Forza,* scheduled for the same period, was canceled.

The outcry from the press was long and shrill. Article after article proclaimed the end to Pavarotti's glorious career, or, even worse, his ignominious descent into tacky casinos and sports arenas.

When Pavarotti published his autobiography in 1995, he called one chapter "Some Rain Must Fall." No matter how famous he was, no matter how much money he earned, Pavarotti's apparently carefree life had been troubled for a long time. What set him apart from most of his colleagues was his admission of this. He was not, by that time, interested in projecting the image of a career pursued without miscalculations. That would not have been an accurate picture, and Pavarotti is an honest man.

Perhaps that is what made him the most famous singer since Caruso. His openness in front of an audience is obvious: he clutches his signature giant white handkerchief not just to mop his perspiration but because he gets terribly nervous. His entire stage personality seems to plead for the audience's love.

Pavarotti acknowledges his flaws. When he was vilified for lip-synching a concert in his hometown of Modena, he conceded that he had been wrong. He uses a score in concerts, because he has trouble remembering the words even to songs he has been singing for thirty years. He regretfully admits that he can hardly read music. And the audience loves him all the more for his human failings.

Pavarotti is outspoken, too, about his vocal crises, of which he has had several. In the early 1980s, right after his burst of superstardom, he began having vocal problems—not large ones, but a source of worry in a man still under fifty. "I took too many sleeping pills," he cheerfully told a reporter from the *Times.* "When you take them every day as I did, there comes *una lenza nelle corde vocale*—the vocal cords were sleepy. But it is now three years that I don't take any. I don't sleep as good, but I feel very healthy."

For years, he shared with the public his battle with his weight. Each new diet began in a blaze of publicity. There were performances of *Tosca* in Paris when he was too heavy to stand for the whole opera. He sat down whenever the story line permitted and was mortified when, in act 2, the chair he lowered himself onto collapsed in pieces on the stage.

He has a passion for riding and horses, and one weight-loss regime was launched when he became too heavy for his horse. For years, he traveled with his own masseuse and nutritionist, although there was always reasonable doubt that he paid attention to their advice. He also traveled with a complete set of his own pots and pans so that he could cook meals for himself and his friends. Not everyone looked forward to these dinners; several artists reported that Pavarotti's cuisine was close to inedible.

But the personal flaw that has attracted the most attention, of course, is his taste not for food but for women. Here again, he has not acted like his colleagues. Many a singer has a well-earned reputation as Don Giovanni offstage, and there is little overt disapproval unless extramarital affairs caused pain to the artist's family. Pavarotti was never indiscriminate. Since the late 1970s, he has regularly been accompanied by a woman, only one at a time. His three or four mistresses over the years have all been beautiful, articulate, educated women, who appeared to be deeply in love with him as a man, not as a celebrity.

His wife, Adua, came from Modena to visit him on rare occasions, sometimes with their three daughters, sometimes by herself. The current girlfriend would then tastefully absent herself and revert to her official role, that as a member of his staff.

Often, the wives of famous singers have personalities as strong as their husbands', and Adua Pavarotti is an excellent example. She fell in love with Luciano and he with her when they were teenagers, and in 1961, after a seven-year engagement, during which the tenor tried to launch a career, they married. This was a banner year for Pavarotti. Not only did he make his operatic debut and marry Adua, but he also bought his first car. In reading his autobiography, it is hard to tell which excited him the most.

Adua stopped traveling with her husband when their three daughters were little. She stayed involved with his career by becoming his business manager. She bought property and invested his large fees, and she became so good at the business that she started her own company, Stage Door, to manage other artists.

Then, except for finances, their lives began to separate. Inevitably, however, Pavarotti's companions left him when they saw no hint that he would divorce Adua. What they didn't consider was the age factor—and the waning career factor.

Marriage in the opera world is a tricky feat. Women singers have problems finding men willing to give up their own careers for the constant traveling, and those men who are willing are often not the strong support these powerful women need. Children are usually out of the question or neglected or the cause of great sacrifice. Male singers who do have children must accept that their wives will not be able to travel with them while the children are young. Any opera production often requires a stay of three months in a faraway city, and this happens several times a year. It is a very strong marriage that can survive that kind of separation.

In recent years, several famous male singers who turned sixty have, with astonishing uniformity, left their wives, including Sherrill Milnes and Samuel Ramey. But Pavarotti's decision to leave his wife has been the most publicized. For years, people had wondered at Adua's seeming acceptance of her husband's philandering. Her response was that he might "look at another bowl of pasta or a pretty face, but there is still plenty of linguine at home." But then, *Chi,* an Italian tabloid, published pictures of Pavarotti capering with and kissing his latest secretary, Nicoletta Mantovani.

Previously, the tenor had joked about his two-year relationship, calling Nicoletta his favorite among his entire harem. But this time, in the article accompanying the photographs, Pavarotti said, "Nicoletta and I are very happy and it shows. To hide or deny it would be a crime." Nor did he bother to deny that she was younger than his youngest daughter.

Adua, through her lawyer, issued a statement that her husband had made "the choice of going beyond the point of no return. . . . For every person . . . just like the road of life, that of success ends." She attributed his infatuation to his advancing age and diminishing career, and warned that he was about to throw away a happy old age with her.

Undaunted, Pavarotti continued to appear everywhere with Mantovani, who maintained that she had not expected this affair. She had become the tenor's temporary secretary in 1993, interrupting her college studies in natural sciences. "I was bored by opera. Insects are my passion." She expected to stay in the job for three months, but she became involved despite herself. "When I started working for him, he didn't have a busy heart, if you know what I mean." Adua, still firmly in control of the family finances, began to separate assets.

In November 1995, to celebrate his sixtieth birthday, Pavarotti decided to re-create the role at the Met that had made him a star in 1973. _La Fille du Régiment,_ the opera that had proved Kathleen Battle's downfall, is especially risky for the tenor lead, who must sing nine high Cs in the first-act aria, "Ah! mes amis." Pavarotti's brilliant, carefree performance of this aria the first time he sang it at the Met had earned him the title King of the High Cs (while Plácido Domingo was dubbed by Pavarotti fans as King of the High B-flats). Now, twenty-two years older, considerably heavier, and in constant pain from deteriorating hip and knee joints, Pavarotti had the music world wondering aloud and, often, in print, about his wisdom in reviving this challenging part. But the controversy only strengthened the tenor's resolve, although he did decide to sing an alternate version of the aria, with the Cs transposed down to Bs. At the first performance, a Saturday evening, everything went fine.

The second performance was the following Wednesday. Afterward, Pavarotti would say he had started the first act with a fever, but as a point of honor he refused to have the Met announce that he was ill, a gambit other singers frequently use when they are in questionable voice. The previous season he had sung _Tosca_ with a fever of 103 from strep throat. The _Fille_ indisposition did not seem as serious.

But as the first act progressed, Pavarotti noticed that phlegm was building up on his vocal cords. This is not something a singer can predict while warming up in his dressing room. And the stress of going onstage and singing in front of four thousand people can easily worsen any physical symptom.

But Pavarotti persevered, even as the killer aria at the end of the first act came nearer. He launched into it, and when the first high C came (now, actually, a high B), he went for it. The note cracked.

Pavarotti took the remaining eight high notes down an octave. The audience, completely on his side, gave him a rousing ovation, but he could not be consoled. He did not take his curtain call after act 1, and he withdrew from the rest of the performance, letting his cover replace him. "I was sick, but I was very sorry," he said. "Very, very, very, very."

Less than six months later, Pavarotti appeared in recital at Foxwoods Resort, a gambling casino in southern Connecticut. His name was embossed in gold on the evening's program, which contained such operatic insights as a description of *La Bohème*'s Rodolfo as "a poor poet who lives in poverty." Ticket prices ranged from $175 to $500, far more expensive than a prime seat at the Met, and the singing was electronically amplified. One critic was of the opinion that "he didn't phone in the performance, he faxed it." He also performed at one of Trump's casinos in Jersey City; on that occasion, he sang so badly that Trump asked for the fee back and Pavarotti agreed to sing a second time gratis. Many questioned Pavarotti's artistic integrity in giving these casino concerts; surely, he didn't need the enormous fees after all the money he had made over his long career.

Pavarotti sang a new production of Giordano's *Andrea Chénier* at the Met the following month to mixed reviews, and his difficulties continued. That spring, he had been scheduled to record Verdi's *I Lombardi* with Levine and the Met Orchestra, but because of the tenor's frail health and the demands of *Chénier*, the recording was left unfinished. Then came the announcement that he was canceling *Forza*.

Despite the critics' outcry, the audience flocked to the substitute *Ballo* performances. They leaped to their feet in standing ovations every time their beloved Luciano appeared. He was there, smiling that exuberant yet slightly terrified smile, and this mattered more to his public than the state of his voice.

The pope was not so forgiving. After Pavarotti's acknowledgment of his affair, His Holiness declined the tenor's offer to sing at the pontiff's mass in New York's Central Park. What may have hurt Pavarotti more deeply was that he was replaced by Domingo.

In the fall of 1997, Pavarotti returned to the Met to sing six *Turandot*s. Although this opera contains one of the tenor's all-time great hits, the aria "Nessun dorma," he had not performed the complete opera in twenty years. Franco Zeffirelli's production has the stage steeply raked, and

Pavarotti looked uncomfortable throughout the run. But considering the part's difficulties and his trouble getting around onstage, he was pleased with the results. At one performance, after a triumphant high C during the judgment scene, he was seen to hit a high five with one of the choristers.

In between performances, he retreated to his sumptuous apartment on Central Park South, which had belonged previously to Sophia Loren, and is in the same building as the New York homes of Plácido Domingo and José Carreras. One of his favorite ways to relax is to watch cartoons, which he regards as masterpieces. He also loves to paint, although even this innocent hobby has led him into trouble. He took up painting while preparing for the role of the artist Mario Cavaradossi in *Tosca,* and for several years visitors to his dressing room would find him in front of an easel, hard at work on his latest painting. In 1993, twenty-two of his works were reproduced and sold as silk-screen prints at $25,000 for each set. During the publicity, Mary I. Hicks, an eighty-seven-year-old pensioner from Colorado, noticed a striking similarity to three of the paintings in her book, *Adventures in Europe,* a teach-yourself-to-paint volume published in 1972. She sued Pavarotti for plagiarism and won.

His fiancée, meanwhile, was devoting herself to Luciano's well-being. She began to monitor his eating, snatching away second helpings. Pavarotti raged, but she persevered, and eventually he lost fifty pounds. Adua may have had control of the family purse, but Nicoletta emerged victorious in their kitchen.

In January 1998, the Met's annual Pension Fund Gala was a tribute to the memory of Sir Rudolf Bing, who had died the previous September. Pavarotti was among several of the house's leading singers who performed a selection of arias and ensembles. After singing a trio from Verdi's *Luisa Miller* with the soprano June Anderson and the baritone Dwayne Croft, the tenor felt light-headed. By intermission, he was so dizzy that Joseph Volpe summoned the company doctor, who examined Pavarotti and advised him to drop out of the rest of the performance. Pavarotti was on his way back to his apartment when Volpe went out in front of the curtain and announced the tenor's withdrawal to the audience.

He had surgery on his right hip and left knee in New York during the summer of 1998, which forced him to cancel several performances of

Tosca at the Met that fall. But he did sing a gala marking the thirtieth anniversary of his Met debut.

In the winter of 2001, Pavarotti returned to the Met to sing several performances of _Aida_. As always, there were dark mutterings that the role was now beyond him, probably had always been too heavy for him, and that he would cancel. He did not cancel; he sang the scheduled performances, including one attended by former President Bill Clinton in one of his first public appearances after leaving the White House. No one, least of all the tenor himself, would claim that these were definitive performances: his mobility on stage has been severely limited by his orthopedic problems, and the role was clearly difficult for him vocally. Even Levine, the ever-accommodating accompanist, had problems holding the ensembles together as he tried to compensate for Pavarotti's problems with technique. But as Peter Davis wrote in _New York_ magazine, "in the less heroic moments he can still spin an elegant phrase . . ."

Many assumed that _Aida_ would mark Pavarotti's farewell to the Met, but he had never announced this. In March 2001, the Met released the company's 2001–2 schedule of performances. Pavarotti would be singing again, this time in _Tosca_.

Pavarotti feels no need to preserve and sanctify his musical heritage. "I never sang for legend," he said. But retirement is far away. He has contracts at the Met and recital bookings, and the Three Tenors tour seems to have a life of its own. Not to mention a concert on April 29, 2001. That date had special significance for Pavarotti as well; he made his professional operatic debut on April 29, 1961. The concert in Parma marked his fortieth anniversary as one of the world's most beloved musicians. Perhaps other singers would choose to leave the stage differently, but his audiences still adore Pavarotti, and with his singing, he pours out his gratitude to them.

Chapter Thirty-six

THE NEW STARS

No sooner did Kathleen Battle disappear from the firmament than new young singers came, seemingly from nowhere, to try to replace her as the Met's most-publicized box office attraction. Ironically, those who tried the hardest failed the fastest; the young singers who relied on their music-making rather than the news-making were more readily embraced by the public.

In the early 1990s, only two singers could guarantee a sold-out house: Luciano Pavarotti and Plácido Domingo. So the opera world became obsessed with finding a young tenor to replace the aging stars. All a record company had to do was suggest that its artist was a possible successor, and immediately the name became one to reckon with—until he actually appeared onstage at the Met.

Perhaps the most egregious misjudgment surrounded the Met debut of the French-Sicilian tenor Roberto Alagna. Only a few years earlier, he had been discovered literally singing for his supper in a Paris restaurant. But he had risen so fast that for his New York debut, EMI Classics mounted a marketing campaign comparing Alagna not only to his illustrious predecessors but also to such teen idols as Leonardo DiCaprio. Bus stops around New York City were emblazoned with Alagna's sultry photos, and huge advertisements for his recordings appeared in every publication. But when Alagna finally got around to singing his first *La Bohème,* he had a cold and made a debut that was far below expectations. His Mimi was a glamorous Romanian soprano, Angela Gheorghiu, who had made her little-noted Met debut during the previous season.

It is a tribute to Alagna's staying power that he did not immediately vanish into the limbo reserved for overpromoted tenors. Shortly after his disastrous debut, in a ceremony conducted by Mayor Rudolph Giuliani of New York, he married Angela Gheorghiu. Something about these two young singers created electricity, not, however, of the artistic kind.

Gheorghiu is a woman of almost palpable ambition. She was married previously to a Romanian plumber, and Alagna, her new husband, was so smitten with her that he even accompanied her to the ladies' room. Suspicion had it that she had married him to advance her career. Certainly, the two of them became a force in the opera world that she could never have achieved by herself. Unfortunately, that force was not benevolent. The Alagnas, who booked themselves as an inseparable pair years into the future, soon acquired a host of nicknames, of which the Love Couple was the most charitable. Gheorghiu was known around the Paris Opera as La Draculette, and she and Alagna together were routinely referred to as the Ceauşescus or Bonnie and Clyde.

Much of this dislike was fostered by Gheorghiu's charmless pushiness. Alagna tended to follow meekly in her wake. Her notoriety had begun when she walked out on a recording session with Sir Georg Solti, because, she said, "I don't like being ordered around." When Alagna was hired to replace Pavarotti in an English performance of the Verdi Requiem, he demanded twice Pavarotti's fee and he got it. The two of them engaged in a loud feud with the director Jonathan Miller over a Paris Opera production of _La Bohème,_ and were soon battling the managements at the Vienna State Opera and La Scala.

In Monte Carlo, during a performance of Mascagni's _L'Amico Fritz,_ Gheorghiu had a memory slip and decided to stop the performance. The conductor, obviously a believer that the show must go on, ignored her and went right ahead with the music—until Alagna stopped and started waving frantically at him. He had no choice but to stop; Alagna blew a kiss at his wife, and the audience applauded wildly. Soon afterward, the Love Couple signed up with Pavarotti's press agent, Herbert Breslin.

Anyone could have predicted a clash between the Alagnas and Joseph Volpe; it took place on a Met tour to Japan in 1997. Gheorghiu, who was to sing the role of Micaëla in _Carmen_, had appeared in the premiere of the Zeffirelli production, for which she wore a blond wig covering her jet-black hair. In Japan, she decided not to wear the wig. Rather than explaining to Volpe quietly why she hated it, Gheorghiu made a loud scene, screaming that she would not wear the wig under any circumstances.

Volpe's reply was to the point: "That wig is going onstage, whether you're in it or not." And so it did, perched on the head of Gheorghiu's cover. The soprano spent the performance sitting in the lobby of the Tokyo theater.

Volpe thought this incident made clear his lack of patience with the artistic temperament. The Alagnas were booked to appear in future seasons in _Roméo et Juliette_ and a new production of _La Traviata_ in November 1998. The _Traviata_ contract was issued in 1996, but by the spring of 1998, the Alagnas, who were at the Met doing _Roméo_, still had not signed. They asked Volpe to show them the production designs, and he told them to sign the contract first. They then informed him that they wanted approval of the design and produced sketches done by Alagna's brother for a production in Madrid. Volpe repeated that they were to sign the contracts, and gave them a deadline. When they had not signed by that date, Volpe dismissed them from the production. He made it clear he was not banning them from the Met, as he had Battle, but he pointed out that "when I say there is a deadline, there is a deadline." Volpe instructed the artistic department to book a new Violetta and a new Alfredo.

Volpe was as good as his word. He offered the Alagnas the lead parts in a 1999–2000 production of _L'Elisir d'Amore_, and this time they signed promptly. When they arrived for the production, their behavior was impeccable. Strewing gifts around the opera house, they were cooperative and sang with charm.

The same season, another much-heralded young tenor made his Met debut. José Cura, a former Argentinean rugby player whose hobbies included the martial arts and body-building, appeared on opening night in a double bill of _Cavalleria Rusticana_ and _Pagliacci_, sharing top tenor billing with Plácido Domingo. Once again, his face was familiar long before his voice was heard in New York. He was already tangled in a feud with Alagna, who, he said, was "discovered in a pizza restaurant and invented by the record company." Ironically, Alagna had won the Pavarotti Vocal Competition, and Cura the Domingo Competition. His strapping good looks, which his record company was busy exploiting, were combined with an arrogance that seemed a little premature. "I have to be careful about the press," he boasted to an English reporter. "If I have dinner with a girl-friend, they write I'm having an affair. If I have dinner with a man, they write I'm gay, and if I'm seen walking my dog, they write that I have sex with animals."

Cura claims that Domingo is his mentor, but he is already singing Otello, a role Domingo did not attempt until much later in his career. But his making his debut on the same night that Domingo celebrated his eigh-teenth opening night at the Met—a company record—did not help his cause. The evening opened with *Cavalleria*, and almost every critic in at-tendance praised Cura's looks. His voice was a different matter. The con-sensus was that important tenor talent lurked somewhere in the blaringly loud interpretation Cura offered, but that his technique was inadequate, his musicianship nonexistent, and his tone already showing signs of wear. After intermission, Domingo took the stage in *Pagliacci*, and gave the au-dience a lesson in what a well-nurtured voice, belonging to a trained mu-sician, could sound like in a man twenty-five years older.

During all the fuss over Alagna and Cura, the Canadian tenor Ben Heppner was quietly developing a career far beyond the dreams or physi-cal abilities of either of his young colleagues. He had begun singing pro-fessionally only in the late 1980s, when he was thirty, and at the time thought that he was a lyric tenor, capable of singing only relatively light roles. But his teacher heard something of more consequence and urged him into the lightly populated world of dramatic tenors. He did not win ei-ther the Pavarotti or Domingo Competition, but he did win the Met's 1988 National Council Auditions, and soon began to specialize in the German repertory. The opera world may have wondered where the successor to Domingo and Pavarotti was hiding, but it had long since given up on dis-covering a new Wagnerian heldentenor. And then, as if out of nowhere, appeared Ben Heppner.

True, Heppner's appearance does not lend itself to smoldering album covers or magazine pinups. He is tall but hefty, and his demeanor is friendly but self-effacing. He truly is happily married, and rushes home between performances whenever possible to be with his wife and children in Toronto. He is also hardworking, and for him it takes very hard work to learn his demanding roles. When he sang Ghermann in the 1996 new production of *Pique Dame,* he struggled with the Russian up to the day of the dress rehearsal. When, at the Seattle Opera, he sang Tristan for the first time, he took the traditional cuts in the role because he had not yet developed the stamina to sing all of it. But by the time he brought Tristan to the Met, in 1999, he had learned how to develop and husband his strength to carry through the role he calls the most demanding in the repertory. At rehearsals, he always sang full out, even when the other singers were "marking" or singing with less than their full voice. Heppner's performances of Tristan were superb. For the first time in several generations, the critics raved that there was a tenor who could actually sing this role, not bark it, not shout it, but sing it with effortless lyricism. When he stepped out for his curtain call after the premiere, he received an ovation that almost shook the theater. Heppner, the audience realized, may not be as handsome as a movie star, as lithe as an athlete, or much of an actor. He will never become a ubiquitous superstar, because he limits himself to three or four productions a year so that he can conserve his voice and spend time with his family. But he is something far more important: he is the real thing, a tenor who is making musical history.

The opera world needs its icons, and if there were not obvious tenorial candidates, these rare creatures would have to be found elsewhere. And so it happened that new stars emerged from the most unlikely vocal categories.

Bryn Terfel, a Welsh bass-baritone, made his Metropolitan Opera debut in the fall of 1994, and that was preceded not by a record company promotion but by a prominent profile in the *New York Times*. The imprimatur of the country's most important paper sells more tickets than bus stop shelters and magazine ads, and by the time Terfel made his debut, all his performances were sold out.

Terfel, too, proved to be the real thing. Early in his career, he was frequently mistaken on the street for Meatloaf; he is a brawny, unaffected man from north Wales, where he grew up on a farm and where he still lives when he isn't singing around the world. Like Pavarotti, he combines a natural voice and seemingly effortless technique with a down-to-earth presence. And his manner onstage keeps the audience's eyes on him no matter what else is happening. His singing is musical and intelligent; he can move with ease from the Mozart operas to Verdi to Wagner.

Offstage, he is as content listening to pop music as to lieder, and one of his best-selling disks was a collection of Rodgers and Hammerstein songs. He almost always includes Welsh folk songs on his recital programs, a tribute to the national heritage that encouraged him to sing when he was a small child. He is looking forward to cutting back his career by his early forties so that he can spend more time with his family at his sheep farm. If he keeps to this plan, the audience that buys every available ticket to his performances will be able to say that they heard the young Terfel, but it will be small consolation for the loss of this free spirit.

Cecilia Bartoli did not need a promotional campaign when she made her Metropolitan Opera debut; at the age of only twenty-eight, she was known throughout the opera world. One book about her had already been published; another was in the works; her CDs sold on a level with those of the Three Tenors; and her short life story was already the stuff of myth—although not particularly lively.

She grew up in Rome, the child of two choristers with the Rome Opera, and her mother was her only teacher. Her career had taken off with an exclusive Decca recording contract. And her only eccentricity was her fear of flying.

As quiet as she was offstage, once she was onstage or in front of a microphone, she, like Terfel, mesmerized the audience. Call it charisma, call it star quality, what she possesses is so rare that it defies description. She is not a beautiful woman, but she exudes energy, optimism, and confidence. Jonathan Miller said of her that she is "like some wonderful, beautifully made piece of confectionery."

Her first opera at the Met was a new production of Mozart's _Così fan_

Tutte in February 1996. She had made an unlikely choice for her debut; she was not even singing the primary mezzo-soprano role. Instead she chose the role of Despina, the conniving maid. Many singers have angrily rejected such lesser roles when the Met first asked them to appear, choosing instead to wait for a starring part. Bartoli did not have to wait; whatever role she took became the focus of the evening.

She finally arrived in New York after rehearsals had begun, and some of the other singers were resentful. But their anger melted. Bartoli proved, again like Terfel, to be unpretentious and undemanding, and she worked hard and seriously at rehearsals. She endeared herself to James Levine, who was conducting. The feeling was completely mutual.

When Levine became ill shortly before the Saturday broadcast of *Così*, Bartoli withdrew. She insisted that she had strained her back, and that the presence of a less-distinguished conductor in Levine's place had nothing to do with her departure. Other singers in the cast were also in poor condition. Both the tenor and baritone leads had canceled before Levine's illness, and there was no question about their indisposition. But gossip at the opera house immediately contradicted Bartoli's story of a bad back. Instead, the story went, she was unhappy with the conductor and was reluctant to sing after so few rehearsals with the cover cast.

Bartoli did not help her case by appearing at a Met performance the night before she canceled, and by meeting a compact disk singing commitment the day after the broadcast.

Volpe, although he was on vacation, did not hesitate to make his feelings known. "She withdrew from the performance, and I'm not going to comment on her reasons," Volpe told the *Times*. "That will tell you whatever there is to tell you. Yes, I was upset that she withdrew."

Levine was not at all upset. When he recovered, he and Bartoli immediately began rehearsing for a series of recitals that they were to give over the next few weeks. "There's nothing controversial about this girl, but she's in the public eye, so everyone asks why does she cancel. She cancels because she's sick."

And Levine broke his tradition of never conducting Rossini when, the following season, Bartoli was the star of a new production of *La Cenerentola*. This was a tribute to her enormous box office appeal; she had been awarded her own new production at an age when most singers are still dreaming of singing at the Met. The *Cenerentola* performances exceeded expectations, and, once again, everyone loved Bartoli.

Bartoli refers to herself as the "anti-diva," but she is far from lacking in temperament. When she performed in a new Met production of *Le Nozze di Figaro*, in 1998, she infuriated her former fan, Jonathan Miller, who was directing. Not only did she show up late for many rehearsals, she insisted on singing obscure alternative arias in several of the performances. Miller was adamantly against the idea because he rightly thought the arias were inferior to the originals, for which he had already done the staging, but Levine and Volpe agreed to the substitutions. Miller was outraged. "Jimmy's a big baby who has no sense of the stage and wears a diaper over his shoulder," he said. "Volpe's a thug." Volpe's reaction was characteristic. "Big deal," he said. "Big deal."

During the fuss over the interpolated arias in *Figaro*, Volpe reiterated that he left artistic decisions to Levine. But it was Volpe, not Levine, who created an uproar when, in the fall of 1997, he announced Valery Gergiev was to be the Met's principal guest conductor. It was a brand-new title.

During an orchestra rehearsal right before the press conference announcing Gergiev's new position, Levine gave the news to orchestra members. The general impression among them was that he was not pleased. He also told them some major news of his own: he was about to become music director of the Munich Philharmonic.

Chapter Thirty-seven

THE CURSE OF *CARMEN*

Joseph Volpe has never made a secret of his admiration for Franco Zeffirelli. Time and again, over the years, when a planned production has fallen through, as happens far too often, he has turned to Zeffirelli. After all, in 1966, Zeffirelli was one of the first to benefit from Volpe's talent in solving technical problems. That was the year of *Antony and Cleopatra*.

Although the Met liked to plan productions of its classic repertory that will last a generation, there are miscalculations. One was the Peter Hall production of *Carmen* that starred Maria Ewing in 1986.

The most caustic criticism James Levine voices is "I don't prefer that." But when Hall's production of *Carmen* came up for a discussion at a press conference in 1996, Levine exploded with "Yuck!"

The assembled press, accustomed to Levine's evasiveness, was astonished. Volpe grinned at Levine with almost paternal pride, and then gave a glowing description of the Met's new *Carmen,* slated for the following month.

Volpe disliked the Hall production as much as Levine. Levine described the sets as "meaninglessly heavy"; Volpe limited himself to "Really ugly!" Levine had often said that he wanted to forget the once-every-twenty-years guidelines and do a new production as soon as possible. Those guidelines necessitated the heavy-duty scenery, constructed from the best materials and painstakingly maintained. The same was true of the costumes. When board members questioned the astronomical cost of costumes, they were reminded that these articles had to survive major alterations for different singers, as well as the wear and tear they were subjected to by people performing under great stress and bright lights.

No one argued about the need for a new *Carmen*, but the extensive time needed to engage singers of world stature meant that once the decision was made to build a new production, years passed before it was staged. *Carmen*, one of the most frequently performed operas in the Met's repertory, was rarely seen between the mid-eighties and the mid-nineties because the Hall version was so unpopular. The search for a new director and design team began.

In 1989, the Italian stage director Gian Carlo del Monaco had been acclaimed for his new production of Puccini's *La Fanciulla del West*, a difficult opera to design and direct. Levine and Volpe, both impressed, immediately approached him about several new productions scheduled for the next few seasons, including *Madama Butterfly, Stiffelio, Simon Boccanegra*, and *La Forza del Destino*. There were even rumors that Levine had chatted informally with Del Monaco about a new *Ring* cycle. And since he seemed well suited for designing traditional productions, *Carmen* was added to the list.

While Levine was conducting at the Bayreuth Festival in the summers, he had come to admire the mezzo-soprano Waltraud Meier. She sang mostly German repertory, especially Wagner, and was, many thought, courageous in singing Isolde, a part that had proved ruinous for a number of mezzos. But she brought a rare fervor to her performances, which convinced Levine that she might sing a fascinating Carmen. When he approached her with the idea, she demurred. She had sung the role once when she was a student and had decided it was not for her.

But Levine is not easy to deter. When he talks with one person, his intensity is compelling. Even behind his trademark aviator glasses, his blue eyes can be tender, fierce, beseeching, or enthusiastic as they draw his listener in. Meanwhile, his words pour out: soothing, complimentary, promising support and excitement in the venture he is concentrating on. It is never a matter of discussion; there is only one side to the conversation.

Levine worked hard and finally convinced Meier that, with her beauty and passion, she could overcome any problems she might have with Carmen. She had the reaction everyone experiences: she wanted to please him.

Meier's doubts about her suitability were soothed when she heard that Del Monaco had been engaged as producer. Many thought him temperamental and quixotic, but she got along well with him. Levine would be conducting, and Plácido Domingo, the Don José, would be another stalwart ally. Reassured, she began work on the role, studying with language and voice coaches.

When her casting was announced, the opera world was intrigued. She was not an obvious choice, but there were few Carmens around, and she was an intelligent and magnetic singer. Anticipation and curiosity were high.

Many changes take place during the five years between the decision to do a new production and the premiere. Singers get sick, undergo crises, change repertory, shift voice category. It is rare for a cast to remain unchanged over such a long period. In the case of _Carmen_, it did. But it was the only element of the production to do so.

Del Monaco's first production after _Fanciulla_ was Verdi's early opera _Stiffelio_. It was also a success. Then, in 1994, came _Madama Butterfly_. His version of Puccini's beloved opera, a repertory staple, was to take the place of one of the most venerable productions the Met owned. Del Monaco was sure he knew that the Met wanted a production that would function for the next quarter-century, something lavish but not gaudy, utilitarian while looking exactly the opposite.

Butterfly was not the success he had hoped for. Del Monaco's idea of Pinkerton was even more louche than Puccini intended; during the love duet, the tenor stripped to the waist. And the director had Butterfly commit suicide right in front of her tiny son. But these small matters could have been corrected, and were, in subsequent revivals. It was Del Monaco's personal style during rehearsals that made everyone wary. It involved more yelling than the company expected, even from an Italian opera director, no less one who stalked out and sulked. The Met's operations are too complex and expensive to be reliant on a temperamental director.

His next production, *Simon Boccanegra,* fell flat, and its lack of success, underscored by Del Monaco's behavior, led Volpe to retract the *Carmen* offer, a decision strengthened by Del Monaco's last Met assignment, a dreary and stolid *Forza* in the spring of 1996, only six months before the scheduled *Carmen* premiere.

Volpe's affection for Zeffirelli is shared by many. Everyone has a "Franco horror story," but everyone regards him as a quick and thorough professional. So he was the first one to whom Volpe turned to salvage the new *Carmen.* Zeffirelli, in the middle of a political campaign for public office in Italy, expressed sincere doubts about directing Waltraud Meier in the title role. When Volpe and Levine made a joint decision that Meier would stay in the cast, Zeffirelli declined the offer.

Volpe's next choice provoked groans throughout the opera house. Piero Faggioni had given the company a lovely but rarely played production of Zandonai's *Francesca da Rimini.* Then, like Del Monaco, he had stumbled badly in his next assignment, a new production of *Un Ballo in Maschera.* It was ridiculously staged, complete with commedia dell'arte figures Verdi never envisioned, and topiary trees that actually danced onstage. The audience had laughed aloud. The handsome Faggioni, a former Italian stage actor, had the requisite personality. He catapulted around the opera house, spewing charm—unless something displeased him. Then he would slump against walls, clutching at his expensively clad chest, swooning with disbelief at whatever bad news he had just received. Although he screamed as much as Del Monaco, he was not cruel, so he was not disliked. But he wasn't respected.

Faggioni wanted to design his own *Carmen* sets in addition to directing, but the Met had already engaged Dante Ferretti as production designer. Predictably, Faggioni immediately began fighting with Ferretti. Although Volpe had his own reservations about Ferretti's designs, he feared the fighting was a bad omen, so he fired Faggioni and kept Ferretti.

It was April 1996. Under normal circumstances, construction on the *Carmen* sets and costumes would long have been under way. Volpe now engaged Liliana Cavani, an Italian film director. She and Ferretti quickly produced sketches that Volpe and Joe Clark thought feasible but that needed changes. For example, there were no mountains surrounding the

Smugglers' Hideaway in the third act. "Where's the mountains? I don't see any mountains!" Volpe complained. Cavani and Ferretti indignantly refused to change a thing, so Volpe fired them both.

There were five months to go before the premiere. Volpe and Joe Clark went to Italy, and when they returned, Zeffirelli was the new director of *Carmen*. Since he designed all the operas he directed, there was no designer to fight with. Zeffirelli knew the house extremely well, and his track record at the Met was first-class. Also, he had just finished a production of *Carmen* in Vienna. What Levine thought is unknown, but he had long ago resigned himself to working with Zeffirelli. "Jimmy and Franco fight all the time," said a former technical staffer. "You can't have two stars in one show."

Critics have complained loud and long about the size of Zeffirelli's *Tosca*, *La Bohème*, and *Turandot*. They are so big, the carping goes, that they dwarf the singers. They are so huge that the expense of presenting them is embarrassing for an opera house engaged in perpetual fund-raising.

The Met has a different view. Zeffirelli's productions are "singer-proof." Even if the theater has a bad night, the audience goes home happy. Zeffirelli's sets may be enormous, but they are filled with the director's exuberance. Street scenes teem with urban life, winter scenes are delicately sculpted of snow and ice, crowd scenes are played with the lights up and the stage full of glitter. The *Bohème* is nineteenth-century Paris; *Tosca* is a travelogue of Rome; *Turandot* incites gasps of incredulity at the lavishness.

Zeffirelli's productions sell tickets, and no Met season is without a Zeffirelli or two; they are among the most popular shows the company owns. As a result, they have proved to be bargains for the Met even though the initial costs were high.

One would have thought that the sheer size of most Zeffirelli efforts would have discouraged Volpe from engaging him at such a late date. But the director, an experienced realist, described his vision of *Carmen* as "stark." Volpe had heard Franco use that word in connection with *Turandot*, one of the largest productions the Met owns, so he was not surprised when Zeffirelli revised his original description. "It's a complex opera," he said. "It says in the score that there are seven horses. Seven are needed, and seven there will be."

Zeffirelli loves animals—some even suggest he prefers them to people—and most of his productions are populated by several species. There are dogs and horses in the double bill of *Cavalleria Rusticana* and *Pagliacci;* horses, dogs, and burros in *La Bohème;* and dogs in *Falstaff. Tosca* and *Turandot* have no creatures, probably because Zeffirelli thought his monumental sets too hazardous for animals.

Zeffirelli always travels with animals of his own. In Italy, he lives with seven or eight Jack Russell terriers, and for years, he was inseparable from his favorite, Bambina. Bambina became the first animal to eat lunch in the Met cafeteria. But Bambina aged and passed on, and her daughter, Blanche, became his new companion. Blanche came to New York for *Carmen* rehearsals in September 1996. She had her own seat in the auditorium for each rehearsal, as her mother had, and Zeffirelli lovingly, if unwisely, fed her scraps of chocolate during scene changes.

In the autumn of 1996, the press was unusually optimistic about the state of the Met. What journalists had perceived as a secretive company was now about to open its portals. During the summer, François Giuliani, an experienced press representative and former journalist, left the United Nations to head the Met's press office. Giuliani had been the press spokesman for several of the secretaries-general at the UN, including Waldheim, Pérez de Cuéllar, and Boutros-Ghali. After working with these men, he was not to be intimidated by opera singers, and opera company crises were not going to faze a man who had dealt with famines, ethnic wars, and rebellions.

There was no problem getting coverage for the new *Carmen* once rehearsals began. Zeffirelli loved publicity, as did Domingo, and whatever trepidation she may have felt privately about her new role, Waltraud Meier was also ready for interviews.

Justin Davidson, a relative newcomer to the cultural staff of *Newsday,* asked the Met for permission to write about the production. His intention was to attend as many rehearsals as possible and chronicle the production's development. Other writers had requested such backstage access, and the Met press office had always refused. The rehearsal of any new production is a minefield of potential disasters, and a reporter scrutinizing so sensitive a situation might cause problems. Over the years, a few writers from the *New York Times,* the *New Yorker, Time,* and *Newsweek* had been allowed to attend only an occasional rehearsal. Now, in the spirit of the new openness, Giuliani and Volpe decided to let *Newsday* attend the *Carmen* rehearsals.

They began in late September, and from the first day, Zeffirelli and Meier clashed. She was nervous and insecure, and he had always thought she was wrong for the part. Maybe because he didn't know how to help her, he approached the rehearsal in a more defensive posture than was usual for him.

There were still indications of his usual enthusiasm. Zeffirelli is extremely fussy about the look of the supernumeraries, or extras, and frequently has casting calls to get the types he wants. For *Carmen,* he demanded "real" Gypsies, and one of the Met's artistic administrators, in desperation, searched the Yellow Pages under "Fortune Tellers." In the end, Zeffirelli settled for people who, in his opinion, looked like Gypsies. He did not want this *Carmen* to have a glossy operatic sheen, so he chose people who were a bit bedraggled. He rejected trained dancers for the flamenco scenes, and had the choreographer work with supers who did not resemble dancers at all. Then he set to work on his elaborate staging of the supers and chorus.

Zeffirelli smoked incessantly, even in the sacrosanct Met auditorium, and he saw nothing wrong with drinking Scotch while he rehearsed. But during the *Carmen* rehearsals, something was different. Zeffirelli didn't act intoxicated, he just seemed unfocused. He spent more time with the chorus and supers than he did with the principal artists, and he prowled around the stage, pushing through the chorus, spouting forth a colorful mixture of compliments and insults. "Too old," he said to one singer; "Too fat," to another. It was a measure of the chorus's affection for him that no grievances were lodged with the union. Even the animals had specific roles to play; in addition to two donkeys and three dogs, there were the seven horses to control crowds in the fight scene, to pull carriages, and to participate in the toreador procession in the last act. The animals had been chosen for their good looks and placidity, the latter a requisite in any animal's venturing onto the distinctly unplacid Met stage, with its bright lights and blaring sounds.

Waltraud Meier watched with growing irritation as her director focused his considerable energy on the chorus, supers, and animals— "atmospheric personnel," as they were called. To make matters worse, Zeffirelli sometimes shortened or skipped "room rehearsals," those in which he worked alone with the principals. Unlike Meier, Domingo was not distressed; he had sung Don José countless times and, in any case, intended to stay with his own interpretation. But Meier became more and more upset at the lack of attention she was receiving. The final straw came when Zeffirelli turned to her one day, at a rehearsal, and commanded "Don't sing!" because she was interrupting his directions to the supers. No longer able to control her anger, she stormed offstage in frustration.

She hated the idea of walking out on a difficult role; yet she was being given no reassurance by the director. Volpe began to spend as much time with her as he could—he relished the chance to stretch his artistic duties, and took her out for meals to calm her nerves. Levine gave her pep talks, too, but no one was able to induce Zeffirelli to work his charms on the German mezzo.

Volpe's dinners with Meier did not go unnoticed; little does in an opera house. However he accomplished it, Volpe managed to keep Meier in New York for opening night. One of his clever moves was to fly over an assistant stage director Meier knew from the Vienna State Opera to work with her privately, and he even allowed her to set up her own rehearsals with the supers so that she could stage her "Habanera" for herself, a staging that Zeffirelli would not see until opening night.

Opening night, Thursday, October 31, was the season's first Metropolitan Opera Guild benefit. The opera house was banked with urns of flowers, and the audience was filled with women in designer gowns and important jewelry. In front, the atmosphere was festive and electric. Zeffirelli productions lend themselves to gala evenings, and the director's extravagant life ensures that glamorous figures from the world of film, politics, and the theater will make their rare appearances at the opera house.

Backstage, the mood was less ebullient. The dress rehearsal had gone well, and Meier was more comfortable after the ministrations of her personal stage director. Audiences for galas, while not particularly knowledgeable or enthusiastic, are seldom ungracious. Everything seemed calm.

The performance was without incident. The animals behaved, the children remembered the staging, the chorus sang lustily, the orchestra played brilliantly, and the principals worked hard. But unlike previous Zeffirelli productions, the scenery elicited no applause. The gold curtain swept up on each act and the audience sat in silence.

At the end of the opera, the company members held their breaths. The chorus received a curtain call, and the audience cheered. Then the principals stepped out, first all together, then one by one. They were received politely, as was James Levine. At last, Zeffirelli appeared with his lighting designer. The director always takes a curtain call at Met premieres; it is usually a signal for approval or disapproval from the audience. Again, the applause was merely courteous.

The mood backstage turned gray. Those who had been invited to the Guild benefit party made themselves go; both there and at a few private parties the champagne flowed until the mood lightened, but everyone knew the performance had not worked.

They were right. Of the twenty-odd reviews that appeared over the next few days, one was enthusiastic. Most were scathing. The production was described as thrown together; Domingo was said to be past the point of singing Don José; the Escamillo was clumsy, the crowd scenes were cluttered; there were too many animals; the scenery was large and clumsy with no sense of drama. Waltraud Meier took the heaviest blows. She was called charmless, ungainly, inept stylistically, and, worst of all, a hausfrau trying to pass as a seductress.

No one in the company was surprised, but Meier was devastated, especially about the review calling her a hausfrau. "Is it possible that in New York I should be criticized for being German?" she asked. Once again, the administration tried to console her, worried that she would leave. The artistic administrators spent most of the weekend on the phone with her, as did Joseph Volpe and some of the music staff.

Waltraud Meier had worked hard on the role, and once the hurt passed, she became angry. Furthermore, she knew exactly on whom to focus her anger. She told the Met press office that she would be available to be interviewed by any reporters who wished to speak to her. Justin Davidson, of *Newsday,* spoke to Meier. "Responding to a barrage of negative reviews, Waltraud Meier . . . said that she had never been happy with the director, Franco Zeffirelli, and had tried to back out just ten days before opening night." She told Davidson, "My Carmen is a woman of total independence, total refusal to compromise, no fear of anything but her own emotions. . . . I think in a more sober production, it would be clear what I am doing."

Davidson went to Volpe to ask whether he could get Zeffirelli's view, and this was the first that Volpe learned of his press department's setting up this controversial interview. He was angry, but he understood his obligation. He told Davidson that "this production makes it difficult for the audience to see what [Meier] is doing."

Zeffirelli, reached by telephone in Rome, declared, "This is not a show for a single singer. It is a show for the Met." And, ever modest, he added, "It is not possible to do a better *Carmen.*"

He went on to speculate that the American singer Denyce Graves, who was scheduled as the next Carmen, might be more comfortable in his production. She "is more animal, more Gypsy—it's something that comes out of the fact that she's black." Zeffirelli expanded his theory: "What I'm saying is not racist. Graves is a great artist, and each one has an interpretation that derives from her own culture. Blacks have this fierce quality, and since Meier was criticized for being too Teutonic, I see that Americans want something more *selvaggio* [savage]. . . ."

He then announced publicly that he had always thought Meier wrong for the part. In yet another *Newsday* piece, he told Davidson, "Once I understood that she was going to do it her way, I didn't even bother going to rehearsals she was in. She began by disobeying by leaving her hair red instead of dyeing it black as I asked. . . . She looked like a lady from Munich at a costume ball."

Meier chose not to respond to this assault. She finished singing the *Carmen* performances for which she was contracted, but her bad luck continued. On the last night, she slipped onstage in the last act and sprained her ankle. With great relief, she took off for Europe at six o'clock the next morning to sing in a production of *Wozzeck*, conducted by Daniel Barenboim. The life of a diva is rarely dull.

But Meier and Carmen were not yet through. The telecast of the opera was scheduled to be taped in March 1997. Zeffirelli declared, "If [Meier] wants to do the television broadcast, she will have to apologize to me first."

Denyce Graves, meanwhile, had come to New York to begin rehearsals. Zeffirelli made a special trip from Europe to work with her, and she gave her first performance on Tuesday, November 26, four days after Meier left. "The mezzo-soprano Denyce Graves has not only taken over the title role of the Metropolitan Opera's new *Carmen*, she has taken over the whole show. And more power to her." Anthony Tommasini wrote in the *Times* to castigate Zeffirelli, referring to the production as "hapless" and "overblown." "Unlike Waltraud Meier," Tommasini wrote, "Ms. Graves is an experienced Carmen. . . . Through her vibrant performance, she seemed to be saying, 'I don't care what kind of clunky production is going on around me, these people came to see *Carmen*, and they're going to get one.' Few Carmens bring such beauty and unselfconsciousness to the role."

The key word in this assessment was "unselfconsciousness." All of Waltraud Meier's work on the part contributed to the audience's sense that she was working too hard. For Carmen is a woman of sensuality, no matter what her motivations, and it is impossible to produce sensuality through laborious effort. Ironically, for many men, Meier abundantly possesses this quality in real life.

In the end, Meier exercised her rights and sang the telecast of *Carmen*. It was no more successful than the premiere. Although she was soon booked to appear again at the Met, she was never again to sing Carmen. Zeffirelli maintained a wounded silence, but he then was engaged to direct and design a new *La Traviata* in the 1998–99 season to replace an older production of the work that he had also designed. Zeffirelli went to work on *Traviata*, and in October 1998, two years after *Carmen*, he and Blanche were back in New York.

Chapter Thirty-eight

THE PRINCIPAL GUEST CONDUCTOR

On a bright September morning in 1997, the cultural press gathered in the boardroom of the Metropolitan Opera House to hear that Valery Gergiev, artistic director of the Kirov Mariinsky Opera and Ballet in St. Petersburg, had been named principal guest conductor of the company. No one was in doubt why the press conference was being held, because the *New York Times* that morning had run a story about the appointment.

That the Met was holding a press conference would have been a story in itself two years earlier. But in September 1996, James Levine and Joe Volpe had presided over the first press conference the Met had given in almost twenty years. Volpe was determined to get rid of the aura of secrecy associated with the Met. Levine was less enthusiastic, and, after the 1996 press conference, was mystified by the press's behavior. "They're always saying they want time with me," he said, "and we gave them a press conference and practically no one even asked a question." He was right; the cultural press is not known for its investigative reporting, and much as they had complained about Levine's inaccessibility, when faced with him directly, their questions were puffballs.

Levine must have been even less happy about the 1997 gathering. He was seated next to a smiling Joseph Volpe, on whose other side sat the new principal guest conductor. "I'm in heaven!" Volpe exclaimed, flanked by two of the most powerful conductors in the world. The conductors were diametric opposites in appearance. Levine wore his usual chipper smile, his face was rosy, and curls sprang all over his head. Gergiev was a grim presence, pale and somber, like a medieval Russian icon.

Once again, there were few questions asked aloud, but there were unspoken issues on everyone's mind. What did the Gergiev appointment signify for Levine and his position at the Met? Was he finally running out of the enormous energy needed to run a large opera company? Or was this a power play by Volpe to force Levine to retreat or even resign?

Volpe was careful to say that Gergiev's new job was an attempt to solve the company's difficulty in engaging prominent conductors. "Getting strong conductors has always been a problem," Volpe said that morning. "I have had discussions with Seiji Ozawa, Zubin Mehta, Kurt Masur, and Giuseppe Sinopoli, but they all have trouble finding the kind of time the Met demands."

"When Joe told me that he wanted to hire Valery," Levine chimed in, "I said, 'Go for it!'" But later, in his office, he was less blithe. "Everyone asks, 'What does Gergiev's coming mean?'" he snapped in an atypical display of irritation. "It means he's coming. That's all it means."

After the press conference, the Met served lunch to the press. Gergiev, always overbooked and always late, was hurrying to catch a plane to Moscow, where officials were said to be highly irritated that he had accepted the new job without consulting them. But he took time to pose for pictures. Volpe, too, seemed everywhere, dealing with reporters the way he always did, teasing and joking in his New York–accented growl. Levine skipped the lunch. He had a rehearsal, and that, as always, was his priority.

"Jimmy says he hates publicity," Volpe said. "Well, now we've got Valery. He loves it."

The press loved Gergiev right back. Throughout the time he has been at the Met, interspersed with Opera House appearances by his Mariinsky company, concerts with the Kirov Orchestra, and guest conductor stints at the New York Philharmonic, Gergiev has received consistently rave reviews from the opinionated New York critics. He is alluringly photogenic and his sad face and eyes make their appeal from newspapers, magazines, and the covers of his many CDs. And he himself seems to be everywhere, touring with his company, making recordings, guest-conducting so frantically that those close to him fear for his physical health.

From the start, the Met Orchestra musicians had a mixed reaction to

Gergiev. They are intrigued by him, in part because his podium style is so different from Levine's. Gergiev is all spur-of-the-moment emotion, while Levine is far more reliable and controlled. Gergiev also does not share Levine's exacting rehearsal technique. He seems to know what he wants but lacks the ability to convey it to the orchestra. "He'll say he wants a 'silvery tone,'" one musician said. "I can understand, 'You're sharp, you're flat, you're too loud, you're too fast,' but I don't understand 'silvery tone.'"

"He keeps you on your toes," another musician said, "because we never know what he's going to do next. There's no mystery left for us with Jimmy. Gergiev gets a visceral response from us."

Unlike the orchestra, the Met management was dazzled by Gergiev. His future plans at the Met include productions of Verdi and Wagner that Levine had previously saved for himself. Since Levine started at the Met, no one else has conducted *Parsifal*, but Gergiev will do so during the 2002–3 season. Gergiev has also conducted a concert with the Met Orchestra, something no conductor other than Levine has done.

There is a clear logic to Gergiev's appointment. The Met has rarely ventured into Russian opera, an occasional *Boris Godunov, Eugene Onegin,* or *Khovanshchina* aside, and Gergiev brings with him a rich and largely untouched repertory. He is also more sociable than Levine, who can rarely be coaxed to fund-raising events. He enjoys meeting the wealthy patrons, whom he invariably charms. Volpe even seemed untroubled by the fact that one of his major donors, Alberto W. Vilar, has now extended his largesse to the Kirov, underwriting new productions, funding Gergiev's White Nights Festival in St. Petersburg, and even opening a "White Nights" office in Manhattan with Gergiev and Plácido Domingo, chairman of the International Friends of the Kirov.

No one, however, thinks Gergiev will have an easy time fitting into the clockwork efficiency of the Met schedule. Flexibility is not characteristic of the company. An opera house whose rehearsal schedules are set years in advance is hardly a natural environment for a conductor who often changes his program the day of the performance. "Valery doesn't understand that he can't change rehearsals at whim," one of his managers said fondly. "Time means nothing to him."

One night in St. Petersburg, after a steady snow had fallen on the city's icy darkness, a passerby at four in the morning might have noticed a lone car parked near the stage door of the Mariinsky Theater, motor running, lights dim, exhaust spiraling up through the cold air. Behind the car's fogged-up windows, huddled in what warmth the heater could provide, was Gergiev. The Mariinsky Theater was shut for the night, and Gergiev had moved to his car to hold the endless administrative appointments essential to running the company. Next to the car, threading back through drifts of snow, was a line of people, stamping their feet and rubbing their hands, waiting patiently for a chance to meet their leader.

His inner clock is thoroughly Russian in its elasticity. He is famous for missing planes, skipping rehearsals, and arriving at the theater seconds before concert time. He is always unshaven and, according to the Met Orchestra, often unbathed. The tardiness worries the Met. In a union theater, the curtain must go up on schedule to avoid expensive overtime. "His manipulation of time is a crucial element of his success," said the director Elijah Moshinsky, who has frequently worked with Gergiev. "Chaos is important to him, because he gets control that way. Look at the Met. The one thing that keeps it in such a dominant position is the scheduling. The efficiency is impenetrable—except by Valery. He is the one person who has been able to crack it."

The premiere of *Pique Dame* by Tchaikovsky in 1995 had been a great triumph for Gergiev and set the stage for his new position. But the revival four years later proved troublesome. At the first orchestra rehearsal, the musicians were astonished to be greeted not by Gergiev but by one of his assistants. Orchestra readings are sacrosanct at the Met, and most conductors beg for more time. Gergiev did not even bother to come.

He skipped not only orchestra readings but most of the staging rehearsals as well. Many conductors consider staging rehearsals optional, but in this case two of the principal roles were being sung for the first time by major artists, Elisabeth Söderström and Plácido Domingo. Both were nervous: Söderström, a beloved Met soprano since the days of Bing, was worried about taking on the demanding role of the Countess so late in her career, and Domingo was having trouble with the Russian language.

Söderström was disappointed to receive little help from Gergiev. "He's a very attractive man," she said. "I just wish I'd seen more of him in rehearsals." She is half-Russian, and had spent a good deal of time studying the original Pushkin text. "Pushkin is my Russian soul," she said, but Gergiev showed little interest into delving into the text. "The idea of exploring the text was something he didn't understand," said one member of the company. "He basically doesn't care at all about what goes on onstage. And that's hard for the singers. Instead of dealing with Söderström's insecurities, he ignored her." In fact, Gergiev paid little attention to anyone except Domingo. Recognizing the difficulty the tenor was having with the Russian, he worked with him for hours after the rest of the cast had left for the day.

Joseph Volpe laughed when asked about the problems during the revival. While acknowledging that there had been some minor difficulties, he said about Gergiev, "The wonderful thing about the guy is that you can talk to him. He's a delight, very much like Jimmy in that way. He understands situations and can see the implications. You can work things out with him. That's probably the only way he's like Jimmy. Jimmy is very easy to work with as far as overall temperament. Valery is a more emotional kind of guy."

Aside from Söderström and Domingo, most members of the *Pique Dame* cast were Kirov singers. Others at the Met were astonished to see the Russian singers cash their paychecks and turn over some of the money to Larissa Gergieva, one of Gergiev's two sisters. Gergieva, a pianist and vocal coach, runs the Kirov's Young Artists' Program, and apparently has financial responsibilities as well. Russian singers were accustomed to paying a percentage of their earnings in the old days to Gosconcert, the Soviet bureau that oversaw classical music. Now their commission goes to the Kirov, in the hard currency for which the company is starved. Even Kirov artists who have major international careers, like Olga Borodina and Dmitri Hvorostovsky, contribute. They know how important it is; 80 percent of the Kirov's income comes from outside Russia.

There were suspicious mutterings about how much of the money might be going into Gergiev's own pocket, and stories were told about the Gergiev sisters clad in mink as they rode through St. Petersburg in limousines. But Gergiev lives like a man with no interest in money; how he would have time to spend it is more of a mystery. And, in 1999, he got married, to Natalya Debisova, a very young accordion virtuoso from his native Ossetia. She was reportedly chosen by his mother. The Gergievs are now parents of a small son.

His life has been a whirlwind of international conducting commitments. And he has promoted touring and recording for the Kirov, which have made his company the most traveled and recorded musical institution in the world. "He's done a phenomenal job for his company," said one American conductor. "His only problem is that he's a lousy conductor. I don't see how people can be taken in."

Although, on the record, Levine speaks only of his delight at having Gergiev at the Met, many feel he agrees with that evaluation. "Come on," said one Met insider. "With his icy shrewdness in assessing other conductors, Jimmy knows the orchestra has little use for Gergiev. Jimmy knows Gergiev is a fraud, and either everyone else will catch on or they won't."

Gergiev is an ambitious man, so it is hard not to imagine him thirsting after the Met, which many people consider the world's prime artistic position. "He's mad on power," said one artist. "It's a drug to him. He could never turn down the Met. He has a messianic belief in himself and in his own extraordinary destiny that will carry him through anything."

One member of the Met Orchestra recounted a conversation with Volpe in which the general manager implied that he would like Gergiev to be the Met's music director. "But how could Gergiev pull it off?" this musician asked. "He has to know that technically he couldn't handle all the repertory he'd need to run a major international company."

Richard Dyer, the outspoken music critic of the *Boston Globe,* also sees Gergiev as limited. "He's a profoundly provincial musician. He's good in his own little slice of the repertory and not even competent otherwise." Other critics, however, are entranced by Gergiev and consider him exceptionally gifted. They exalt him for more than just his considerable musical talents. "James Levine for all [his] gifts seems to be unable to generate much personal charisma," Peter Davis of *New York* magazine commented. "The city positively hungers for the kind of musical glamour Gergiev dispenses with such ease and flair."

Volpe laughs off any suggestion Gergiev might want to succeed Levine. "Valery will *never* leave the Kirov. He's married to the Kirov just the way Jimmy is married to the Met."

Norman Lebrecht, the British critic, Gergiev enthusiast, and author of the book *The Maestro Myth,* agrees. "Valery is just using the Met," he says. "He's made it quite clear to Joe Volpe that he has no interest in being artistic director. What he wants for his staff and himself is the knowledge of how to run a modern opera house. There's no ulterior motive. He's been offered every post there is, and he hasn't taken any of them."

Some see Gergiev using the Met, and some see Volpe using Gergiev in his struggle with Levine for artistic control of the company. Gergiev says that he will never give up the Kirov. But in the opera world, full of intrigue, double meanings, and devious dramatics, even a direct statement can be ambiguous. Perhaps doubters should take a look at Gergiev's wristwatch. No matter where he is in the world, whether conducting at the Met or touring in Japan or recording in Germany, Gergiev's watch is set to St. Petersburg time.

But the decision may not be Gergiev's to make. Volpe has made a dramatic turnaround from his original hints about Gergiev's rosy future with the company. When asked about Gergiev replacing Levine, he said, "He won't be Jimmy's successor, because, as long as I'm here, Jimmy will be here." If that wasn't direct enough, he added, "You can say he'll become music director over my dead body."

Chapter Thirty-nine

THE EVOLUTION OF JAMES LEVINE

At about the same time as the Gergiev appointment, James Levine began to make a number of changes in his own life. It almost seemed that, with a strong and consistent general manager like Volpe running the Met, he could relax his overriding commitment to the institution—at least to some extent.

When, in 1995, Levine took over the podium for the Three Tenors, nothing seemed more remote from the aesthetic values to which he had devoted his life. Since 1990, when Carreras, Domingo, and Pavarotti teamed up with Zubin Mehta to televise the original concert, the Three Tenors had become a cultural phenomenon that quickly moved beyond the world of classical music. Opera finally made a definitive move into the popular culture of the twentieth century. The recording of that first concert became the best-selling classical recording of all time, and the video did almost as well. In the summer of 1992, the Tenors' concert, led by Mehta at the Hollywood Bowl, was heard and seen by a billion people around the globe.

No one had expected the first concert to be so successful, and it was said that Domingo in particular was annoyed that he had promised most of his fee to Carreras's charity. He and Pavarotti were determined that if this success were to endure, they would profit, and they did. Estimates of their concert fees, not including television and recording rights, were millions of dollars for each performance. "There's nothing wrong with being commercial," Domingo declared at a press conference. "It would be hypocrit-ical to say we're not looking forward to success."

Levine had become wealthy over his years as a major conductor, but his financial profile improved perceptibly when he took over the Three Tenors, starting with a world tour. Although he would not earn anything like the sums the tenors garnered, it was estimated that his fee for each concert would be $500,000.

Levine was immediately accused of selling out. In order to fit in all the Three Tenors tour engagements, he had to cancel several prestigious per-formances, including concerts with the Boston Symphony. "[He was] probably hoping his great mentor George Szell would not hurl a bolt of lightning at him," wrote Richard Dyer in the *Boston Globe*.

But Levine knew the energizing effect these concerts would have on the operatic world. It is always difficult to say how many people who went to Giant Stadium for a Three Tenors concert became Met subscribers. But certainly the air of elitism surrounding opera began to dissipate with the great success of the Three Tenors. During the 1990s, opera became the only performing art to make substantial gains at the box office, in sharp contrast to what was happening to symphony concerts and ballet presenta-tions. The audiences at opera performances became noticeably younger. While some of this new vigor may be attributable to opera's being a visual art that appeals to generations trained as television viewers, the Three Tenors certainly helped to lighten the operatic perception.

Levine struggled to explain his involvement; occasionally, he sounded defensive. There was his real concern about keeping two of his most im-portant singers happy and performing at the Met. (José Carreras rarely sings opera anymore, although he has scheduled future engagements at the Met.) After all, Domingo and Pavarotti both sold out the opera house.

But Levine also pointed out that there is plenty of historical precedent for a serious musician becoming involved in more-commercial ventures. "In the old days, no one would have questioned this at all. . . . The world I grew up in, Toscanini was without doubt the conducting example, a force of nature by which you can measure a certain standard. Toscanini . . . was coaxed out of retirement to conduct a radio orchestra [the NBC sym-phony] in a dry studio. He did it because the possibility existed to interest a lot of people in the music that interested him. Heifetz used to play at Lewisohn Stadium [an outdoor concert pavilion in New York City], [and] Stokowski introduced important works and also conducted _Fantasia_.

"I saw the _Fantasia_ film at a young enough age to be very impressed by it, [and] I'm very proud to be the conductor of the new _Fantasia_ movie."

That movie became Levine's next excursion into the commercial world of popular music. It opened in December 1999, again with a world tour, Levine conducting London's Philharmonic Orchestra. Even in a production from the powerful Disney organization, the influence of Ronald Wilford was very much in evidence through his protégé, Peter Gelb. In an article in London's _Independent_ newspaper, Gelb, now head of Sony International, takes credit for Levine's involvement: "Many conductors would have fought shy of the populism of this project, but James has an instinctive knowledge of what the medium is about."

As _Fantasia_ opened in theaters around the world, and the sound track hit the top of the best-seller charts, surpassing even recordings by Pavarotti, the Three Tenors phenomenon peaked and began to fade. The concerts were no longer automatic sellouts, and the tenors had tax problems with their enormous earnings, as did their producer. Levine has remained above reproach in the tax area.

Levine has no patience with the criticism of his new populism. "I was brought up to take responsibility for myself, to obey the natural laws of my personality and gifts." One can hear the echo of the young man whose father once told him that, to become a successful conductor, he would have to cut his hair and lose twenty pounds. Levine's response to his father was that he had to be who he was.

At the same time that he was involved with the Three Tenors and Disney's _Fantasia_, Levine was simultaneously launching more serious projects, projects that he had been developing in his own mind for years. He arranged a chamber music series with members of the Metropolitan Opera Orchestra at Weill Recital Hall in Carnegie Hall, at which he presented difficult and demanding programs to sold-out audiences. And his concerts with the Met Orchestra in the main hall at Carnegie began to include programs as challenging as the chamber music he was doing. "He always said what he wanted to do was just play contemporary chamber music," one critic said in astonishment, "and now that's just what he's doing."

In 1999, Levine finally achieved the new production of *Moses und Aron* that he had talked about for twenty-five years. He judged that now the chorus and orchestra were so excellent that this difficult piece could be rehearsed without upsetting the rest of the schedule. The resulting production, directed by Graham Vick, was a critical success, especially for Levine, the chorus, the orchestra, and the principal artists. Again, as with the Met Titles, the company had taken a long time to see the project through to the end, and, again, the production was all the better for the care and time it had been given.

For twenty-five years, Levine had also wanted to participate in a festival that would gather many of the great musicians of the world and, at the same time, provide a chance for talented younger musicians to work with them, and have both groups perform in an area of great natural beauty. In July 2000, this dream of Levine's came true when he began an association with the Verbier Festival in Switzerland. In this mountain village, orchestra concerts by the Verbier Festival Youth Orchestra, under various conductors, including Levine, alternated with opera master classes, chamber music concerts, and solo recitals. In addition, the musicians played impromptu performances in tents and cafés throughout the town, and the artists, student musicians, audience members, and local people mingled in the shops, restaurants, and streets. The list of artists involved was impressive, including several who, like Levine, are not usually so accessible: Martha Argerich, Yuri Bashmet, Evgeny Kissin, Lynn Harrell, Dmitri Hvorostovsky, Gil Shaham, Mischa Maisky, and Zoltán Kocsis. "Look over your shoulder at those mountains," Levine told a visitor. "Boy, are we hungry to come here, feel this sort of air and see those sights. It affects your whole state of mind." Verbier reminded him of Aspen, where he spent so many of his own happy and formative years, and where, in his first professional disappointment, he had once lost the chance to direct that festival. Perhaps, in addition to everything else, Verbier was a long-overdue vindication.

One of Levine's pet projects, however, had vanished from his agenda: the ever-elusive Mini-Met. Perhaps the importance of this vision of Levine's had subsided when other parts of his life blossomed. "If Jimmy really wanted it," Bruce Crawford said in the late 1990s, "we would have it." "Touring, recording, and the orchestra," mused Joseph Volpe, "have taken the Mini-Met's place in Jimmy's heart."

Levine's decision to take on the music directorship of the Munich Philharmonic seemed, at first glance, incomprehensible. Several American orchestras were looking for a music director. Even a curious Bruce Crawford asked Levine why, when he had supposedly been offered the Philadelphia Orchestra. Levine explained that it was important to keep part of his artistic life in Europe. With the end of his work at Salzburg, and his temporary hiatus from Bayreuth, Munich had come along at just the right time.

But why the Munich Philharmonic? Munich has three orchestras: the Bavarian Radio Symphony Orchestra, the Orchestra of the Bavarian State Opera, and the Philharmonic, the least well known. The other two are in the hands of Lorin Maazel and Zubin Mehta. Didn't this make Levine feel like third choice?

At the 1997 press conference announcing Gergiev's appointment and Levine's probable move to Munich, one intrepid reporter had asked Levine why he was taking on such a poor orchestra. "Oh," Gergiev airily answered for him, "it's not _that_ bad." Levine bristled. "What did the Met Orchestra sound like when I came here?" he asked. Obviously, he cannot resist the challenge of building another great orchestra; it is more stimulating to Levine than taking on an orchestra with a more illustrious reputation.

But his move to Munich was to be traumatic. Although, throughout the fall of 1997, Levine maintained he was unaware of what was going on when his appointment was first leaked to the press, the German reporters were vitriolic. The conductors had been caught in the middle of a local political battle, since the orchestra was supported by the government.

The musicians in the orchestra, who had been leaderless since the death of Sergiu Celibidache the preceding year, had unanimously asked for Levine as their new music director after his debut concert with the orchestra. Up to that point, Levine had not considered this. Only when the orchestra members came to him after that first concert and literally begged him to consider becoming their regular conductor did he begin to consider the idea. At first, he resisted, and, then, the idea began to appeal to him. He figured out that he could do thirty weeks at the Met, twelve weeks in Munich, and still have ten weeks for vacation and special projects. That's when Munich began to seem to him like a real possibility.

After Levine decided he wanted to go to Munich, his contract was negotiated between Ronald Wilford and the mayor of Munich. It stipulated twenty-four concerts a year at DM 60,000 per concert, plus a salary of DM 500,000—which amounted to more than $1 million. This sum was to come from municipal tax funds.

The radical Green Party in Munich exploded at this deal and the financial burden it would put on the city. The Social Democrats, trying to negotiate, suggested that Levine be given a probationary period, something he never would have accepted. The newspapers pounced upon the altercation, and one decreed that Levine was not young enough, slim enough, or "Bavarian" enough for the job. Immediately, in response, cries of anti-Semitism arose. Finally, the rumors about Levine's private life crept into the press, and some Green Party politicians suggested that the city demand a certificate of good conduct from the New York City Police Department. Levine remained aloof from the fray, although he was kept informed by Wilford; his only response was to stress that he had never campaigned for this job.

Why, then, did he decide to go ahead with negotiating for the position in the face of all the uproar? There were two reasons, he said. First, he wanted a chance to perform new music with a symphony orchestra. This isn't feasible at the Met, and guest-conducting engagements are too limited in rehearsal time to enable him to program contemporary works. Second, he needed an outlet to perform orchestral repertory over and over, as he has done with the Mozart operas at the Met. Repeating works is not an option for a guest conductor—artistic administrators ask Levine to do different programs each time he goes back to an orchestra, and a brief engagement doesn't allow him to achieve the level of depth he wants. Previously, Ravinia had filled these needs for him, as had his seventeen summers with the Vienna Philharmonic at Salzburg. But now he missed these elements of his musical life.

After weeks of contention, the city council finally voted to give Levine the job. Apparently, the German politicians, in a country where artists are venerated in a way that is inconceivable to Americans, decided that letting Levine get away would be a black mark on Munich, and this led to a peaceful conclusion. In the fall of 1999, Levine began his tenure.

But the experiment was troubled. Despite a good response from the Munich public, the Philharmonic continued to have to struggle for funding from the city and state. The lack of money, as always, was frustrating to Levine, who disliked having to compromise his artistic instincts to accommodate a shrinking budget. Even an orchestra builder as experienced as Levine found it difficult to work the same miracle with Munich that he had with the Met Orchestra, given the much shorter amount of time he spent in Germany; a tour of Europe he undertook with the Philharmonic in 2000 was not a success.

At almost the same time, Seiji Ozawa had announced his resignation from the podium of the Boston Symphony in order to become music director of the Vienna State Opera. Levine, who had grown up idolizing the partnership of the Boston orchestra and Serge Koussevitzky, was a frequent guest conductor in Boston, and he was uniquely popular with the musicians. Boston is only two hundred miles north of New York; Levine, frustrated in Munich, began to think about moving his symphonic career closer to home.

Chapter Forty

THE MET AT THE MILLENNIUM

Around the world, other opera companies now look at the Metropolitan Opera with envy. During the many crises, financial and artistic, facing London's Royal Opera in the last few years, one of the English newspapers ran an article about Joseph Volpe entitled "The Right Way to Run an Opera House." The writer used Volpe's management at the Met as a direct contrast to the hapless Covent Garden board and administration.

Volpe outlined the simple plan that had succeeded so well. He had improved the Met's relationship with the public by a customer service campaign, had sold more than $1 million of tickets over the Internet on the new Met site in its first year alone, had installed a new $5 million computer system that would track tickets and contributions.

He has also programmed more operas than in the past, but for fewer performances. This policy produced anguished complaints from the company members, who simply could not see how they could rehearse up to thirty operas a year. But, somehow, rehearsal time was worked out, and the new policy has meant that the company can now sell difficult operas like *The Makropulos Case* and *Billy Budd* at over 90 percent capacity. *Wozzeck* and *Pelléas* have sold out their runs.

Volpe is also responsible for the newly eclectic mixture of designers and directors working at the theater. Gone are the days when three or four directors ruled the Met stage—now Volpe is eager to try directors who have made news in Europe, and the Met is beginning to generate some of the creative excitement felt during the Dexter years. "The most interesting night in the theater these days," said one theater critic, "is an evening at the Met." As the box office has grown stronger, many have rushed to take credit for the evolution of the company's theatrical side. "Other people at the Met try to build up this mythology that they are responsible for all this new talent," said Elijah Moshinsky, "but it is really Joe Volpe."

Volpe's commitment to expanding the repertory led to the Met premiere of Janáček's _The Makropulos Case_. The production was directed by Elijah Moshinsky and starred Jessye Norman in one of her infrequent Met appearances. The first-night audience on January 5, 1996, was excited about the new work and the curtain went up on time. But less than two minutes after the curtain rose, the tenor Richard Versalle, perched on a towering ladder, sang the line "You can only live so long," and then fell, his arms outstretched, fifteen feet to the stage floor. The audience gasped, not sure if this was part of the staging or an accident. The conductor called out, "Richard, are you all right?" but there was no response. The curtain fell.

Volpe came out onstage and announced a twenty-minute intermission. Backstage, however, it was obvious to everyone that Versalle was dead. He was rushed to nearby St. Luke's–Roosevelt Hospital, where it was determined that he had died of a massive heart attack, probably just before he fell. He had been on the Met roster intermittently since 1978.

There are times when the show must not go on, and this was one of them. Volpe called the audience back into the auditorium, announced the sad news and the cancellation of the performance. The audience applauded this appropriate gesture. What was never made public was that Volpe called Versalle's widow to tell her the news and also to reassure her that the sixty-three-year-old tenor's fees would be paid for the entire run of the opera.

Although Volpe, like all the general managers, has had some problems with the new administrators he has brought in, he has had no such trouble with the singers. He is perhaps most proud of the close collaborations he has forged with the principal artists. He is always backstage, at rehearsals and performances, and makes a point of going into every dressing room to greet each singer, in striking contrast to his predecessors.

The singers respond to Volpe's compassionate side, which offsets his sometimes-brusque demeanor. He is close to Renée Fleming, a young soprano who has made her career the old-fashioned way—slowly. Since her debut in 1991 as the Countess in *Le Nozze di Figaro,* the Met public's appetite for her appearances has increased gradually but steadily, as has been the case with her audiences all over the world. Now she is edging close to being a singer who can sell out an opera house, and frequently does so. She is not one to knock an audience flat by her intensity; she is far more subtle. Her voice is rich and beautiful, and she is an elegant musician. She believes that her voice did not reach its potential until 1995, when she sang Desdemona at the Met's opening night opposite the Otello of Plácido Domingo. She had given birth to her second daughter just three weeks before.

After years of study and amassing experience, it seemed that overnight Fleming was in demand everywhere, in this country and in Europe. And although she has planned her career with intelligence, in 1998, she took on too much. During the fall, she sang three new roles in three months: Strauss's *Arabella,* Donizetti's *Lucrezia Borgia,* and the world premiere of André Previn's *A Streetcar Named Desire. Lucrezia Borgia* at La Scala was a particularly painful experience. She found the company's music director, Riccardo Muti, difficult to get along with, and the Milan public reacted badly to her performance: she was booed.

Then she was off to San Francisco and the long and intense rehearsal period for *Streetcar.* Next came a new production of *Figaro* at the Met, with a cast that included Cecilia Bartoli and Bryn Terfel. By this time, she was so emotionally exhausted that she dreaded each performance. Yet she held her own in this supercharged cast.

A year earlier, when the Alagnas had pulled out of the new Zeffirelli *Traviata* to be presented during the 1998–99 season, Fleming had felt comfortable enough with Volpe to call him and admit she had been longing to add Violetta to her repertory. Volpe loved the idea, and she was cast. But by the end of the *Figaro* run, Fleming was completely spent. In addition to her exhausting professional schedule, her marriage was breaking up. In November 1998, she called her friend Volpe again, and asked to withdraw from *Traviata*. Although this meant finding a new Violetta, a difficult role to cast, at very short notice, Volpe agreed. He reassured Fleming that this would have no effect on her future Met career, and it hasn't. He understands that to comfort great singers, who have difficult patches in their lives just like everyone else, is to ensure that they will repay his understanding with loyalty to the Met.

Volpe's custom is to be omnipresent at the opera house. He attends most performances, entertains donors at intermission, freely gives interviews, meets with the unions, the board, and the artists, putting in eighteen-hour days at home and frequently traveling to other theaters in the United States and in Europe. All this has taken some toll on his health, although he is a big, robust man. In the winter of 1994, he collapsed while attending a performance at the Brooklyn Academy of Music. He was diagnosed with an "episode of the vagal nerve controlling respiration and digestion." Since then, he has had various other ailments, including back problems and a hernia operation. The job of general manager historically has been hard on the men who have held it.

In the late 1990s, New York City moved into an era of affluence that far outstripped the 1980s. Suddenly, the definition of wealth changed: no longer were personal fortunes computed by millions of dollars but rather by billions.

Going back to the robber barons, the new rich had quickly targeted the Metropolitan as a means to social acceptance. And in this age of instant and glorified celebrity, the Met became a means to the end of fame and recognition.

Sybil Harrington had set an elegant precedent for future donors: the chief demands she made were that the productions she endowed would be to her taste. The next major donor, Cynthia Wood, who died prematurely of cancer in the early 1990s, was a self-effacing woman who particularly loved Levine and the Met Orchestra. Wood was admired by the company for her quiet dignity; she actually had first come to the Met as a mere assistant stage director, although one with a trust fund in the millions and her own private plane. Her will left a bequest that will fund the orchestra's tours and Carnegie Hall series for years to come.

In September 1998, the Met kicked off another endowment drive to supplement the funds raised during the 1980s. This time, the plan was to raise $200 million and end up with a total of $300 million in income-producing investments. Just as the Centennial Endowment Drive had generated the benevolence of Sybil Harrington, the 1998 drive centered around a new and very different kind of donor.

Alberto W. Vilar was discovered by Marilyn Shapiro and her relentless research staff as they went about their task of matching ticket-buyers to their donations. She noted a pattern of large gifts from Vilar, and her interest was piqued. She made a point of meeting up with Vilar.

Vilar's father had owned a sugar plantation in Cuba, and the family had fled the Cuban Revolution as penniless refugees. The young Alberto had come to New York because he believed that the United States would not tolerate Castro's regime in its own backyard. While he waited out Castro, he joined Citibank as a trainee in their overseas division. About the time he realized that Cuba was not going to change, he became sick of banking, and moved to London, where he began his career as an investor.

In London, while he amassed an impressive fortune, he went often to the Royal Opera at Covent Garden, and became fascinated by opera. His father did everything possible to discourage his son's interest in the arts, but Vilar became a passionate connoisseur. Vilar's first contribution to the Met came in 1987, the year he moved back to New York; it was $1,500. His next gift was $3,000, and he then joined the Golden Horseshoe circle of donors.

A slender, elegant, soft-spoken man, he soon became known in the company as eccentric. He lived in a thirty-room apartment at United Nations Plaza. The decor alone has caused much comment: his dining room ceiling is a replica of the ceiling of the Mozarteum concert hall in Salzburg, and he has also installed chandeliers that are exactly like the crystal lamps that ornament the Met.

Within a few years, Vilar was underwriting new productions. Meanwhile, the Met was not the only beneficiary of his generosity: he gave $16 million to Covent Garden, including $2 million to fund the Royal Opera's Young Artists' Program. In gratitude, the main foyer in the reconstructed opera house was renamed the Vilar Floral Hall. He gave $5 million to Carnegie Hall, over $2 million to the Vienna Philharmonic, several million to Valery Gergiev's Kirov, the Kennedy Center, the Lyric Opera of Chicago, the Baden-Baden Festival, the Spoleto Festival, the Salzburg Festival, the Lyric Opera of Chicago, the Los Angeles Opera, run by his friend Plácido Domingo, and Operalia, Domingo's vocal competition. He also funded a conducting competition to be overseen by his friend Lorin Maazel, the new music director of the New York Philharmonic. Maazel's appointment led some to speculate that Vilar's money had entered into the Philharmonic's decision.

When the Met decided to launch the new endowment campaign, Vilar was the obvious person for the company to turn to. He responded with a pledged gift of $25 million, instantly becoming one of the largest contributors in Met history: with this gift, he almost matched Sybil Harrington's entire contribution. In gratitude, the Met renamed the Grand Tier level of the opera house the Vilar Grand Tier. Even the signs in the theater's elevators were changed to reflect the new name.

But Vilar was no Sybil Harrington, and trouble began almost immediately because he was a very hands-on donor. He was appalled to discover that the Met's investment philosophy was to sell any stock that they were given rather than let the shares grow. When he decided to make his endowment gift, he spent months in legal negotiations to make sure that his contribution was treated differently. As a result, he said with satisfaction, "the Met has benefited enormously, and my gift will be worth substantially more than when I gave it."

After making this gift to the Met, Vilar began to strew his billions even more generously throughout the music world. He continued to fund the Kirov, donated substantially to the Salzburg Festival, and gave the Vienna State Opera several million to create the "Vilar Titles," a supertitling system modeled on Met Titles that is even more technologically advanced. He gave La Scala $2 million to fund three operas in celebration of Verdi's centenary, becoming the first individual and the first non-Italian to make a major contribution to the company. In all, it is estimated he has given some $150 million to musical institutions around the world. "I think anyone will tell you that I'm the largest supporter of classical music, opera and ballet in the world," he proudly told a *New York Times* reporter.

Vilar announced that he was determined to bring U.S.-style arts patronage to other parts of the world. Almost immediately, however, the dangerous side of support from private individuals became obvious in the restrictions he placed on his gifts. Reportedly, he promised a substantial donation to the San Francisco Opera, but only if the company chose as its new intendant one of the two people he wanted. When they chose someone else, he withdrew the gift and gave the money instead to the Los Angeles Opera, headed by his friend Domingo. At Salzburg, every program contains a color photograph of Vilar, along with a flowery pronouncement of thanks for his gift of $6 million. At Bayreuth, where a power struggle had developed between Wolfgang Wagner and his board, who were supporting the takeover of the festival by his niece, Nike, or his daughter, Eva, Vilar donated the money for a new production, making clear that he was taking Wagner's side against his daughter and his niece. Wolfgang Wagner released a statement thanking Vilar but admonishing that he would be given no artistic authority. Few believed this would be the case. The English music critic Rodney Milnes stated flatly, "It's starting to look as though the future of opera will depend on the whim of a Cuban-American stockmarket investor with a love of music."

Joseph Volpe has no intention of giving Vilar all the perks he receives automatically from other companies, and this infuriates the Cuban patron. His most frequent complaint about the Met is the lack of what he refers to as "donor recognition." "The old families are dying out," he said. "Where is capital now being generated? The engine of growth is technology, particularly Internet technology. The question is, does the Met have access to this technology? The only way they do is through people like me. The old line of money is paling in contrast. . . . There is a whole new generation of donor."

Vilar has made his own money and this gives him the right, he believes, to a strong opinion about how he is recognized. "To give this way is to set an example," he said. "They're in the business of opera and also the business of raising money. Fifty percent of the revenues are raised privately. The Met is, in effect, two businesses, and if you want to raise money, you have to think like a money manager." For example, for a long time he has been irritated by the small print in the Met program in which he was acknowledged for his production contributions. "You look . . . at the program for, say, *The Marriage of Figaro* and it starts with 'Libretto by . . .' Well, who cares who wrote the libretto? How about the guy who wrote the check?"

The Met, in fact, did redesign the program's face page to give production donors a far more prominent placement and larger type size. But this has not placated Vilar. He complained that he had to use his lawyers to get the signs in Met elevators changed to "Vilar Grand Tier." And, in comparison, at Salzburg and at the Mariinsky, he receives a full page of recognition in the house programs, including a color portrait.

Sitting in his office, also festooned with Met chandeliers, Vilar ruminated on the changing role of arts patrons.

> This [the Met] is a marriage between two forces—the artist and the donor. The donors are considered second-class citizens. The realization must come that the donors and the artistic side of the Met are two equal forces. The Met has a potentially phenomenal fundraising machine. But they are reluctant to come out of the closet and say they are in the money business.
>
> I don't understand why I should be treated like a second-class citizen. What makes me less important than Plácido Domingo? Why shouldn't I take curtain calls?

Volpe makes no secret of how appalled he is at this kind of declaration. "I'm going to take his name off the Grand Tier," he threatened, joking at least on the surface. But he has to admit that "if [Vilar] is not our biggest donor, he certainly will be in time." He also acknowledges that Sybil Harrington influenced artistic planning by, for example, enthusiastically underwriting Zeffirelli productions and refusing to endow more contemporary stagings. "There are some people who give a lot of money and don't want credit . . . I do agree that [Vilar] should receive credit, that one should recognize what he is doing. And I think we have made some changes here to do that."

Around this time, Bruce Crawford was tired of trying to please everyone. "I can't deal with another *arriviste*," he said. Whatever the precipitating cause, he resigned as board president. A man who gets bored easily, by the time Vilar's influence began to blossom, he felt he had put the house into good order, raising the money to refurbish the standard repertory, stabilizing day-to-day operations, and instituting a more-adventurous repertory. He had no wish to involve himself with the company's new fund-raising imperatives, although he has stayed closely involved with other aspects of the company—for example, overseeing the modernization of the Met archives.

Crawford was succeeded by Paul Montrone, chairman and chief executive officer of Fisher Scientific International. Although Montrone had been a Met ticket-buyer and supporter for thirty years, he has been a managing director only since 1991, so he can be considered the kind of new blood on the board that Volpe feels is so important. "Today no one can rely on the old WASP families," Volpe said. "The money is gone. Now the board members are much more real people." Montrone, who says his love of the Met is "genetic," referring to his Italian-American heritage, is also a self-made man who contributes to the Met because he loves opera. In the old days, wealthy patrons understood that support of culture was part of the obligation of wealth; now the wealthiest board members, like Vilar and Montrone, are avid supporters and donors because they just love opera. Montrone has also pledged to put an end to intra-Met antagonisms—such as those between the opera company and the Guild, its volunteer and educational arm; the National Council; and the Opera Club—that are so reminiscent of the long battle between the Opera Company and Real Estate Company boards. "We're in the twenty-first century and we have to admit that, both on the artistic side, where we've done a lot, and, especially, the business side. What do we expect of our board? What do we do for our donors? The landscape has changed and become much more competitive, and our lifestyle has changed." Montrone admires Volpe: "I would not have taken the job without Joe there. For its size, the Met is more complex than a regular business with a $200 million budget and Joe is very good at dealing with the artistic temperament." He also likes Vilar and understands his need for recognition. "We get along well because we are on the same wavelength as to how things should be run," Montrone says. "He's a big supporter and the Met has to do everything it can to make him feel appreciated. All the donors must be treated as well as possible: this is supposed to be an enriching experience; this is supposed to be an enjoyable experience."

The new attitude toward major donors was obvious when, in the summer of 1999, the Met broke with one of its long-standing traditions and allowed its stage to be used for a gaudy private event given by two of its leading patrons. Mr. and Mrs. George Lindemann have a family fortune derived from cell phones and cable TV estimated by _Forbes_ magazine at $1.5 billion. They have given the Met so much money—over $10 million—that the program for young singers is now known as the Lindemann Young Artists' Development Program. Previously, the Lindemanns had been infamous because their son, George, Jr., had been convicted of killing several valuable racehorses in order to collect the insurance. The crime inspired widespread revulsion, but the Lindemanns airily ascribed the whole imbroglio to anti-Semitism in the racing world.

The Lindemann daughter, who goes by the name of Sloan, has been more successful than George, Jr. She is a former Manhattan assistant district attorney who now writes consumer affairs pieces for the _Daily News_ and is the host of a cable TV shopping show. In 1999, she became engaged to Roger Barnett, an Internet mogul who specializes in beauty products. The elder Lindemanns decided to have Sloan's wedding rehearsal dinner onstage at the Met.

Volpe, despite his distaste for trading the Met's prestige for contributions, was well aware that there were few families able to give the company $10 million. So he agreed that the Lindemanns could have their party onstage.

The party that finally took place was a throwback to the days of Mrs. Vanderbilt and Mrs. Astor. It incurred stagehand costs of over $100,000 and arrangements became so complicated that a twelve-page memo was issued from the technical department to cover all eventualities. The set for

the second act of *Die Fledermaus* was erected, and two orchestras performed, including one flown in from Paris, as did a trumpet ensemble that
provided ceremonial flourishes. The party decor included such unusual
facets as an actress costumed as Marie Antoinette (the irony surely unin-
tended) and several pretend Blackamoors. There were also live red birds
and small performing monkeys, and the technical memo instructed the
props department to assist with the animals' cages and to cover the cages
to keep the animals calm.

The evening included performances by young Met singers who had
been trained by the Lindemann Young Artists' Development Program,
which presumably lifted the evening's tone, however briefly. But then the
dancing resumed, and the waiters were positioned around the dance floor
(i.e., the Met main stage) to offer the perspiring guests lavender-scented
hand towels proffered from silver trays by silver ice tongs. The used hand
towels were deposited into a silver chafing dish.

The evening ended at 2:00 A.M., and at 3:00 A.M., the animals were
scheduled to leave, hopefully still breathing. Somewhere, Mrs. Vanderbilt
was smiling.

The always precarious balance between the social, the artistic, and the
financial elements of the Metropolitan can be seen as slipping as the latest
ilk of nouveaux riches attempt to wield their power and influence. But
Volpe and Levine are determined that the artistic side remain unaffected.
Almost always, the Met has managed to combine its essential thirst for
money with artistic integrity.

By the end of 1999, the general consensus was that Volpe and Levine
had reached harmony. Each spoke of the other with the respect they had
always felt and, now, with a new affection. They joked about each other's
idiosyncrasies—Volpe about Levine's hatred of publicity, and Levine
about the influence of Volpe's Sicilian roots.

Levine seems excited about the future; he points out that, after the age
of sixty, Toscanini had conducted far more symphonic music than opera,
and it was clear that Levine expected his own career to make a similar ad-
justment. Speculation concentrated around major American orchestras,

with most attention centered on the Boston Symphony Orchestra. But should Levine decide to take on the institution once known as "the aristocrat of orchestras," he would be unlikely to give up his role as artistic director of his beloved Met.

> I don't have any plan to leave in the foreseeable future. We have arrived at a certain quality and I want to take that as far as possible. Any moment now, that orchestra will be without weaknesses anywhere, and then we shall play even better. I can imagine wanting to work with this ensemble and this company always. It has become like my own voice.

Volpe is also in demand. He was offered the intendant's position at Covent Garden and turned it down, saying that he wanted his young daughter to stay at school in New York. But there was a ruefulness in his refusal: "Now, if I were ten years younger . . . ," he told friends.

But, at any age, Volpe seems genetically unable to stay away from controversy, a characteristic that has endeared him to New Yorkers and made him the most charismatic general manager since Bing. He has already taken on temperamental singers, dismissive board members, and an independent-minded and stubborn artistic director; now he is prepared for what may become his biggest and most complex battle with Lincoln Center, the Met's home for over thirty-five years.

In June 1999, officials of the performing arts complex admitted publicly that they were in the planning stage of a vast project to overhaul the cultural center and its crumbling and inadequate buildings. In the 1960s, the world seemed to view buildings as disposable, and there were quiet murmurings that the Lincoln Center complex had never been meant to hold up longer than twenty-five years.

Thirty-seven years after Avery Fisher Hall, the first building in the complex had opened, Lincoln Center was in terrible shape. Despite an almost complete gutting, Avery Fisher Hall's acoustics were still impossible; the New York State Theater's acoustics were so bad for opera—the hall had been designed originally only for dance—that the New York City Opera had been forced to amplify the singers; the granite of the giant plaza was cracked; and the marble facing of most of the buildings was degenerating. One New York Philharmonic board member said direly, "Other than the Met, I'd take them [the constituent buildings] down."

As usual, the Met stands apart: the company had conducted its own capital drive ten years previously to patch its building; the opera house is also the only theater at Lincoln Center to be generally considered as without problems. Almost. Although the acoustics and sight lines in the auditorium are superb, there are still many adverse results from Anthony Bliss's decision long ago to reduce the size of the building. The public areas of the house are so limited that the lengthy intermissions become exercises in crowd control; space for administrative offices ran out long ago and capacity for the vastly expanded Met staff is a combination of jerry-building and imaginative use of closets. Like all the other constituents, the Met could make good use of any funds raised for the Center's rebuilding.

But when in 2001 Lincoln Center would finally organize its $1.5 billion renovation project under a nonprofit corporation and receive a commitment of $240 million from New York City (thanks to opera fanatic Rudolph Giuliani), the Met would balk. In a scenario startlingly reminiscent of Rudolf Bing's antagonism toward Lincoln Center in general, and the New York City Opera in specific, Joseph Volpe and Paul Montrone co-signed a letter withdrawing from the joint construction project and announcing that the Met would do its renovating on its own.

At the core of the complicated dispute is the historic distrust the Met has had for the conglomerate of Lincoln Center. Believing itself to be better run and better financed, the Met board and administration regard Lincoln Center and the other constituents with a combination of mistrust and disdain. With its annual budget approaching $200 million, the Met towers over the other member organizations fiscally, and is responsible for 30 percent of the Center's operating costs, in return receiving the same percentage of joint fund-raising. Yet Volpe and Montrone believe that Lincoln Center had neglected to consult the Met on many of the most important aspects of the renovation and the company had received only one seat on the redevelopment corporation, the same recognition received by such tiny constituents as the Film Society and the School of American Ballet.

Another major stumbling block is the idea of building a new opera house for the New York City Opera. Tentative plans would place this structure just south of the Met in Damrosch Park. Although the City Opera had made great gains both in fund-raising and in prestige under the management of its elegant general director, Paul Kellogg, Volpe and Montrone were worried that the smaller company was not yet ready to support its own opera house. If financial disaster threatened, the Met, because of its current position as a Lincoln Center constituent, would be drawn into the fiscal rescue.

The conflict between the Met and Lincoln Center is ongoing and probably always will be. The situation will remain that, on Lincoln Center Plaza, one constituent is more equal than the others, and some have hypothesized that, in the future, the Met might even consider seceding from Lincoln Center altogether. Somewhere, Sir Rudolf must be smiling as he says, "I told you so." Volpe, who has modeled his career as general manager on Bing's, would certainly agree.

The Met celebrated the last month of the twentieth century with two new productions, just weeks apart. The world premiere of *The Great Gatsby*, by John Harbison, was the third world premiere the company had produced in less than ten years. Levine conducted, and although reviews were mixed and the production did not have the public success of *Ghosts of Versailles*, it was an important artistic effort, indicative of the new Met and its priorities.

And also in the early winter of 1999, the Met was finally able to do something James Levine had wanted from the beginning. The company, now probably in the best condition ever, was ready to do a new production of *Tristan und Isolde*. He had dreamed of this for twenty-five years.

Levine had done revivals of the previous production, but the casting had never felt right to him. He swore that he would not attempt a new production until he could cast it correctly, and so *Tristan* disappeared from the Met schedule for fifteen years. Now, with the ascendance of the English soprano Jane Eaglen and the heldentenor Ben Heppner, he had the cast he wanted. He had his magnificent orchestra. And he himself was generally acknowledged as the prime Wagnerian conductor of the day.

The production by Dieter Dorn was stark by Met standards. Dorn, understanding Levine's priorities, placed the singers at the front of the stage, from where they rarely strayed, and thus they were able to communicate directly with Levine. Dorn opted for an understated production, coolly lit, that required the singers to move very little. The music, which always threatens to swamp the stage in this opera, was thus left to frame the drama of the doomed lovers, and Levine, who conducts Wagner as though he hates to think it could ever end, chose slow and measured tempos. He decided to present the opera uncut. Throughout its six hours, *Tristan*, like the Met itself, balances the characters' intimate conflicts against its gigantic breadth.

Tristan und Isolde is one of the great masterpieces, a seminal work that is central to any opera house's repertory, and its long absence from the Met surrounded this new production with intense interest and speculation. Even the company's most severe critics admitted that, artistically, the Met had never been in better condition, and Eaglen and Heppner fitted securely into the Met tradition of heroic Wagnerians.

All performances quickly sold out in advance. On opening night, Monday, November 22, the excitement in the Met's crowded lobbies was palpable. Special nights at the Met have a special flavor, a sense that something historic is about to occur, a chance that this evening would join other legendary nights, an event each audience member would someday be proud to have been part of. This *Tristan* had become the most eagerly anticipated Wagner performance in years.

Volpe was in his box, accompanied by his wife, and also Eva Wagner, the composer's great-granddaughter, who is the Met's European representative. Elsewhere in the auditorium was Eva's father, Wolfgang, Wagner's grandson and intendant of the Bayreuth Festival, from whom she is estranged and with whom she is battling for control of the Bayreuth Festival.

Backstage, too, there was an unusual hush—everyone understood the momentousness of this performance. James Levine waited in his dressing room just off the entrance to the orchestra pit. This *Tristan* had been his fantasy since childhood, a fantasy that was about to be fulfilled. On the speaker in his dressing room, over the sounds of the orchestra tuning up, and the singers testing their voices, came the voice of the stage manager.

"Thirty seconds to curtain," he said. "Conductor to the pit." It was an ordinary announcement on an extraordinary occasion.

Levine straightened his white tie, and then walked into the pit. He wove his way through his musicians as the audience roared a welcoming ovation. Hopping up on the podium, he bowed briefly to the public, acknowledged the orchestra, and then turned to face the stage. The red light on his music stand glowed, indicating it was time to start. Then, slowly and splendidly, the huge gold curtain parted, the stage lights glowed on, and the opera began.

ACKNOWLEDGMENTS

I am indebted to the many people at the Metropolitan Opera who made this book possible: James Levine, artistic director; Joseph Volpe, general manager; Paul Montrone, president and chief executive officer of the Metropolitan Opera; Bruce Crawford, chairman of the Metropolitan Opera board; Mrs. Gilbert W. Humphrey, chairman emeritus; and Mrs. Ezra K. Zilkha, vice chairman.

In addition, I would like to thank Robert Tuggle, director of the Metropolitan Opera Archives for his endless kindness, suggestions, corrections, and bottomless reservoir of knowledge. John Pennino, assistant archivist, was generous in his patient help, and invaluable in my photo and performance history research. The Met's press department was never too busy to answer my questions, to set up interviews, or to find long-lost newspaper articles, and I would like to thank François Giuliani, Peter E. Clark, Jonathan Tichler, and Charles C. Sheek, as well as the Met's official photographer, Winnie Klotz. Robert Sirinek, the orchestra manager, kindly helped me understand the workings of the Met Orchestra and arrange interviews with the players.

I am also grateful to the family of the late Anthony A. Bliss, especially Barbara Bliss and Sally Brayley Bliss.

Other present and former Met board and company members to whom I am grateful are Cecilia Bartoli, Sarah Billinghurst, Stephen Brown, the late Richard Cassilly, Joseph Clark, Thomas H. Connell III, George Darden, Edo de Waart, John Ferrillo, Jonathan Friend, Lawrence Glazener, Mark Gould, Peter J. Hall, Ben Heppner, Richard Horowitz, Alfred Hubay, Raymond Hughes, Kenneth Hunt, Joan Ingpen, David Kneuss, Julie Landsman, Hilary Ley, Lawrence D. Lovett, Catherine Malfitano, Peter McClintock, William McCourt, Fabrizio Melano, Aprile Millo, Ken Noda, Stewart Pearce, Paul Plishka, David Reppa, David M. Reuben, Gail Robinson, the late Leonie Rysanek, Marilyn Shapiro, Smeeta Sharon, James S. Smith, Patrick J. Smith, Frank E. Taplin, Carol Vaness, Alberto W. Vilar, Eva Wagner-Pasquier, Gil Wechsler, and Wendy Westwood.

Others who were of great assistance are Alison Ames, Katrine Ames, the late John Ardoin, Martin Bernheimer, Ralph Blumenthal, Herbert Breslin, Justin Davidson, Peter G. Davis, David Hamilton, Jocelyn Herbert, Merle Hubbard, Albert Innaurato, Judie Janowski, Joela Jones, Norman Lebrecht, Nancy Malitz, Jonathan Miller, Elijah Moshinsky, James Oestreich, Riggs O'Hara, Tim Page, John Rockwell, Craig Rutenberg, Elisabeth Söderström, Terry Teachout, Ronald A. Wilford, Jeannie Williams, Francesca Zambello, and David Zauder.

My family, who have become heartily sick of opera, bolstered me: my sister and brother-in-law, Ned and Deborah F. Stiles; my brother and sister-in-law, Peter and Dieuwke Fiedler; and my aunts May K. Bottomley and Lydia Fuller Bottomley.

I could not have survived the long process of producing this book without the patience and unending support of my friends: Donna Ahlstrand, Richard Cohen, Richard Dyer, Jane Hermann, Manuela Hoelterhoff, Julia C. Markham, Gerard and Jody Schwarz, David Patrick Stearns, Sissy and Max Strauss, and Allyn Thompson. My writers' group read and reread sections of the manuscript and I want to thank them: Mark Alpert, Stephen Goldstone, Nalini Jones, Dave King, Eva Mekler, and Cheryl Morrison. Thanks also to Jesse Cohen, who was supportive in developing the concept of this book.

Molto Agitato *would not have been written without the invaluable help of Nan A. Talese, my editor and publisher, who never lost faith; Lorna Owen, the assistant editor; Frances Apt, one of the copy editors and morale booster; my agent, Gloria Loomis; and Stephen E. Rubin, the publisher of Doubleday.*

NOTES

PROLOGUE: THE LONGEST CONCERT

p. 4   Author's interview with Miriam Gilbert, high school classmate in Cincinnati of James Levine.

CHAPTER ONE: THE BOXHOLDERS

p. 10   Controversy between Opera Company and Real Estate Company: The correspondence between Eliot Gregory and Henry Hyde, preserved in the Metropolitan Opera Archives, provides a rare glimpse into the personal rivalries and tastes of the Met board as the directors struggled to establish equilibrium between finance and art. All of the documents from the Met Archives are used by permission.

p. 11   *Salome* controversy: Henry H. Krehbiel, one of the leading music critics of the day, quoted by Irving Kolodin in his comprehensive history of the Metropolitan Opera up to 1966, p. 186.

p. 11   Met's first approach to Arturo Toscanini: Letter from Heinrich Conried to Henry Hyde, May 14, 1907; Metropolitan Opera Archives.

p. 11   Engagement of Gustav Mahler: Cable from Heinrich Conried to Henry Hyde, July 1907; Metropolitan Opera Archives.

p. 11   Mahler's reaction to the Met: From *Gustav Mahler: Memories and Letters*, by Alma Mahler, p. 129.

p. 12   Met's reaction to Mahler: *Evening Sun*, January 12, 1908, quoted by Robert Tuggle in "Mahler at the Met," liner notes for a New York Philharmonic recording of Mahler performances.

p. 12   Anti-Semitism of early board members: Letter from Eliot Gregory to Henry Hyde, January 15, 1908; Metropolitan Opera Archives.

p. 13   Evaluation of Kahn: Anonymous board member; used by permission of the Metropolitan Opera Archives.

CHAPTER TWO: MAHLER AND TOSCANINI

p. 15   Toscanini's attitude toward Mahler's presence at the Met: Arturo Toscanini quoted by Harvey Sachs in his biography of the conductor.

p. 15   Mahler's attitude toward Toscanini's arrival at the Met: *Gustav Mahler: Memories and Letters*, op. cit., p. 146.

p. 18   Affair between Toscanini and Geraldine Farrar: *Such Sweet Compulsion*, Geraldine Farrar's autobiography.

p. 21   Toscanini's departure: Although Toscanini never conducted an opera again at the Met, he subsequently did appear there in concert, conducting first his orchestra from La Scala and later the New York Philharmonic between 1920 and 1923.

CHAPTER THREE: WORLD WAR I AND THE 1920S

p. 22   Press supports Gatti's stand on anti-German issue: *New York Sun*, September 15, 1917.

CHAPTER FOUR: THE GREAT DEPRESSION

p. 28   Newspaper coverage of Met's financial crisis: Robert Tuggle, *The Golden Age of Opera*, p. 8.

p. 29   Controversy about whether the wealthy should control Met policies: Artur Bodanzky quoted by John Dizikes in *Opera in America*, p. 436.

p. 31   Mrs. Belmont's attitude toward domination of the Met by the wealthy: Eleanor Robson Belmont quoted by Martin Mayer in *The Met*, p. 193.

CHAPTER FIVE: EDWARD JOHNSON, WORLD WAR II,
        AND THE AMERICAN OPERA SINGER; RUDOLF BING ARRIVES

p. 36   Rudolf Bing becomes general manager: The material on Sir Rudolf Bing is taken from several sources: *5000 Nights at the Opera*, a memoir by Bing; an unpublished memoir by Anthony A. Bliss, used by permission of Sally Brayley Bliss; Bing's correspondence on file in the Metropolitan Opera Archives; the author's interviews with Barbara Bliss, Herman Krawitz, and Joseph Volpe; an oral history about the founding of Lincoln Center by Anthony Bliss, used by permission of Sally Brayley Bliss; *The Metropolitan Opera*, a definitive history of the company by Irving Kolodin; and *The Met*, another Met history published on the occasion of the company's Centennial season by Martin Mayer.

p. 45   Maria Callas's affair with Aristotle Onassis: Franco Zeffirelli quoted by Rupert Christiansen in *Prima Donna*, p. 248.

CHAPTER SIX: RUDOLF BING AND ANTHONY BLISS;
        THE BIRTH OF A NEW OPERA HOUSE

Throughout this chapter, Bing quotes are excerpted from his memoir, *5000 Nights at the Opera*, op. cit.

p. 47   Bliss's first meeting with Bing: From unpublished memoir by Anthony Bliss, op. cit.

p. 48   Information about Anthony Bliss's early life and family from his entry in *Current Biography,* April 1979; Bliss obituary in *New York Times,* August 12, 1991; Bliss's unpublished memoir; and author's interviews with Barbara Bliss, Bliss's daughter.

p. 56   Bliss's trip to meet with Arthur Goldberg: Unpublished memoir by Bliss, op. cit.

p. 56   Orchestra's reaction to settlement from author's interview with Sandor Balint, longtime chairman of the Met Orchestra committee.

CHAPTER SEVEN: THE NEW HOUSE

p. 60   Bing's attitude toward Lincoln Center: Memo from Rudolf Bing to Anthony Bliss, Metropolitan Opera Archives.

p. 61   From unpublished memoir by Anthony Bliss, op. cit.

p. 62   Bing's attitude toward National Company: *5000 Nights at the Opera,* op. cit.

p. 62   Bliss rebukes Bing on National Company: Memo from Bliss to Bing, Metropolitan Opera Archives.

p. 64   Bing snipes at Bliss: Letter from Bing to Reginald Allen, member of the Met administration, Summer 1963, Metropolitan Opera Archives.

p. 64   Bing suggests appointment of Schippers: Memo from Bing to Bliss, December 17, 1963, Metropolitan Opera Archives.

p. 65   Bliss's reaction to Schippers's suggestion: Memo from Bliss to Bing, December 27, 1963, Metropolitan Opera Archives.

p. 65   Bing begins to have doubts about Schippers: These quotes are from Bing letters (some undated) to Thomas Schippers, Metropolitan Opera Archives.

p. 65   Overscheduled first season: Bing, *5000 Nights at the Opera,* op. cit.

p. 67   Leontyne Price and opening of *Antony and Cleopatra:* Unpublished Bliss memoir, op. cit.

p. 69   George S. Moore on financial crisis: As reported by the Associated Press, November 12, 1966.

CHAPTER EIGHT: BING VS. BLISS REDUX

P. 71   Bing's reaction to Bliss idea about ballet evenings: Letter from Bing to Bliss, December 12, 1966; Metropolitan Opera Archives.

p. 72   Krawitz on Bliss/Brayley romance and further quotes from Krawitz in this chapter: From author's interview with Krawitz in November 1996.

p. 72   Sally Bliss on beginning of her romance with Bliss: Author's conversation with Sally Brayley Bliss, Summer 1995.

p. 72   Bing on Bliss's close relationship to Met Ballet: Letter from Bing to Bliss, December 23, 1966; Metropolitan Opera Archives.

p. 73   Bing asks board to accept his resignation and then sees Bliss resign: Bing gives an account of these events in his memoir, op. cit.

p. 74   Bliss votes against Bing's reappointment: Letter from Bliss to Bing, June 23, 1968; Metropolitan Opera Archives.

p. 74   Bing's reply to Bliss: Letter from Bing to Bliss, July 1, 1968; Metropolitan Opera Archives.

CHAPTER NINE: STAR POWER

p. 80   Bing tells Domingo he will make his Met debut: From Plácido Domingo's autobiography, *My First Forty Years*, p. 70.

CHAPTER TEN: THE BING ERA ENDS

p. 83   Nilsson's sense of humor: Bing memoir, op. cit.

p. 83   Bing's reaction to Karajan's lighting: ibid.

p. 83   Nilsson on Karajan's lighting: Nilsson quoted by Donal Henahan in *New York Times*.

p. 84   Met musicians' attitude toward 1969 strike: Author's interview with Sandor Balint, violinist in the Met Orchestra and orchestra committee chairman during several labor negotiations, January 1998.

p. 84   Bing's attitude toward orchestra musicians: Bing memoir, op. cit.

p. 85   Met seeks government support: Theodore Strongin in *New York Times*, December 11, 1970.

p. 87   Gentele's attitude toward role of an opera company: Gentele interviewed by Donal Henahan in *New York Times*, December 11, 1970.

p. 88   Volpe and Bing: Jane Boutwell, *New Yorker*, September 1971.

CHAPTER ELEVEN: THE YOUNG JIMMY

p. 90 Marriage of James Levine's parents: Author's interview with Levine, October 1998.

p. 91 Levine as a baby: Barbara Rowes, *People,* October 1983.

p. 91 Levine's father makes him practice: From "James Levine, New Baton at the Met," by Speight Jenkins, *Stereo Review,* May 1975.

p. 91 Levine's first trip to New York: Author's interview with Levine, November 1997.

p. 92 Levine as a young music student: *Dialogues and Discoveries: James Levine: His Life and His Music,* by Robert C. Marsh, p. 20.

p. 93 Levine's years in Cleveland: The author had many conversations with people who were in Cleveland at the same time as Levine: current members of the Met Orchestra and the Cleveland Orchestra, and former students at the Cleveland Institute. Some people agreed to interviews and then canceled. No one would repeat specific rumors except in vague terms, but several implied that the gossip had been unsavory. Levine has always inspired great discretion from his friends and associates.

p. 94 Levine on his desire for personal privacy: "Musician of the Month: James Levine," Robert C. Marsh, *Musical America,* March 1974.

p. 95 Levine's desire to stay in one situation professionally: Author's interview with Levine, December 1996.

CHAPTER TWELVE: TRAGEDY

p. 98 Gentele's tenure as general manager: The Met's fiscal year runs from July 1 to June 30. Thus Gentele only became general manager officially on July 1, 1972, since his contract began with the 1972–73 season.

p. 100 Krawitz's enduring bitterness: Author's interview with Krawitz, op. cit.

p. 101 Board's reluctance to appoint Chapin: *Musical Chairs,* a memoir by Schuyler Chapin, p. 328.

p. 102 Chapin engages mostly American artists: Allen Hughes in *New York Times,* September 6, 1973.

p. 103 Costs of canceling *Tristan:* The only time the Metropolitan Opera ever gives refunds for tickets purchased is when the opera is changed.

p. 104 Leinsdorf's irritation at the Met administration: Leinsdorf quoted by Donal Henahan in *New York Times,* January 8, 1974.

p. 104   Kubelik reason for resigning: Kubelik quoted by Donal Henahan in *New York Times*, February 13, 1974.

p. 104   Chapin's attitude toward William Rockefeller: *Musical Chairs*, op. cit., p. 15.

CHAPTER THIRTEEN: THE DARK TUNNEL

P. 106   Press conference on Bliss's return: Quotes from this press conference are from an article by Hubert Saal in *Newsweek*, December 2, 1974.

p. 106   Rockefeller defines the new chain of command: From unpublished Bliss memoir, op. cit.

p. 107   Levine offers to take over artistic control: From unpublished Bliss memoir, op. cit.

p. 108   Bliss and Chapin conversation about chain of command: From Bliss oral history about early years of Lincoln Center.

p. 108   John Dexter's philosophy of stage direction and design: *The Honourable Beast*, the diaries of John Dexter, p. 9.

p. 108   Bliss's enthusiasm for smaller productions: Bliss quoted by Bob Micklin in *Newsday*, March 9, 1975.

p. 109   Levine defines Met division of responsibilities: Levine quoted by Speight Jenkins in *New York Post*, May 22, 1975.

p. 109   Bliss's pessimism about Met's future: Micklin interview, op. cit.

p. 109   "Musical Chairs at the Met," Schuyler Chapin, *Saturday Review*, February 2, 1976.

CHAPTER FOURTEEN: JIMMY AND JOHN, AND JOE

p. 117   Bliss reassures Dexter and Levine: From unpublished Bliss memoir, op. cit.

p. 118   John Dexter's arrest and imprisonment: "The Birth of Shylock and the Death of Zero Mostel" by Arnold Wesker.

p. 119   Dexter enjoys his first years at the Met: Dexter quoted by John Higgins, *Times* (London), February 7, 1977.

p. 119   Dexter on self-examination: Dexter quoted by Harriett Johnson, *New York Post*, October 15, 1978.

p. 119   Dexter's lack of self-confidence: Dexter in his diaries, *The Honourable Beast*, op. cit.

p. 120   Levine's belief that he is essential to orchestra: Unpublished Bliss memoir, op. cit.

p. 120   The material on Joseph Volpe's early career and direct quotes from Volpe come from the following sources:

Several lengthy interviews with Volpe by the author between 1996 and 1999; "Met Appoints a General Manager," John Rockwell, *New York Times*, August 12, 1990; "Singing the Cancellation Blues, Again," John Rockwell, *New York Times*, August 16, 1990; "Behind the Gold Curtain," Walter Price, *Connoisseur Magazine*, December 1989; interview with Volpe by Mike Silverman, the AP, September 21, 1990; "Managing the Met," Allan Kozinn, *New York Times*, June 15, 1993; "The Volpe Method: Perfection at the Met or Else," Ralph Blumenthal, *New York Times*, October 31, 1995; "The Twilight of the God?," Fredric Dannen, *New Yorker*, October 3, 1994; "The Imperial Stagehand," David Remnick, *New Yorker*, February 22 and March 1, 1999; "The Met's Joseph Volpe," Patrick Smith, *Opera News*, September 1994; "The Right Way to Run an Opera House," Rupert Christiansen, *Daily Telegraph* (London), December 13, 1997.

p. 121   Volpe's unique understanding of the new Met: Author's interview with a former Met resident designer who wishes to remain anonymous.

p. 122   Dexter expresses his unhappiness with Met technical department: *The Honourable Beast*, op. cit., p. 126.

p. 123   Dexter and Levine talk about their shared aesthetic: Interview with Levine and Dexter by Robert Jacobson, *Metropolitan Opera Souvenir Book*, 1977–78 season.

p. 124   Dexter's concept for the new *Aïda: The Honourable Beast*, op. cit., p. 133.

p. 124   Dexter and Levine discuss new *Aïda:* Jacobson interview, op. cit.

CHAPTER FIFTEEN: SYBIL AND JOHN

p. 128   Sybil Harrington's attitude toward charitable contributions for the arts: Harrington quoted in her obituary by Anthony Tommasini, *New York Times*, September 19, 1998.

p. 129   Bliss suggests that Dexter may leave: Bliss quoted by Donal Henahan in *New York Times*, April 20, 1979.

p. 129   Bliss decision whether or not to replace Dexter: Ibid.

p. 129   Levine on the size of the Met: Levine quoted by Stephen Wadsworth, *Opera News*, October 1976.

p. 130   Kathleen Battle's early success: Nicholas Kenyon, *New Yorker*, April 29, 1980.

p. 131   Dexter designs a new educational program for the Met: *The Honourable Beast*, op. cit., p. 140; outline for program drafted by John Dexter, used by permission of the Metropolitan Opera Archives.

p. 131   Bliss's lack of faith in Michael Bronson: Bliss unpublished memoir, op. cit.

p. 131   Dexter's thoughts on his deteriorating relationship with Levine: *The Honourable Beast*, op. cit., p. 167.

p. 132   Dexter on Zeffirelli's extravagance: Ibid.

p. 132   Dexter's fury on decision to have Zeffirelli direct *Bohème:* Ibid., p. 167.

CHAPTER SIXTEEN: THE MET GETS ORGANIZED

P. 136   Material on Joan Ingpen's Met career taken from the author's interview with Ingpen, September 1996.

p. 138   Bliss expresses new confidence in the Met's financial status: Interview with Bliss by Robert McFadden, *New York Times*, December 13, 1977.

CHAPTER SEVENTEEN: THE SUMMER OF 1980: MONEY AND MURDER AT THE MET

p. 142   Taplin on drop in Met attendance: Taplin interviewed by Donal Henahan, *New York Times*, December 5, 1979.

p. 143   Information on Helen Hagnes's murder taken from newspaper coverage of the crime in 1980–81, and *Murder at the Met*, by David Black.

CHAPTER EIGHTEEN: THE LAST STRIKE AND THE PRICE OF PEACE

p. 150   Sally Bliss on her husband's unpretentiousness: From "Anthony Bliss: Culture and Commerce at the Met," Bernard Holland, *New York Times Magazine*, September 20, 1981.

p. 150   Musicians tell Met management to raise more money: Notes on negotiating meeting, August 12, 1980; Metropolitan Opera Archives.

p. 150   Musicians protest Met's arrogant attitude: Ibid.

p. 150   Labor problems as class issue: "Class Distinctions Add to Discord Complicating Met Labor Problem," William Serrin, *New York Times*, October 15, 1980.

p. 151   Levine declines to take sides in labor problems: Ibid.

p. 151   Levine depressed: John Rockwell in *New York Times*, December 16, 1980, and author's interview with Levine, April 2001.

p. 151   Bliss on opening night after strike: Bliss quoted by John Rockwell, *New York Times*, December 11, 1980.

p. 152   Philip Sipser warning about next labor negotiation: Sipser quoted by John Rockwell in *New York Times,* December 16, 1980.

p. 152   Bliss puts Volpe in charge of labor matters: Unpublished Bliss memoir, op. cit.

p. 152   Bliss lack of confidence in Bronson: Unpublished Bliss memoir, op. cit.

p. 153   Orchestra tells Bliss they trust Volpe: Ibid.

p. 153   Taplin on Bliss's depression after strike: Author's interview with Frank Taplin, February 1999.

p. 153   Board loses confidence in Bliss: Author's interview with negotiating committee member who wishes to be anonymous.

p. 155   Bergonzi hurt by Met's attitude: *Daily News,* March 5, 1981.

p. 155   Erich Leinsdorf criticizes the Met ambience: Leinsdorf quoted by Martin Mayer in *The Met,* op. cit.

p. 155   Bliss defends number of performances conducted by Levine: Letter from Bliss to Leinsdorf, May 20, 1976; Metropolitan Opera Archives.

p. 156   Leinsdorf praises Ingpen: Letter from Leinsdorf to Bliss, May 12, 1979; Metropolitan Opera Archives.

p. 156   Leinsdorf on cancellation of his *Ring* cycle: Letter from Leinsdorf to Ingpen, April 5, 1981; Metropolitan Opera Archives.

p. 158   Bliss tells Sutherland and Bonynge that the Met is reluctant to produce *The Merry Widow:* Letter from Bliss to Sutherland and Bonynge, July 1978; Metropolitan Opera Archives.

p. 158   Bliss informs Dexter and Levine about his *Merry Widow* decision: Memo from Bliss to Levine and Dexter, June 1978; Metropolitan Opera Archives.

p. 158   Bonynge and Sutherland express their disappointment: Letter from Sutherland and Bonynge to Bliss, July 1978; Metropolitan Opera Archives.

p. 159   Sutherland and bel canto opera: Maria Callas brought a dramatic intensity to these same roles that Sutherland could not match, but technically Sutherland sang them better. In the case of both singers, it was revelatory to hear these parts sung by sopranos with dramatic-sized voices; previously, they had been performed by singers with much lighter voices.

p. 159   Met's reluctance to stage operetta: Later, the company would successfully produce Strauss's *Die Fledermaus,* and, in 1999–2000, *The Merry Widow,* mounted for Frederica von Stade and Plácido Domingo.

p. 159   Bliss definitively cancels *Merry Widow:* Letter from Bliss to Sutherland and Bonynge, Fall 1978; Metropolitan Opera Archives.

p. 159   Sutherland defends her decision to pull out of some Met contracts: Letter from Sutherland to Bliss, October 25, 1978; Metropolitan Opera Archives.

p. 160   Bliss and Sutherland declare their mutual affection: Speight Jenkins, *New York Post,* January 22, 1979.

CHAPTER NINETEEN: THE DEFEAT OF JOHN DEXTER

p. 161   Dexter wants to give up administrative duties: *The Honourable Beast,* op. cit., p. 162.

p. 161   Press notices Dexter's absence from Met decision-making: John Rockwell, *New York Times,* July 1980.

p. 161   Dexter expresses feeling left out: *The Honourable Beast,* op. cit., p. 172.

p. 162   Dexter denies that he wants power: Ibid., p. 173.

p. 162   Bliss on Zeffirelli *Bohème:* Unpublished Bliss memoir, op. cit.

p. 163   Dexter feels Mrs. Harrington is now controlling productions at the Met: *The Honourable Beast,* op. cit., p. 182.

p. 163   Dexter expresses irritation at Levine: Ibid., p. 181.

p. 164   Dexter on Volpe's perceived disloyalty: Ibid., pp. 183, 185.

p. 164   Dexter on Levine's inability to make decisions: Ibid., p. 188.

p. 164   Dexter on Volpe's reluctance to hire him for revival of *Parade:* Ibid., p. 190.

p. 165   Volpe on his relationship with Dexter: Author's interview with Volpe, Winter 1999.

p. 166   Riggs O'Hara's bitterness toward the Met: Author's interview with O'Hara, September 1995.

CHAPTER TWENTY: THE HOUSE SOPRANO

p. 167   Scotto on Callas: Scotto interview by Stephen E. Rubin, *New York Times,* November 18, 1972.

p. 168   Levine on Scotto: Levine quoted by Stephen E. Rubin, op. cit.

p. 169   Francis Robinson on singers' weight: Robinson quoted by Mary Campbell, the AP, January 6, 1980.

p. 169   Marilyn Horne on role of eating in singers' lives: Horne quoted by Stephen E. Rubin, *New York Times Magazine,* February 12, 1978.

p. 170   Scotto in San Francisco: "The Opera Star They Love to Hate," Caroline Seebohm, *Saturday Review,* March 1982.

p. 171   Reviews of Scotto's *Norma:* Bill Zakariasen in *Daily News,* September 23, 1981, and Peter Goodman in *Newsday,* September 23, 1981.

p. 172   Scotto would go on to many professional triumphs: she became a venerated mentor and teacher, both privately and as part of the Met's Lindemann Young Artists' Program; she directed opera all over the world; and she continued to add new roles to her repertory, including Clytemnestra in Strauss's *Elektra* in the fall of 2000.

CHAPTER TWENTY-ONE: WHITHER THE MET?

p. 174   Failure of Peter Hall's *Macbeth:* Donal Henahan in *New York Times,* October 1982.

p. 177   Material on Carlo Bini's travails taken from newspaper articles about the debacle and the author's interviews with Met company members who were at the performance.

p. 181   Bliss reads performance report on Bini's *Gioconda:* A report on every performance is made by the stage manager and distributed to the appropriate administrators the following morning.

p. 182   Bini on his *Gioconda* experience: Bini quoted by John Rockwell, *New York Times,* October 20, 1982.

CHAPTER TWENTY-TWO: JAMES LEVINE IN ASCENDANCE

p. 183   Levine on performing contemporary opera: Levine quoted by John Rockwell, *New York Times,* September 19, 1981.

p. 183   Ingpen complains about conservative Met audience: Author's interview with Ingpen, September 1996.

p. 184   Levine hints that Bliss should retire: Author's interview with board member who wishes to remain anonymous.

p. 184   Bernstein on Levine's *Parsifal:* "Maestro of the Met," *Time* cover story, January 1983.

p. 185   Levine on why he conducts at Bayreuth: Ibid.

p. 185   Ingpen on inviting renowned conductors to the Met: Author's interview with Ingpen, September 1996.

p. 186   Levine on who conducts at the Met: "How the Plots Thickened at the Metropolitan Opera," Richard Dyer, *Boston Globe,* April 6, 1980.

p. 186   Levine on why music directors should stay with their orchestras as much as possible: Ibid.

p. 187   Met musician on Levine's rehearsal technique: Author's interview with a principal player in Met Orchestra, February 1999.

p. 188   Bliss tries to set limits on artistic costs: Ezio Frigerio is an Italian set designer known for his lavish and expensive productions.

p. 189   Bliss complains about television repertory for following seasons: Bliss memo to Levine, Ingpen, Dexter, and Volpe, September 30, 1981; Metropolitan Opera Archives.

p. 189   Bliss warns Levine about expenses: Letter from Bliss to Levine, July 9, 1982; Metropolitan Opera Archives.

p. 191   Rockefeller discusses search for new general manager: "Levine Said to Seek Artistic Control of the Met," by Harold C. Schonberg, *New York Times*, June 15, 1983.

p. 191   Levine named artistic director: John Rockwell in *New York Times*, September 16, 1983.

p. 192   Taplin on board's relationship with artistic director: Ibid.

CHAPTER TWENTY-THREE: THE MET'S ONE HUNDREDTH BIRTHDAY
AND THE YEARS OF TRANSITION

p. 194   Bliss announces cost-cutting: "Met Opera Deficit May Be $4 Million," John Rockwell, *New York Times*, March 3, 1984.

p. 195   Everding turns down position of general manager: "Everding Rules Out Met Opera Manager Job," Harold C. Schonberg, *New York Times*, June 9, 1984.

p. 195   Ingpen decides to retire: Author's interview with Ingpen, September 1996.

p. 196   Ingpen on her successor: Ibid.

p. 197   Levine on Crawford's appointment as general manager: *New York Times*, October 5, 1984, unsigned article.

p. 198   Bliss's private reaction to Crawford: Author's interview with a member of Bliss's family.

p. 198   Crawford on his early opera experience: "Hands-On Manager," Robert Jacobson, *Opera News*, September 1985.

p. 198   Leonie Rysanek on Crawford: Author's interview with Rysanek, January 1996.

p. 200   Levine on *Porgy and Bess:* Levine quoted by Samuel G. Freedman, *New York Times*, February 3, 1985.

p. 201   Personal information on Behrens from article by John Rockwell in *New York Times*, December 10, 1983.

p. 201 Behrens on her intensity: Behrens quoted by Michael Walsh in *Time*, December 19, 1983.

p. 202 Critics disapprove of lavish Zeffirelli *Tosca:* Peter G. Davis in *New York*, October 7, 1985.

p. 203 Bliss thanks Harrington for her support: Kathy Larkin, *Daily News*, February 27, 1985.

p. 204 Crawford cancels Met tour: Crawford quoted by Nancy Malitz in *Detroit News*, May 9, 1985.

CHAPTER TWENTY-FOUR: BRUCE CRAWFORD TAKES COMMAND

p. 207 Chapin on return of elegance to the Met: Chapin quoted by Carol Lawson in *New York Times*, September 24, 1985.

p. 207 Crawford on Chanel sponsorship of opening night: Ibid.

p. 207 Cecile Zilkha on her fund-raising efforts: Author's interview with Zilkha, February 1999.

p. 209 Louise Humphrey on her executive style: Humphrey quoted by *Cleveland Magazine*, May 1986.

p. 210 Crawford's attitude toward Met's problems: Crawford quoted by Robert Jacobson in *Opera News*, September 1985.

CHAPTER TWENTY-FIVE: DIVAS IN DISTRESS

p. 211 Trio of Mozart operas directed for Met by Jean-Pierre Ponnelle: The first two operas in the trio, *Idomeneo* and *La Clemenza di Tito*, had been given in previous seasons.

p. 216 Liz Smith on opening night of *Carmen:* Liz Smith, *Daily News*, March 16, 1986.

p. 217 Levine on difficulty in Met casting: Levine quoted by Will Crutchfield, *New York Times*, April 15, 1987.

CHAPTER TWENTY-SIX: JAMES LEVINE, ARTISTIC DIRECTOR

p. 219 Controversy on Levine conducting at Bayreuth: Anthony Lewis, op-ed page, *New York Times*, June 12, 1986.

p. 223 Marton on her injury during *Tosca:* Harold C. Schonberg, *New York Times*, October 1986.

p. 224 Marton's decision to finish *Tosca:* Interview with Garcia Navarro, WQXR-FM, October 1986.

p. 225 Marton's husband protests the cancellation of her Brünnhilde contract: Will Crutchfield, *New York Times*, August 1989.

CHAPTER TWENTY-SEVEN: THE IMPERIAL MET

p. 230 Photograph on last night of *Turandot:* Marton quoted by John Rockwell in *New York Times*, April 11, 1987.

p. 230 Levine on frustrations of his position: Quoted by Peter G. Davis in *New York*, April 29, 1987.

p. 232 Levine on the importance to him of the Mini-Met: Ibid.

p. 233 Rumors about Levine: The author interviewed several board members on this subject. All denied that the payoff ever happened. One former director, who had been depicted as the one most likely to talk about the matter, expressed extreme anti-Levine sentiments, based mostly on the amount of power he had amassed. In this man's opinion, the directors had conceded too much to Levine, and this was why he had resigned from the board. But he, too, denied that there had ever been a payoff.

p. 234 Article on changes in Met balance of power by John Rockwell, *New York Times*, July 23, 1987.

p. 234 Levine talks about the rumors: Ibid.

p. 235 Crawford talks on more artistic responsibility: Ibid.

CHAPTER TWENTY-EIGHT: THE PHANTOM OF THE OPERA

p. 238 The information on Rudolf Bing's romance and marriage to Carroll Douglass comes from the following newspaper articles: Harry Haun's column, *Daily News*, January 8, 1987; "Judge Bars Bride from 'Senile' Opera Czar's Fortune," *New York Post*, February 5, 1987; "Met's Bing Ailing," *Daily News*, February 5, 1987; " 'Senile' Bing and Bride Vanish in Virginia," *New York Post*, February 6, 1987; "Bride of Bing Sought Will," *Daily News*, February 6, 1987; "A Mere Phantom of the Opera Boss," *Daily News*, un-dated article by Tony Burton; "Bing and Bride Found in Secret Island Love Nest," *New York Post*, February 10, 1987; "Rudy and Carroll Sing Out," *Daily News*, February 11, 1987; "Runaways Bing, Wife Go Public," *New York Post*, February 11, 1987; "Won't Go to New York . . . Lady B.," *Daily News*, February 12, 1987.

"Attorney Ponders Action," *Daily News*, February 12, 1987; "Rings False," *Daily News*, February 13, 1987; "She's a Liar: Rickenbacker," *Daily News*, February 13, 1987; "In Rudolf Bing Affair, a New Turn," *New York Times*, February 14, 1987; "Bing's Mrs. Had Crush on Pontiff: Kin," *New York Post*, February 14, 1987; "The Sad Truth," *Daily News*, February 15, 1987; "About Lady Bing," *New York Post*, February 15, 1987; "Lady Bing:

Love Foe Battling for Rudy," *New York Post*, February 17, 1987; "Brother Defends Lady B.," *Daily News*, February 17, 1987; "At Home with the Bings," *New York Post*, February 18, 1987.

"Lost Together in Paradise," *Time*, February 21, 1987; "How Lady Bing Landed Sir Rudolf," *New York Post*, March 11, 1987; "A Court Plea by Lady Bing," *Daily News*, March 13, 1987; "Sir Rudolf Bing Reportedly in England," *New York Times*, April 28, 1987; "Bings Ignore Date in Court; Judge Is Irate," *Daily News*, June 4, 1987; "Court Raps Bing's Wife," *Daily News*, June 14, 1987; "Rudolf Bing, Titan of the Met, Dies at 95," *New York Times*, September 3, 1997; "Met Legend Bing Dies at 95," *Daily News*, September 3, 1997; "Opera Chief Rudolf Bing is Dead at 95," *New York Post*, September 3, 1997; "Lady Bing—Forever," *Daily News*, September 7, 1997.

p. 239 Bing's honeymoon: *New York Post*, February 14, 1987.

CHAPTER TWENTY-NINE: THE THREE TENORS

p. 244 Pavarotti complains about Domingo: Interview with Pavarotti by Susan Margolis, *Playboy*, November 1981.

p. 244 Domingo complains about Pavarotti: Quoted by Harriett Johnson, *New York Post*, October 8, 1982.

p. 245 Domingo's Wagner roles: Domingo has said he will never sing Tristan onstage; he has, however, recorded the role.

p. 247 Carreras taken ill during *Bohème* filming: *New York Times*, August 8, 1987.

p. 248 Carreras returns to singing: Quoted by Tim Page, *Washington Post*, October 29, 1995.

CHAPTER THIRTY: MORE CHANGE

p. 252 Crawford on time to leave a job: Quoted by Martin Mayer in "From BBDO to Bel Canto," *Across the Board*, Winter 1986.

p. 253 Bliss on Crawford's style: Ibid.

p. 253 Crawford on his job as general manager: Ibid.

p. 257 Levine on next music director of Berlin Philharmonic: Quoted by John Rockwell, *New York Times*, April 26, 1989.

p. 258 Levine never sought Berlin position: "Staying Power: An Interview with James Levine," Martin Kettle, *Guardian*, November 17, 2000.

p. 258   Volpe on Louise Humphrey's father: Author's interview with Volpe, February 20, 1999.

p. 258   Volpe on board's selection of Hugh Southern instead of himself: Ibid.

p. 260   Southern fired: "Met Officials Say Southern Was Dismissed," John Rockwell, *New York Times,* June 17, 1990.

CHAPTER THIRTY-ONE: JOSEPH VOLPE TAKES OVER

p. 264   Opinion about Joseph Clark's way of working: Most of the resident designers interviewed by the author would not speak for attribution.

p. 264   Volpe on difficulties with productions of Italian operas: Author's interview with Volpe, February 1999.

p. 265   Volpe on Crawford as board president: Ibid.

p. 265   Volpe on his attitude toward the staff: Ibid.

p. 265   Material on Anthony Bliss's final days taken from author's interviews with his daughter, Barbara Bliss, 1996–98, and with Sally Brayley Bliss in 2001.

p. 266   Metropolitan Opera press release announcing Volpe's new title in 1993.

CHAPTER THIRTY-TWO: JAMES LEVINE IN HIS MIDDLE YEARS

p. 270   Levine's friendliness: Author's interview with Richard Dyer, 1998.

p. 271   Levine on aging process: Author's interview with Levine, October 1998.

p. 271   Levine on marginalizing of culture in today's world: Ibid.

p. 272   Bartoli on Levine: Author's interview with Bartoli, October 1997.

p. 272   Leonie Rysanek on working with Levine: Author's interview with Rysanek, January 1996.

p. 272   Plácido Domingo on working with Levine: Fax message to author from Plácido Domingo, December 1997.

p. 272   Levine on his positive attitude: Author's interview with Levine, October 11, 1997.

p. 273   Jonathan Miller on atmosphere at the Met: Author's interview with Miller, October 1999.

p. 273   Levine on maintaining personal privacy: Author's interview with Levine, October 1997.

p. 273   Levine on rumors: Ibid.

p. 274   Rysanek on Levine: Author's interview with Rysanek, op. cit.

CHAPTER THIRTY-THREE: BACKSTAGE WITH PLÁCIDO DOMINGO

p. 276   Domingo on difficulties of new roles: Quoted by Peter Goodman, *Newsday,* October 16, 1983.

p. 277   Domingo on attention he receives from women: Quoted by Susan Chenery in *Daily Telegraph* (London), April 18, 1998.

p. 278   Domingo on difficulties in his marriage: "I Am Hurt for My Family," an interview with Domingo by Jan Moir, *Daily Telegraph* (London), October 16, 2000.

CHAPTER THIRTY-FOUR: IS IT A POWER STRUGGLE?

p. 283   The material on Kathleen Battle's dismissal is culled from several sources as well as the author's interviews with those involved: "Nights at the Opera: Twilight of the God?," Fredric Dannen, *New Yorker,* October 3, 1994; *When the Music Stops: Managers, Maestros and the Corporate Murder of Classical Music,* Norman Lebrecht, London: Simon & Schuster, 1996; "Battle Royale," Annalyn Swan, *Vanity Fair,* May 1994; "Met Men Screech Over Kathleen Battle; The Diva Sings 'Myself I Shall Adore,' " Phoebe Hoban, *New York Observer,* March 20, 1994; interviews with Bruce Donnell, Richard Dyer, Raymond Hughes, Joan Ingpen, James Levine, Sissy Strauss, Joseph Volpe, Larry Woodard.

CHAPTER THIRTY-FIVE: THE LONG CAREER OF LUCIANO PAVAROTTI

p. 290   Pavarotti on one of his vocal crises: Quoted by Will Crutchfield, *New York Times,* September 24, 1985.

p. 292   Adua Pavarotti on her husband's flirtations: *My World,* a memoir by Luciano Pavarotti, New York: Crown Publishers, 1995, p. 237.

p. 292   Pavarotti on his romance with Nicoletta Mantovani: Quoted by *Times* (London), February 28, 1996.

p. 292   Adua Pavarotti on her husband's affair: *Daily Telegraph* (London), February 28, 1996.

p. 293   Mantovani on the beginning of her relationship with Pavarotti: Interview with Mantovani by Elizabeth Grice, *Daily Telegraph* (London), June 13, 1998.

p. 294   Pavarotti on *La Fille du Régiment* debacle: Interview with Ralph Blumenthal, *New York Times,* October 21, 1997.

p. 294   Pavarotti's poor performance at Foxwoods: "Gambling on a Career? Say It Ain't So, Luciano," Katrine Ames, *Newsweek,* March 23, 1996.

CHAPTER THIRTY-SIX: THE NEW STARS

p. 298   Angela Gheorghiu on her fight with Solti: Interview by Alexander Chancellor in the *Daily Telegraph* (London), April 11, 1998.

p. 299   Volpe on his dispute with the Alagnas: Interview with Volpe in *New York Times*, April 4, 1998.

p. 300   José Cura on Alagna: Interview with Cura by Joanna Pittman, *Times* (London), October 12, 1999.

p. 300   Cura on the price of fame: Ibid.

p. 302   Jonathan Miller praises Bartoli: "The Anti-Diva," Alexander Chancellor, *Daily Telegraph* (London), October 6, 1998.

p. 303   Volpe on Bartoli cancellation: Interview by Allan Kozinn, *New York Times*, March 18, 1997.

p. 303   Levine defends Bartoli: Author's interview with Levine, October 11, 1997.

p. 304   Jonathan Miller expresses disillusionment with Met: Author's interview with Miller, October 1999.

p. 304   Volpe dismisses Miller's opinion: "The Imperial Stagehand," by David Remnick in the *New Yorker*, February 22 and March 1, 1999.

CHAPTER THIRTY-SEVEN: THE CURSE OF *CARMEN*

The material on Franco Zeffirelli's 1996 production of *Carmen* is taken from the following sources: "Singers, Supers and Bales of Silk," Justin Davidson, *Newsday*, October 27, 1996; "Tensions On, Offstage at *Carmen*," Justin Davidson, *Newsday*, November 26, 1996; "*Carmen* Director Fires Back," Justin Davidson, *Newsday*, November 28, 1996; and author's interviews with Met staff members who wished to remain anonymous.

CHAPTER THIRTY-EIGHT: THE PRINCIPAL GUEST CONDUCTOR

p. 317   Levine on Gergiev's appointment: Author's interview with Levine, October 1997.

p. 318   Gergiev conducts concert with Met Orchestra: Sir Georg Solti was scheduled to conduct a concert with the Met Orchestra in the spring of 1998, but died before he could fulfill the engagement.

p. 319   Gergiev holds appointments in his car: Author's interview with Peter J. Hall, August 1999. Mr. Hall, who was the Met's resident costume designer, has designed costumes for all the major opera companies, including the Kirov.

p. 319   Söderström's problems with Gergiev: Author's interview with Söderström, August 1999.

p. 320   Volpe on Gergiev: Author's interview with Volpe, August 1999.

p. 321   Gergiev's conducting ability: Author's interview with Richard Dyer, August 1999.

p. 321   Peter Davis on Gergiev's glamour and charisma: Articles in *New York*, January 23, 1995, and February 8, 1999.

p. 322   Gergiev's lack of interest in Met position: Author's interview with Norman Lebrecht, August 1999.

p. 322   Volpe on Gergiev's future at the Met: Author's interview with Volpe, August 1999.

CHAPTER THIRTY-NINE: THE EVOLUTION OF JAMES LEVINE

p. 324   Domingo on money he earns on Three Tenors concerts and recordings: Quoted by Tim Page, *Washington Post*, October 29, 1995.

p. 324   Levine on his entry into a more commercial kind of music-making: Author's interview with Levine, October 11, 1997.

p. 325   Peter Gelb on Levine's sense about populist projects: Gelb quoted in "Decline and Fall of the Classical Empire," Michael Church, *Independent* (London), December 15, 1999.

p. 325   Levine on his sense of responsibility for his actions: Author's interview with Levine, October 11, 1997.

p. 326   Levine on the Verbier Festival: Quoted by Rob Cowan, *Independent* (London), August 4, 2000, and interview with the author, April 2001.

p. 327   Crawford and Volpe on the demise of the Mini-Met idea: Author's interviews with Crawford and Volpe.

p. 329   Levine's appointment to Munich Philharmonic: Discussion taken from author's interview with Levine, January 19, 1998.

CHAPTER FORTY: THE MET AT THE MILLENNIUM

p. 330   Growing interest in Met's repertory expansion: Author's conversation with David Patrick Stearns, former theater critic for *USA Today* and current classical music critic for the *Philadelphia Inquirer.*

p. 330   Volpe is responsible for bringing in new directors and designers: Author's interview with Elijah Moshinsky, August 1999.

p. 333   Volpe's diagnosis was specified in "The Volpe Method: Perfection at the Met, or Else," Ralph Blumenthal, *New York Times*, October 31, 1995.

p. 335   Quotes by Alberto W. Vilar from author's interview with Vilar, May 4, 2000.

p. 336   Vilar quoted in "So You Can Buy Love After All: An Interview with Alberto Vilar," Allan Kozinn, *New York Times*, October 8, 2000.

p. 336   Vilar's goal to bring U.S.-style arts patronage to rest of world: "La Scala Meets $2 Million Man," Jennifer Clark, Reuters, July 23, 2000.

p. 336   Vilar's attempt to control choice of new general manager at San Francisco Opera: Allan Kozinn, *New York Times*, October 8, 2000.

p. 336   Vilar's presence in Salzburg: "Dazzled by Salzburg's Bill," Rodney Milnes, *Times* (London), August 9, 2000.

p. 337   Vilar on necessity for Met to think in a more businesslike way: Author's interview with Vilar, op. cit.

p. 337   Vilar on Met's lack of recognition: "The Imperial Stagehand," David Remnick, *New Yorker*, February 22 and March 1, 1999.

p. 337   Vilar on Met's lack of recognition: Author's interview with Vilar, op. cit.

p. 337   Volpe jokes about Vilar's demands: Author's interview with Volpe, August 1999.

p. 338   Crawford drops out of fund-raising: Author's conversation with Crawford.

p. 338   Volpe on new blood on board: Author's interview with Volpe, February 1999.

p. 338   Quotes from Paul Montrone: Author's interview with Montrone, December 17, 2000.

p. 340   Levine's symphonic future?: Author's interview with Levine, April 2001.

p. 341   Levine's desire to stay at Met: "Staying Power: An Interview with James Levine," Martin Kettle, *Guardian*, November 17, 2000.

p. 343   The Met also celebrated the Millennium with a gala concert in the spring of 2000 that featured the Three Tenors performing together for the first time at the Met. But this was not a repeat of their stadium concerts. Each sang separately in an operatic scene. James Levine conducted.

BIBLIOGRAPHY

Books

Alda, Frances. *Men, Women and Tenors*. Boston: Houghton Mifflin, 1937.

Bing, Sir Rudolf. *5000 Nights at the Opera*. Garden City, New York: Doubleday, 1972.

————. *A Knight at the Opera*. New York: G. P. Putnam's Sons, 1981.

Black, David. *Murder at the Met*. New York: Dial Press, Doubleday, 1984.

Bliss, Anthony A. Unpublished memoir, by permission of Sally Brayley Bliss.

Chapin, Schuyler. *Musical Chairs: A Life in the Arts*. New York: G. P. Putnam's Sons, 1977.

Christiansen, Rupert. *Prima Donna: A History*. London: Pimlico, Random House, 1995.

Conrad, Peter. *Romantic Opera and Literary Form*. Berkeley: University of California Books, 1977.

————. *A Song of Love and Death: The Meaning of Opera*. New York: Poseidon Press, 1987.

Davis, Peter G. *The American Opera Singer*. New York: Doubleday, 1997.

Dexter, John. *The Honourable Beast: A Posthumous Autobiography*. New York: Theater Arts Books, Routledge, 1993.

Dizikes, John. *Opera in America: A Cultural History*. New Haven and London: Yale University Press, 1993.

Domingo, Plácido. *My First Forty Years*. New York: Alfred A. Knopf, 1983.

Epstein, Helen. *Music Talks: Conversations with Musicians*. New York: Penguin Books, 1987.

Farrar, Geraldine. *Such Sweet Compulsion*. New York: Greystone Press, 1938.

Harries, Meirion, and Susie Harries. *Opera Today*. New York: St. Martin's Press, 1986.

Harewood, Earl of. *The Definite Kobbé's Opera Book*. New York: G. P. Putnam's Sons, 1987.

Hiley, Jim. *Theater at Work: The Story of the National Theatre's Production of Brecht's "Galileo."* London, Boston, and Henley: Routledge & Kegan Paul, 1981.

Hoelterhoff, Manuela. *Cinderella & Company: Backstage at the Opera*. New York: Alfred A. Knopf, 1998.

Horowitz, Joseph. *Understanding Toscanini*. New York: Alfred A. Knopf, 1987.

Kolodin, Irving. *The Metropolitan Opera 1883–1966: A Candid History*. New York: Alfred A. Knopf, 1968.

————. *The Opera Omnibus*. New York: E. F. Dutton, 1976.

Lebrecht, Norman. *The Maestro Myth: Great Conductors in Pursuit of Power*. Secaucus, New Jersey: Birch Lane Press Book, Carol Publishing Group, 1991.

————. *When the Music Stops: Managers, Maestros and the Corporate Murder of Classical Music*. London: Simon & Schuster, 1996.

————. *Covent Garden: The Untold Story*. London: Simon & Schuster, 2000.

Leinsdorf, Erich. *Cadenza: A Musical Career*. Boston: Houghton Mifflin, 1976.

Lewis, Marcia. *The Private Lives of the Three Tenors: Behind the Scenes with Plácido Domingo, Luciano Pavarotti, and José Carreras*. Secaucus, New Jersey: Birch Lane Press, 1996.

Lipman, Samuel. *The House of Music: Art in an Era of Institutions*. Boston: David R. Godine, 1984.

Mahler, Alma. *Gustav Mahler: Memories and Letters*. Edited by Donald Mitchell. New York: Viking Press, 1946.

Marsh, Robert C. *Dialogues and Discoveries: James Levine: His Life and His Music.* New York: Lisa Drew, Scribner, 1998.

Martner, Knud, ed. *Gustav Mahler: Selected Letters.* New York: Farrar, Straus, Giroux, 1976.

Matheopoulos, Helena. *Maestro: Encounters with Conductors of Today.* New York: Harper & Row, 1982.

Matz, Mary Jane. *The Many Lives of Otto Kahn.* New York: Macmillan, 1965.

Mayer, Martin. *The Met: One Hundred Years of Grand Opera.* New York: Simon & Schuster, Metropolitan Opera Guild, 1983.

Monson, Karen. *Alma Mahler: Muse to Genius.* Boston: Houghton Mifflin, 1983.

Pavarotti, Luciano, with William Weaver. *My World.* New York: Crown Publishers, 1995.

Peltz, Mary Ellen. *Behind the Gold Curtain: The Story of the Metropolitan Opera 1883–1950.* New York: Farrar, Straus & Company, 1950.

Porter, Andrew. *Music of Three Seasons: 1974–1977.* New York: Farrar, Straus, Giroux, 1978.

———. *Musical Events: A Chronicle: 1983–86.* New York: Summit Books, 1989.

Robinson, Francis. *Celebration: The Metropolitan Opera.* New York: Doubleday, Metropolitan Opera Association, Metropolitan Opera Guild, 1983.

Rubin, Stephen E. *The New Met in Profile.* New York: Macmillan, 1974.

Sachs, Harvey. *Toscanini.* Philadelphia and New York: J. B. Lippincott, 1978.

———. *Reflections on Toscanini.* Rocklin, California: Prima Publishing, 1993.

Schuller, Gunther. *The Compleat Conductor.* New York and Oxford: Oxford University Press, 1997.

Shanet, Howard. *Philharmonic: History of New York's Orchestra.* New York: Doubleday, 1975.

Smith, Patrick. *A Year at the Met.* New York: Alfred A. Knopf, 1983.

Spotts, Frederic. *Bayreuth: A History of the Wagner Festival.* New York and New Haven: Yale University Press, 1994.

Tuggle, Robert. *The Golden Age of Opera.* New York: Holt, Rinehart and Winston, 1983.

Waleson, Heidi. *The Metropolitan Opera Guide Book.* New York: Metropolitan Opera Guild, 1988.

Wesker, Arnold. *The Birth of Shylock and the Death of Zero Mostel: Diary of a Play 1973–1980.* Quartet Books, 1997.

Wharton, Edith. *The Age of Innocence.* New York: D. Appleton and Company, 1920; reprinted by Charles Scribner's Sons, 1968.

Major Articles

Ames, Katrine. "Gambling on a Career? Say It Ain't So, Luciano." *Newsweek,* March 23, 1996.

Blumenthal, Ralph. "Gray Eminence of Classical Music's Stars." *New York Times,* May 23, 1995.

———. "The Volpe Method: Perfection at the Met, or Else." *New York Times,* October 31, 1995.

———. "A High-Voltage Dynamo Named Domingo." *New York Times,* November 7, 1996.

———. "40 Years and No Swan Song, Vows Pavarotti." *New York Times,* October 21, 1997.

———. "Maestro Manager's New Title Sets the Music World Humming." *New York Times,* January 3, 2001.

———. "Met Rejects Plan for Renovation of Lincoln Center." *New York Times,* January 24, 2001.

———. "Boston Is Said to Broach Conductor's Job to Levine." *New York Times,* February 3, 2001.

Blumenthal, Ralph, and Robin Pogrebin. "Lincoln Center Renovation Plan Has Opera Houses at Odds." *New York Times,* January 25, 2001.

Chancellor, Alexander. "The Anti-Diva." *Daily Telegraph* (London), October 6, 1998.

Chapin, Schuyler. "Musical Chairs at the Met." *Saturday Review,* February 7, 1976.

Chenery Susan. "Charm Alert." *Daily Telegraph* (London), April 18, 1998.

Christiansen, Rupert. "Don't Mess with the Met Man." *Observer* (London), January 11, 1997.

———. "The Right Way to Run an Opera House." *Daily Telegraph* (London), December 13, 1997.

Church, Michael. "Decline and Fall of the Classical Empire." *Independent* (London), December 15, 1999.

Clark, Andrew. "Playing It Safe with Jimmy at the Met." *Financial Times* (London), March 20, 1995.

Clark, Jennifer. "La Scala Meets $2 Million Man." Reuters, July 23, 2000.

Cohen, Laurie P. "That Delicate Voice: A Singer's Nemesis." *Saturday Review,* March 1982.

Crutchfield, Will. "James Levine: A New Era at the Met." *New York Times Magazine,* September 22, 1985.

———. "Pavarotti Reflects on 'The Voice.'" *New York Times,* September 24, 1985.

———. "The Metropolitan Opera Orchestra." *New York Times,* November 11, 1990.

Dannen, Fredric. "Nights at the Opera: Twilight of the God?" *New Yorker,* October 3, 1994.

Davidson, Justin. "James Levine's Silver Season." *Newsday,* April 21, 1996.

———. "Jimmy Levine, King of the Met." *Newsday,* April 21, 1996.

———. "Singers, Supers and Bales of Silk." *Newsday,* October 27, 1996.

———. "Tensions On, Offstage at *Carmen.*" *Newsday,* November 26, 1996.

———. "*Carmen* Director Fires Back." *Newsday,* November 28, 1996.

Davis, Peter G. "Jimmy's Met." *New York,* April 29, 1987.

———. "Days of Levine and Roses." *New York,* May 13, 1996.

Denby, David. "James Levine Is Recasting the Met for the 80s." *New York,* September 28, 1981.

Dyer, Richard. "How the Plots Thickened at the Metropolitan Opera." *Boston Globe,* April 6, 1980.

———. "Controversy Swirls Around Met's Levine." *Boston Globe,* July 7, 1980.

———. "Levine of the Met: Optimistic *and* Demanding." *Boston Globe,* June 26, 1983.

———. Interview with James Levine. *Boston Globe,* February 24, 1992.

———. "James Levine Makes a Rare BSO Appearance." *Boston Globe,* November 11, 1994.

———. "James Levine Comes to Town This Week—And Then What?" *Boston Globe,* January 28, 2001.

———. "Levine Conducts Himself Accordingly." *Boston Globe,* February 7, 2001.

Gould, Gordon. "James Levine: Honoring Ravinia's Half-Century." *Chicago Magazine,* July 1985.

Harris, Dale. "The Met, Then and Now." *Ovation,* September 1983.

Henahan, Donal. Interview with Goeran Gentele. *New York Times,* December 11, 1970.

———. "Hard Road for Native Conductors." *New York Times,* April 26, 1987.

Higgins, John. Interview with John Dexter. *Times* (London), February 1977.

Hoelterhoff, Manuela. "What's Wrong with the Metropolitan Opera." *Wall Street Journal,* May 23, 1985.

Holland, Bernard. "Anthony Bliss: Culture and Commerce at the Met." *New York Times Magazine,* September 20, 1981.

———. "James Levine's Upbeat Libretto for the Met." *New York Times,* January 17, 1982.

———. "The Well-Tempered Tenor." *New York Times Magazine,* January 30, 1983.

Innaurato, Albert. "Mighty Joe Opera." *Forbes,* June 15, 1998.

Jacobson, Robert. "Hands-on Manager." *Opera News,* September 1985.

Jenkins, Speight. "James Levine, New Baton at the Met." *Stereo Review,* May 1975.

———. "James Levine: Catalyst of the Revitalized Met." *Ovation,* April 1980.

Kettle, Martin. "Staying Power: An Interview with James Levine." *Guardian,* November 17, 2000.

Kozinn, Allan. "Managing the Met." *New York Times,* June 15, 1993.

———. "A Busy Man of Opera Gets Even Busier." *New York Times,* November 9, 1998.

———. "So You Can Buy Love After All: An Interview with Alberto Vilar." *New York Times,* October 8, 2000.

Kupferberg, Herbert. "Simply Levine." *American Way,* May 1984.

Lebrecht, Norman. "Opera Lessons from Abroad." *Daily Telegraph* (London), June 27, 1998.

———. "Could Silver Fox, the Manager of Maestros, Be Losing His Grip?" *Daily Telegraph* (London), January 24, 2001.

Levine, James. "The Conductor at the Opera." *BBC Music Magazine,* November 1996.

Malitz, Nancy. "He Can't Let Go of Mozart. Or the Met." *New York Times,* April 21, 1996.

Marsh, Robert C. "Musician of the Month: James Levine." *Musical America,* March 1974.

Mayer, Martin. "From BBDO to Bel Canto." *Across the Board Magazine,* Winter 1986.

———. "Managing the Met." Unpublished, April 1989. Used by permission of the author.

McFadden, Robert. Interview with Anthony Bliss. *New York Times,* December 13, 1977.

Meyers, William. "Bruce Crawford Changes His Tune." *M Magazine,* February 1985.

Micklin, Robert. Interview with James Levine. *Newsday,* February 25, 1974.

Moss, Stephen. "House Proud." *Guardian,* February 18, 2000.

Page, Tim. "Metropolitan Opera Picks New Director." *Newsday,* August 2, 1990.

Price, Walter. "Behind the Gold Curtain." *Connoisseur Magazine,* December 1989.

Rauch, Rudolph S. "Three-Cornered Hat." *Opera News,* July 27, 1999.

Remnick, David. "The Imperial Stagehand." *New Yorker,* February 22 and March 1, 1999.

Rich, Alan. "How Stars Are Made, or the Business of Music Management." *Newsweek,* February 24, 1986.

Rockwell, John. Analysis of Met's labor problems. *New York Times,* December 16, 1980.

———. "Repertory Is the Key to the 'New' Met." *New York Times,* September 19, 1982.

———. "Bliss Looks Back on Years at the Met." *New York Times,* July 29, 1985.

———. "Met Opera Changes Managerial Balance." *New York Times,* July 25, 1987.

———. "Music World Has Room at the Top, But Who'll Fill It?" *New York Times,* March 13, 1989.

———. "Met Appoints a General Director." *New York Times,* August 2, 1990.

Rothstein, Mervyn. "Master of the Met." *Cigar Aficionado Magazine,* November 1998.

Schauer, John. Interview with James Levine. *Advocate,* October 18, 1978.

Schonberg, Harold C. "Levine Said to Seek Artistic Control of the Met." *New York Times,* June 15, 1983.

Seebohm, Caroline. "The Opera Star They Love to Hate." *Saturday Review,* March 1982.

Smith, Patrick J. "The Met Today and Tomorrow: An Interview with General Manager Joseph Volpe." *Opera News,* September 1994.

———. "This Side of Heaven." *Opera News,* September 1994.

———. "Silver Salute: James Levine Celebrates 25 Years at the Met." *Opera News,* September 1997.

Swan, Annalyn. "Levine Lights Up the Met." *Newsweek,* October 11, 1982.

———. "Battle Royale." *Vanity Fair,* May 1994.

Tommasini, Anthony. "A Tenor Who Knows No Bounds." *New York Times,* September 27, 1998.

Wadsworth, Stephen. "Brave New World? James Levine Projects a Fresh Concept for the Metropolitan Opera." *Opera News*, October 1976.

Walsh, Michael. "Making Opera Grand: James Levine, America's Top Maestro." *Time*, January 17, 1982.

———. "Snake and the Fat Man." *New York*, November 13, 1995.

White, Lesley. "Love Is in the Aria." *Sunday Times* (London), September 26, 1999.

PHOTO CREDITS

Insert 1

PAGE 1
(top) Culver Pictures

(top insert) The Metropolitan Opera Archives

(center left) © Bettmann/Corbis

(bottom right) The Metropolitan Opera Archives

PAGE 2
(top) The Metropolitan Opera Archives

(center) The New York Public Library for the Performing Arts, Music Division.
Astor, Lenox and Tilden Foundations

(bottom) The Metropolitan Opera Archives

PAGE 3
(top) Irving Newman/Photograph courtesy of The Metropolitan Opera Archives

(bottom) © Henry Grossman

PAGE 4
(top) © Henry Grossman

(bottom) Photograph courtesy of The Metropolitan Opera Archives

PAGE 5
(top) Frank Dunand/The Metropolitan Opera Guild

(bottom) © Henry Grossman

PAGE 6
Copyright © Beth Bergman, 2000. All Rights Reserved

PAGE 7
Koichi Miura/The Metropolitan Opera Press Department

PAGE 8
Copyright © Beth Bergman, 2001. All Rights Reserved

Insert 2

PAGE 1
The Metropolitan Opera Archives

PAGE 2
(both) The Metropolitan Opera Archives

PAGE 3
(top) Copyright © Beth Bergman, 2001. All Rights Reserved

(bottom left) Copyright © Beth Bergman, 2000. All Rights Reserved

(bottom right) Courtesy Janis J. Mintiks

PAGE 4
(top left) Linda Cataffo/copyright © 1999 by New York Daily News L.P.

(top right) © Henry Grossman

(bottom) Ruby Washington/NYT Pictures

PAGE 5
(top) © Harry Heleotis 2001/The Metropolitan Opera Press Department

(bottom) © Steve J. Sherman. All Rights Reserved

PAGE 6
(top) Copyright © Beth Bergman, 2000. All Rights Reserved

(bottom left) © 1995 Jack Vartoogian

(bottom right) © Steve J. Sherman. All Rights Reserved

PAGE 7
(top) The Metropolitan Opera Archives

(bottom) © Jack Vartoogian

PAGE 8
(top) © Steve J. Sherman. All Rights Reserved

(center) Bruce Cotler/AP/Wide World Photos

(bottom) Suzanne DeChillo/NYT Pictures

ENDPAPERS
© 1988/Steve J. Sherman. All Rights Reserved

INDEX

NOTE ABOUT THE AUTHOR

Johanna Fiedler is the daughter of Arthur Fiedler, the long-time conductor of the Boston Pops, and has worked in the field of classical music for many years. She is the author of *Arthur Fiedler: Papa, the Pops, and Me*. She lives in New York City.

NOTE ON TYPE

This book was typeset in Fournier. The youngest son of a French printing family, Pierre Simon Fournier started out engraving woodblocks and large capitals, then moved on to fonts of type. In 1736 he began his own foundry and made several important contributions in the field of type design; he is said to have cut 147 alphabets of his own creation. Fournier is probably best remembered as the designer of St. Augustine Ordinaire, a face that served as the model for Monotype's Fournier, which was released in 1925.